The PRESBYTERIAN ENTERPRISE

Sources of American Presbyterian History

Edited by

MAURICE W. ARMSTRONG, PH.D.
Ursinus College

LEFFERTS A. LOETSCHER, PH.D.
Princeton Theological Seminary

CHARLES A. ANDERSON, M.A.
Presbyterian Historical Society

Wipf & Stock
PUBLISHERS
Eugene, Oregon

Wipf and Stock Publishers
199 West 8th Avenue, Suite 3
Eugene, Oregon 97401

The Presbyterian Enterprise
Edited by Armstrong, Maurice W. , Loetscher, Lefferts A.
and Anderson, Charles A.
ISBN: 1-57910-749-4
Publication date 9/10/2001
Previously published by Westminster John Knox, 1956

THE PRESBYTERIAN ENTERPRISE

CONTENTS

Foreword *by Charles A. Anderson*   7

Part I
COLONIAL PRESBYTERIANISM (1706–1783)

1. The Foundations (1706–1729)   11
2. The Great Awakening (1730–1754)   33
3. Religion and Empire (1755–1783)   62

Part II
AMERICAN PRESBYTERIANISM IN MID-PASSAGE (1784–1869)

4. The National Impulse (1784–1811)   95
5. The Age of Benevolence (1812–1828)   121
6. Old School–New School (1829–1838)   146
7. Parallel Expansion (1839–1860)   172
8. The Irrepressible Conflict (1861–1869)   199

Part III
RECENT PRESBYTERIANISM (1870–1956)

9. Reconciled and Expanding (1870–1886)   225
10. Resistance to Social and Cultural Change (1887–1899)   244
11. Adjustment to Social and Cultural Change (1900–1936)   268
12. Intimations of Fresh Creativity (1937–1956)   293

Appendix: *List of Documents Quoted*   323

Index   331

FOREWORD

This book supplies evidence that Americans have given a superior position to moral and spiritual values. The variety and interrelation of the life of a representative American Church will surprise many readers. The religious documents presented here touch on many phases of our common life—the isolation of early colonists, the need for education, the struggle for freedom, and mass developments as threats to the individual, to mention only a few.

The book makes no narrow denominational emphasis. It will be equally enjoyable to the scholar and to the average reader. Here we see the fear of change, the struggle for religious security, the adjustment to the advance of science, the broadening church.

In this collection of letters, journals, diaries, periodicals, minutes, and other documents certain attitudes and trends emerge. The thread of religious liberty weaves itself into the Church from start to finish. Throughout its history the Church has laid a strong emphasis on an educated ministry. Again and again we find the Church making a vigorous effort to spiritualize American life. Knowing that their fathers had suffered grievous persecution in Europe, the colonists continued vigorous opposition to all attempts to plant State Churches in this country. Tensions between liberals and conservatives have sometimes risen to high pitch. Early in our American history Presbyterians adopted a Confession of Faith which allows for wide differences in interpretations of beliefs. Tolerance is a delicate plant which still needs cultivation.

Co-operation has been characteristic of Presbyterians in America. Although occasionally they have competed with others or glorified their own name, they have not thought of their denomination as an end in itself, but as a means to advance the common welfare, or, to put it in other words, to further the Kingdom of God.

This book is the fruition of an idea that has long been in the minds of the Board of Directors of the Presbyterian Historical Society. For two years an Editorial Committee has been gathering manuscripts and planning for publication. It is fitting that this book should appear in connection with the celebration in 1956 of the 250th Anniversary of the founding of the first Presbytery in America in 1706. The Committee consists of the Doctors Maurice W. Armstrong, Lefferts A. Loetscher, and Charles A. Anderson. Unfortunately the limitations of space have necessitated the elimination of many documents that rightfully should be included.

The editors have gathered about one hundred seventy manuscripts through their extensive and painstaking labor. Each item received the careful scrutiny of the Committee before it was accepted.

The Committee chose documents because they contributed to the better understanding of the influence of the Church on the life of the nation. Most of the manuscripts and other selections in this book, which are printed here with their original spelling and punctuation, are housed in the rich and extensive Library of the Presbyterian Historical Society (P.H.S.). The introductory or explanatory material at the head of each item or group has purposely been kept brief in order to permit the documents to speak for themselves. The general arrangement has followed the historical development of our national life.

The book is designed for the general reader who wants to know the facts behind historical stories. Facts often prove to be more fascinating than fiction. It should be useful in college and university courses on American civilization. It will probably prove to be indispensable to seminary courses on Church history. Ministers will find in it many stimulating ideas and illustrations. Laymen will discover answers to numerous questions about the Presbyterian way.

The Committee and the Board of the Historical Society hope that other readings in Presbyterian historical sources will be forthcoming.

CHARLES A. ANDERSON
Secretary, Presbyterian Historical Society

Philadelphia, Pa., 1955

PART

I

COLONIAL PRESBYTERIANISM
1706–1783

CHAPTER

1

THE FOUNDATIONS
1706–1729

1. The First American Presbytery

Early colonial records indicate the presence of Presbyterian ministers and people in the Middle Colonies before 1650. It was not, however, until 1706 that seven ministers (F. Makemie of Rehoboth, Md.; N. Taylor of Patuxent, Md.; S. Davis of Lewes, Del.; J. Wilson of New Castle, Del.; J. Andrews of Philadelphia; J. Hampton and G. McNish, recently arrived from the British Isles) arranged to meet together in Philadelphia "to consult the most proper measures for advancing religion and propagating Christianity" in this part of the American wilderness. Unfortunately, the first page of the manuscript minutes of this first Presbytery is missing. The record begins in the middle of a sentence relating to an expository sermon by John Boyd, a candidate for ordination. This was at Freehold, N. J., on December 26, 1706. At the next meeting, March 22, 1707, elders as well as ministers were present. The significant fact, however, is that this New World Presbytery was entirely independent of any Old World Synod. The minutes reveal that the familiar procedures of Scottish Presbyterianism were followed in respect to lay representation, excuses, absences, calls, and overtures, but, beyond that, the Presbytery was an American creation, shaped by the needs of "the desolate places" of the New World.

De regimine ecclesiae, which being heard was approved of and sustained. He gave in also his thesis to be considered of against next *sederunt.*

Sederunt 2d. 10 bris. 27.
Post preces sederunt, Mr. Francis McKemie, Moderator, Messrs. Jedediah Andrews, and John Hampton, Ministers.

Mr. John Boyd performed the other parts of his trials, viz. preached a popular sermon on John i. 12; defended his thesis; gave satisfaction as to his skill in the languages, and answered to extemporary questions; all which were approved of and sustained.

Appointed his ordination to be on the next Lord's day, the 29th inst., which was accordingly performed in the public meeting house of this place, before a numerous assembly; and the next day he had the certificate of his ordination.

March 22d, 1707.

At a meeting of the Presbytery held at Philadelphia, *post preces sederunt*, Messrs. John Wilson, Jedediah Andrews, Nathaniel Taylor, George McNish, *Ministers*. Joseph Yard, William Smith, John Gardener, James Stoddard, *Elders*.

Master John Wilson, by plurality of votes was chosen Moderator, George McNish was chosen Clerk of the Presbytery.

This day a letter sent by Mr. Samuel Davis to the Presbytery, was presented to them; it being moved by one of the members that the letter might be read, it was accordingly read and considered, and Mr. Davis his reasons for excusing his absence from this and the preceding meeting of the Presbytery, were *not* sustained by the Presbytery.

Ordered that the next dyet of the Presbytery be held upon Tuesday, at four o'clock, in the afternoon.

Mr. Francis McKemie and Mr. John Wilson, are appointed to preach upon Tuesday, upon the subjects appointed them at the last Presbytery, from Heb. i. 1, 2v., by way of exercise and addition.

March 25th.

Post preces sederunt, John Wilson, &c. This day Mr. Francis McKemie and Mr. John Wilson delivered their discourses according to appointment, and were approved by the Presbytery.

Ordered, that a letter be writ, and sent to Mr. Samuel Davis in the name of the Presbytery, by Master John Wilson, requiring him to be present at our next meeting in this place. . . .

Appointed that the Presbytery meet to-morrow at ten o'clock, and that Mr. Andrews and Mr. John Boyd, prepare some overtures to be considered by the Presbytery, for propagating religion in their respective congregations.

March 26th. *Post preces sederunt,
the moderator, &c.*

Ordered by the Presbytery, that Mr. Francis McKemie write to Scotland, to Mr. Alexander Coldin, minister of Oxam, of the Presbytery of ——, and to give an account of the state and circumstances of the dissenting Presbyterian interest among the people in and about Lewistown, and to signify the earnest desires of that people, for the said Mr. Coldin's coming over to be their minister; and that Mr. McKemie make report of his diligence herein against the next Presbytery.

The Presbytery appoints Mr. John Wilson to write to the Presbytery of ——, to the effect aforesaid, and make report of his care herein against the next Presbytery.

Overtures proposed to the Presbytery and agreed upon, for propagating the interest of religion:

First, That every minister in their respective congregations, read and comment upon a chapter of the Bible every Lord's day, as discretion and circumstances of time, place, &c., will admit.

Second over: That it be recommended to every minister of the Presbytery to set on foot and encourage private Christian societies.

Third over: That every minister of the Presbytery supply neighbouring desolate places where a minister is wanting, and opportunity of doing good offers.

The Presbytery do appoint Mr. Jedediah Andrews and Mr. Nathaniel Taylor, to prepare a Presbyterial sermon, each of them to be delivered against the next Presbytery. Mr. Andrews to discourse from Heb. i. chap. 3. v. the *first*, and Mr. Taylor from *latter* part of the verse.

Appointed that the Presbytery meet upon the first Tuesday of April, 1708, at Philadelphia, and this meeting was concluded. (*Records of the Presbyterian Church U.S.A.*, W. H. Roberts, ed., Philadelphia, 1904, 9–10.)

2. Freedom of Religion

Rev. Francis Makemie was sent to the eastern shore of Chesapeake Bay in 1683 by the Irish Presbytery of Laggan. He is generally believed to have been the chief promoter of an American presbytery. A letter to the Bishop of London describes him as "a great Pillar of that Sect, who travels thro' all the main like a Bishop, having Pupills to attend him, and, where he comes, Ordains Ministers and exercises all the Powers of a Bishop." In January, 1707, Makemie and John Hampton were arrested for preaching in New York without a license from the Governor, Lord Cornbury. Although he was imprisoned for six weeks, and compelled to pay excessive court charges, Makemie's spirited defense of religious liberty aroused much popular support, and his final acquittal by a jury was hailed by Cotton Mather as "a triumph for Non-Conformity" in America.

A. Warrant for Arrest

Whereas I am informed, that one Mackennan, and one Hampton, two Presbyterian Preachers, who lately came to this City, have taken upon them to Preach in a Private House, without having obtained My Licence for so doing, which is directly contrary to the known Laws of England; and being likewise informed, that they are gone into Long-Island, with intent there to spread their Pernicious Doctrine and Principles, to the great disturbance of the Church by Law Established, and of the Government of this Province. You are therefore hereby Required and Commanded, to take into your Custody the Bodies of the said Mackennan and Hampton, and them to bring with all convenient speed before me, at Fort-Anne in New-York. And for so doing, this shall be your sufficient Warrant: Given under my Hand, at Fort Anne this 21st day of January, 1706, 7.

Cornbury.

To Thomas Cardale Esqr. High-Sheriff of Queens-County on Long-Island, or his Deputy.

A true Copy Examined per
Thomas Cardale.

And being late when Apprehended they were Prisoners upon Parole, at the Houses of two Neighbours for that night, and next day, instead of carrying them to Fort-Anne, according to the directions of said Precept, they were carried by said Sheriffs to Jamaica, seven or eight miles out of their direct way to York, and there detained all that day & night; as if they were to be carried about in Triumph to be insulted over, as Exemplary Criminals, and put to further Charge. The 23d day about Noon, they were carried to Fort-Anne in York; and after sundry hours attendance, appeared before Lord Cornbury in the Council-Chamber, about three or 4 of the Clock, who charged them with taking upon them to Preach in his Government without his Licence.

B. Interlocutory Conference

Lord Cornbury. How dare you take upon you to Preach in my Government, without my Licence?

Mr. Makemie. We have Liberty from an Act of Parliament, made the First Year of the Reign of King William and Queen Mary, which gave us Liberty, with which Law we have complied.

Ld. C. None shall Preach in my Government without my Licence?

F. M. If the Law for Liberty, my Lord, had directed us to any particular persons in Authority for Licence, we would readily have observed the same; but we cannot find any directions in said Act of Parliament, therefore could not take notice therof.

Ld. C. That Law does not extend to the American Plantations, but only to England.

F. M. My Lord, I humbly conceive, it is not a limited nor Local Act, and am well assured, it extends to other Plantations of the Queens Dominions, which is evident from Certificates from Courts of Record of Virginia, and Maryland, certifying we have complied with said Law.

Both Certificates were produced and read by Lord Cornbury, who was pleased to say, these Certificates extended not to New-York.

Ld. C. I know it is local and limited, for I was at making thereof.

F. M. Your Excellency might be at making thereof, but we are well assured, there is no such limiting clause therein, as is in Local Acts, and desire the Law may be produced to determine this point.

Ld. C. Turning to Mr. Attorney, Mr. Bekely, who was present, ask'd him, Is it not so, Mr. Attorney?

Mr. Attorney. Yes, it is Local, my Lord, and producing an Argument for it, further said, that all the Paenal Laws were Local, and limited, and did not extend to the Plantations, and the Act of Toleration being made to take off the edge of the Paenal Laws; therefore the Act of Toleration does not extend to any Plantations?

F. M. I desire the Law may be produced; for I am morally perswaded, there is no limitation or restriction in the Law to England, Wales, and Berwick on Tweed; for it extends to sundry Plantations of the Queens Dominions, as Barbadoes, Virginia, and Maryland; which was evident from the Certificates produced, which we could not have obtained, if the Act of Parliament had not extended to the Plantations.

And Mr. Makemie further said, that he presumed New-York was a part of Her Majesties Dominions also; and that sundry Ministers on the East-end of Long-Island, had complied with said Law, and qualifyed themselves at Court, by complying with the directions of said Law, and have no Licence from your Lordship.

Ld. C. Yes, New-York is of Her Majesties Dominions; but the Act of Toleration does not extend to the Plantations by its own intrinsick vertue, or any intention of the Legislators, but only by her Majesties Royal Instructions signifyed unto me, and that is from Her Prerogative and Clemency. And the Courts which have qualifyed those men, are in error, and I shall check them for it.

F. M. If the Law extends to the Plantations any manner of way, whether by the Queens Prerogative, Clemency, or otherwise, our Certificates were a demonstration we had complied therewith. . . .

Ld. C. That act of Parliament was made against Strowling Preachers, and you are such, and shall not Preach in my Government.

F. M. There is not one word, my Lord, mentioned in any part of the Law, against Travelling or Strowling Preachers, as Your Excellency is pleased to call them; and we are to judge that to be the true end of the Law, which is specifyed in the Preamble thereof, which is for the satisfaction of Scrupulous Consciences, and Uniting the Subjects of England, in interest and affection. And it is well known, my Lord, to all, that Quakers, who also have Liberty by this Law, have few or no fixed Teachers, but chiefly taught by such as Travel; and it is known to all such are sent forth by the Yearly Meeting at London, and Travel and Teach over the Plantations, and are not molested.

Ld. C. I have troubled some of them, and will trouble them more.

F. M. We hear my Lord, one of them was Prosecuted at Jamaica, but it was not for Travelling or Teaching, but for particulars in Teaching, for which he suffered.

Ld. C. You shall not spread your Pernicious Doctrines here?

F. M. As to our Doctrines, my Lord, we have our Confession of Faith, which is known to the Christian World, and I challenge all the Clergy of York to show us any false or pernicious Doctrines therein; Yea, with those exceptions specifyed in the Law, we are able to make it appear, they are in all Doctrinal Articles of Faith agreeable to the Established Doctrines of the Church of England.

Ld. C. There is one thing wanting in your Certificates, and that is Signing the Articles of the Church of England.

F. M. That is the Clerks omission, my Lord, for which we are no way accountable, by not being full and more particular; but if we had not complied with the whole Law, in all the parts thereof, we should not have had Certificates pursuant to said Act of Parliament. And Your Lordship may be assured, we have done nothing in complying with said Law, but what we are still ready to perform, if your Lordship require it, and that ten times over: And as to the Articles of Religion, I have a Copy in my Pocket, and am ready at all times to Sign with those exceptions specifyed in the Law.

Ld. C. You Preached in a Private House, not certifyed according to Act of Parliament.

F. M. There were endeavours used for my Preaching in a more publick place, and (tho' without my knowledge) your Lordships permission was demanded for my Preaching in the Dutch Church; and being denied, we were under a necessity, of assembling for Public Worship in a Private House, which we did, in as publick a manner as possible, with open doors: And we are directed to certify the same to the next Quarter Sessions, which cannot be done, until the Quarter Sessions come in course; for the Law binds no man to impossibilities; and if we do not certifie to the next Quarter Sessions, we shall be culpable, but not till then: For it is evident, my Lord, that this Act of Parliament was made, and passed the Royal Assent, May 24th. And it being some time before the Quarter Sessions came in course, and all Ministers in England continued to Preach without one days cessation or forbearance; and we hope the practice of England, should be a president for America.

Ld. C. None shall Preach in my Government, without my Licence, as the Queen has signifyed to me, by her Royal Instructions.

F. M. Whatever direction the Queens Instructions may be to Your Lordship, they can be no Rule or Law to us, nor any particular persons who never saw, and perhaps never shall see them: for Promulgation is the life of the Law.

Ld. C. You must give Bond and Security for your good Behaviour, and also Bond and Security to Preach no more in my Government?

F. M. As to our Behaviour, tho' we have no way broke it, endeavouring always so to live, as to keep a Conscience void of offence, towards God and Man: Yet if his Lordship required it, we would give Security for our Behaviour; but to give Bond and Security to Preach no more in your Excellency's Government, if invited and desired by any people, we neither can, nor dare do.

Ld. C. Then you must go to Goal?

F. M. We are neither ashamed nor affraid of what we have done; and we have complied, and are ready still to comply with the Act of Parliament, which we hope will protect us at last: And it will be unaccountable to England, to hear, that Jews, who openly blaspheme the Name of the Lord Jesus Christ, and disown the whole Christian Religion; Quakers who disown the Fundamental Doctrines of the Church of England, and both Sacraments; Lutherans, and all others, are tolerated in Your Lordships Government; and only we, who have complied, and are still ready to comply with the Act of Toleration, and are nearest to, and likest the Church of England of any Dissenters, should be hindered, and that only in the Government of New-York and the Jersies. This will appear strange indeed.

Ld. C. You must blame the Queen for that?

F. M. We do not, neither have we any reason to blame Her Majesty, for She molests none, neither countenances or encourages any who do; and has given frequent assurances, and of late in Her Gracious Speech to Her Parliament, That she would inviolably maintain the Toleration.

While Lord Cornbury was writing Precepts for discharging us from the custody of Cardale, High Sheriff of Queens County in Long-Island, and another for our Commitment in York; Mr. John Hampton demanded a Licence of Lord Cornbury, but he absolutely denied it.

And before finishing of said Mittimus, for their Commitment, Mr. Francis Makemie moved, that it was highly necessary before their Commitment, the Law should be produced, to determine that point, whether it is local and limited, or not: And it is not to be doubted, but Mr. Attorney was soon able to produce the Law: And he further offered to pay Mr. Attorney for a Copy of that Paragraph, in which the limiting Clause is, if any. But every thing relating hereunto was declined and disregarded.

Ld. C. You Sir, Know Law.

F. M. I do not my Lord, pretend to know Law, but I pretend to know this particular Law, having had sundry disputes thereon. The Mittimus being finished, they were commited to the Custody of Ebenezer Wilson, High Sheriff of York City and County, and carried to his Dwelling-House, as the place of their Confinement; and after sundry demands, they had upon the 25th day, the following Copy of the Precept, for their Commitment.

(Seal) You are hereby Required and Commanded to take into your Custody the Bodies of Francis Makemie and John Hampton, and them safely keep till further Orders; and for so doing, this shall be your Warrant. Given under my Hand and Seal, this 23d day of January, 1706, 7.

Cornbury.

(*A Narrative of a New and Unusual American Imprisonment Of Two Presbyterian Ministers . . . One of Them for Preaching One Sermon at the City of New-York, By a Learner of Law and a Lover of Liberty,* 1707, 2 ff.)

3. A Learned Ministry

From the beginning, the Presbytery insisted on maintaining the traditional Scottish ideal of a learned ministry, even in the face of a great shortage of preachers. It was four years from the time David Evans was forbidden to preach until he was considered sufficiently well grounded in the ancient languages and in theology to be a Presbyterian minister.

Upon information that David Evan, a lay person, had taken upon him publicly to teach or preach among the Welch in the Great Valley, Chester county, it was unanimously agreed that the said Evan had done very ill, and acted irregularly in thus invading the work of the ministry, and was thereupon censured.

Agreed that the most proper method for advancing David Evan in necessary literature to prepare him for the work of the ministry is, that he lay aside all other business for a twelve month, and apply himself closely to learning and study, under the direction of Mr. Andrews, and with the assistance of Mr. Wilson and Anderson, and that it be left to the discretion of the said ministers when to put said Evan on trials, and license him publicly to teach or preach.

Ordered, That Mr. Wilson write to the Welch, in the Welch Tract, and Mr. Andrews to those in the Great Valley. (*Records of Pres. Ch.*, 1710, 17.)

MEMORANDUM

It being appointed the last Presbytery, that the ordination of Mr. David Evans should be left to the discretion of diverse ministers mentioned in the minutes; the said members having heard him preach a popular sermon on Romans iii, 31, received his *exegesis* on a question *de necessitate specialis Spiritus Sancti operationis ad conversionem*, taken an account of his skill in the original languages, and likewise of his attainments and orthodoxy in the theological matters, to their satisfaction, did on the third day of November, 1714, ordain the said Mr. Evans to the work of the ministry. (*Letter Book of Presbytery*, 1714.)

4. "This Remote Corner"

The following letter was written in 1716 to the Principal of Glasgow College, Scotland, by Rev. James Anderson (later minister of the First Presbyterian Church of New York). His reference to the use of the Scottish Directory is the earliest information available on the order of worship in the American Church. As a result of this and similar appeals, collections were received at the church doors in Scotland "for encouraging ministers to preach the gospel among the poor of God" in America.

There are in all, of minrs, who meet, in a presbytry once a year, sometimes att Philadelphia, sometimes here att Newcastle, seventeen, & two probationers from ye north of Irland whom we have under tryall for ordination, twelve of qch, I think, have had the most & best of their education at your famous University of Glasgow; We are mostly but young raw heads, yet glory to our God he magnifies & perfects his strength in our weaknesse, and makes it evident yt he can work wonders of grace by poor mean & insignificant instruments. As to our proceedings in matters of publick worship & discipline, we make it our businesse to follow ye directory of ye Church of Scotland, qch (as well we may) we oun as our moyr church. We make it our businesse to settle & to make settlements, for minrs of our perswasion yt join with us, in places where ye Gospell has either never att all been preached, or else in places where there are wicked, prophane, debauched, carelesse creatures of the bishop of London of qch there has been not a few, & yet are some, within ye bounds of these provinces, where some of our brethren meet, which is ye reason of our meeting with pritty many hardships & difficulties both from ye inconveniences of our congregations & ye opposition of inveterate enemies.

In some of our places ye hearers, by reason of their poverty & paucity, are scarce att all able, tho' never so willing, to allow a competent creditable subsistence for their minrs, which is the reason for some contempt amongst some; which I humbly think might be, in some measure, easily remedied by our moyr ye Church of Scotland and her adherants in Brittain. And I doubt not but she readily would use her care & endeavors this way, if she were but sensible of the inconveniences yt her poor children in this remote corner lye under upon this account. (Quoted in C. A. Briggs, *American Presbyterianism*, New York, 1885, lxxi–lxxii.)

5. The Organization of a Synod

By 1716 the number of ministers and congregations had increased to such an extent that the original Presbytery could be divided into four subsidiary presbyteries, the whole body still continuing to meet once a year as a general Synod. The effect of this was to increase the strength of the Church in the local areas, yet to maintain the unity of the whole.

It having pleased Divine Providence so to increase our number, as that, after much deliberation, we judge it may be more serviceable to the interest of religion, to divide ourselves into subordinate meetings or Presbyteries, constituting one annually as a synod, to meet at Philadelphia or elsewhere, to consist of all the members of each subordinate Presbytery or meeting for this year at least: Therefore it is agreed by the Presbytery, after serious deliberation, that the first subordinate meeting or Presbytery, to meet at Philadelphia or elsewhere, as they shall see fit, do consist of these following members, viz: Masters Andrews, Jones, Powell, Orr, Bradner, and Morgan. And the second t meet at New Castle or elsewhere, as they shall see fit, to consist of those, viz: Masters Anderson, McGill, Gillespie, Witherspoon, Evans, and Conn. The third to meet at Snow-Hill or elsewhere, to consist of these, viz: Masters Davis, Hampton, and Henry. And in consideration that only our brethren Mr. McNish and Mr. Pumry, are of our number upon Long-Island at present, we earnestly recommend it to them to use their best endeavours with the neighbouring brethren that are settled there, which as yet join not with us, to join with them in erecting a fourth Presbytery. And as to the time of the meeting of the respective Presbyteries, it is ordered that that be left to their own discretion.

Ordered, That a book be kept by each of the said Presbyteries, containing a record of their proceedings, and that the said book be brought every year to our anniversary Synod to be revised. (*Records of Pres. Ch.*, 1716, 45.)

6. "Two Hundred Families from Ireland"

In the half century following 1717 it has been estimated that some two hundred thousand Scotch-Irish emigrated to America. Poor, land-hungry, boisterous and contentious, these people were also tenaciously Presbyterian. The following letter written by a frontier minister to a friend in Scotland indicates some of the problems presented by the new arrivals. "Grossly scandalous" behavior, especially drunkenness among the clergy, continued to be a matter of grave concern to frontier presbyteries throughout the colonial period.

Reverend Sr

Being well acquainted wth your publick spirit, for the Interest of Glorious Christ, I have embraced this opportunity, now presented, to send you this letter.

As to the affairs of Christ in our parts of the world: There are a great many congregations erected, and now errecting; for wthin the space of five years by gone, near to two hundred Families have come into our parts from Ireland, and more are following: They are generally Presbyterians. So, it would appear, yt Glorious Christ hath great designs in America; tho' I am afraid not to be effectuated in my days: for the mirs and congregations be multiplied wth us; yet alas, there is little of the power and life of Religion wth either: The Lord disappoint my fears. There are not above 30 ministers & probationer preachers in our Synod, and yet six of the said number have been grossly scandalous;

Suspension for 4 Sabbaths hath been the greatest censure inflicted as yet.

Mr Alexander Hutchison was ordained upon the 6th of June last: I preached his ordination sermon, his congregation is contiguous to mine, he answers the character given of him by the Revd Presbytery of Glasgow. One Mr Robert Laing who left Scotland about the same time with Mr. Hutchison is to be censured at our Presbytery of New-Castle upon the first Wednesday of August ensueing for Washing himself upon the Lord's day: he is the first from Scotland grossly scandalous in our parts.

Revd Sr be mindfull in your prayers of the Infant church of Christ in America, and that the Lord would purifie the sons of Levi. May the faithfull God hasten the time when he will fulfill his promse in Isa: 59. 19 That they shall fear his name from the West. Sr, I desire in particular, yt you may be mindfull of me in your prayers That I may be an honest and faithfull minister of Christ and that I may have many seals of my miry. Remember my love and Service to the Revd Mr John Simpson Professor of Theology in ye Colledge of Glasgow—and to ye laborious and diligent Mr. Gersham Carmichal, who was my Regent.

The Lord be nigh unto you in Mercy & love These from, Revd Sr
Your lover and humble Servant
GEORGE GILLESPIE.

July ye 16. 1723 at ye head of
Christiana Creek 12 miles West
from New-Castle in Pennsilvania
of America.

(Quoted in Briggs, *American Presbyterianism*, lxxxiv.)

7. The Session as a Moral Court

Session records reveal the fact that much of the time was occupied by cases of discipline. In the absence of civil courts, local sessions were frequently called upon to settle cases involving horse-trading, trespassing, indentured servants, assault and battery, as well as the more recognizable breaches of the Ten Commandments, Sabbathbreaking, swearing, lying, and adultery. There are even a few cases of witchcraft in the minutes of colonial sessions. The strength of the Presbyterian system is shown in the following examples from the records of New Londonderry (Fagg's Manor, Pa.), in the willingness of the offenders to carry out the sentence of making a public confession of their guilt before the entire congregation. Further examples of the session as a moral court may be found in G. S. Klett, Presbyterians in Colonial Pennsylvania, *Philadelphia, 1937.*

January 5th 1741/2. We the church-session, the Minister & Elders of this congregation of New-Londonderry having lately, to our grief, had to deal wt some persons on account of their being guilty of ye great & scandalous sin of excess in strong Drink, and finding it has been generally at publick Vendues they were guilty of this evil, we look upon it our Duty in this publick manner, to testify against the corrupt practice of giving & drinking spirituous Liquor on such occasions; inasmuch as ye shameful & unmanly, as well as unchristian & ungodly sin of Drunkenness, more or less, is generally the consequence of it; so that it is likely to corrupt & Debauch the Land, & make bad men much worse, to ye great endangering of ye everlasting perdition of souls, the prophanation of God's Holy Name, & wounding of his church. . . .

Furthermore, we think it convenient to give this general Notice, that all such under our care & Inspection as shall be found guilty for ye time to come of being so publickly Intoxicated and sensibly disorder'd by strong Drink shall, before they be admitted to ye distinguishing privileges of the visible church, make publick confession of their sin, and profession of their grief & sorrow for it before God, as an evidence of ye Truth of their Humiliation, as a greater Bond and Restraint upon them afterwards, as a fuller satisfaction to ye church concerning their after-admission, and that all Israel may hear & fear & do no more so wickedly. N:B: This Act for the more effectual suppressing of Drunkenness was pr order read in ye open congregation. . . .

Febry 2d 1741/2. John Shiels being call'd before the session upon a Report of his having been publickly guilty of excess in strong Drink, and being this day present, confesses guilt, and declares his sorrow for it. The session judge it needful yt he make a publick acknowledgement the next Lord's Day.

Likewise, William McFerren having been publickly guilty of excess in strong Drink twice, the Session also order that he make a publick acknowledgement next Lord's Day.

N.B. Both these orders were comply'd with. . . .

Jul. 16th 1742. William McKinny & Jane his Wife and John Woodside being called before ye Session to give an account of several sinful unchristian expressions & actions that sometime ago fell out among them, it does appear to ye session yt Jane McKinny did treat John Woodside wt very sinful unchristian Language which the session judges she ought to acknowledge her sin in before them, and to declare her grief & humiliation for it, as likewise yt she ought to be sharply Rebuk'd for it by ye session.

As to Willm McKinny: The Session finds yt he was guilty of swearing vainly by the Dread Name of God, & of other sinful expressions: as also, of assaulting John Woodside in such a manner wt a stick that John was obliged to strike him in his own defence, especially, finding himself endanger'd by one or both of William's sons, John & William, who offer'd to strike him wt sticks; and afterwards one, or both, threw stones at him.

The session, considering, both, ye heinousness of these crimes, and, their being so publick in the Country, does judge it necessary for him to acknowledge penitently his sin therein before ye congregation. And that his two sons shall give such satisfaction as ye Session shall judge convenient. . . .

Nov. 8, 1743. Isabel Wilson appear'd before ye session, who had been guilty of ye crime of fornication wt William Erwin, in order to know what satisfaction the Session Judged necessary to her being admitted again to ye privileges of ye church. It appear'd to ye session that ye sd Willm Erwin had a wife living at ye same time in Ireland and ye sd Isabel was warned of it at ye time that he pretended to be in courtship of her before she was with child to him. The Session on these considerations, and considering moreover, her former profession & privilege at being a communicant at the Lord's Table, Judged it necessary, as a proportionable censure for ye aggravated crime, and satisfactory evidence of her Humiliation & Repentance, and Warning to all others, that she in a publick manner before ye congregation, humbly acknowledge her aggravated sin & profess hearty sorrow for it as an offence against God & scandal to his church, for three several Sabbath Days Viz: the 2d & 4th Sabbaths of this month, and the 2d Sabbath of the next.

N.B. This order was comply'd with. . . .

May 4, 1744. Esther McClosky appear'd this day again before the session . . . and appear'd to make a serious (unre)-served confession of her heinous crime; and testify'd her willingness to make an open acknowledgement before ye congregation. But upon Examination she was found to be too Ignorant of ye Doctrines of Religion to be admitted to ye distinguishing privileges of ye visible Church; and therefore we think proper to Defer her publick acknowledgement till she appear better qualify'd with knowledge to have her child baptized.

N.B. After taking pains with her for awhile from time to time in instructing her, she was at length admitted to publick confession & the Baptism of her child. (*Records of Old Londonderry Congregation,* manuscript in P.H.S., 7 ff.)

8. A Colonial Ordination

Alexander Hutchinson was a graduate of a Scottish university and had been supplying vacant congregations on the frontier of southeastern Pennsylvania. The following account of his examination and ordination is of particular interest because of the part played by the congregation in the ordination.

June ye 5th 1723. At ye meeting house of Bohemia and Broad-Creek the Presbytery met according to appointmt. ubi post preces sederunt. . . .

Mr. Alexander Hutchinson having delivered a sermon on Psal. 63.8 & an Exegesis de Resurrectione Corporis, and also having undergone ye usual pieces of tryal in the learned languages & Extemporaries in order to his ordination, in all wch he was unanimously approved of.

Adjourned till to Morrow at ten of ye Clock ante meridiem.
                                        Concluded wth prayer.

At 10 of ye Clock ante Meridiem met according to appointmt & post preces sederunt qui supra. . . .

A proclamation being made three times at the door of Bohemia & Broad-Creek meetinghouse by Mr. David Evans yt if any had anything to object against ye ordaining of Mr. Hutchinson they shd make it known to ye Presbytery now sitting & no objection being made, the sd Mr. Hutchinson was solemnly set apart to ye work of the Ministry by fasting & prayer with ye imposition of ye hands of ye Presbytery.

Mr. George Gillespie preached the Ordination sermon.

Mr. Hutchinson desiring to joyn to our Presbytery was accordingly received by the Modr & Members.

Ordered that Mr. Alexandr. Hutchinson preach to ye people of Canestoga on ye 2d Sabbath of July next. (*Records of the Presbytery of New Castle Upon Delaware,* mss. in P.H.S., I, 84–86.)

9. "Open the Doors of the Church as Wide as Christ Opens the Gates of Heaven"

The founders of the first Presbytery and Synod were more interested in uniting the various types of Presbyterians into an effective missionary and Christian Church than they were in doctrinal definition and conformity. To many of the newer Scotch-Irish immigrants this tendency appeared dangerous. It is not surprising, therefore, to find that there was a movement in the Synod to require all ministers to subscribe to the Westminster Confession of Faith. The champion of the older way was Rev. Jonathan Dickinson of Elizabethtown, N.J., whose Puritan background led him to resist any infringement upon the liberty of conscience. In 1722, Dickinson preached a sermon at the opening of the Synod in which he took his stand upon the ground that the Scriptures are the only rule of faith and worship for the Church, and that no man-made interpretation of them is binding upon the Christian conscience.

There has no one thing had an equal hand in the many Heresies, Schisms, Convulsions and Confusions, which the Church of God has always laboured under, with HUMANE INVENTIONS and INSTITUTIONS, in the affairs of God's House. . . .

It's a bold invasion of Christ's *Royal Power*, and a rude reflection upon his *Wisdom* and *Faithfulness*, for *proud Worms* to make any Addition to that perfect Pattern, which he has given us: For how artful soever this Mischief may be painted over, with the fair Colours of *Apostolick Tradition, Antiquity, Order and Decency,* The band of Union and Communion, The Well Government or greater Good of the Church, or whatever other Pretence; it may be justly challanged with a WHO HAS REQUIRED THIS AT YOUR HANDS, Since he who is faithful to him that appointed him . . . has given us a complete Rule of Doctrine, Worship and Discipline. . . .

If we make any Laws for the Discipline of the Church, they must be made either by Authority derived from Christ, or by our own Authority. I'm sure it's imperious enough to claim such an Authority of our own, and I challange the World to produce any such *Dedimus potestatem* from Christ, or the least lisp in the Bible that countenances such Royal Power. I add,

Whatever Constitutions can be formed for Church-Government must be either of a Religious Nature or meerly Humane Politicks and Prudentials. . . .

Could we make Acts never so innocent in themselves, and never so agreeable to the State and Circumstances of our Churches, the *Law-making* Faculty would still be an Usurpation.

Let us make never so many Pretences to found such Constitutions upon the Word of God, all the Churches in the World may put in the same Plea, and even the *Papal Hierarchy* and the *Canons of Trent,* pretend to the same Foundation, and have as much claim to this *Legis-*

lative Authority from such Pretences, as we can have; that is none at all. . . .

But I'll hasten forward and consider, That any authorative obligatory *Interpretation* of the Laws of Christ, is a *Law-making Faculty* that we are not entitled to. . . . It's true the Ministers of Christ have Commission to *Interpret* his Laws, and it concerns them with utmost application to study his Mind and Will, that they may declare his whole Counsel to his People. But then these having no claim to *Infallibility,* can have no Authority to impose their *Interpretations;* nor is any Man absolutely obliged to receive them, any farther than they appear to him just and true. The Reason of this are obvious.

Whatever Subjection is either required or performed unto such *Interpretations*, must be in obedience either to God or Man. Obedience to God cannot be, when our Consciences (whether Regular or Erring, it's the same thing) tell us that God requires no such thing at our hands. And if we owe Obedience to Man in this case, it must be because he has an *absolute legislative Power,* and is *Lord over our Consciences.* . . .

But to make this Case, if possible a little plainer:

Though some plain and comprehensive Creed or Confession of Faith (for distinguishing such as receive, from those who reject *the Faith once delivered to the Saints*) may be useful and necessary since the worst Heresies may take shelter under the express Words of Scripture. Yet we are by no means to force these *credenda,* upon any of differing Sentiments.

We may not so much as shut out of Communion, any such Dissenters, as we can charitably hope Christ won't shut out of Heaven: But should open *the Doors of the Church* as wide as Christ opens *the Gates of Heaven;* and *receive one another,* as Christ also received us, to the Glory of God.

And tho' we ought to reject both the Heresy, and the Communion of those, who deny what we esteem the Fundamental Truths of our holy Religion; yet even these essential Articles of Christianity, may not be imposed by Civil Coercions, temporal Penalties, or any other way whatsoever. (J. Dickinson, A *Sermon Preached at the Opening of the Synod at Philadelphia: September 19, 1722, etc.,* Boston, 1723, 1–2, 13, 17–19, 22–23.)

10. "A Church Without a Confession, What Is It Like?"

Many of the Scotch-Irish ministers in America felt that the broad doctrinal basis of the Synod was an invitation to abuse. Following a similar movement in Ireland, they therefore began to advocate subscription to the Westminster Confession of Faith as a requirement for membership in presbyteries and synod. In 1727 the following overture on this subject was brought into the Synod by the New Castle Presbytery. The author was probably Rev. John Thomson of Lewes, Del., an able controversialist and the acknowledged leader of the subscriptionist, and later of the antirevival, party in the Church. A direct result of this overture was the famous Adopting Act of 1729.

An overture humbly offered to the consideration of the reverend Synod; wherein is proposed an expedient for preventing the ingress and spreading of dangerous errors, among either ourselves or the flocks committed to our care.

Reverend Fathers and Brethren:

. . . First, it seemes to me that we are too much like the people of Laish, in a careless defenceless condition, as a city without walls; (or perhaps my unacquaintedness with our records may cause me to mistake). For as far as I know, though we be an entire particular church, as has been observed, and not a part of a particular church, yet we have not any particular system of doctrines, composed by ourselves, or others, which we, by any judicial act of our church, have adopted to be the articles or confession of our faith, &c. Now a church without a confession, what is it like? It is true, as I take it, we all generally acknowledge and look upon the Westminster Confession and Catechisms to be our confession, or what we own for such; but the most that can be said is, that the Westminster Confession of Faith is the confession of the faith of the generality of our members, ministers and people; but that it is our confession, as we are a united body politic, I cannot see, unless, First, it hath been received by a conjunct act of the representatives of our church; I mean by the Synod, either before or since it hath been *sub forma synodi.* Secondly, unless due care be, and hath been taken that all intrants into the ministry among us hath subscribed the said confession, or by some equivalent solemn act, *coram auctoritate ecclesiastica,* testified their owning it as the confession of their faith; which how far it is observed within the bounds of our Synod, I am ignorant. Now, if this be so, (for upon this supposition I speak,) I think we are in a very defenceless condition. For if we have no confession which is ours by synodical act, or if any among us have not subscribed or acknowledged the confession, *ut supra,* then—First, there is no bar provided to keep out of the ministry those who are corrupt in doctrinals; they may be received into the ministry without renouncing their corrupt doctrines. Secondly, those that are in the ministry among us may propagate gross errors and corrupt many thereby without being discovered to preach any thing against the received truth, because (*supposito ut supra*) the truth was never publicly received among us.

Secondly, another of our present circumstances is, that we are surrounded by so many pernicious and dangerous corruptions in doctrine, and these grown so much in vogue and fashion, even among those whose ancestors, at the beginning of the reformation, would have sealed the now despised truth with their blood. When Arminianism, Socinianism, Deism, Freethinking, &c., do like a deluge overflow even the reformed churches, both established and dissenting, to such a degree, have we not reason to consult our own safety?

Tum tua res agitur paries cum proximus ardet.

A third circumstance we are in, which increaseth our danger of infection by error, is partly the infancy, and partly the poverty of our circumstances, which render us unable to plant a seminary of learning among ourselves, and so to see to the education of our young candidates for the ministry, and therefore we are under the necessity of depending upon other places for men to supply our vacancies in the church, and so are in danger of having our ministry corrupted by such as are leavened with false doctrines before they come among us.

Fourthly, I am afraid there are too many among ourselves, who, though they may be sound in the faith themselves, yet have the edge of their zeal against the prevailing errors of the times very much blunted, partly by their being dispirited, and so by a kind of cowardice are afraid, boldly, openly, and zealously to appear against those errors that show themselves in the world under the patronage and protection of so many persons of note and figure; partly by a kind of indifference and mistaken charity, whereby they think they ought to bear with others, though differing from them in opinion about points which are mysterious and sublime, but not practical nor fundamental, such as predestination. Now, although I would grant that the precise point of election and reprobation be neither fundamental nor immediately practical, yet take predestination completely, as it takes in the other disputed points between Calvinists and Arminians, such as universal grace, the non-perseverance of the saints, foreseen faith, and good works, &c., and I think it such an article in my creed, such a fundamental of my faith, that I know not what any other articles would avail, that could be retained without it.

Now the expedient which I would humbly propose you may take is as follows: First, that our Synod, as an ecclesiastical judicature of Christ, clothed with ministerial authority to act in concert in behalf of truth and opposition to error, would do something of this kind at such a juncture, when error seems to grow so fast, that unless we be well fortified, it is like to swallow us up.

Secondly, that in pursuance hereof, the Synod would, by an act of its own, publicly and authoritatively adopt the Westminster Confession of Faith, Catechisms, &c., for the public confession of our faith, as we are a particular organized church. Thirdly, that further the Synod would make an act to oblige every Presbytery within their bounds, to oblige every candidate for the ministry, to subscribe, or otherwise acknowledge *coram presbyterio*, the said confession of theirs, &c., and to promise not to preach or teach contrary to it. Fourthly, to oblige every actual minister coming among us to do the like. Fifthly, to enact, that if any minister within our bounds shall take upon him to teach or preach any thing contrary to any of the said articles, unless, first, he propose the said point to the Presbytery or Synod to be by them discussed, he shall be censured so and so. Sixthly, let the Synod recommend it to all their members, and members to their flocks, to entertain the truth in love, to be zealous and fruitful, and to be earnest with God by prayer, to preserve their vine from being spoiled by those deluding foxes; which if the Synod shall see cause to do, I hope it may, through the divine blessing, prevent in a great measure, if not altogether, our being deluded with the damnable errors of our times; but if not, I am afraid we may be at last infected with the errors which so much prevail elsewhere. . . .

Thus, brethren, I have offered to your consideration some serious thoughts, in a coarse dress. May it please the Master of assemblies to preside among us, and direct and influence us in all things, for his glory, and the edification of his church. So prays your unworthy fellow labourer in Christ's vineyard. (Quoted in C. Hodge, *The Constitutional History of the Presbyterian Church in U.S.A.*, Philadelphia, 1851, Part I, 136–141.)

11. The Adopting Act, 1729

The action of the Synod of 1729, whereby the Westminster Confession and Catechisms were adopted as "the confession of our faith," has been the subject of much learned controversy. Obviously the act was a compromise between those who wanted unqualified subscription to the creed and those who objected to such a limitation of divine revelation

THE FOUNDATIONS 31

to one man-made formula or interpretation. Thus, the act begins by disclaiming all power to legislate over men's consciences. No claim to infallibility is made for the Westminster Divines, but each minister is to be free to state his own conscientious scruples. All are to agree that "in all the essential and necessary articles of faith," the Westminster Assembly devised "good forms of sound words and systems of Christian doctrine." Acceptance of the Confession of Faith as "a system of doctrine taught in the Holy Scriptures," rather than as a detailed statement of required belief, continues to be a part of the ordination service for both ministers and elders. These broad standards have attracted both men of conservative attitudes and men of liberal tendencies, and have formed the basis for the development of a great Church. (Cf. Ch. 8, art. 9; Ch. 11, arts. 7 and 9.)

The committee brought in an overture upon the affair of the confession, which, after long debating upon it, was agreed upon *in haec verba*.

Although the Synod do not claim or pretend to any authority of imposing our faith upon other men's consciences, but do profess our just dissatisfaction with, and abhorrence of such impositions, and do utterly disclaim all legislative power and authority in the Church, being willing to receive one another as Christ has received us to the glory of God, and admit to fellowship in sacred ordinances, all such as we have grounds to believe Christ will at last admit to the kingdom of heaven, yet we are undoubtedly obliged to take care that the faith once delivered to the saints be kept pure and uncorrupt among us, and so handed down to our posterity; and do therefore agree that all the ministers of this Synod, or that shall hereafter be admitted into this Synod, shall declare their agreement in, and approbation of, the Confession of Faith, with the Larger and Shorter Catechisms of the Assembly of Divines at Westminster, as being in all the essential and necessary articles, good forms of sound words and systems of Christian doctrine, and do also adopt the said Confession and Catechisms as the confession of our faith. And we do also agree, that all the Presbyteries within our bounds shall always take care not to admit any candidate of the ministry into the exercise of the sacred function but what declares his agreement in opinion with all the essential and necessary articles of said Confession, either by subscribing the said Confession of Faith and Catechisms, or by a verbal declaration of their assent thereto, as such minister or candidate shall think best. And in case any minister of this Synod, or any candidate for the ministry, shall have any scruple with respect to any article or articles of said Confession or Catechisms, he shall at the time of his making said declaration declare his sentiments to the Presbytery or Synod, who shall, notwithstanding, admit him to the exercise of the ministry within our bounds, and to ministerial communion, if the Synod or Presbytery shall judge his scruple or mistake to be only about articles not essential and necessary in doctrine, worship, or government. But if the Synod or Presbytery shall judge such ministers or candidates erroneous in essential and necessary articles of faith, the Synod or Presbytery shall declare them uncapable of communion with them. And the Synod do solemnly agree, that none of us will traduce or use any opprobrious terms of those that differ from us in these extra-essential and not necessary points of doctrine, but treat them with the same friendship, kindness, and brotherly love, as if they had not differed from us in such sentiments.

Mr. Morgan sent a letter to the Synod giving his reasons for his absence, which were sustained.

Adjourned till three o'clock, P.M.

At three o'clock, P.M. post preces sederunt qui supra.

Ordered, That the minutes of our last *sederunt* be read.

All the ministers of this Synod now present, except one that declared himself not prepared, viz. Masters Jedidiah Andrews, Thomas Craighead, John Thomson, James Anderson, John Pierson, Samuel Gelston, Joseph Houston, Gilbert Tennent, Adam Boyd, Jonathan Dickinson, John Bradner, Alexander Hutchinson, Thomas Evans, Hugh Stevenson, William Tennent, Hugh Conn, George Gillespie, and John Willson, after proposing all the scruples that any of them had to make against any articles and expressions in the Confession of Faith, and Larger and Shorter Catechisms of the Assembly of Divines at Westminster, have unanimously agreed in the solution of those scruples, and in declaring the said Confession and Catechisms to be the confession of their faith, excepting only some clauses in the twentieth and twenty-third chapters, concerning which clauses the Synod do unanimously declare, that they do not receive those articles in any such sense as to suppose the civil magistrate hath a controlling power over Synods with respect to the exercise of their ministerial authority; or power to persecute any for their religion, or in any sense contrary to the Protestant succession to the throne of Great Britain.

The Synod observing that unanimity, peace, and unity, which appeared in all their consultations and determinations relating to the affair of the Confession, did unanimously agree in giving thanks to God in solemn prayer and praises. (*Records of Pres. Ch.*, 1729, 94 f.)

CHAPTER

2

THE GREAT AWAKENING
1730–1754

1. "The Log College"

While the subscriptionist party within the Presbyterian Church was urging stricter doctrinal requirements for the ministry, another group, centering around Rev. William Tennent, Sr., and his sons, was stressing the importance of a vital religious experience of conversion. About 1727, Mr. Tennent began to educate young men for the ministry in his own home at Neshaminy, Pa., and in 1735 he erected a log cabin for his students. This has been called "the most important event in colonial Presbyterian history." Some eighteen young men were trained in the "Log College," and went out to the churches, filled with an intense spirit of evangelism and a warm personal piety. Their enthusiasm was contagious, and soon their congregations began to experience the revivals of religion which are known as the Great Awakening. The following description of the "school of the prophets" was written by the great English evangelist Rev. George Whitefield.

Thursday, November 22. Set out for *Neshamini* (twenty miles distant from Trent-Town) where old Mr. Tennent lives, and keeps an Academy, and where I was to preach to Day, according to Appointment. About Twelve we came thither, and found above 3000 people gather'd together in the Meeting-House Yard; and Mr. *William Tennent,* an eminent Servant of Jesus Christ, preaching to them, because we had stayed beyond the Time appointed. When I came up, he soon stopp'd, and sung a Psalm, and then I began to speak as the Lord gave me Utterance.—At first the People seem'd unaffected, but in the midst of my Discourse, the Power of the Lord Jesus came upon me, and I felt such a Struggling within myself for the People, as I scarce ever felt before. The Hearers began to be melted down immediately, and cry much; and we had good Reason to hope the Lord intended Good for many. After I had finished, Mr. *Gilbert Tennent* gave a word of Exhortation to confirm what had been deliver'd. At the End of his Discourse, we sung a Psalm, and then dismiss'd the People with a Blessing. *Oh that the Lord may say Amen to it!* After our Exercises were over, we went to old Mr. *Tennent,* who entertain'd us like one of the ancient Patriarchs. His wife to me seemed like *Elizabeth,* and he like *Zacchary;* both, as far as I can find, walk in all the Ordinances and Commandments of the Lord blameless.—Tho' God was pleased to humble my Soul, so that I was obliged to retire for a while, yet we had sweet Communion with each other, and spent the Evening in concerting what measures had best be taken for promoting our dear Lord's Kingdom. It happens very providentially, that Mr. *Tennent* and his Brethren are appointed to be a Presbytery by the Synod, so that they intend breeding up gracious Youths, and sending them out from Time to Time into our Lord's Vineyard. The place wherein the young Men study now is in contempt call'd *the College.* It is a Log-House, about Twenty Feet long, and near as many broad; and to me it seemed to resemble the Schools of the old Prophets.—For that their Habitations were mean, and that they sought not great Things for themselves, is plain from that Passage of Scripture wherein we are told that at the Feast of the Sons of the Prophets, one of them put on the Pot, whilst the others went to fetch some Herbs out of the Field. All that can be said of most of our publick Universities is, they are all glorious *without.* From this despised Place Seven or Eight worthy Ministers of Jesus have lately been sent forth; more are almost ready to be sent, and a Foundation is now laying for the Instruction of many others. The Devil will certainly rage against them, but the Work, I am persuaded, is of God, and therefore will not come to nought. Carnal Ministers oppose them strongly; and because People, when awaken'd by Mr. *Tennent,* or his Brethren, see through, and therefore leave their Ministry, the poor Gentlemen are loaded with Contempt, and look'd upon (as all faithful Preachers will be) as Persons that turn the World upside down.—A notable War I believe is commencing between *Michael* and the Dragon, we may easily guess who will prevail. —*The Seed of the Woman shall bruise the Serpent's Head.* (Whitefield's Fifth Journal, Nov. 22, 1739, 43 f.)

2. "Prevent Errors Young Men May Imbibe by Reading Without Direction"

In an effort to undermine the influence of the Log College men, the subscriptionist and antirevivalist element presented the following overture to the Synod in 1738. While the principle of requiring candidates for the ministry who had no college degree to submit to an examination by a committee of the Synod seems reasonable, it deepened the gulf between those in the Church who emphasized intellectual achievement and those who insisted on religious experience.

A proposal was made by the Presbytery of Lewes to this Synod, which is as follows: That this part of the world where God has ordered our lot, labours under a grievous disadvantage for want of the opportunities of universities, and professors skilled in the several branches of useful learning, and that many students from Europe are especially cramped in prosecuting their studies, their parents removing to these colonies before they have an opportunity of attending the college, after having spent some years at the grammar school; and that many persons born in the country groan under the same pressure, whose circumstances are not able to support them to spend a course of years in the European, or New England colleges, which discourages much, and must be a detriment to our church; for we know that natural parts, however great and promising, for want of being well improved, must be marred of their usefulness, and cannot be so extensively serviceable to the public, and that want of due pains and care paves the way for ignorance, and this for a formidable train of sad consequences. To prevent this evil, it is humbly proposed as a remedy, that every student who has not studied with approbation, passing the usual courses in some of the New England, or European colleges, approved by public authority, shall, before he be encouraged by any Presbytery for the sacred work of the ministry, apply himself to this Synod, and that they appoint a committee of their members yearly, whom they know to be well skilled in the several branches of philosophy, and divinity, and the languages, to examine such students in this place, and finding them well accomplished in those several parts of learning, shall allow them a public testimonial from the Synod, which, till better provision be made, will in some measure answer the design of taking a degree in the college. And for encouragement of students let this be done, without putting them to further expenses than attending. And let it be an objection against none, where they have read, or what books, but let all encouragement be only according to merit. And 'tis hoped this will fill our youth with a laudable emulation, prevent errors young men may imbibe by reading without direction, or things of little value, will banish ignorance, fill our infant church with men eminent for parts and learning, and advance the glory of God, and the honour of our Synod both at home and among our neighbours, who conceive a low opinion of us for want of such favourable opportunities. 'Tis further proposed, that all that are not licensed to preach the gospel, what university or college soever they come from, may undergo the same trials. But inasmuch as this act cannot be put in force this year, without discouraging such as may not be apprized of it, 'tis ordered, that there be two standing committees to act in the above affair for this year, one to the northward and the other to the southward of Philadelphia. (*Records of Pres. Ch.,* 1738, 141.)

3. Narratives of Revivals of Religion

The Great Awakening in the Middle Colonies had its beginnings among the Dutch Reformed congregations in northern New Jersey. During the ministry of John Tennent at Freehold, N.J. (1730–1732), the revival spread among the Presbyterians. What happened is described by William Tennent, Jr., who succeeded his brother in 1732. In the second narrative, Samuel Blair describes the revival in his congregation at New-Londonderry (Fagg's Manor, Pa.). Blair's narrative is particularly valuable for the insight it gives into the methods and techniques of the Log College evangelists. It will be noted that the awakening was preceded by six months of doctrinal preaching, and was followed by careful pastoral guidance. The best treatment of the whole movement is in The Forming of an American Tradition (*Philadelphia, 1949*), *by Prof. L. J. Trinterud.*

A. THE REVIVAL AT FREEHOLD, N.J.

During his [John Tennent's] short Time, his Labours were greatly blessed; so that the Place of public Worship was usually crouded with People of all Ranks and Orders, as well as Professions that obtain'd in that Part of the Country, and they seem'd to hear generally as for their Lives: yea, such as were won't to go to those Places for their Diversion, viz. To hear News or speak to their Trades-Men & even on the Lord's-Day, as they themselves have since confess'd, were taken in the Gospel Net: a solemn Awe of God's Majesty possessed many, so that they behav'd themselves as at his Bar while in his House. Many Tears were usually shed, when he preached, and sometimes the Body of the Congregation was mov'd or affected. I can say, and let the Lord alone have the Glory of it, that I have seen both Minister and People wet with their Tears as with a bedewing Rain. It was no uncommon Thing to see Persons in the Time of Hearing, sobbing as if their Hearts would break, but without any public Out-cry; and some have been carry'd out of the Assembly (being overcome) as if they had been dead. . . .

Religion was then the general Subject of Discourse, tho' they did not all approve of the Power of it: the holy Bible was searched by People on both Sides of the Question, and Knowledge surprizingly increased! The Terror of God fell generally upon the Inhabitants of this Place; so that Wickedness as ashamed in a great Measure hid it self; Frolicking, Dancing, Horse-racing, with other profane Meetings were broken up.

Some of the jolly Companions of both Sexes, were constrained by their Consciences to meet together, the Men by themselves, and the Women by themselves, to confess privately their Abominations before God, and beg the Pardon of them.

Before my Brother's Death, by Reason of his bodily Weakness, and Inability on that Account to officiate publickly, I preached here about six Months. In which Time, many came enquiring what they should do to be saved, and some to tell what the Lord had done for their Souls. But the Blessing on his Labours to the Conviction and Conversion of Souls, was more discernible some Months after his Death, than any Time in his Life; almost in every Neighbourhood, I cannot say in every House, there were Sin sick Souls, longing for and seeking after the dear Physician Jesus Christ: several of whom I no Ways doubt have since that Time sincerely closed with him, and are healed: Glory, Glory to his holy Name be given for ever and ever, Amen! (*The Christian History, Containing Accounts of the Revival and Propagation of Religion in Great-Britain, America & for the Year 1744*, Boston, 1744, 300–301.)

B. THE REVIVAL AT NEW-LONDONDERRY, PA.

The first sermon I preached after my return to them was from Matthew, vi. 33. *Seek ye first the kingdom of God and his righteousness.* After opening up and explaining the parts of the text, when in the improvement, I came to press the injunction in the text, upon the unconverted and ungodly, and offered this as one reason, among others, why they should now henceforth first of all *seek the kingdom and righteousnes of God,* viz. that they had neglected too, too long to do so already. This consideration seemed to come and cut like a sword upon several in the congregation, so that while I was speaking upon it, they could no longer contain, but burst out in the most bitter mourning. I desired them, as much as possible, to restrain themselves from making a noise that would hinder themselves or others from hearing what was spoken: and often afterwards I had occasion to repeat the same counsel. I still advised people to endeavour to moderate and bound their passions, but not so as to resist or stifle their convictions. The number of the awakened increased very fast, frequently under sermons there were some newly convicted, and brought into deep distress of soul about their perishing estate. Our sabbath assemblies soon became vastly large: many people from almost all parts around inclining very much to come where there was such appearance of the divine power and presence. I think there was scarcely a sermon or lecture preached here through that whole summer, but there was manifest evidences of impressions on the hearers; and many times the impressions were very great and general: several would be overcome and fainting; others deeply sobbing, hardly able to contain, others crying in a most dolorous manner, many others more silently weeping; and a solemn concern appearing in the countenance of many others. And sometimes the soul exercises of some, though comparatively but very few, would so far affect their bodies, as to occasion some strange, unusual bodily motions. I had opportunities of speaking particularly with a great many of those who afforded such outward tokens of inward soul concern in the time of public worship and hearing of the word; indeed many came to me of themselves in their distress for private instruction and counsel; and I found, so far as I can remember, that, with by far the greater part, their apparent concern in public was not just a transient qualm of conscience, or merely a floating commotion of the affections; but a rational fixed conviction of their dangerous perishing estate. . . .

The main scope of my preaching through that summer, was, laying open the deplorable state of man by nature since the fall, our ruined, exposed case by the breach of the first covenant, and the awful condition of such as were not in *Christ,* giving the marks and characters of such as were in that condition: and moreover, laying open the way of recovery in the new covenant, through a Mediator, with the nature and necessity of faith in *Christ,* the Mediator, &c. I laboured much on the last mentioned heads, that people might have right apprehensions of the gospel method of life and salvation. I treated much on the way of a sinner's closing with *Christ* by faith, and obtaining a right peace to an awakened wounded conscience; shewing, that persons were not to take peace to themselves on account of their repentings, sorrows, prayers, and reformations, nor to make these things the ground of their adventuring themselves upon *Christ* and his righteousness, and of their expectations of life by him: and, that neither were they to obtain or seek peace in extraordinary ways, by visions, dreams, or immediate inspirations; but by an understanding view and believing persuasion of the way of life, as revealed in the gospel, through the suretyship, obedience, and sufferings of Jesus Christ, with a view of the suitableness and sufficiency of that mediatory righteousness of *Christ* for the justification and life of law-condemned sinners: and thereupon freely accepting him for their Saviour, heartily consenting to, and being well pleased with, that way of salvation; and venturing their all upon his mediation, from the warrant and encouragement afforded of God thereunto in his word, by his free offer, authoritative command, and sure promise to those that so believe. I endeavoured to shew the fruits and evidences of a true faith, &c.

In some time many of the convinced and distressed afforded very hopeful, satisfying evidence that the Lord had brought them to a true closure with *Jesus Christ,* and that their distresses and fears had been in a great measure removed in a right gospel-way by believing in the Son of God; several of them had very remarkable and sweet deliverances this way. It was very agreeable to hear their accounts, how that, when they were in the deepest perplexity and darkness, distress and difficulty, seeking God as poor condemned hell-deserving sinners, the scene of the recovering grace, through a Redeemer, has been opened to their understandings, with a surprising beauty and glory, so that they were enabled to believe in Christ with joy unspeakable and full of glory. . . . Much of their exercise was in self-abasing and self-loathing, and admiring the astonishing condescension and grace of God towards such vile and despicable creatures, that had been so full of enmity and disaffection to him: then they freely and sweetly, with all their hearts, chose the ways of his commandments; their inflamed desire was to live to him forever, according to his will, and to the glory of his name. (S. Blair, *A Short and Faithful Narrative of a Remarkable Revival of Religion in the Congregation of New Londonderry and other Parts of Pennsylvania, etc.* Reprinted, Baltimore, 1836, 73–77.)

4. An Act to Control Itinerants

The popularity of the new type, revivalist preaching resulted in a demand for the services of the Log College men beyond the bounds of their own congregations. Frequently Old Side ministers found their own churches deserted. The following resolutions were an attempt to prevent the disorders arising from wandering itinerant preachers.

The debate concerning ministers preaching without the bounds of their own Presbyteries, to vacancies in the bounds of another Presbytery, without the consent of some of the members, was reassumed, and overtured upon it, that no minister belonging to this Synod shall have liberty to preach in any congregation belonging to another Presbytery whereof he is not a member, after he is advised by any minister of such Presbytery, that he thinks his preaching in that congregation will have a tendency to procure divisions and disorders, until he first obtain liberty from the Presbytery or Synod so to do. This being put to the vote, was approved.

Overtured, That in order to obviate some mistakes, that it is supposed some of the members of the Synod were in, with respect to the preceding overture, that it be voted that every minister belonging to this Synod, has liberty to preach in any vacant congregation where he shall be occasionally and providentially called, even though he is out of the bounds of the Presbytery to which he belongs, unless he be first advised by some minister of such Presbytery, that his preaching there is likely to procure divisions and disorders in such congregation; and even when he is so advised by any minister of such Presbytery, he may yet preach in such congregation, if by liberty first obtained from such Presbytery or from the Synod, but not otherwise. Agreed *nemine contradicente*. (*Records of Pres. Ch.*, 1738, 138.)

5. "The Danger of an Unconverted Ministry"

No Presbyterian sermon was more famous in its day than that preached by Gilbert Tennent to a vacant congregation at Nottingham, Pa., on March 8, 1740. In it the acknowledged leader of the New Side not only vented his scorn of the "letter-learned," and unconverted college men of the Old Side, but openly criticized congregations which were content to put up with such "dead Dogs," and encouraged the people to attend services where they could hear live preaching. As an example of the pungency, vigor, and emotionalism of the new preaching it is outstanding. Reading it, one understands the bitterness of the controversy over itinerants and education, and the final division of the Church in 1741. In later years, as pastor of the Second Presbyterian Church of Philadelphia, Tennent repudiated the extreme position he had taken at Nottingham.

As a faithful Ministry is a great Ornament, Blessing, and Comfort, to the Church of God; even the Feet of such Messengers are beautiful: So on the contrary, an ungodly Ministry is a great Curse and Judgment: These Caterpillars labour to devour every green Thing.

THERE is nothing that may more justly call forth our saddest Sorrows, and make all our Powers and Passions mourn, in the most doleful Accents, the most incessant, insatiable, and deploring Agonies; than the melancholy Case of such, who have no faithful Ministry! This Truth is set before our Minds in a strong Light, in the Words that I have chosen now to insist upon; in which we have an Account of our LORD's Grief, with the Causes of it.

WE are informed, That our dear Redeemer was moved with Compassion towards them. The Original Word signifies the strongest and most vehement Pity, issuing from the innermost Bowels.

BUT what was the Cause of this great and compassionate Commotion in the Heart of Christ? It was because he saw much People as Sheep having no Shepherd. Why, had the People then no Teachers? O yes! they had Heaps of Pharisee-Teachers, that came out, no doubt after they had been at the Feet of Gamaliel the usual Time, and according to the Acts, Canons, and Traditions of the Jewish Church. But notwithstanding of the great Crowds of these Orthodox, Letter-learned and regular Pharisees, our Lord laments the unhappy Case of that great Number of People, who, in the Days of his Flesh, had no better Guides: Because that those were as good as none (in many Respects) in our Saviour's Judgment. For all them, the People were as Sheep without a Shepherd. . . .

Pharisee-Teachers, having no Experience of a special Work of the Holy Ghost, upon their owns Souls, are therefore neither inclined to, nor fitted for Discoursing, frequently, clearly, and pathetically, upon such important Subjects. The Application of their Discourses, is either short, or indistinct and general. . . . No! They carelessly offer a common Mess to their People, and leave it to them, to divide it among themselves, as they see fit. This is indeed their general Practice, which is bad enough: But sometimes they do worse, by misapplying the Word, through Ignorance, or Anger. . . . These foolish Builders do but strengthen Men's carnal Security, by their soft, selfish, cowardly Discourses. They have not the Courage, or Honesty, to thrust the Nail of Terror into sleeping Souls; nay, sometimes they strive with all their Might, to fasten Terror into the Hearts of the Righteous, and so to make those sad, whom GOD would not have made sad! And this happens, when pious People begin to suspect their Hypocrisie, for which they have good Reason. I may add, That inasmuch as Pharisee-Teachers seek after Righteousness as it were by the Works of the Law themselves, they therefore do not distinguish as they ought, between *Law* and *Gospel*, in their Discourses to others. They keep Driving, Driving, to Duty, Duty, under this Notion, That it will recommend natural Men to the Favour of GOD, or entitle them to the Promises of Grace and Salvation: And thus those blind Guides fix a deluded World upon the false Foundation of their own Righteousness, and so exclude them from the dear Redeemer. All the Doings of unconverted Men, not proceeding from the Principles of Faith, Love, and a new Nature, nor being directed to the divine Glory as their highest End, but flowing from, and tending to Self, as their Principle and End; are doubtless damnably wicked in their Manner of Performance, and do deserve the Wrath and Curse of a Sin-avenging GOD; neither can any other Encouragement be justly given them, but this, That in the Way of Duty, there is a Peradventure or Probability of obtaining Mercy. . . .

Poor Christians are stunted and starv'd, who are put to feed on such bare Pastures, and such dry Nurses; as the Rev. Mr. Hildersham justly calls them. It's only when the wise Virgins sleep, that they can bear with those dead Dogs, that can't bark; but when the LORD revives his People, they can't but abhor them! O! it is ready to break their very Hearts with Grief, to see, how luke-warm those Pharisee-Teachers are in their publick Discourses, while Sinners are sinking into Damnation, in Multitudes! . . .

Is a blind Man fit to be a Guide in a very dangerous Way? Is a dead Man fit to bring others to Life? a mad Man fit to give Counsel in a Matter of Life and Death? . . . a Leper, or one that has Plague-sores upon him, fit to be a good Physician? Is an ignorant Rustick, that has never been at Sea in his Life, fit to be a Pilot, to keep Vessels from being dashed to Pieces upon Rocks and Sand-banks? Isn't an unconverted Minister like a Man who would learn others to swim, before he has learn'd it himself, and so is drowned in the Act, and dies like a Fool?

I may add, that sad Experience verifies what has been now observed, concerning the Unprofitableness of the Ministry of unconverted Men. Look into the Congregations of unconverted Ministers, and see what a sad Security reigns there; not a Soul convinced that can be heard of, for many Years together; and yet the Ministers are easy; for they say they do their Duty! . . .

And alas! what poor Guides are natural Ministers to those, who are under spiritual Trouble? they either slight such Distress altogether, and call it Melancholy, or Madness, or dawb those that are under it, with untemper'd Mortar. . . . Be these Moral Negroes never so white in the Mouth, (as one expresseth it) yet will they hinder, instead of helping others, in at the strait Gate. . . .

But let such hireling murderous Hypocrites take Care, that they don't feel the Force of a Halter in this World, and an aggravated Damnation in the next. . . .

THE IMPROVEMENT of this Subject remains. And, 1. If it be so, That the Case of those, who have no other, or no better than Pharisee-Teachers, is to be pitied: Then what a Scrole and Scene of Mourning, and Lamentation, and Wo, is opened! because of the Swarms of Locusts, the Crowds of Pharisees, that have as covetously as cruelly, crept into the Ministry, in this adulterous Generation! who as nearly resemble the Character given of the old Pharisees, in the Doctrinal Part of this Discourse, as one Crows Egg does another. It is true some of the modern Pharisees have learned to prate a little more orthodoxly about the New Birth, than their Predecessor *Nicodemus,* who are, in the mean Time, as great Strangers to the feeling Experience of it, as he. They are blind who see not this to be the Case of the Body of the Clergy, of this Generation. And O! that our Heads were Waters, and our Eyes a Fountain of Tears, that we could Day and Night lament, with the utmost Bitterness, the doleful Case of the poor Church of God, upon this account.

2. From what has been said, we may learn, That such who are contented under a dead Ministry, have not in them the Temper of that Saviour they profess. It's an awful Sign, that they are as blind as Moles, and as dead as Stones, without any spiritual Taste and Relish. And alas! isn't this the Case of Multitudes? If they can get one, that has the Name of a Minister, with a Band, and a Black Coat or Gown to carry on a Sabbath-days among them, although never so coldly, and insuccessfully; if he is free from gross Crimes in Practice, and takes good Care to keep at a due Distance from their Consciences, and is never troubled about his Insuccessfulness; O! think the poor Fools, that is a fine Man indeed; our Minister is a prudent charitable Man, he is not always harping upon Terror, and Sounding Damnation in our Ears, like some rash-headed Preachers, who by their uncharitable Methods, are ready to put poor People out of their Wits, or to run them into Despair; O! how terrible a Thing is that Despair! Ay, our Minister, honest Man, gives us good Caution against it. Poor silly Souls! consider seriously these Passages, of the Prophet *Jeremiah,* c. 5. 30, 31. . . .

4. If the Ministry of natural Men be as it has been represented; Then it is both lawful and expedient to go from them to hear Godly Persons; yea, it's so far from being sinful to do this, that one who lives under a pious Minister of lesser Gifts, after having honestly endeavour'd to get Benefit by his Ministry, and yet gets little or none, but doth find real Benefit and more Benefit elsewhere; I say, he may lawfully go, and that frequently, where he gets most Good to his precious Soul, after regular Application to the Pastor where he lives, for his Consent, and proposing

the Reasons thereof; when this is done in the Spirit of Love and Meekness, without Contempt of any, as also without rash Anger, or vain Curiosity. . . .

To bind Men to a particular Minister, against their Judgment and Inclinations, when they are more edified elsewhere, is carnal with a Witness; a cruel Oppression of tender Consciences, a Compelling of Men to Sin: . . .

Besides it is an unscriptural Infringment on Christian Liberty; 1 *Cor.* 3. 22. It's a Yoke worse than that of *Rome* itself. . . .

If the great Ends of Hearing may be attained as well, and better, by Hearing of another Minister than our own; then I see not, why we should be under a fatal Necessity of hearing him, I mean our Parish-Minister, perpetually, or generally. . . . *Faith* is said to come by *Hearing*, Rom. 10. But the Apostle doesn't add, *Your Parish-Minister*. . . .

From such as have a Form of Godliness, and deny the Power thereof, we are enjoined to turn away, 2 Tim. 3. 5. And are there not many such? . . .

I would conclude my present Meditations upon this Subject, by Exhorting All those who enjoy a faithful Ministry, to a speedy and sincere Improvement of so rare and valuable a Privilege; lest by their foolish Ingratitude the Righteous GOD be provok'd to remove the Means they enjoy, or his Blessing from them, and so at last to expose them in another State to Enduring and greater Miseries. . . .

And let those who live under the Ministry of dead Men, whether they have got the Form of Religion or not, repair to the Living, where they may be edified. Let who will, oppose it. . . . But tho' your Neighbours growl against you, and reproach you for doing your Duty, in seeking your Souls Good; bear their unjust Censures with Christian Meekness, and persevere. (Gilbert Tennent, *The Danger of an Unconverted Ministry*, Philadelphia: Printed by Benjamin Franklin, in Market-street, 1740.)

6. "An Epidemical Distemper"

To the Old Side Presbyterians, the emotional extravagances of the revivalists appeared like some dreadful social disease. In the following passages from a sermon preached at New Londonderry, Pa., October 14, 1741, Rev. John Caldwell seeks to prove that the loud talking, censoriousness, and lack of charity among the so-called converted could not be the fruits of the Holy Spirit. The savageness of his attack helps to explain the highhanded action of the Old Side men in expelling the

New Side party from the Synod in 1741. Caldwell's sermon was reprinted in Glasgow and widely distributed in the British Isles.

I shall, with the greatest Caution, and a sincere Regard to Truth and Holiness, to the Glory of God and the Good of humane Souls, proceed to consider the Nature, Effects and Evidences of the present supposed Conversion in this Part of the World, that we may all be the better able to judge of the Nature of the Spirit from whence it flows.

To any Person, that with an unprejudiced Mind hath viewed the same for these six Months past, or more, I presume its Nature will appear to be this, or very near, *viz.* A sudden and terrible Fear of Divine Wrath, or the Miseries of Hell, occasioning in some a Sensation of Cold, in most a very extraordinary Warmth all over the Body; causing People to cry as if distracted; to shed Tears in great Plenty; throwing many into Convulsions, and a few for some Time into Despair. This continues with the generality but for a very short Season, (tho' some few feel it a little longer). In a few Days or less, the Cloud blows, for ordinary, over; the Terror is at an End, and a more than common Chearfulness succeeds; all their Difficulties and Doubts are removed, and immediately a Certainty that all their Sins are pardoned, and that they shall be saved, takes place; and that all their after Sins, how many or heinous soever they be, will be overlooked, upon their confidently relying on the Merits of our Redeemer.

Its Effects, in general are, a bold talking of Experiences, as soon as the Terror is over; by which if we judge as we would in other Cases, we are to understand their Righteousness; tho' in the mean Time that they are filling our Ears with such Discourse, they would have us believe them the most humble and self-denied of Mankind; a Contempt of all others, especially such as seem to question any thing of what they say of their Experiences; boldly calling such carnal, and sentencing them to eternal Misery, who demand more Evidence than they think proper to give, to convince them their Spirit is from God; refusing to reason upon their Principles, telling the World none are capable to judge of their Doctrines or Experiences but spiritual Men; i.e. such as are of their Opinions. Its Effects upon many of their Teachers are very uncommon, divesting them of all Charity to such as oppose, tho' ever so conscientiously, this present Scheme; moving them to shut the Gates of Heaven against the whole humane Race, but themselves and a few of their friends, whose Sins God will not be offended at, as he will not approve the righteous and Christian Behaviour of others: To despise or lightly esteem the great Duties of Morality, so clearly taught, so powerfully enforced, and declared by our Saviour, to be necessary Conditions of Salvation.

Some of them it moves to leave their own particular Congregations destitute of the Ordinances of Christ, and travel to and fro upon the Earth, spiriting People against their Pastors, who are not of their Stamp, by representing them as carnal and dead Men, who have no more Right to preach than the Devil; to declare that many Errors in Judgment, Delusions of the Devil, and direct Opposition to God's Word, are no Proof of Mens being guided by a wrong Spirit; to reproach People for not being affected with what they say, i.e. because they do not shed Tears, fall down into Convulsions, scream, and prevent others from being benefited; to declare such as oppose them are guilty of Blasphemy against the Holy Ghost; to neglect the Information of the Judgment, and apply to the Passions, especially Fear; by almost constantly insisting upon Subjects of Terror, Hell and Damnation, with Pathos and moving Gestures; to declare such Things as God declares he will condemn Men for, may yet be found in God's own Children.

Its Effects upon People, are Censoriousness and Uncharitableness to such as differ from them in that Point; speaking evil of their Neighbours, despising a holy and religious Life in all but themselves; fancying they are obliged to persuade as many as they can, to despise and leave the Ministry of their Pastors, if not agreeable to them; pretending to God's peculiar Prerogative, *searching the Heart;* taking deluded Imaginations for heavenly Visions; fancying their Noise and Uncharitableness, Religion; preferring the Discourses of an ignorant Person among them, to the most judicious and learned of such as differ from them; becoming Teachers of others, praying in public, and some laying aside all Labour for the Support of themselves and Dependents.

The Evidences upon which the Certainty of their Conversion is founded, are their being able to point out the Time of their first Convictions, or remembering how some Expressions in a Sermon or Texts of Scripture, tho' not understood, filled them with Terror, caused them to weep, scream, or fall into epileptic-like Fits; thus finding by some unknown Cause, or Text of Scripture, or humane Expressions, or Imaginations, called Visions; and attributed to the divine Spirit, this Uneasiness removed, and Chearfulness succeed: From these and such like Things, they judge that their own, and the Conversion of others, are undoubtedly certain.

This I think a just Account of the Nature, Effects and Evidences of the present Conversion, when stripped of a Set of Phrases and Gestures, to which it owes no small Part of its Success. It spreads like an epidemical Distemper, catches at the Eyes, and by a kind of Sympathy, prevails over all Ages and Sexes, but especially the younger Women and Children. (J. Caldwell, *A Trial of the Present Spirit*, Boston, 1742, 21–25.)

7. The Protestation of 1741

The increasingly bitter battle between the Log College men and the antirevival subscriptionist forces reached its climax in the Synod of 1741, when, "to save this swooning Church from a total expiration," Robert Cross introduced a carefully prepared Protestation. *It was asserted that only those who had subscribed to the Confession of Faith and the Directory (Ch. 1, art. 11), and had obeyed all the other rules of the Synod (e.g., Ch. 2, art. 4), should sit and vote in the Synod. The Log College men had broken these rules, hence, they had forfeited their right to membership. The reasons for this highhanded procedure are stated in the portion of the* Protestation *printed below.*

Reverend and dear Brethren, we beseech you to hear us with patience, while we lay before you as briefly as we can, some of the reasons that move us thus to protest, and more particularly why we protest against our protesting brethren's being allowed to sit as members of this Synod.

1. Their heterodox and anarchial principles expressed in their Apology, . . . where they expressly deny that Presbyteries have authority to oblige their dissenting members, and that Synods should go no further, in judging of appeals or references, &c. than to give their best advice. . . .

2. Their protesting against the Synod's act in relation to the examination of candidates, together with their proceeding to license and ordain men to the ministry of the gospel, in opposition to, and in contempt of said act of Synod.

3. Their making irregular irruptions upon the congregations to which they have no immediate relation, without order, concurrence, or allowance of the Presbyteries or ministers to which congregations belong, thereby sowing the seeds of division among people, and doing what they can to alienate and fill their minds with unjust prejudices against their lawfully called pastors.

4. Their principles and practice or rash judging and condemning all who do not fall in with their measures, both ministers and people, as carnal, graceless, and enemies to the work of God, and what not, as appears in Mr. Gilbert Tennent's sermon against unconverted ministers, . . . which rash judging has been the constant practice of our protesting brethren, and their irregular probationers, for above these

twelve months past, in their disorderly itinerations and preaching through our congregations, by which, (alas! for it,) most of our congregations, through weakness and credulity, are so shattered and divided, and shaken in their principles, that few or none of us can say we enjoy the comfort, or have the success among our people, which otherwise we might, and which we enjoyed heretofore.

5. Their industriously persuading people to believe that the call of God whereby he calls men to the ministry, does not consist in their being regularly ordained and set apart to that work, according to the institution and rules of the word; but in some invisible motions and workings of the Spirit, which none can be conscious or sensible of but the person himself, and with respect to which he is liable to be deceived, or play the hypocrite; that the gospel preached in truth by unconverted ministers, can be of no saving benefit to souls; and their pointing out such ministers, whom they condemn as graceless by their rash judging spirit, they effectually carry the point with the poor credulous people, who, in imitation of their example, and under their patrociny, judge their ministers to be graceless, and forsake their ministry as hurtful rather than profitable.

6. Their preaching the terrors of the law in such a manner and dialect as has no precedent in the word of God, but rather appears to be borrowed from a worse dialect; and so industriously working on the passions and affections of weak minds, as to cause them to cry out in a hideous manner, and fall down in convulsion-like fits, to the marring of the profiting both of themselves and others, who are so taken up in seeing and hearing these odd symptoms, that they cannot attend to or hear what the preacher says; and then, after all, boasting of these things as the work of God, which we are persuaded do proceed from an inferior or worse cause.

7. Their, or some of them, preaching and maintaining that all true converts are as certain of their gracious state as a person can be of what he knows by his outward senses; and are able to give a narrative of the time and manner of their conversion, or else they conclude them to be in a natural or graceless state, and that a gracious person can judge of another's gracious state otherwise than by his profession and life. That people are under no sacred tie or relation to their own pastors lawfully called, but may leave them when they please, and ought to go where they think they get the most good.

For these and many other reasons, we protest, before the Eternal God, his holy angels, and you, Reverend Brethren, and before all here present, that these brethren have no right to be acknowledged as members of this judicatory of Christ, whose principles and practices are so diametrically opposite to our doctrine, and principles of government and order, which the great King of the Church hath laid down in his Word. (*Records of Pres. Ch.*, 1741, 1904 edition, 157–160 n.)

8. A Presbyterian Mystic

No life inspired his own and later generations with a spirit of devotion and missionary zeal more than that of David Brainerd (1718–1747). A product of the Great Awakening in New England, he was ordained by the Presbytery of New York to be a missionary to the Delaware Indians. Though dying of tuberculosis, he underwent tremendous hardships and discouragements for the sake of his "beloved people," crossing the "howling wilderness" between the Delaware and Susquehanna Rivers four times. His greatest success was among the New Jersey Indians at Crossweeksung near Freehold. The following passages from his diary refer to his arrival among the Delawares, near Easton, Pa., his journeys to the Susquehanna, his contact with an Indian medicine man, and his work at Crossweeksung. Especially notable is the deep mystical quality of Brainerd's piety. His "practice of the presence of God" makes his diary a classic of Christian mysticism.

June 28 (1744). Spent the morning in reading several parts of the holy scripture, and in fervent prayer for my Indians, that God would set up his kingdom among them, and bring them into his church. About nine, I withdrew to my usual place of retirement in the woods; and there again enjoyed some assistance in prayer. My great concern was for the conversion of the Heathen to God; and the Lord helped me to plead with him for it. Towards noon, rode up to the Indians, in order to preach to them; and while going, my heart went up to God in prayer for them; could freely tell God, he knew that the cause in which I was engaged was not mine; but that it was his own cause, and that it would be for his own glory to convert the poor Indians: and blessed be God, I felt no desire of their conversion, that I might receive honour from the world, as being the instrument of it. Had some freedom in speaking to the Indians. . . .

Towards night my burden respecting my work among the Indians began to increase much; and was aggravated by hearing sundry things which looked very discouraging; in particular, that they intended to meet together the next day for an idolatrous feast and dance. Then I began to be in anguish: I thought that I must in conscience go and endeavour to break them up; yet knew not how to attempt such a thing.

However, I withdrew for prayer, hoping for strength from above. In prayer I was exceedingly enlarged, and my soul was as much drawn out as I ever remember it to have been in my life. I was in such anguish, and pleaded with so much earnestness and importunity, that when I rose from my knees I felt extremely weak and overcome; I could scarcely walk straight; my joints were loosed; the sweat ran down my face and body; and nature seemed as if it would dissolve. So far as I could judge, I was wholly free from selfish ends in my fervent supplications for the poor Indians. I knew that they were met together to worship devils, and not God; and this made me cry earnestly, that God would now appear, and help me in my attempts to break up this idolatrous meeting. My soul pleaded long; and I thought that God would hear, and would go with me to vindicate his own cause: I seemed to confide in God for his presence and assistance. And thus I spent the evening, praying incessantly for divine assistance, and that I might not be self-dependent, but still have my whole dependence upon God. What I passed through was remarkable, and indeed inexpressible. All things here below vanished; and there appeared to be nothing of any considerable importance to me, but holiness of heart and life, and the conversion of the Heathen to God. All my cares, fears, and desires, which might be said to be of a worldly nature, disappeared; and were, in my esteem, of little more importance than a puff of wind. I exceedingly longed that God would get to himself a name among the Heathen; and I appealed to him with the greatest freedom, that he knew I "preferred him above my chief joy." Indeed, I had no notion of joy from this world; I cared not where or how I lived, or what hardships I went through, so that I could but gain souls to Christ. I continued in this frame all the evening and night. While I was asleep, I dreamed of these things; and when I waked, (as I frequently did,) the first thing I thought of was this great work of pleading for God against Satan. . . .

Oct. 1. Was engaged this day in making preparations for my intended journey to the Susquehannah. Withdrew several times to the woods for secret duties, and endeavoured to plead for the divine presence to go with me to the poor Pagans, to whom I was going to preach the gospel. . . .

Oct. 2. Set out on my journey, in company with dear brother Byram, and my interpreter, and two chief Indians from the Forks of Delaware. Travelled about twenty-five miles, and lodged in one of the last houses on our road; after which there was nothing but a hideous and howling *wilderness.*

Oct. 3. We went on our way into the wilderness, and found the most difficult and dangerous travelling, by far, that ever any of us had seen. We had scarce any thing else but lofty mountains, deep valleys, and hideous rocks, to make our way through. However, I felt some sweetness in divine things, part of the day, and had my mind intensely engaged in meditation on a divine subject. Near night, my beast on which I rode, hung one of her legs in the rocks, and fell down under me; but through divine goodness, I was not hurt. However, she broke her leg; and being in such a hideous place, and near thirty miles from any house, I saw nothing that could be done to preserve her life, and so was obliged to kill her, and to prosecute my journey on foot. This accident made me admire the divine goodness to me, that my bones were not broken, and the multitude of them filled with strong pain. Just at dark, we kindled a fire, cut up a few bushes, and made a shelter over our heads, to save us from the frost, which was very hard that night; and committing ourselves to God in prayer, we lay down on the ground, and slept quietly. . . .

Oct. 5. We reached the Susquehannah river, at a place called *Opeholhaupung,* and found there twelve Indian houses. After I had saluted the king in a friendly manner, I told him my business, and that my desire was to teach them *Christianity.* . . .

Oct. 6. Rose early and besought the Lord for help in my great work. Near noon, preached again to the Indians; and in the afternoon, visited them from house to house, and invited them to come and hear me again the next day, and put off their hunting design, which they were just entering upon, till Monday. "This night," I trust, "the Lord stood by me," to encourage and strengthen my soul: I spent more than an hour in secret retirement; and was enabled to "pour out my heart before God," for the increase of grace in my soul, for ministerial endowments, for success among the poor Indians, for God's ministers and people, for distant dear friends, &c. "*Blessed be God!*" . . .

Oct. 9. We rose about four in the morning, and commending ourselves to God by prayer, and asking his special protection, we set out on our journey homewards about five, and travelled with great steadiness till past six at night; and then made us a fire, and a shelter of barks, and so rested. I had some clear and comfortable thoughts on a divine subject, by the way, towards night.—In the night, the wolves howled around us; but God preserved us. . . .

Lord's day, Feb. 17 (1745). Preached to the *white* people, my *Interpreter* being absent, in the wilderness upon the sunny side of a hill; had a considerable assembly, consisting of people who lived, at least many of them, not less than thirty miles asunder; some of them came near twenty miles. I discoursed to them all day from John v11.37. *Jesus stood and cried, saying, if any man thirst,* &c. In the afternoon, it pleased God to grant me great freedom and fervency in my discourse; and I was enabled to imitate the example of Christ in the text, who *stood and cried.* . . . Afterwards, I was enabled earnestly to invite the children of God to come renewedly, and drink of this fountain of the water of life, from whence they have heretofore derived unspeakable satisfaction. It was very comfortable to me. There were many tears in the assembly; and I doubt not that the Spirit of God was there, convincing poor sinners of their need of Christ. . . .

Lord's Day, Sept 21. Spent the day with the Indians on the island (below Shaumoking on the Susquehanna). As soon as they were up in the morning, I attempted to instruct them, . . . but soon found they had something else to do, for near noon they gathered together all their powows, or conjurers, and set about half a dozen of them playing their juggling tricks, and acting their frantic distracted postures, in order to find out why they were then so sickly upon the island, numbers of them being at that time disordered with a fever and bloody flux. In this exercise they were engaged for several hours, making all the wild, ridiculous and distracted motions imaginable; sometimes singing; sometimes howling; sometimes extending their hands to the utmost stretch, and spreading all their fingers,—they seemed to push with them as if they designed to push something away, or at least keep it off at arm's-end; sometimes stroking their faces with their hands, then spurting water as fine as mist; sometimes sitting flat on the earth, then bowing down their faces to the ground; then wringing their sides as if in pain and anguish, twisting their faces, turning up their eyes, grunting, puffing, &c.

Their monstrous actions tended to excite ideas of horror, and semed to have something in them, as I thought, peculiarly suited to raise the devil, if he could be raised by any thing, odd, ridiculous and frightful. . . . I sat at a small distance, not more than thirty feet from them, though undiscovered, with a bible in my hand, resolving, if possible, to spoil their sport, and prevent their receiving any answer from the infernal world. . . .

After they had done pow-wowing, I attempted to discourse with them about Christianity; but they soon scattered, and gave me no opportunity for any thing of that nature. . . .

But of all the sights I ever saw among them, or indeed anywhere else, none appeared so frightful, or so near a kin to what is usually imagined of *infernal powers,* none ever excited such images of teror in my mind, as the apperance of one who was a devout and zealous Reformer, or rather, restorer of what he supposed was the ancient religion of the Indians. He made his appearance in his *pontifical garb*, which was a coat of *boar skins*, dressed with the hair on, and hanging down to his toes; a pair of bear skin stockings; and a great *wooden face* painted, the one half black, the other half tawny, about the colour of an Indian's skin, with an extravagant mouth, cut very much awry; the face fastened to a bear skin cap, which was drawn over his head. He advanced towards me with the instrument in his hand, which he used for music in his idolatrous worship; which was a dry *tortoise shell* with some corn in it, and the neck of it drawn on to a piece of wood, which made a very convenient handle. As he came forward, he beat his tune with the rattle, and danced with all his might, but did not suffer any part of his body, not so much as his fingers to be seen. No one would have imagined from his appearance or actions that he could have been a human creature. . . . When he came near me, I could not but shrink away from him, although it was then noon day, and I knew who it was; his appearance and gestures were so prodigiously frightful. . . . I discoursed with him about Christianity. Some of my discourse he seemed to like, but some he disliked extremely. He told me that God had taught him his religion, and that he would never turn from it; but wanted to find some who would join heartily with him in it; for the Indians, he said, were grown very degenerate and corrupt. . . . He seemed to be sincere, honest, and conscientious in his own way, . . . which was more than I ever saw in any other Pagan. . . .

Crossweeksung, Oct. 1745.

Oct. 5. Preached to my people from John xiv. 1–6. The divine presence seemed to be in the assembly. Numbers were affected with divine truths, and it was a comfort to some in particular. O what a difference is there between these, and the Indians with whom I lately treated upon the Susquehanna! To be with those seemed to be like being banished from God and all his people; to be with these, like being admitted into his family, and to the enjoyment of his divine presence! (J. Edwards, *Memoirs of the Rev. David Brainerd; Missionary to the Indians etc.*, S. E. Dwight ed., New-Haven, 1822, 151–153; 156–157; 162–165; 193; 235–40.)

9. The New London Synodical Academy

The need for an institution of higher learning was widely felt in the Middle Colonies. In 1743 the Old Side Synod of Philadelphia established the first Presbyterian Academy at New London, Pa., with Rev. Francis Alison as master. The school is sometimes credited with being the beginning of both the University of Pennsylvania and the University of Delaware.

The minutes of a committee held at the Great Valley, November 16th, 1743, by a private agreement between the Presbyteries of Philadelphia, New Castle, and Donegall, were laid before us, showing that the said committee considered the necessity of using speedy endeavours to educate youth for supplying our vacancies. But the proper method for this end cannot be so well compassed without the Synod; they refer the further consideration of the affair to that reverend body, but agree that in the mean time a school be opened for the education of youth. And the Synod now approve that design, and take the said school under our care, and agree upon the following plan for carrying on that design:

1. That there be a school kept open where all persons who please may send their children and have them instructed gratis in the languages, philosophy, and divinity.

2. In order to carry on this design, it is agreed that every congregation under our care, be applied to for yearly contributions, more or less, as they can afford, and as God may incline them to contribute, until Providence open a door for our supporting the school some other way.

3. That if any thing can be spared besides what may support a master and tutor, that it be employed by the trustees for buying books and other necessaries for said school, and for the benefit of it, as the trustees shall see proper. And Mr. Alison is chosen master of said school, and has the privilege of choosing an usher under him to assist him. (*Records of Pres. Ch.*, 1743, 175.)

10. The College of New Jersey

The great need of a college nearer than New England, where candidates for the ministry might be educated, led a number of New Side Presbyterians to secure a charter for the College of New Jersey in 1746. Classes were begun in 1747 in the home of Rev. Jonathan Dickinson at

Elizabethtown, N.J. While not organically connected with the Synod of New York, this college, which eventually became known as Princeton, received both leadership and financial assistance from the Presbyterian Church. Collections were ordered to be taken in every congregation, and in 1754, Rev. Samuel Davies and Rev. Gilbert Tennent carried the following petition from the Synod to the churches of Great Britain. As a result, they collected more than £4000 for the College of New Jersey. The petition gives a clear picture of conditions in the Middle Colonies in 1754.

To the very venerable and honourable the moderator and other members of the General Assembly of the Church of Scotland, to meet at Edinburgh, May, 1754. The petition of the Synod of New York, convened at Philadelphia, October 3, 1753, humbly showeth:

That a college has been lately erected in the province of New Jersey by his majesty's royal charter, in which a number of youth has been already educated, who are now the instruments of service to the church of God; and which would be far more extensively beneficial were it brought to maturity. That after all the contributions that have been made to the said college, or can be raised in these parts, the fund is far from being sufficient for the erection of proper buildings, supporting the president and tutors, furnishing a library, and defraying other necessary expenses; that the trustees of said college, who are zealous and active to promote it for the public good, have already sent their humble petition to this venerable house for some assistance in carrying on so important a design; and also petitioned this Synod to appoint two of their members, the Rev. Messrs. Gilbert Tennent and Samuel Davies, to undertake a voyage to Europe in behalf of said college.

Your petitioners, therefore, most heartily concur in the said petition of the trustees to the Reverend Assembly, and appoint the said Messrs. Tennent and Davies to be their commissioners for that purpose. . . .

In the colonies of New York, New Jersey, Pennsylvania, Maryland, Virginia, and Carolina, a great number of congregations have been formed upon the Presbyterian plan, which have put themselves under the Synodical care of your petitioners, who conform to the constitution of the Church of Scotland, and have adopted her standards of doctrine, worship, and discipline. There are also large settlements lately planted in various parts, particularly in North and South Carolina, where multitudes are extremely desirous of the ministrations of the gospel; but they are not yet formed into congregations, and regularly organized for want of ministers.

These numerous bodies of people, dispersed so wide through so many colonies, have repeatedly made the most importunate applications to your petitioners, for ministers to be sent among them; and your petitioners have exerted themselves to the utmost for their relief, both by sending their members and candidates to officiate some time among them, and using all practicable measures for the education of pious youth for the ministry.

But alas! notwithstanding these painful endeavours, your petitioners have been utterly incapable to make sufficient provision for so many shepherdless flocks; and those that come hundreds of miles crying to them for some to break the bread of life among them, are often obliged to return in tears, with little or no relief, by reason of the scarcity of ministers.

Though every practicable expedient, which the most urgent necessity could suggest, has been used to prepare labourers for this extensive and growing harvest; yet the number of ministers in this Synod is far from being equal to that of the congregations under their care. Though sundry of them have taken the pastoral charge of two or three congregations for a time, in order to lessen the number of vacancies; and though sundry youth have lately been licensed, ordained, and settled in congregations, that were before destitute; yet there are no less than forty vacant congregations at present under the care of this Synod, besides many more which are incapable at present to support ministers; and the whole colony of North Carolina, where numerous congregations of Presbyterians are forming, and where there is not one Presbyterian minister settled.

The great number of vacancies in the bounds of this Synod, is owing, partly, to the new settlements lately made in various parts of this continent, partly to the death of sundry ministers belonging to this Synod, but principally to the small number of youth educated for the ministry, so vastly disproportionate to the numerous vacancies; and unless some effectual measures can be taken for the education of proper persons for the sacred character, the churches of Christ in these parts must continue in the most destitute circumstances, wandering shepherdless and forlorn through this wilderness, thousands perishing for lack of knowledge, the children of God hungry and unfed, and the rising age growing up in a state little better than that of heathenism, with regard to the public ministrations of the gospel.

The numerous inconveniences of a private, and the many important advantages of a public education are so evident, that we need not inform this venerable assembly of them, who cannot but be sensible from happy experience, of the many extensive benefits of convenient colleges.

The difficulty, (and in some cases impossibility,) of sending youth two, three, four, or five hundred miles or more, to the colleges in New England, is also evident at first sight. Now it is from the college of New Jersey only, that we can expect a remedy of these inconveniences; it is to *that* your petitioners look for the increase of their number; it is on *that* the Presbyterian churches, through the six colonies above mentioned, principally depend for a supply of accomplished ministers; from *that* has been obtained considerable relief already, notwithstanding the many disadvantages that unavoidably attend it in its present infant state; and from *that* may be expected a sufficient supply when brought to maturity.

Your petitioners, therefore, most earnestly pray, that this very reverend Assembly would afford the said college all the countenance and assistance in their power. The young daughter of the Church of Scotland, helpless and exposed in this foreign land, cries to her tender and powerful mother for relief. The cries of ministers oppressed with labours, and of congregations famishing for want of the sincere milk of the word, implore assistance. And were the poor Indian savages sensible of their own case, they would join in the cry, and beg for more missionaries to be sent to propagate the religion of Jesus among them.

Now as the college of New Jersey appears the most promising expedient to redress these grievances, and to promote religion and learning in these provinces, your petitioners most heartily concur with the trustees, and humbly pray, that an act may be passed by this venerable and honourable Assembly, for a national collection in favour of said college. And your petitioners as in duty bound shall ever pray, &c. (*Records of Pres. Ch.*, 1753, 256 ff.)

11. "Renew the Covenants with a Drawn Sword"

The disorganization following the schism of 1741 had the effect of bringing to the surface various submerged elements in American Presbyterianism. In 1742, Rev. Alexander Craighead demanded that the New Side Presbytery should renew the historic Scottish National Covenant (1581) and the Solemn League and Covenant (1643), thus committing themselves to the extreme Covenanter position of opposition to the existing British Government. When the Presbytery declared his views to be full of "treason, sedition and distraction," he withdrew from them, and on Nov. 11, 1743, led his congregation at Middle Oc-

torara, Pa., in a solemn ceremony of renewal of the covenants, with four swords pointed to the four winds, as described in the following remarkable document. This was the beginning of the Covenanter or Reformed Presbyterian Church in America.

THE DECLARATION, PROTESTATION, AND TESTIMONY OF A SUFFERING REMNANT OF THE ANTI-POPISH, ANTI-LUTHERIAN, ANTI-PRELATICK, ANTI-ERASTIAN, ANTI-LATITUDINARIAN, ANTI-SECTARIAN, TRUE PRESBYTERIAN CHURCH OF CHRIST, IN AMERICA.

We for our own Sins, and the Sins of our Fathers, being given up of a long Season by the righteous Judgment of God, to go on in Apostacy, Perjury and Defection from our reformed and covenanted Principles, have now come to be convinced by the Word and Spirit of God, of this heinous Guilt, together with the Sin of all these that have gone on in the like pernicious back-sliding Courses, and as an Evidence of our unfeigned Repentance and true Reformation, we do, in the Strength and by the Grace of God, lift up the following Testimony.

First, We find ourselves under a Necessity from the Word of God, and from a true covenanted Reformation and our baptismal Vows, by this our Testimony, in the Name of our Lord Jesus Christ, to declare a defensive War against all Usurpers of the Royal Prerogative of the glorious Lamb of God: against all Usurpers of an unscriptural Power over the Church of Christ, or the Consciences of Men; against all Maintainers and Helpers of these or any of them; all Continuers in Subjection to them or Connivers at them; the Partakers or Partners, by the Law of God and Man, being equal with the Thief in Transgression. We also declare, that we look upon ourselves as bound both by the Law of God, and the Law of Nature, to endeavour to defend our religeous Liberties wherewith Christ hath made us free, and our Bodies and Goods, from all kind of false Impositions, Intrigues, Snares, treacherous Deceitfulness, or whatever kind of perverse Dealing of any of them, with our best Skill, Power, bodily Strength and Activity.

2dly, We profess sincerely to own and adhere to the true Reformed Presbyterian Religion, in Doctrine, Worship, Discipline and Government, as it is contained at large in the Word of God, the Old and New Testaments, and briefly summ'd up in our *Westminster* Confession of Faith, Catechisms larger and shorter, Sum of Saving Knowledge, Directory for Worship, Propositions of Church Government, and to our Covenants National and Solemn League. . . .

9thly, We do likewise enter our Testimony against *George* the I. his having any legal Right to rule over this Realm, because he being an outlandish Lutheran; and likewise against *George* the II. for their being sworn Prelaticks, the Head of Malignants, and Protectors of Sectarian Hereticks, and Electory Princes of *Brunswick,* in chusing of new Emperors, which is their giving their Power to the Beast; and for their Confederacy with Popish Princes, directly contrary to the second Commandment; and for want of their Scriptural and national Qualifications, as is above said; and for their being established Head of the Church by the Laws of *England.*

10thly, We likewise state our Testimony against all that shall succeed them under these Limitations to the Crown. . . .

14thly, We lift up our Testimony against that constituting Act of the Year 1729, composed by a number of pretended Presbyterian Ministers, met in *Philadelphia,* under the name of a Synod; which Act is contrary to the true Constitution of the Presbyterian Reformed Church of Christ, as is evident by the Act itself; and this Constitution they walk agreeably to, this Day, or worse, which appears from their almost boundless Terms of Church Communion.

N.B. This our active Testimony commences from the Year 1680, altho' we have spoken something concerning some Defections before said Period; yet, in regard to our active Testimony, we do date it from said Period.

Given at Middle Octorara, *upon the* 11th Day *of November,* 1743. Let *King* JESUS *reign, and let all his Enemies be scattered.* Amen. . . .

The Covenants were renewed by Solemn Swearing to them, with an uplifted Hand to Almighty God: During the Time of reading the Testimony, and Renewal of the Covenants, the Sword was drawn. About this there are many Conjectures: Some imagine that the Sword was drawn for fear of Man, but this is certainly false; again, some pretend that it was drawn in Rebellion, and such like Notions; but the Reason of the Sword's being drawn at that Time was: I. Because no War is proclaimed without a drawn Sword, and there is no Reason that this should be singular in this particular. 2. Because our renowned Ancestors were constrained to draw the Sword in the Defence of their own Lives, and for the maintaining of a true Presbyterian Covenanted Reformation. On the Account of this alone, *to wit,* their adhering unto a true Presbyterian Reformation, they were persecuted by that cruel Tyrant *Charles the Second,* by taking away their Lives, if they would not forsake their Religion, and turn with the Tyrant; and they choosed rather to draw the Sword in Defence of their Lives and their Religion, than to relinquish their Religion: And our drawing the Sword, is to testify to the World; that we are one in Judgement with them, and that we are to this Day willing to maintain the same defensive War in defending our Religion and ourselves against all Opposers thereof, altho' the Defence of these should cost us our Lives, or any Thing that is most dear to us; and this we have sufficient Warrant for, *Psal.* XCIV. 16. *Who will rise up for me against the Evil-doers? Or who will stand up for me against the Workers of Iniquity?* If these be not Evil-doers, who punish Persons for adhering to the true Cause of God, we know not who are, *Matth.* X. 28. *And fear not them which kill the Body, but are not able to kill the Soul; but rather fear him which is able to destroy both Body and Soul in Hell.* Luke XXii, 36. *And he that hath no Sword, let him sell his Garments and buy one.* Acts iv. 19, 20. Rev. xii, 11. The 3rd Reason why the Sword was drawn at the Time, was, because it hath been the Practice of the faithful witnessing Remnant, to renew the Covenants with a drawn Sword, and we are commanded to follow the Footsteps of the Flock, *Cant.* i, 8. We look upon those who resisted unto Blood, striving against Sin, to be the only true Flock of Christ in their Day; and as such we desire to follow their Example in this. This War is not offensive, but defensive; not for falling upon Persons to take away their Lives, but a defending our Religion and ourselves from all unjust Assaults of others; which is allowable unto every Creature that hath life. (*Renewal of the Covenants, National and Solemn League; A Confession of Sins; An Engagement to Duties; and a Testimony; as they were carried on at Middle Octorara in Pennsylvania, November 11, 1743,* n.p., 1748.)

12. A Call to a Frontier Church

By 1754 the frontier had been pushed westward to the Appalachian range. The following call from the congregations of Paxtang and Derry (near modern Harrisburg, Pa.) are a reminder that one of the foundation stones of the Presbyterian way was the right of the people to choose their own pastor. The call was mediated to the minister through, and with the approval of, the Presbytery. John Elder later became known as "the fighting pastor." When eighty members of his congregation were either killed or captured by the Indians, he organized the famous Paxton Rangers for the defense of the frontier.

To the Reverend Mr. John Elder: Sir—We, the inhabitants in the Township & Congregation of Paxtang & Derry, Being now Destitute of a Settled Gospel minister amongst us; Being also Deeply Sensible of the great loss & Disadvantage we & ours may sustain, In regard of our souls

& spiritual Concerns by our living in such a Condition in this Wilderness; & having had Sufficient Proof of, & being well pleased & satisfied with the ministerial abilities & qualifications of y'u, the Rev. Jno. Elder, Do unanimously Invite and Call y'u to take the Pastoral Care & oversight of us, Promising all due subjection, submission & obedience to the Doctrine, Discipline & Government & Ordinances Exercised & administered by y'u as our Pastor in the Lord. And that y'u may be the Better Enabled to attend upon y'r Pastoral & ministerial work amongst us, without Anxious and Distracting Cares about y'r worldly Concerns, We Do hereby Cheerfully Promise & Engage to take Care of y'r Support and maintenance for an Honourable & Creditable manner Suitable to & befitting y'r Honourable Function & office as a Minister of the Gospel of Jesus Christ amongst us; Knowing that the Lord hath ordained that they who Preach the Gospel should live by the Gospel. (Quoted in M. W. Mc Alarney, *History of the Sesqui-Centennial of Paxtang Church,* Harrisburg, 1890, 65–66.)

CHAPTER
3

RELIGION AND EMPIRE
1755–1783

1. "The Curse of Cowardice"

The full brunt of the savage Indian raids of the Seven Years' War (1756–1763) was borne by the Scotch-Irish settlers on the frontiers of Pennsylvania and Virginia. During those years Presbyterian pastors and people went armed to church. Among those who gave leadership in inspiring the people to defend the settlements was Samuel Davies of Hanover, Va. (later president of the College of New Jersey). He had been largely responsible for the Great Awakening in Virginia, and for the founding of the first southern presbytery. He had also fought for religious toleration in Virginia. Young Patrick Henry is said to have acquired many of his ideas of liberty, as well as his style of eloquence, from the great preacher. The following sermon, preached at a general muster of the militia of Hanover County in 1758 received wide publicity. In it, Davies presents the Presbyterian argument for self-defense. The text was Jer. 48:10.

Nothing can be more agreeable to the God of Peace, than to see universal harmony and benevolence prevail among his creatures, and he has laid them under the strongest obligations to cultivate a pacific temper towards one another, both as individuals and as nations. *Follow peace with all men*, is one of the principal precepts of our holy religion. And the great Prince of Peace has solemnly pronounced, *Blessed are the peacemakers.*

But when, in this corrupt, disordered state of things, where the lusts of men are perpetually embroiling the world with wars and fightings, throwing all into confusion; when ambition and avarice would rob us of our property, for which we have toiled, and on which we subsist; when they would enslave the free-born mind, and compel us meanly to cringe to usurpation and arbitrary power; when they would tear from our eager grasp the most valuable blessing of heaven, I mean our religion; when they invade our country, formerly the region of tranquility, ravage our frontiers, butcher our fellow-subjects, or confine them in a barbarous captivity in the dens of savages; when our earthly all is ready to be seized by rapacious hands, and even our eternal all is in danger by the loss of our religion: when this is the case, what is then the will of God? Must peace then be maintained, maintained with our perfidious and cruel invaders? maintained at the expense of property, liberty, life, and every thing dear and valuable? maintained, when it is in our power to vindicate our right, and do ourselves justice? Is the work of peace then our only business?

No: in such a time, even the God of Peace proclaims by his Providence, "To arms!" Then the sword is, as it were, consecrated to God; and the art of war becomes a part of our religion. Then happy is he that shall reward our enemies as they have served us. Psalm cxxxvii. 8. Blessed is the brave soldier: blessed is the defender of his country, and the destroyer of its enemies. Blessed are they who offer themselves willingly in this service, and who faithfully discharge it. But on the other hand "Cursed is he that doth the work of the Lord deceitfully; and cursed is he that keepeth back his sword from blood." . . . Cowardice and treachery are now as execrable as ever.

Cursed be he that keepeth back his sword from blood.—This denunciation, like the artillery of heaven, is levelled against the coward, who, when God, in the course of his providence, calls him to arms, refuses to obey, and consults his own ease and safety more than his duty to God and his country.

Cursed be he that doth the work of the Lord deceitfully.—This seems to be levelled against another species of cowards; sly, hypocritical cowards, who undertake the work of the Lord; that is, take up arms; but they do the work of the Lord deceitfully; that is, they do not faithfully use their arms for the purposes they were taken up. They commence soldiers, not that they may serve their country, and do their duty to God, but that they may live in ease, idleness, and pleasure, and enrich themselves at the public expense. *Cursed is he that doth the work of the Lord deceitfully,* and serves himself under pretence of serving his country. . . .

Need I inform you what barbarities and depredations a mongrel race of Indian savages and French papists have perpetrated upon our frontiers? How many deserted or demolished houses and plantations? How wide an extent of country abandoned? How many poor families obliged to fly in consternation, and leave their all behind them? What breaches and separations between the nearest relations? What painful ruptures of heart from heart? What shocking dispersions of those once united by the strongest and most endearing ties? Some lie dead, mangled with savage wounds, consumed to ashes with outrageous flames, or torn and devoured by the beasts of the wilderness, while their bones lie whitening in the sun, and serve as tragical memorials of the fatal spot where they fell. Others have been dragged away captives, and made the slaves of imperious and cruel savages: others have made their escape, and live to lament their butchered or captivated friends and relations. In short, our frontiers have been drenched with the blood of our fellow subjects, through the length of a thousand miles: and new wounds are still opening. . . .

And will these violences cease without a vigorous and timely resistance from us? Can Indian revenge and thirst for blood be glutted? or can French ambition and avarice be satisfied? No, we have no method left, but to repel force with force, and to give them blood to drink in their turn, who have drank ours. If we sit still and do nothing, or content ourselves, as, alas! we have hitherto, with feeble, dilatory efforts, we may expect these barbarities will not only continue, but that the Indians, headed by the French, will carry their inroads still farther into the country, and reach even unto us. By the desertion of our remote settlements, the frontiers are approaching every day nearer and nearer to us: and if we cannot stand our ground now, when we have above a hundred miles of a thick-settled country between us and the enemy, much less shall we be able, when our strength is weakened by so vast a loss of men, arms and riches, and we lie exposed to their immediate incursions. Some cry "let the enemy come down to us, and then we will fight them." But this is the trifling excuse of cowardice or security, and not the language of prudence and fortitude. Those who make this plea, if the enemy should take them at their word, and make them so near a visit, would be as forward in flight as they are now backward to take up arms.

Such, my brethren, such, alas! is the present state of our country: it bleeds in a thousand veins; and without timely remedy, the wound will prove mortal. And in such circumstances is it not our duty in the sight of God; is it not a work to which the Lord loudly calls us, to take up arms for the defence of our country? Certainly it is: and *cursed is he* who, having no ties sufficiently strong to confine him at home, *keepeth his sword from blood.* The man that can desert the cause of his country in such an exigency; his country, in the blessings of which he shared while in peace and prosperity; and which is therefore entitled to his sympathy and assistance in the day of its distress; that cowardly, ungrateful man sins against God and his country, and deserves the curse of both. Such a conduct in such a conjuncture, is a moral evil, a gross wickedness; and exposes the wretch to the heavy curse of God both in this and the eternal world.

And here I cannot but observe, that among the various and numberless sins under which the country groans, and which must be looked upon as the cause of our public calamities, by every one that believes a divine Providence: a doctrine so comfortable, and so essential both in natural and revealed religion; an article in the creed of heathens and Mahometans, (as well as Jews and Christians;) I say, among these various sins, cowardice and security are none of the least. He that hath determined the bounds of our habitations, hath planted us in a land of liberty and plenty; a land, till lately, unalarmed with the terrors of war, and unstained with human blood; indeed, all things considered, there are but few such happy spots on our globe. And must it not highly provoke our divine Benefactor, to see a people thus distinguished with blessings, so insensible of their worth, so ungrateful for them, and so unacquainted with their own unworthiness to receive them? . . .

May we not suppose, that divine Providence has permitted our body politic to suffer wound after wound, and baffled all our languid efforts, in order to give it sensibility, and rouse us to exert our strength in more vigorous efforts? Has not the curse of God lain heavy upon our country, because we have "done the work of the Lord deceitfully, and kept back our swords from blood?" (S. Davies, *Sermons on Important Subjects,* A. Barnes, ed., New York, 1854, III, 84 ff.)

2. Plan of Reunion, 1758

By 1758, under the pressure of war and the failure of the Old Side to propagate itself, the heated opinions of the Great Awakening had cooled. The following Plan of Union completely disregards the Protestation of 1741 (see Ch. 2, art. 7). The questions of itinerancy, the examination of candidates, and the rights of individuals are charitably treated. On the vexed matter of subscription the reunited Church returned to the plan of the Adopting Act of 1729 (Ch. 1, art. 11), and required adherence to the system and not to the letter of the Westminster Standards.

That no jealousies or grounds of alienation may remain, and also to prevent future breaches of like nature, we agree to unite and do unite in one body, under the name of the Synod of New York and Philadelphia, on the following plan.

I. Both Synods having always approved and received the Westminster Confession of Faith, and Larger and Shorter Catechisms, as an orthodox and excellent system of Christian doctrine, founded on the word of God, we do still receive the same as the confession of our faith, and also adhere to the plan of worship, government, and discipline, contained in the Westminster Directory, strictly enjoining it on all our members and probationers for the ministry, that they preach and teach according to the form of sound words in said Confession and Catechisms, and avoid and oppose all errors contrary thereto.

II. That when any matter is determined by a major vote, every member shall either actively concur with, or passively submit to such determination; or, if his conscience permit him to do neither, he shall, after sufficient liberty modestly to reason and remonstrate, peaceably withdraw from our communion, without attempting to make any schism. Provided always, that this shall be understood to extend only to such determinations as the body shall judge indispensable in doctrine or Presbyterian government.

III. That any member or members, for the exoneration of his or their conscience before God, have a right to protest against any act or procedure of our highest judicature, because there is no further appeal to another for redress; and to require that such protestation be recorded in their minutes. And as such a protest is a solemn appeal from the bar of said judicature, no member is liable to prosecution on the account of his protesting. Provided always, that it shall be deemed irregular and unlawful, to enter a protestation against any member or members, or to protest facts or accusations instead of proving 1em, unless a fair trial be refused, even by the highest judicature. And it is agreed, that protestations are only to be entered against the public acts, judgments, or determinations of the judicature with which the protester's conscience is offended.

IV. As the protestation entered in the Synod of Philadelphia, *Ann. Dom.* 1741, has been apprehended to have been approved and received by an act of said Synod, and on that account was judged a sufficient obstacle to an union; the said Synod declare, that they never judicially adopted the said protestation, nor do account it a Synodical act, but that it is to be considered as the act of those only who subscribed it; and therefore cannot in its nature be a valid objection to the union of the two Synods, especially considering that a very great majority of both Synods have become members, since the said protestation was entered.

V. That it shall be esteemed and treated as a censurable evil, to accuse any member of heterodoxy, insufficiency, or immorality, in a calumniating manner, or otherwise than by private brotherly admonition, or by a regular process according to our known rules of judicial trial in cases of scandal. And it shall be considered in the same view, if any Presbytery appoint supplies within the bounds of another Presbytery without their concurrence; or if any member officiate in another's congregation, without asking and obtaining his consent, or the session's in case the minister be absent; yet it shall be esteemed unbrotherly for any one, in ordinary circumstances, to refuse his consent to a regular member when it is requested.

VI. That no Presbytery shall license or ordain to the work of the ministry, any candidate, until he give them competent satisfaction as to his learning, and experimental acquaintance with religion, and skill in divinity and cases of conscience; and declare his acceptance of the Westminster Confession and Catechisms as the confession of his faith, and promise subjection to the Presbyterian plan of government in the Westminster Directory.

VII. The Synods declare it is their earnest desire, that a complete union may be obtained as soon as possible, and agree that the united Synod shall model the several Presbyteries in such manner as shall appear to them most expedient. Provided nevertheless, that Presbyteries, where an alteration does not appear to be for edification, continue in their present form. As to divided congregations it is agreed, that such as have settled ministers on both sides be allowed to continue as they are; that where those of one side have a settled minister, the other being vacant, may join with the settled minister, if a majority choose so to do; that when both sides are vacant they shall be at liberty to unite together.

VIII. As the late religious appearances occasioned much speculation and debate, the members of the New York Synod, in order to prevent any misapprehensions, declare their adherence to their former sentiments in favour of them, that a blessed work of God's Holy Spirit in the conversion of numbers was then carried on; and for the satisfaction of all concerned, this united Synod agree in declaring, that as all mankind are naturally dead in trespasses and sins an entire change of heart and life is necessary to make them meet for the service and enjoyment of God; that such a change can be only effected by the powerful operations of the Divine Spirit; that when sinners are made sensible of their lost condition and absolute inability to recover themselves, are enlightened in the knowledge of Christ and convinced of his ability and willingness to save, and renouncing their own righteousness in point of merit, depend upon his imputed righteousness for their justification before God, and on his wisdom and strength for guidance and support; when upon these apprehensions and exercises their souls are comforted, notwithstanding all their past guilt, and rejoice in God through Jesus Christ; when they hate and bewail their sins of heart and life, delight in the laws of God without exception, reverently and diligently attend his ordinances, become humble and self denied, and make it the business of their lives to please and glorify God and to do good to their fellow men; this is to be acknowledged as a gracious work of God, even though it should be attended with unusual bodily commotions or some more exceptionable circumstances, by means of infirmity, temptations, or remaining corruptions; and wherever religious appearances are attended with the good effects above mentioned, we desire to rejoice in and thank God for them.

But on the other hand, when persons seeming to be under a religious concern, imagine that they have visions of the human nature of Jesus Christ, or hear voices, or see external lights, or have fainting and convulsion-like fits, and on the account of these judge themselves to be truly converted, though they have not the Scriptural characters of a work of God above described, we believe such persons are under a dangerous delusion. And we testify our utter disapprobation of such a delusion wherever it attends any religious appearances, in any church or time. . . .

The Synod agree, that all former differences and disputes are laid aside and buried; and that no future inquiry or vote shall be proposed in this Synod concerning these things; but if any member seek a Synodical inquiry, or declaration about any of the matters of our past differences, it shall be deemed a censurable breach of this agreement, and be refused, and he be rebuked accordingly.

Adjourned till to-morrow morning at nine o'clock. Concluded with prayer. (*Records of Pres. Ch.*, 1758, 285 ff.)

3. "Enlarging the Bounds of Christ's Kingdom and Extending the British Empire"

In 1757 the Synod of Philadelphia, "deeply sensible that among other things, the small and uncertain stipends of ministers and the poverty and distress of their widows and children were great discouragements to many pious and able men," established a relief fund to be administered by a Charitable Corporation. The following appeal to the British churches gives an exceptionally clear picture of social conditions among Presbyterians at this time and of the problems presented to the Church by the lure of the frontier. Substantial amounts were received from Great Britain, and today, under the name of The Presbyterian Ministers' Fund, the Corporation makes the proud claim of being "the first Life Insurance Company in America and the oldest in the world."

The Representation of the Corporation to all pious & well Disposed persons in Brittain & Ireland was read & approved & ordered to be subscribed by the President & Secretary, & is as follows.

To all pious & charitable Christians in Great Brittain & Ireland.

The Representation of the Corporation for ye Releif of poor & distressed Presbyterian Ministers & their Widows & children in the Province of Pensilvania, & of the Counties of New Castle Kent & Sussex upon Delaware Humbly Sheweth.

That Pensylvania, a Province Distinguished for civil & religious Liberty has been peopled with numbers from England, Scotland, Ireland, Wales, Sweden, Germany & Holland & some French refugees. That those in general who held a parity among all Gospel Ministers (the Dutch excepted) united and formed Churches after Presbyterian Plan, both in this & the neighbouring Provinces of New York, New Jersey, Maryland &C and at length their Ministers agreed to hold a Synodical Meeting once a Year in the City of Philadelphia.

As the first Settlers were generally in low Circumstances & were obliged by the Force of hard industry to make new Settlements on our Frontiers, they were unable to do much for the support of a Gospel Ministry. And many worthy protestant Ministers who left Europe with a truely Catholic Spirit to promote the Kingdom of Christ in this Wilderness, and many educated in this Country, have had great & uncommon Difficulties to struggle with. Many of the lower Ranks who flocked in thither were ignorant, vicious and intractable, readier to learn the vices of their Indian Neighbours, than to teach them the more perfect ways of God. They were soon elated with the Name of Plantations, tho' their greatest Wealth was no more than the necessaries of Life; they were not easily brought to the more strict and civilized Conduct which the Gospel requires; and were highly pleased with the prevailing principles that Gospel Ministers should work for their livings, and Preach for Charity. With these and many other Difficulties of the like Nature, have many of our pious Ministers struggled & earned their Bread in a great Measure with the Sweat of their Brows, and thro' the Grace of God have laboriously preached the Gospel, and have been examples of Industry, of Hospitality, of Patience and of every good work to their Flock. But as they had but small and very uncertain Incomes from the good will of their people, joined with their own labour; and as their Stations prevented them from following the more gainfull Employments of Life; they always found it difficult to make any tolerable Provision for their Families, We have often with Sorrow and Regret, seen the Widows and Children of great and good Ministers extremely pinched and distressed by want and Poverty, without being able to afford them any suitable Releif.

These things have always been great Discouragements to Pious and good men in the Ministry; they have also been great Hindrances to Parents from educating their Children for this necessary, and honourable, but laborious Employment; and must bring the Gospel into Contempt, by its falling into weak hands; and deprive many Congregations in this wide extended Wilderness of the Benefit of Ministers and Ordinances.

To Remedy these evils, as far as our Circumstances may permit, the Synod of Philadelphia, encouraged by the laudable Example of the Church of Scotland, came to a Resolution in the Year 1754 to promote a Fund out of their narrow Incomes with the Assistance of any charitable Contributions which they might obtain. But having made a Tryal they were soon convinced, that they could not in their Circumstances succeed without the aid of a Law in their favour; or without Letters of Incorporation. The Synod therefore, Ano. 1757 applied to Our Honorable Proprietaries of this Province residing in England, Praying for their Approbation and Countenance, and for Letters of Incorporation.

These honorable Gentlemen, sensible that this Reverend Body were distinguished for Loyalty to the best of Kings; and that they had lived peaceably, and had been useful to promote Religion, Virtue and Industry among the People under their Care, and to defend their Country, Out of their great Benevolence and Humanity erected a Charitable Corporation by Letters Patent dated January the Eleventh 1759, for the Relief of distressed Presbyterian Ministers, their Widows and Children. . . .

While these Measures were taken to obtain a Relief for the distressed a yet severer Dispensation of Providence greatly encreased our Calamities. An Indian War broke forth. A Savage & barbarous Enemy, prompted by the perfidious French, like prowling Wolves fell on the Peaceful Habitations of many on our Frontier Inhabitants, and in the Night, time after time, murdered and scalped without regard to Age or Sex; and led numbers of our people into Captivity, who are many of them in Bondage a-mong the Heathen at this Day. As the Frontier Counties of Pennsylvania and Virginia were mostly settled by people of our Denomination, we felt the Blow severely; several of our Congregations were entirely broken up; the Ministers removed to other Provinces, or sought Shelter in the innermost parts of the Provinces distressed by the War, or went forth with their People to repell the Enemy. Among these our Worthy Agent, the Reverend Mr Charles Beaty distinguished himself by his public Spirit, Love to his Country and true Courage. He of his own Accord went with our honourable Governor Robert Hunter Morris Esqr. and some other of our Chief Gentlemen, who exposed themselves to the Inclemency of a severe Winter, and to all the dangerous Incursions of the Indians, till they built Forts for the Defence of the Frontiers. He also continued as a Chaplain exposed to dangers till the French were obliged to fly from Ohio & untill Fort Duquesne (now Pitts Burgh) was in his Majesty's Possession; and he as an Eye Witness, can inform what Congregations were laid waste by this War. From these Ministers in general & from their distressed People we can expect little Assistance to our present Undertaking; many of whom stand in the greatest need of our charitable Contributions.

Another Circumstance which greatly discourages us, even now when an incorporated Body, arises from the Nature of the Country. The Inhabitants are inconstant and unsettled, and are always shifting their Habitations, either from a Love of variety, or from the fair Prospect of more commodious Settlements on the Frontiers of this, or the Neighbouring Provinces; So that we can have no Certainty of any fixed Number of Parishes, or Ministers in the Bounds of this or the Neighbouring Provinces. When our People remove they are generally Succeeded by Strangers from Europe, who incline at their first arrival to purchase or hire cultivated Lands; but as all religious Denominations of Christians equally flourish here one of our most promising Settlements of Presbyterians or Episcopals, may in a few Years, be entirely possessed by German Menomists, and Longbeards or Moravians; or any other Society of Christians; And were every Minister now in the Bounds of our Synod to become a Contributor, we can have no certainty that we shall have the same Number for any given Space of Time, & hence all Calculations must in a great Measure fail us, when we attempt a Fund after the Example of the Church of Scotland.

As oft as Indian Wars may distress our Frontiers, which may be for many Years to come, so oft will all our Plans of Contribution be broken, for the only safety in the Inhabitants will ever consist in flight, untill the Country be able by Arms to pursue these Murderers into their own Country, and reduce them to terms of Peace. And in all our new Settlements unless there be something done to help the first Adventurers to the Wilderness, to support Gospel Ministers among them, they, and their Children must for many Years continue like the Indians, without the Gospel Ordinances; and in such Cases the rising Generation, without the Benefit of Public Instructions, are apt to become too like the Heathens. To relieve such distresses the Society for propagating the Christian Religion in England yearly bestow a considerable Sum on their Missionaries. And the hardy, frugal Germans were under a Necessity to apply both to Holland & England for relief and were assisted by charitable Donations from the King and many of the English Nobility, and others; and even by a general Collection from the Church of Scotland.

No Denomination of Christian Ministers in this vast Continent are more regular and industrious, or stand in greater need of some charitable Assistance than the Presbyterians, for themselves & poor Families; their Number is great; and they and their People are every Day enlarging the Bounds of Christs Kingdom & extending the British Empire in America, and they never had the Aid of a Public Fund, nor the Countenance of the great or the Powerful, untill they were in great Compassion by the Proprietaries of this Province favour'd with the Powers of a charitable Corporation for their Relief; tho the greater Number that are now in Arms contending for the rights of British Subjects against French and Indians are of yt Denomination.

From this Enumeration of Matters of fact, it (as we hope) appears evident, that a Fund for the Relief of so many and so great Distresses is necessary. And that unless the charitable Corporation can raise a Capital to pay off Contributions, even tho' the Number of annual Contributors should sometimes fail or be greatly diminished, their Endeavours will be all to no Purpose. But if this can be procured, (for which we earnestly sollicit your Charity) then Numbers will be always encouraged to contribute yearly, from an Assurance that this Corporation are able to make good the Annuities convenanted to be paid to their Families after their Decease. . . .

We beg that our Christian Friends & Brethren, would regard us as a Sort of Guardians taking Care of a part of this infant Church, who is in great Distresses; and that we plead for Ability to spread the Gospel of Peace thro the dark Places of the Earth that have long been the Habitations of Cruelty: we that plead for the distressed Ministers of our Lord & Master Christ Jesus, and for the Widows & the Fatherless; whose Hearts your Charity may fill with Joy. Charity covers a Multitude of Sins; it is a most exalted Grace, it is highly beneficial to Mankind, and will be loudly applauded, and receive an ample Reward in the great Day of Recompense. (*Minutes of the Corporation for Relief of Poor and Distressed Presbyterian Ministers etc., mss. in P.H.S., 16–20.*)

4. Relief to Victims of Indian Warfare

In 1763 the outbreak of Pontiac's War once more brought disaster to the Presbyterian churches on the frontiers of Pennsylvania. The following minutes indicate how the Corporation for Relief came to the assistance of distressed families regardless of denomination. Large sums were spent to ransom captives and to provide for the homeless. With an eye to the future, missionaries were sent to the frontier, "to report how we may best promote the Kingdom of God among them and the Indian nations in their neighbourhood."

Catherine Crow applied for Relief to this Corporation, who as appears by good Certificates, was taken Captive the fourth of June last from Cumberland County, her husband was scalped & Murdered & four Children led with her into Captivity, who are still Among the Indians; She after great Sufferings made her Escape, & being stript of all partly by the Savage Indians and partly by her husbands Creditors, She requested this board to pity her distresses, & to enable her to take out a Warrant for her Land which she is in danger of losing. Tis agreed that the Treasurer advance as much money for her as will pay for a warrant for a Plantation not exceeding two hundred acres; and That messrs. Humphreys and Alison apply to the office to obtain A Warrant in favor of her & her children. . . .(Oct. 9, 1764.) . . .

April ye: 28 1766. At the request of Thomas Smiley a poor distressed man whose daughter has been long in Captivity among the Indians, the Committee of the Corporation and all the Members living in this City were invited to a Meeting.

Present. Messrs Humphreys, Chevalier, Hodge, Ewing, Bryan, Bayard, Wallace, Redman, Ehea, Harris & Alison.

The distress of Thomas Smiley was taken Under Consideration, whose daughter now above thirty nine years of age, has been eight years in Captivity among the Savage Indians, & she earnestly longs & desires to Obtain her liberty & to be restored to her parents & Children & to the Churches of Christ. As we find we have no authority to dispose of any publick money, because our Meeting has not been publickly advertized, yet we cannot but pity the distress both of the parent & of the Child, now in Captivity & agree that our treasurer pay him the Sum of fifteen pounds to Redeem his daughter. And we submit these our proceedings to this Corporation at their Next Meeting. We also enjoin it as a duty on said Thomas Smiley or his Son to enquire what Number of white people are still in Captivity, & among what Indian Nations, and on what terms they may be redeemed & the Names of the Captives, and that either one of them, or the Daughter when Redeemed come & inform this Corporation concerning these affairs. (*Minutes of the Corporation for Relief,* ms. 54–55, 59–60.)

5. Across the Alleghenies

The visit of Rev. Charles Beatty and Rev. George Duffield to the Ohio country in 1766 is a landmark in the history of the westward movement of Presbyterianism. Their report on the new settlements and the possibilities of Indian missions led the Synod to send annual missionaries across the Alleghenies to evangelize the west. The following selections from Beatty's Journal describe the condition of the settlers in the Juniata Valley.

Tuesday 26. Crossed the River [Juniata] early this morning to Andrew Brattons where we breakfasted, & preached at Hollidays Mill to a Considerable number of People who were very attentive. Baptised 3 Children we are incommoded by the rain & were obligded to croud into a little house—as many as could, in time of sermon a Ratle Snake creep in the house which alarmed the people but was hapily Discovered and killed before it did any damage, a little after a Snake of another kind, came in which was also killed, after Sermon rode to Robt. Samuel's 4½ miles and lodged.

Wedensday 27. Baptized a child which was brought to my lodging. rode to Jno. Karmichels about 8 Miles to the mouth of Aughweek where I preached to a small number of People, and Baptized 4 Children— lodged at Jno. Carmichaels, there is fine Bottom land on this River & good upland, tho broken by the hils.

The Setlement on both sides River Juniata are new, extending 25 Miles from the narrows to the mouth of aughweek & about 7 miles Broad, in the center, containing at present about 80 families, a numbr more expected to setle thre in a litle time—they purpose to build a meeting House near Hollidays mill which is about the center, & to Join Kishaqulla or great valley, which is about 4 Miles from the center of Juniata setlement, this valley is about 30 miles long & 5 or 6 miles wide & mostly very good land, at present there are but 5 or 6 families setl'd in it but more expected next spring—there never was any sermon preached in this setlement before. (C. Beatty, *The Journal of a Two Months Tour,* ms. in P.H.S.)

6. "They Sang the Old Scotch Version"

In 1772–1773 Rev. David Mc Clure was appointed by the Presbytery of Donegal to supply vacant congregations west of the Alleghenies. His Diary is one of the most readable sources of the period. In the following passages Mc Clure describes the worship, religious education, and mode of travel of the new settlers.

August 9, 1772 (Big Spring, Pa.).

Sabbath went to the place of worship. It was a large log house. The congregation being great, I preached on a stage erected in a large shady grove. The people sat on the ground which was covered with verdant grass. The Assembly was solemn & attentive. They seemed all to unite their voices in psalmody. They sang the old Scotch version & all on the tenor. The Clerk read the lines. There was much solemnity in the sound of the high praises of Jehovah, in their united & elevated voices. . . .

April 8, 1773.

The inhabitants west of the Appalachian mountains are chiefly Scotch Irish presbyterians. They are either natives of the North of Ireland, or the descendents of such & removed here from the middle Colonies. There are some Germans, English & Scotch. The presbyterians are generally well indoctrinated in the principles of the christian religion. The young people are taught by their parents & school masters, the Larger and Shorter Catechisms, & almost every family has the Westminster Confession of Faith, which they carefully study. . . .

April 24, 1773.

Saturday. Reached Ligonier. In this journey we overtook several families removing from the old settlements in the State, and from Maryland and New Jersey, to the western country. Their patience and perseverence in poverty and fatigue were wonderful. They were not only patient, but cheerful and pleased themselves with the expectation of seeing happy days, beyond the mountains.

I noticed, particularly, one family of about 12 in number. The man carried an ax and gun on his shoulders—the Wife, the rim of a spinning wheel in one hand, and a loaf of bread in the other. Several little boys and girls, each with a bundle, according to their size. Two poor horses, each heavily loaded with some poor necessaries, on the top of the baggage of one, was an infant rocked to sleep in a kind of wicker cage, lashed securely to the horse. A Cow formed one of the company, and she was destined to bear her proportion of service, a bed cord was wound around her horns, and a bag of meal on her back. The above is a specimen of the greater part of the poor and enterprising people, who leave their old habitations and connections, and go in quest of lands for themselves and children, & with the hope of the enjoyment of independence, in their worldly circumstances, where land is good & cheap. (*Diary of David Mc Clure*, F. B. Dexter, ed. New York, 1899, 115 ff.)

7. John Mc Millan's First Manse

In 1776 the Presbytery of Donegal ordained John Mc Millan to be the first settled pastor beyond the mountains. Two years later he brought his wife to the log house which the people of Chartiers and Pigeon Creek had helped him prepare. The following description of the first manse in the west was written by Dr. Mc Millan in a letter to Dr. Carahan, March 26, 1832. By 1781 there were enough ministers and congregations in western Pennsylvania to organize the Redstone Presbytery.

When I came to this country, the cabin in which I was to live, was raised, but there was no roof to it, nor any chimney, nor floor. The people, however, were very kind; they assisted me in preparing my house, and on the 16th of December, I removed into it. But we had neither bedstead, nor tables, nor stool, nor chair, nor bucket. All these things we had to leave behind us, as there was no wagon road, at that time, over the mountains. We could bring nothing with us but what was carried on pack-horses. We placed two boxes, one on the other, which served us for a table, and two kegs served us for seats; and having committed ourselves to God, in family worship, we spread a bed on the floor, and slept soundly till morning. The next day a neighbor coming to my assistance, we made a table and stool, and in a little time, had everything comfortable about us. Sometimes, indeed, we had no bread for weeks together; but we had plenty of pumpkins and potatoes, and all the necessaries of life; as for luxuries, we were not much concerned about them. We enjoyed health, the gospel and its ordinances, and pious friends. We were in the place where we believed God would have us to be; and we did not doubt but that He would provide everything necessary, and, glory to his name, we were not disappointed. (Quoted in J. Smith, *Old Redstone*, Philadelphia, 1854, 186.)

8. The Token

The use of Communion tokens was widespread in colonial Presbyterian churches. The following description of the distribution and meaning of tokens is by the hand of Rev. John Murray of Booth Bay, Maine, a pioneer of Presbyterianism in eastern New England. A large collection of tokens are preserved in the Presbyterian Historical Society, Philadelphia.

On the ensuing Saturday in the afternoon a preparatory sermon on the dying love of Christ from John II was preached, and before the congregation was dismissed the Pastor came down from the pulpit, and standing before the Communion table, declared the qualifications of such as should be welcome to approach to the ordinance in view, published a free invitation addressed to particular characters, and then poured out on the table a great number of small square pieces of lead on which the initial letters of his name were stamped in capitals; these he informed us it was the custom of the Presbyterian Church to have delivered by the Pastor, or Elders, into the hands of the Communicants at some convenient time before the administration of the Lord's Supper, as tokens of their admission to the privileges of Christ's disciples by which the Church intends:

1st To guard against the approaches of persons not approved.

2d No one is to sit down at that table without delivering his token into the hand of an Elder who is to be stationed at the end of that table for that purpose . . . every communicant at a previous opportunity of knowing all his fellow . . . at that feast; both that they may have the more particular inducement to . . . together in the bonds of love; and that time may be given them to object to any person who has broken the law of charity towards them is likely to. . . .

3d That this token may be a perpetual monitor to him that takes it as a great obligation, that putting him in mind of his high privileges, it is to him . . . seek with renewed earnestness the inward tokens of his being a member of the Church invisible, by these pledges of redeeming love that are given and sealed to God's children after at this sacred feast by the spirit of God; and finally that he may look on that token as likely to prove a swift witness against him at the last if he comes now without the wedding garment, or should hereafter go about to break the sacramental vow to the public making of which it is a pledge of his admission.

Before the delivering of these tokens he called us to join in solemn prayer in which the covenant was again renewed; and the particular ascension gifts and graces earnestly sought that might be needful and suitable to every case; after which a short exhortation was given, in the time of which the Communicants were desired to come up one by one & receive their tokens from his hand, and then return to their seats again; during the distribution, he continued the exhortation which being finished they concluded by a Psalm, and the congregation dismissed with a blessing. (*Records of the Presbyterian Church of Booth Bay, Maine,* 1767, printed in *Journal of the Presbyterian Historical Society,* XVI, pp. 244-245.)

9. "The Joyful Occasion of the Repeal of the Stamp Act"

The position of the Presbyterian Church on the question of the American Revolution cannot be understood by merely assuming that the War of Independence was "a Presbyterian Rebellion." The first reaction of those brought up on the Bible and the Shorter Catechism was to search for God's will "in the course of human affairs." George III was thanked for repealing the Stamp Act, but Presbyterians were reminded that the act itself was a sign of divine anger, and that "our gracious God is our deliverer." Like the Commonwealth men of old, the Presbyterians waited for Providence to make the way clear.

[May 29, 1766] . . . An overture was made by Dr. Alison, that an address should be made to our Sovereign, on the joyful occasion of the repeal of the Stamp Act, and thereby a confirmation of our liberties, at the same time proposing the copy of such an address for examination; which was read and approved by the Synod. (*Records of Pres. Ch.,* 1766, 360.)

A Pastoral Letter

Dearly Beloved:—We think it our indispensable duty, not only in our particular charges, but in this united and more public capacity, to direct you to some suitable reflections upon the late remarkable and merciful steps of Divine Providence, and to inculcate a becoming improvement of an event, the most interesting and important to the people of this continent. . . .

The faithless French, and their savage allies, were lately the rod of Divine displeasure for our many provocations. Under the calamities of war, and the wasting ravages of Indian cruelty, we were repeatedly brought to approach the throne of grace, with solemn fasting and prayer; and thereby openly professed our resolution to forsake the ways of sin, and turn unto the Lord. But, alas! we rendered not to God according to the multitude of his tender mercies, for no sooner was the rod removed, and the blessings of peace restored, but we became more vain and dissolute than before.

The Almighty thus provoked, permitted counsels of the most pernicious tendency, both to Great Britain and her colonies. The imposition of unusual taxes, a severe restriction of our trade, and an almost total stagnation of business, threatened us with inevitable ruin. A long suspense, whether we should be deprived of, or restored to, the peaceable enjoyment of the inestimable privilege of English liberty, filled every breast with the most painful anxiety. A gloomy cloud thickened over our heads, ready to burst upon us in a desolating storm. Had our gracious Sovereign, the present ministry, and the British Parliament been less wise, just, and good; had they, instead of yielding to a spirit of moderation, unhappily recurred to force, we shudder at the very thoughts of the consequences. We cannot look down the precipice on the brink of which we stood, without horror. We were not without reason apprehensive that the tumultuous outrages, which in some places attended a determined opposition to the disrelished statute, might provoke the resentment of the British legislature.

When we reflect on the public offences of our land against heaven; when we think of the open disregard and violation of the holy Sabbath; the neglect of the ordinances of Divine worship, the abuse of gospel light and privileges, the profane swearing and cursing, intemperance and luxury, the various scenes of uncleaness and lasciviousness, the pride and vanity, and every other evil so shamefully prevalent, what less could we expect than that an offended God would have made the gathering tempest to break upon us, and plunged us and our mother country in all the rueful calamities of a civil war? But how astonishing is the long-suffering patience of Jehovah! He has inclined the hearts of many powerful friends to espouse our cause. He has given us to experience the paternal tenderness of the best of kings, and the moderation of the British Parliament. Our gracious God is our deliverer. He is making a further trial of us. May his unmerited goodness lend us to repentance.

We, therefore, call upon you, who are the dear people of our charge, not only to acknowledge with joy and gratitude the general Providence of God, but also thankfully to adore that particular Providence, wherein, upon special occasions, he directs and controls the course of events by his immediate influence, and whereby he hath on the late interesting occasion, so signally appeared for our protection.

While we thus call upon you to fear God, you will not forget to honour your king, and pay a due submission to his august parliament. Let this fresh instance of royal clemency increase the ardour of your affection to the person, family, and government, of our rightful and gracious sovereign. This you will manifest by a cheerful and ready obedience to civil authority. A spirit of liberty is highly laudable when under proper regulations, but we hope you will carefully distinguish between liberty and licentiousness.

We most earnestly recommend it to you to encourage and strengthen the hands of government, to demonstrate on every proper occasion your undissembled love for your mother country, and your attachment to her true interest, so inseparably connected with our own.

That thus you may become wise and good, as well as free and happy, and that while you enjoy liberty, civil and religious, you may not be the servants of sin and Satan, is the fervent prayer of those who watch for your souls, as men who must give an account. (*Records of Pres. Ch.,* 1766, 362.)

10. A Pastoral Letter on the Eve of Revolution

A month after the Battle of Lexington the Synod issued the first official Presbyterian pronouncement on civil affairs. With great dignity and feeling they laid before the people the reasons for the war, and sought to guide them in ways of Christian conduct during the crisis. It is of interest to note that despite popular ideas about Presbyterian subversiveness, the Synod, with only one dissenting voice, recommended loyalty to George III. The reason for revolt is not lawlessness, but the preservation of the rights of free men. These are not the sentiments of firebrands, but of responsible Christian leaders.

Very dear Brethren—The Synod of New York and Philadelphia being met at a time when public affairs wear so threatening an aspect, and when (unless God in his sovereign Providence speedily prevent it) all the horrors of a civil war throughout this great Continent are to be apprehended, were of opinion, that they could not discharge their duty to the numerous congregations under their care, without addressing them at this important crisis. As the firm belief, and habitual recollection of the power and presence of the living God, ought at all times to possess the minds of real Christians, so in seasons of public calamity, when the Lord is known by the judgment which he executeth, it would be an ignorance or indifference highly criminal not to look up to him with reverence, to implore his mercy by humble and fervent prayer, and, if possible, to prevent his vengeance by unfeigned repentance.

We do therefore, brethren, beseech you in the most earnest manner, to look beyond the immediate authors either of your sufferings or fears, and to acknowledge the holiness and justice of the Almighty in the present visitations. . . .

The Synod cannot help thinking that this is a proper time for pressing all of every rank, seriously to consider the things that belong to their eternal peace. Hostilities, long feared, have now taken place; the sword has been drawn in one province, and the whole continent, with hardly any exception, seem determined to defend their rights by force of arms. If, at the same time, the British ministry shall continue to enforce their claims by violence, a lasting and bloody contest must be expected. Surely, then, it becomes those who have taken up arms, and profess a willingness to hazard their lives in the cause of liberty, to be prepared for death, which to many must be certain, and to every one is a possible or probable event.

We have long seen with concern, the circumstances which occasioned, and the gradual increase of this unhappy difference. As ministers of the gospel of peace, we have ardently wished that it could, and often hoped that it would have been more early accommodated. It is well known to you, (otherwise it would be imprudent indeed thus publicly to profess,) that we have not been instrumental in inflaming the minds of the people, or urging them to acts of violence and disorder. Perhaps no instance can be given on so interesting a subject, in which political sentiments have been so long and so fully kept from the pulpit, and even malice itself has not charged us with labouring from the press; but things are now come to such a state, that as we do not wish to conceal our opinions as men and citizens, so the relation we stand in to you seemed to make the present improvement of it to your spiritual benefit, an indispensable duty.

Suffer us then to lay hold of your present temper of mind, and to exhort, especially the young and vigorous, by assuring them that there is no soldier so undaunted as the pious man, no army so formidable as those who are superior to the fear of death. There is nothing more awful to think of, than that those whose trade is war should be despisers of the name of the Lord of hosts, and that they should expose themselves to the imminent danger of being immediately sent from cursing and cruelty on the earth, to the blaspheming rage and despairing horror of the infernal pit. Let therefore, every one, who from generosity of spirit, or benevolence of heart, offers himself as a champion in his country's cause, be persuaded to reverence the name, and walk in the fear of the Prince of the kings of the earth, and then he may, with the most unshaken firmness, expect the issue either in victory or death.

Let it not be forgotten, that though for the wise ends of his Providence it may please God, for a season to suffer his people to lie under unmerited oppression, yet in general we may expect, that those who fear and serve him in sincerity and truth, will be favoured with his countenance and strength. It is both the character and the privilege of the children of God, that they call upon him in the day of trouble, and he, who keepeth covenant and truth for ever, has said, that his ears are always open to their cry. We need not mention to you in how many instances the event in battles, and success in war, have turned upon circumstances which were inconsiderable in themselves, as well as out of the power of human prudence to forsee or direct, because we suppose you firmly believe that after all the counsels of men, and the most probable and promising means, the Lord will do that which seemeth him good; nor hath his promise ever failed of its full accomplishment; "the Lord is with you while ye be with him, and if ye seek him he will be found of you; but if ye forsake him he will forsake you." 2 Chron. xv. 2.

After this exhortation, which we thought ourselves called upon to give you at this time, on your great interest, the one thing needful, we shall take the liberty to offer a few advices to the societies under our charge, as to their public and general conduct; and,

First. In carrying on this important struggle, let every opportunity be taken to express your attachment and respect to our sovereign King George, and to the revolution principles by which his august family was seated on the British throne. We recommend, indeed, not only allegiance to him from duty and principle, as the first magistrate of the empire, but esteem and reverence for the person of the prince, who has merited well of his subjects on many accounts, and who has probably been misled into the late and present measures by those about him; neither have we any doubt that they themselves have been in a great degree deceived by false information from interested persons residing in America. It gives us the greatest pleasure to say, from our own certain knowledge of all belonging to our communion, and from the best means of information, of the far greatest part of all denominations in this country, that the present opposition to the measures of administration does not in the least arise from disaffection to the king, or a desire of separation from the parent state. We are happy in being able with truth to affirm, that no part of America would either have approved or permitted such insults as have been offered to the sovereign in Great Britain. We exhort you, therefore, to continue in the same disposition, and not to suffer oppression, or injury itself, easily to provoke you to any thing which may seem to betray contrary sentiments: let it ever appear, that you only desire the preservation and security of those rights which belong to you as freemen and Britons, and that reconciliation upon these terms is your ardent desire.

Secondly. Be careful to maintain the union which at present subsists through all the colonies; nothing can be more manifest than that the success of every measure depends on its being inviolably preserved, and therefore, we hope that you will leave nothing undone which can promote that end. In particular, as the Continental Congress, now sitting at Philadelphia, consists of delegates chosen in the most free and unbiased manner, by the body of the people, let them not only be treated with respect, and encouraged in their difficult service—not only let your prayers be offered up to God for his direction in their proceedings—but adhere firmly to their resolutions; and let it be seen that they are able to bring out the whole strength of this vast country to carry them into execution. We would also advise for the same purpose, that a spirit of candour, charity, and mutual esteem, be preserved and promoted towards those of different religious denominations. Persons of probity and principle of every profession, should be united together as servants of the same master, and the experience of our happy concord hitherto in a state of liberty should engage all to unite in support of the common interest; for there is no example in history, in which civil liberty was destroyed, and the rights of conscience preserved entire.

Thirdly. We do earnestly exhort and beseech the societies under our care to be strict and vigilant in their private government, and to watch over the morals of their several members. It is with the utmost pleasure we remind you, that the last Continental Congress determined to discourage luxury in living, public diversions, and gaming of all kinds, which have so fatal an influence on the morals of the people. If it is undeniable that universal profligacy makes a nation ripe for Divine judgments, and is the natural means of bringing them to ruin, reformation of manners is of the utmost necessity in our present distress. At the same time, as it has been observed by many eminent writers, that the censorial power, which had for its object the manners of the public in the ancient free States, was absolutely necessary to their continuance, we cannot help being of opinion that the only thing which we have now to supply the place of this is, the religious discipline of the several sects with respect to their own members; so that the denomination or profession which shall take the most effectual care of the instruction of its members, and maintain its discipline in the fullest vigour, will do the most essential service to the whole body. For the very same reason, the greatest service which magistrates, or persons in authority, can do, with respect to the religion or morals of the people, is to defend and secure the rights of conscience in the most equal and impartial manner.

Fourth. We cannot but recommend, and urge in the warmest manner, a regard to order and the public peace; and as in many places, during the confusions that prevail, legal proceedings have become difficult, it is hoped that all persons will conscientiously pay their just debts, and to the utmost of their power serve one another, so that the evils inseparable from a civil war may not be augmented by wantoness and irregularity.

Fifth. We think it of importance, at this time, to recommend to all of every rank, but especially to those who may be called to action, a spirit of humanity and mercy. Every battle of the warrior is with confused noise, and garments rolled in blood. It is impossible to appeal to the sword without being exposed to many scenes of cruelty and slaughter; but it is often observed, that civil wars are carried on with a rancour and spirit of revenge much greater than those between independent States. The injuries received, or supposed, in civil wars, wound more deeply than those of foreign enemies, it is therefore the more necessary to guard against this abuse, and recommend that meekness and gentleness of spirit, which is the noblest attendant on true valour. That man will fight most bravely, who never fights till it is necessary, and who ceases to fight as soon as the necessity is over.

Lastly. We would recommend to all the societies under our care, not to content themselves with attending devoutly on general fasts, but to continue habitually in the exercise of prayer, and to have frequent occasional voluntary meetings for solemn intercession with God on the important trial. Those who are immediately exposed to danger need your sympathy; and we learn from the Scriptures, that fervency and importunity are the very characters of that prayer of the righteous man that availeth much.

We conclude with our most earnest prayer, that the God of heaven may bless you in your temporal and spiritual concerns, and that the present unnatural dispute may be speedily terminated by an equitable and lasting settlement on constitutional principles. (*Records of Pres. Ch.*, 1775, 466–469.)

11. John Adams Hears a Presbyterian Sermon

It was only a fortnight after the Synod meeting in 1775 that John Adams (later the second President of the United States) attended the Old Pine Street Church in Philadelphia, and was delighted to hear the same type of revolutionary sermon to which he was accustomed in Massachusetts. The preacher was Rev. George Duffield, who later had a price set upon his head by the British. The public endorsement of their cause by the Presbyterian clergy was of great importance to the Continental Congress.

I have this morning been to hear Mr. Duffield, a preacher in this City, whose principles, prayer, and sermons more nearly resemble those of our New England clergy than any I have heard. His discourse was a kind of exposition on the Thirty-fifth Chapter of Isaiah. America was the wilderness, and the solitary place, and he said it would be glad, "rejoice and blossom as the rose." He labored "to strengthen the weak hands and confirm the feeble knees." He "said to them that were of a fearful heart, Be strong, fear not. Behold, your God will come with vengeance, even God with a recompense; he will come and save you." "No lion shall be there, nor any ravenous beast shall go up, but the redeemed shall walk there" etc. He applied the whole prophecy to this country, and gave us as animating an entertainment as I ever heard. He filled and swelled the bosom of every hearer. I hope you have received a letter, in which I inclosed a pastoral letter from the Synod of New York and Philadelphia; by this you will see, that the clergy this way are but now beginning to engage in politics, and they engage with a fervor that will produce wonderful effects. (*Familiar Letters of John Adams to his Wife etc.*, ed. by C. F. Adams, New York, 1876, Letter, June 11, 1775, 65.)

12. "The Cause of Justice, of Liberty, and of Human Nature"

Rev. John Witherspoon, president of the College of New Jersey, a member of the Continental Congress, and a signer of the Declaration of Independence, was the most outstanding Presbyterian leader of the Revolutionary era. The following excerpts are from a sermon he preached at Princeton, May 17, 1776, "being the General Fast ap-

pointed by the Congress through the United Colonies." There is little in these pages to substantiate the Tory Jonathan O'dell's lines about Witherspoon,

"*Fierce as the fiercest, foremost of the first,
He'd rail at kings, with venom well-nigh burst.*"

Instead the emphasis is on solid Presbyterian virtues, orderliness, industry, thrift, and obedience to God in a time of crisis. The reason for revolt lies in the impossibility of just government by a remote and uninformed parliament.

If your cause is just, you may look with confidence to the Lord, and entreat him to plead it as his own.

You are all my witnesses, that this is the first time of my introducing any political subject into the pulpit. At this season, however, it is not only lawful but necessary; and I willingly embrace the opportunity of declaring my opinion without any hesitation, that the cause in which America is now in arms, is the cause of justice, of liberty, and of human nature. So far as we have hitherto proceeded, I am satisfied that the confederacy of the colonies, has not been the effect of pride, resentment, or sedition, but of a deep and general conviction, that our civil and religious liberties, and consequently, in a great measure, the temporal and eternal happiness of us and our posterity, depended on the issue. . . . There is not a single instance in history, in which civil liberty was lost, and religious liberty preserved entire. If, therefore, we yield up our temporal property, we at the same time deliver the conscience into bondage.

You shall not, my brethren, hear from me in the pulpit, what you have never heard from me in conversation; I mean railing at the king personally, or even his ministers and the parliament, and people of Britain, as so many barbarous savages. Many of their actions have probably been worse than their intentions. That they should desire unlimited dominion if they can obtain or preserve it, is neither new nor wonderful. I do not refuse submission to their unjust claims, because they are corrupt or profligate, although probably many of them are so, but because they are *men*, and therefore liable to all the selfish bias inseparable from human nature. I call these claims unjust, of making laws to bind us in all cases whatsoever, because they are separated from us, independent of us, and have an interest in opposing us. Would any man who could prevent it, give up his estate, person, and family, to the disposal of his neighbor, although he had liberty to choose the wisest and the best master? Surely not! This is the true and proper hinge of the controversy between Great Britain and America. It is, however, to be added, that such is their distance from us, that a wise and prudent administration of our affairs is as impossible as the claim of authority is unjust. Such is and must be their ignorance of the state of things here, so much time must elapse before any errors can be seen and remedied, and so much injustice and partiality must be expected from the arts and misrepresentation of interested persons, that for these colonies to depend wholly upon the legislature of Great Britain, would be, like many other oppressive connections, injury to the master, and ruin to the slave. . . .

I have said—If your principles are pure—the meaning of this is, if your present opposition to the claims of the British ministry does not arise from a seditious and turbulent spirit, or a wanton contempt of legal authority, from a blind and factious attachment to particular persons or parties, or from a selfish, rapacious disposition, and a desire to turn public confusion to private profit; but from a concern for the interest of your country, and the safety of yourself and your posterity. On this subject I cannot help observing, that though it would be a miracle if there were not many selfish persons among us, and discoveries now and then made of mean and interested transactions, yet they have been comparatively inconsiderable both in number and effect. In general, there has been so great a degree of public spirit, that we have much more reason to be thankful for its vigor and prevalence, than to wonder at the few appearances of dishonesty and disaffection. It would be very uncandid to ascribe the universal ardor that has prevailed among all ranks of men, and the spirited exertions in the most distant colonies to any thing else than public spirit. Nor was there ever perhaps in history so general a commotion, from which religious differences have been so entirely excluded. Nothing of this kind has as yet been heard, except of late in the absurd, but malicious and detestable attempts of our few remaining enemies to introduce them. At the same time, I must also for the honor of this country observe, that though government in the ancient forms has been so long unhinged, and in some colonies not sufficient care taken to substitute another in its place; yet has there been, by common consent, a much greater degree of order and public peace, than men of reflexion and experience foretold or could expect. From all these circumstances, I conclude favorably of the principles of the friends of liberty, and do earnestly exhort you to adopt and act upon those which have been described, and resist the influence of every other. . . .

1. Give me leave to recommend to you an attention to the public in-

terests of religion, or, in other words, zeal for the glory of God, and the good of others. . . .

This is a matter of the utmost moment, and which ought to be well understood both in its nature and principles. Nothing is more certain, than that a general profligacy and corruption of manners, makes a people ripe for destruction. A good form of government may hold the rotten materials together for some time, but beyond a certain pitch, even the best constitution will be ineffectual, and slavery must ensue. On the other hand, when the manners of a nation are pure, when true religion and internal principles maintain their vigour, the attempts of the most powerful enemies to oppress them are commonly baffled and disappointed. This will be found equally certain, whether we consider the great principles of God's moral government, or the operation and influence of natural causes.

What follows from this? That he is the best friend to American liberty, who is most sincere and active in promoting true and undefiled religion, and who sets himself, with the greatest firmness, to bear down profanity and immorality of every kind. Whoever is an avowed enemy to God, I scruple not to call him an enemy to his country. . . .

2. I exhort all who are not called to go into the field, to apply themselves, with the utmost diligence, to works of industry. It is in your power, by this means, not only to supply the necessities, but to add to the strength of your country. Habits of industry prevailing in a society not only increase its wealth, as their immediate effect, but they prevent the introduction of many vices, and are intimately connected with sobriety and good morals. Idleness is the mother or nurse of almost every vice; and want, which is its inseparable companion, urges men on to the most abandoned and destructive courses. Industry, therefore, is a moral virtue of the greatest moment, absolutely necessary to national prosperity, and the sure way of obtaining the blessing of God. I would also observe, that in this, as well as in every other part of God's government, obedience to his will is as much a natural mean, as a meritorious cause of the advantage we wish to reap from it. Industry brings up a firm and hardy race. He who is inured to the labour of the field, is prepared for the fatigues of a campaign. The active farmer, who rises with the dawn, and follows his team or plow, must, in the end, be an overmatch for those effeminate and delicate soldiers who are nursed in the lap of self-indulgence, and whose greatest exertion is the important preparation for, and tedious attendance on, a masquerade or midnight ball.

3. In the last place, suffer me to recommend to you frugality in your

families, and every other article or expence.

This the state of things among us renders absolutely necessary, and it stands in the most immediate connection both with virtuous industry and active public spirit. Temperance in meals, moderation in dress, furniture, and equipage, have, I think, generally been characteristics of a distinguished patriot. And when the same spirit pervades a people in general, they are fit for every duty, and able to encounter the most formidable enemy. The general subject of the preceding discourse has been—The wrath of man praising God. If the unjust oppression of your enemy, which withholds from you many of the usual articles of luxury and magnificence, shall contribute to make you clothe yourselves and your children with the work of your own hands, and cover your tables with the salutary productions of your own soil, it will be a new illustration of the same truth, and a real happiness to yourselves and country. . . .

Upon the whole, I beseech you to make a wise improvement of the present threatening aspect of public affairs, and to remember, that your duty to God, to your country, to your families, and to yourselves, is the same. True religion is nothing else, but an inward temper and outward conduct, suited to your state and circumstances in providence at any time. And as peace with God, and conformity to him, adds, to the sweetness of created comforts while we possess them, so, in times of difficulty and trial, it is in the man of piety and inward principle that we may expect to find the uncorrupted patriot, the useful citizen, and the invincible soldier. God grant, that in America true religion and civil liberty may be inseparable, and that the unjust attempts to destroy the one may, in the issue, tend to the support and establishment of both. (J. Witherspoon, *The Dominion of Providence Over the Passions of Men*, reprinted, London, 1778, 33 ff.)

13. "We Ask No Ecclesiastical Establishment for Ourselves; Neither Can We Approve of Them When Granted to Others"

The first Church judicatory in America openly to recognize the Declaration of Independence was the Presbytery of Hanover in Virginia. On October 24, 1776, the following memorial was presented to the Virginia Assembly by "the mother of all southern presbyteries." It is of great interest not only for its clear statement of the principle of separation of Church and State, but also for the fact that its arguments are not derived from the Westminster Divines, but from the same eighteenth century political philosophers who influenced Thomas Jefferson.

To the Honorable the General Assembly of Virginia. The Memorial of the Presbytery of Hanover humbly represents:

That your memorialists are governed by the same sentiments which have inspired the United States of America, and are determined that nothing in our power and influence shall be wanting to give success to their common cause. We would also represent that dissenters from the Church of England in this country have ever been desirous to conduct themselves as peaceable members of the civil government, for which reason they have hitherto submitted to various ecclesiastical burdens and restrictions that are inconsistent with equal liberty. But now, when the many and grievous oppressions of our mother-country have laid this Continent under the necessity of casting off the yoke of tyranny, and of forming independent governments upon equitable and liberal foundations, we flatter ourselves, that we shall be freed from all the encumbrances which a spirit of domination, prejudice, or bigotry has interwoven with most other political systems. This we are the more strongly encouraged to expect by the Declaration of Rights, so universally applauded for that dignity, firmness, and precision with which it delineates and asserts the privileges of society, and the prerogatives of human nature; and which we embrace as the Magna Charta of our commonwealth, that can never be violated without endangering the grand superstructure it was designed to sustain. Therefore, we rely upon this Declaration, as well as the justice of our honorable Legislature, to secure us the free exercise of religion according to the dictates of our consciences; and we should fall short in our duty to ourselves, and the many and numerous congregations under our care, were we, upon this occasion, to neglect laying before you a statement of the religious grievances under which we have hitherto labored, that they may no longer be continued in our present form of government.

It is well known that in the frontier counties, which are justly supposed to contain a fifth part of the inhabitants of Virginia, the dissenters have borne the heavy burdens of purchasing glebes, building churches and supporting the established clergy, where there are very few Episcopalians, either to assist in bearing the expense, or to reap the advantage; and that throughout the other parts of the country there are also many thousands of zealous friends and defenders of our State, who, besides the invidious, and disadvantageous restrictions to which they have been subjected, annually pay large taxes to support an establishment from which their consciences and principles oblige them to dissent: all which are confessedly so many violations of their natural rights; and in their consequences, a restraint upon freedom of inquiry, and private judgment.

In this enlightened age, and in a land where all of every denomination are united in the most strenuous efforts to be free, we hope and expect that our representatives will cheerfully concur in removing every species of religious, as well as civil bondage. Certain it is, that every argument for civil liberty, gains additional strength when applied to liberty in the concerns of religion; and there is no argument in favor of establishing the Christian religion, but what may be pleaded, with equal propriety, for establishing the tenets of Mohammed by those who believe the Alcoran; or, if this be not true, it is at least impossible for the magistrate to adjudge the right of preference among the various sects that profess the Christian faith, without erecting a claim to infallibility, which would lead us back to the Church of Rome.

We beg leave farther to represent, that religious establishments are highly injurious to the temporal interests of any community. Without insisting upon the ambition and the arbitrary practices of those who are favored by government, or the intriguing, seditious spirit which is commonly excited by this, as well as by every other kind of oppression, such establishments greatly retard population, and, consequently, the progress of arts, sciences, and manufactures. Witness the rapid growth and improvement of the Northern provinces compared with this. No one can deny that the more early settlement, and the many superior advantages of our country, would have invited multitudes of artificers, mechanics, and other useful members of society, to fix their habitation among us, who have either remained in their place of nativity, or preferred worse civil governments, and a more barren soil, where they might enjoy the rights of conscience more fully than they have a prospect of doing in this. From which we infer that Virginia might have now been the capital of America, and a match for the British arms, without depending on others for the necessaries of war, had it not been prevented by her religious establishment.

Neither can it be made to appear that the Gospel needs any such civil aid. We rather conceive that, when our blessed Saviour declares his kingdom is not of this world, he renounces all dependence upon state power; and as his weapons are spiritual, and were only designed to have influence on the judgement and heart of man, we are persuaded that if mankind were left in the quiet possession of their inalienable religious privileges, Christianity, as in the days of the Apostles, would continue to prevail and flourish in the greatest purity by its own native excellence, and under the all-disposing providence of God.

We would also humbly represent, that the only proper objects of civil government are the happiness and protection of men in the present state of existence; the security of the life, liberty, and property of the citizens, and to restrain the vicious and encourage the virtuous by wholesome laws, equally extending to every individual; but that the duty which we owe to our Creator, and the manner of discharging it, can only be directed by reason and conviction and is nowhere cognizable but at the tribunal of the universal Judge.

Therefore, we ask no ecclesiastical establishment for ourselves; neither can we approve of them when granted to others. This, indeed, would be giving exclusive or separate emoluments or privileges to one set of men, without any special public services, to the common reproach and injury of every other denomination. And, for the reasons recited, we are induced earnestly to entreat that all laws now in force in this commonwealth, which contenance religious domination, may be speedily repealed; that all, of every religious sect may be protected in the full exercise of their several modes of worship; exempted from all taxes for the support of any Church whatsoever, farther than what may be agreeable to their own private choice or voluntary obligation. This being done, all partial and invidious distinctions will be abolished, to the great honor and interest of the State, and every one be left to stand or fall according to his merit, which can never be the case so long as any one denomination is established in preference to others.

That the great sovereign of the universe may inspire you with unanimity, wisdom, and resolution and bring you to a just determination on all the important concerns before you is the fervent prayer of your memorialists. (Quoted in W. H. Foote, *Sketches of Virginia*, Philadelphia, 1850, 323 ff.)

PART
II

AMERICAN PRESBYTERIANISM IN MID-PASSAGE 1784–1869

CHAPTER

4

THE NATIONAL IMPULSE
1784–1811

1. The Making of the General Assembly

The new nationalism of the United States was reflected in the organization of a General Assembly of the Presbyterian Church. The first Presbytery of 1706 had created the Synod of 1717. This Synod was not a delegated body, but always retained the character of a general court or presbytery of the whole. By 1786 an annual meeting of all the ministers had become impractical. The question was, Should there be several regional synods, loosely related, or should there be a national assembly of delegates from the presbyteries? At the same time that the Federalists were drafting a Federal Constitution for the nation, therefore, the Synod prepared and adopted a constitution which provided for a national General Assembly of delegates, but left the ultimate power in the hands of the presbyteries. It will be noted that this is in contrast to the Scottish system where the General Assembly is supreme. The following documents indicate the steps in the making of the constitution. The Constitution *itself is readily available in many editions.*

The following motion was made and seconded, viz: the Synod considering the number and extent of the churches under their care, and the inconvenience of the present mode of government by one Synod, resolved, that this Synod will establish, out of its own body, three or more subordinate Synods, out of which shall be composed a General Assembly, Synod, or Council, agreeably to a system hereafter to be adopted.

Upon the question being put, Will the Synod adopt the resolution aforesaid, or not? it was carried in the affirmative. (*Records of Pres. Ch.,* 1786, 517.)

The Synod took into consideration the last paragraph of the twentieth chapter of the Westminster Confession of Faith; the third paragraph of the twenty-third chapter; and the first paragraph of the thirty-first chapter; and having made some alterations, agreed that the said paragraphs, as now altered, be printed for consideration, together with the draught of a plan of government and discipline. The Synod also appointed the above named committee to revise the Westminster Directory for public worship, and to have it when thus revised, printed, together with the draught, for consideration. And the Synod agreed, that when the above proposed alterations in the Confession of Faith shall have been finally determined on by the body, and the Directory shall have been revised as above directed, and adopted by the Synod, the said Confession thus altered, and Directory thus revised and adopted, shall be styled, "The Confession of Faith, and Directory for public worship, of the Presbyterian Church in the United States of America." (*Records of Pres. Ch.*, 1787, 539.)

The Synod having fully considered the draught of the form of government and discipline, did, on a review of the whole, and hereby do ratify and adopt the same, as now altered and amended, as the Constitution of the Presbyterian Church in America, and order the same to be considered and strictly observed as the rule of their proceedings, by all the inferior judicatories belonging to the body. And they order that a correct copy be printed, and that the Westminster Confession of Faith, as now altered, be printed in full along with it, as making a part of the constitution.

Resolved, That the true intent and meaning of the above ratification by the Synod, is, that the Form of Government and Discipline and the Confession of Faith, as now ratified, is to continue to be our constitution and the confession of our faith and practice unalterable, unless two thirds of the Presbyteries under the care of the General Assembly shall propose alterations or amendments, and such alterations or amendments shall be agreed to and enacted by the General Assembly. (*Records of Pres. Ch.*, 1788, 546.)

2. "The Psalms of David"

Traditionally the only words worthy to be sung in the praise of God were The Whole Psalmes of David in English Metre *prepared by Francis Rouse, a Puritan member of the Long Parliament, and adopted by both the Westminster Assembly and the General Assembly of the Church of Scotland (1649). With the appearance of Isaac Watts's* The Psalms of David Imitated *(1719), and his even more popular paraphrases of other portions of Scripture, a controversy developed which still divides Presbyterian churches in America. As early as 1756 the Synod ruled that "no particular version is of divine authority," and in 1787 the following course was recommended. It was not until 1802 that Theodore Dwight's revision of Watts with an appendix of hymns was officially adopted by the General Assembly.*

In respect to the psalmody; the Synod have allowed the use of the imitation of the Psalms of David for many years, to such congregations as choose them, and still allow of the same, but they are far from disapproving of Rouse's version, commonly called the Old Psalms, in those who were in the use of them and chose them, but are of opinion that either may be used by the churches, as each congregation may judge most for their peace and edification, and therefore highly disapprove of public, severe, and unchristian censures being passed upon either of the systems of psalmody, and recommend it to all ministers in those parts of the Church, to be more tender and charitable on these heads. (*Records of Pres. Ch.*, 1787, 537.)

3. "Old Redstone"

By 1781 there were four Presbyterian ministers settled west of the Alleghenies and steps were taken to organize the Presbytery of Redstone to serve the needs of the vast area of the Old Northwest. Few accounts of early Presbyterian customs excel the following reminiscences of "Old Redstone" by Rev. Joseph Smith.

Many congregations, during the whole summer, when the weather was pleasant, worshipped in groves. These groves were commonly in the immediate vicinity of the churches. Usually a hill-side was selected, where the trees were large and free from undergrowth. A platform, six or eight feet wide and ten or twelve feet long, was erected, about four feet from the ground, on the upper side. This was boarded up a few feet above the platform, having an open doorway, or place of entrance. At the back, on the lower side, the boarding extended much higher, and was connected with the roof, or covering, sloping off from the front. This *tent*, as it was called, was usually placed some distance down the hill-side, on descending ground; seats of logs, or slabs, were arranged in front of the tent, along up the side of the hill for some distance, spreading off considerably to the right and left of this tent-pulpit. Usually a long log, hewn only on the upper side, extended from near the pulpit, directly up through the area of the seats. This was elevated about the common height of a table, supported sometimes by straddling legs, but most generally by blocks of wood. On either side were similar logs, but much lower, for seats, placed sufficiently far from the higher, or table-logs, as to give room for walking between them. Sometimes, also, two other log-tables, with their seats diverged at right angles, to the right and left, all converging to a point some six or eight feet in front of the pulpit, but leaving sufficient room for an ordinary walnut or deal table. These log tables were occupied exclusively by communicants, during the progress of that solemn service. Before that service began, and at other times, they served as a part of the ordinary sitting.

A passing stranger, if not altogether a heathen or a publican, would readily recognise the sacramental sabbath by observing these extended log tables, covered with snowy linen, all radiating from the large common table, containing the vessels of the sacred symbols, and all covered with white napkins. . . . The seats were, of course, without backs, except where the trees furnished that luxury; and such choice seats were reserved for aged ladies and the infirm. . . .

The people are assembling from all directions—many on horseback, more on foot. . . . Some are seen on the ground, or on the logs, putting on their stockings and shoes—for they have walked many miles barefoot, carrying these articles wrapped in their kerchiefs, *in their hands*. . . .

The vast assembly gradually gather round the spot appropriated to the solemnities of that glorious day. They all become, at length, quietly seated. After a short pause, he sees the men all uncovering their heads, and the whole assembly rising to their feet; for the minister has risen in the tent, come forward to its front, and spread his hands in token of prayer. Then the psalm succeeds. . . . Another longer prayer, another psalm, and then the sermon. . . . The communion seasons of our fathers were, from an early period, exceedingly interesting. The Thursday preceding was commonly observed as a day of fasting and prayer. And there was always public worship on Saturday and Monday, in connexion with these occasions. The ministers, of course, aided each other; and many people from surrounding congregations and distant settlements attended. The families residing in the vicinity of the place were usually thronged with lodgers. . . .

For many years, it was not usual to administer the Lord's Supper more than twice a year, and, indeed, generally, as the ministers had more than one pastoral charge, only once in each congregation. But a very large proportion of all the members of their whole charge attended; riding, or walking, as many were compelled to do, ten or fifteen miles. The sermon on the fast-day (which was usually the previous Thursday) was generally long, and was a prayerfully prepared and affecting exhibition of the grounds and reasons for humiliation and prayer. . . .

The *action sermons*, as they were called, on communion Sabbaths, were generally preached by the pastors or resident ministers; this was considered peculiarly proper. . . . Then followed what was called *fencing the tables*. This was often tedious, occupying an hour or more. Not unfrequently there was a regular review of all the sins forbidden in each of the ten commandments. And it was remarked by the profane, that the preacher never stopped till he had solemnly debarred from the ordinance every one of his people, and himself to boot. Our old ministers, however, seldom indulged in such lengthened details as the *seceders* were said to be in the practice of doing, forbidding and debarring various classes of offenders, that were not to be found among them, such as stage-players and visitants of theatres; and yet it must be confessed that, too often, our venerable fathers took this occasion to pour out a great deal "de omnibus rebus, et quibusdem aliis." . . .

The practice of distributing tokens to communicants on Saturday or Sabbath morning, previous to the communion service, universally prevailed. . . . When at our early sacraments, so large a proportion of intending communicants were from surrounding churches, it seemed a highly proper custom. . . .

The ordinance of infant baptism was generally administered on the Sabbath, at the house of God, at as early a time after the birth of the child, as it suited the convenience of parents to attend public worship. The practice of confining the administration of this ordinance to Mondays of Communions, they did not sanction or approve. . . .

They were all in the habit of engaging parents to strict and solemn promises, in reference to the religious training of their children. . . .

Great attention was paid to the "Shorter Catechism." It was usually taught in all the schools. And pious parents required a recitation of it in their families, by old and young, on Sabbath evening. To have neglected this matter would have been regarded as heathenish. . . .

The singing at the church was generally led by one or more persons in front of the pulpit; and very commonly a smaller pulpit was constructed in front of the minister's, a few feet lower, called the Clerk's desk. . . .

The lines were "parcelled" out—sometimes one at a time—generally two. . . . But in those days psalmbooks were scarce, and many would have been scandalized had any attempt been made to sing without "giving out" the lines. . . .

In those times, the people all rose in time of prayer, except the aged and infirm, and stood devoutly till its close. . . .

There was one custom that then prevailed, which was well adapted to the plainness and simplicity of the times, the restoration of which we would almost advocate. When anybody became drowsy or weary with sitting, it was perfectly allowable to get up and stand awhile. And persons of every age and both sexes adopted this custom; so that, on a warm summer day, you might see twenty, fifty, or sixty people, young and old, standing bolt upright, in various parts of the congregation. By this means, sleep was resisted, and drowsiness thrown off. Subjected to various toils and hardships, many, in those days, found it exceedingly difficult, after a week of hard work, to keep themselves awake on the Sabbath, while at church. The services were somewhat long—the sermon would often reach the length of an hour and a half. Their prayers, too, were often long. In the summer, an hour's intermission between sermons was common. . . .

Their custom was, generally, during the period of the year when they preached twice, to make one of the discourses a part of a series of lectures, or expository sermons, on some portion of the Bible. The Psalms, the Prophecy of Isaiah, or one of the Epistles, would be taken up and treated seriatim in this way. (J. Smith, *Old Redstone*, Philadelphia, 1854, 153 ff.)

4. "Where Discipline Is Duly Exercised"

The Presbyterian way ran counter to much of the recreation of frontiersmen. In the two cases following, the Presbytery of Redstone was called upon to condemn the activities of prominent members of the churches in Chartiers and Pittsburgh.

Henry Taylor brought in an appeal from the judgment of the session of Chartiers congregation, with respect to his having and encouraging a *promiscuous dance* at his house. The Presbytery, after hearing both parties, upon mature deliberation, considering the smallness of the number present, (at the meeting of Presbytery,) and the importance of the case, defer the decision of it to the next meeting of the Presbytery. Adjourned to meet at Chartiers, 3d Tuesday of October next. Concluded with prayer. . . .

Therefore, as promiscuous dancing is condemned by the body of the godly and judicious in all ages, as well as by our own standards, and is generally attended with bad effects, we cannot think that the sessions were too rigorous in their judgment; and, therefore, with them, must conclude that Mr. Taylor, in order to admission to church privileges, ought to acknowledge his fault before this Presbytery, or be admonished to be more circumspect for the future. (*Records of the Presbytery of Redstone,* 1784, in Smith, *Old Redstone,* 329, 336.)

The Presbytery cannot but testify, upon this occasion, their disapprobation of card-playing, night-revelling, and using any expressions leading to immodest ideas, as practices very unbecoming in any professor of religion, and such as would lay a just foundation for exclusion from church privileges, in any congregation where discipline is duly exercised; and that, therefore, such of the elders of the church of Pittsburg as have appeared before us to be guilty of such things, ought to be, and are hereby admonished to abstain from such practices for the future—and be informed that, without a reformation, they ought to be further dealt with. Adjourned to meet at Laurel Hill, the third Tuesday of August. Concluded with prayer. (*Records of the Presbytery of Redstone,* 1789, in Smith, *Old Redstone,* 382.)

5. "The First Literary Institution in the West"

Nothing has characterized the Presbyterian way in America more than the founding of academies and colleges almost as soon as new presbyteries were formed on the frontier. Rev. Samuel Doak, who has been called "the apostle of learning and religion in the west," is an example of this tendency. Arriving in east Tennessee in 1775, he built three log houses on his farm, one for himself, one for a church, and one for a school. Incorporated as Martin Academy in 1785, it was chartered as Washington College in 1795, with Mr. Doak as president and the elders of his church as part of the board of trustees. The library consisted of books solicited by the president in the east, and transported by him "in a sack on a pack horse, five hundred miles" over the mountains.

Commencement was the only gala-day in the year with Dr. Doak. On that occasion, he wore his antique wig, his shorts, and his old fashioned shoes: the muscles of his stern brow were relaxed, and he gave himself up to an unusual urbanity and kindliness of manner. He was still grave, —still dignified and venerable; but there was an air of self-complacency, —of benignity blended with conscious self-consequence, which he exhibited on no other occasion. His posture was erect; his movements less ungraceful; his manner calm and most respectful. His Board of Trustees, who were indeed his Faculty, were seated upon plain benches near and around his chair. The candidates for the Academic honours approached him deferentially, slowly, modestly, and with filial regard and consideration bowed to him. Returning the salutation, the old President arose, and holding the diploma in one hand, said in a solemn and impressive tone of voice, and with a paternal pride and solicitude in his eye,—"Praeses et Curatores Washingtoniensis Collegii," &c. The scene was deeply interesting and impressive, and was never forgotten by a graduate. . . . His tuition fee was five dollars a session of five months; and in this was included the use of the college library, and other facilities of instruction. His habits were frugal; his hospitality, though not elegant, was better—it was unpretending and cordial. The primitive simplicity of early times in the West, and of frontier life, was exhibited upon his farm, in his house, in his dress, and in his intercourse with the world. When a young man, the condition of things around him created a necessity of participating actively in the settlement and defence of the country, and in its civil and political affairs. He always voted; and the consideration in which he was held by the people, generally allowed him to open the polls,—in other words, to vote first. (Letter of J. G. M. Ramsey, M.D., 1849, in W. B. Sprague, *Annals of the American Pulpit,* New York, 1868, III, 395 f.)

6. The Plan of Union

The rapid expansion of settlement in Ohio and western New York led the Congregational and Presbyterian Churches to take steps to eliminate wasteful overlapping and competition in home missionary work. The Plan of Union of 1801 was a co-operative scheme far in advance of the times and was an important factor in establishing Presbyterianism in the Old Northwest. The "Presby-gational" churches that came into existence, however, alarmed the purists in both denominations, and led eventually to the division of the Presbyterian Church in 1838. (See Ch. 6.)

The report of the committee appointed to consider and digest a plan of government for the Churches in the new settlements, was taken up and considered, and after mature deliberation on the same, approved, as follows:

Regulations adopted by the General Assembly of the Presbyterian Church in America, and by the General Association of the State of

Connecticut, (provided said Association agree to them,) with a view to prevent alienation, and to promote union and harmony in those new settlements which are composed of inhabitants from these bodies.

1. It is strictly enjoined on all their missionaries to the new settlements, to endeavour, by all proper means, to promote mutual forbearance, and a spirit of accommodation between those inhabitants of the new settlements who hold the Presbyterian, and those who hold the Congregational, form of Church government.

2. If in the new settlements any Church of the Congregational order shall settle a Minister of the Presbyterian order, that Church may, if they choose, still conduct their discipline according to the Congregational principles, settling their difficulties among themselves, or by a council mutually agreed upon for that purpose. But if any difficulty shall exist between the Minister and the Church, or any member of it, it shall be referred to the Presbytery to which the Minister shall belong, provided both parties agree to it; if not, to a council consisting of an equal number of Presbyterians and Congregationalists, agreed upon by both parties.

3. If a Presbyterian Church shall settle a Minister of Congregational principles, that Church may still conduct their discipline according to Presbyterian principles, excepting that if a difficulty arise between him and his Church, or any member of it, the cause shall be tried by the Association to which the said Minister shall belong, provided both parties agree to it; otherwise by a council, one-half Congregationalists and the other Presbyterians, mutually agreed upon by the parties.

4. If any Congregation consist partly of those who hold the Congregational form of discipline, and partly of those who hold the Presbyterian form, we recommend to both parties that this be no obstruction to their uniting in one Church and settling a Minister; and that in this case the Church choose a standing committee from the communicants of said Church, whose business it shall be to call to account every member of the Church who shall conduct himself inconsistently with the laws of Christianity, and to give judgment on such conduct. That if the person condemned by their judgment be a Presbyterian, he shall have liberty to appeal to the Presbytery; if he be a Congregationalist, he shall have liberty to appeal to the body of the male communicants of the Church. In the former case, the determination of the Presbytery shall be final, unless the Church shall consent to a further appeal to the Synod, or to the General Assembly; and in the latter case, if the party condemned shall wish for a trial by a mutual council, the case shall be referred to such a council. And provided the said standing

committee of any Church shall depute one of themselves to attend the Presbytery, he may have the same right to sit and act in the Presbytery, as a Ruling Elder of the Presbyterian Church. (*Minutes of the General Assembly*, 1801, 224.)

7. The Standing Committee on Missions

The erection of a standing committee in 1802 to direct "the missionary business" of the Church marks the beginning of the practice of the General Assembly of operating through authorized agencies. The first standing committee included among its members Elias Boudinot, formerly a president of the Continental Congress, Director of the Mint, and founder of the American Bible Society, and Ebenezer Hazard, formerly Postmaster General.

Resolved, 1. That a committee be chosen annually by the General Assembly, to be denominated the Standing Committee of Missions; that the committee shall consist of seven members, of whom four shall be clergymen and three laymen; that a majority of this Committee shall be a quorum to do business; that it shall be the duty of this Committee to collect, during the recess of the Assembly, all the information in their power relative to the concerns of missions and missionaries; to digest this information, and report thereon at each meeting of the Assembly; to designate the places where, and to specify the periods during which, the missionaries should be employed; to correspond with them, if necessary, and with all other persons on missionary business; to nominate missionaries to the Assembly, and report the number which the funds will permit to be employed; to hear the reports of the missionaries and make a statement thereon to the Assembly, relative to the diligence, fidelity, and success of the missionaries, the sums due to each, and such parts of their reports as it may be proper for the Assembly to hear in detail; to ascertain annually, whether any money remains with the Trustees of the college of New Jersey, which ought to be used for missionary purposes, agreeably to the last will of James Leslie, deceased; that they also engage a suitable person annually, to preach a missionary sermon on the Monday evening next after the opening of the General Assembly, at which a collection shall be made for the support of missions; and superintend generally, under the direction of the Assembly, the missionary business. . . .

3. That this Standing Committee of Missions, in addition to the duties above specified, shall be, and they hereby are, empowered to direct the Trustees of the General Assembly, during the recess of the Assem-

bly, to issue warrants for any sums of money which may become due, in consequence of contracts, appropriations, or assignments of duty made by the Assembly, and for which orders may not have been issued by the Assembly; and on this subject the committee shall report annually to the Assembly. (*Minutes of the G. A.*, 1802, 257.)

8. "Christ Must Increase"

The first promotional publication authorized by the Standing Committee on Missions was a sermon which had been preached before the General Assembly in 1803 by Rev. Henry Kollock of Elizabethtown, N. J. In it the Church's threefold responsibility toward the frontiersman, the Negro, and the Indian is forcibly presented.

Consider, for a moment, for whom we plead, in whose behalf we solicit donations; and then judge whether your liberality can more worthily, more profitably be exercised.

We plead for the persons who inhabit our frontier settlements. They are your brethren; your ancestors are theirs; the same blood which flows in your veins runs also in theirs. They lift to you a supplicating voice; they cry to you, with emphasis and importunity, to pity their distresses, to send to them those ordinances of religion which you enjoy, to have compassion on the souls of their children, who, without your aid, will grow up ignorant of religion, and unprepared for eternity. To their cry God joins his voice, and addresses us in language which cannot be misunderstood, "Since it is well with you, think of your brethren."

We plead for the unhappy blacks that dwell in our land. They are exposed to many calamities; they are labouring under the pressure of many sorrows. Though you, surrounded by so many sources of enjoyment, may not feel the necessity of religion as a comforter of the afflicted, as a cheerer of the desponding soul, yet they need the consolations of piety. Their path through life is dark and dreary; humanity loudly commands you to gild it by the prospect of immortality, by the hopes that it will issue in a world of rest, and of joy.—Besides, they have souls to save as well as we; they must exist for eternity as well as we. Already have we contracted awful guilt in remaining so negligent of their immortal interests; already has this sin cried to heaven for vengeance. It is time for us to strive to avert the judgments which we have deserved; it is time for us to awake from that criminal indifference with which we have seen this miserable race treading the path which conducts to the chambers of woe; it is time for us to stretch forth a succouring hand, and pluck them from eternal damnation.

But especially we plead for the wretched savages who, in a situation still more deplorable, have never heard of a Saviour's love. Think, think, of the misery of their state. Covered with guilt, and ignorant of the atonement provided by eternal love, they pass through life without any solid comfort, they expire without any well-founded hope, and awake with astonishment and anguish in a hell of which they had never heard. Where is the heart so obdurate that it does not compassionate this distress, and sigh to relieve it. The nations of Europe have not been able to consider it without emotion. Their sensibilities and good wishes have reached over the vast Atlantic: and, not contented with barren lamentations, with fruitless desires, many persons have left father, and mother, and house, and home; and have come with the burning zeal of apostles, and the high intrepidity of martyrs, to preach salvation to the Pagans. O! when I think of those generous men, whose devotion led them to sacrifice the pleasures of civilized life, to pass over interposing seas and mountains, and to moisten the turf of America with their blood—when I think that they did all this for the sake of those Indians that are our neighbours, that dwell upon our very borders—when I compare with the heroism of these martyred missionaries our coldness and indifference, I blush for the crimes of my country, I tremble at the account which it must render at the decisive day.—Shall not the liberality of your contributions prove that there are, at least, some hearts in America, which can listen to that cry from the wilderness, which struck the ears of these generous Europeans? (H. Kollock, *Christ Must Increase*, Philadelphia, 1903, 18–21.)

9. Circuit Riders

The following selection from the journal of Rev. William Williamson of the Presbytery of Washington (Ohio) is a reminder that "circuit riders" were not confined to the Methodist Church. For many years the official policy of the Presbyterians was to authorize ministers "to ride as missionaries" among the pastorless settlements of the West. (For objections to this policy, see Ch. 5, art. 5.)

Presbytery of Washington　　　　　　　　Tuesday Novr. 14th 1809

This day, agreably to an appointment of Presbytery, I set out in company with the Revd. James Gilleland on a Mission authorised by the General Assembly.

After proceeding about 8 miles up the Ohio river I was called about 9 miles off my intended rout to celebrate a marriage for which I received two dollars Mr. Gilleland proceed[ed] 10 miles to Mr. Lockhearts at the mouth of Brush Creek at which place he preached.

In the evening I found Mr G—d at said Lockhearts. We spent the remainder of the evening principally in conversation with the heads of the family on the duties they owed to God & their families & the necessaty of an interest in Christ in order to salvation—Neither of them were professors of religion, but both seemed to have some concern on the subject.

We learned from them that there were several families in their vicinity who called themselves Presbyterians. And who probably would attend presbyterian preaching if they had opportunity.

Wednesday 15th. We proceeded we proceeded [sic] 9 miles up the Ohio river to Moses Bairds at whose house I preached to 20 or 30 people. Mr G—d followed the Sermon with an Exhortation. Nothing remarkable appeared in the people.

Thursday 16 Mr G—d preached at Mr Murphy's 2 miles from Bairds. I also prea[c]hed at the same place in the evening between 20 & 30 attended & seemed very serious. It would seem from the best information we could get there are about 20 families in this neighbourhood who have some partiallity for presbyterianism. At present however a majority of them seemed principally engaged in securing their corn which they had left out longer than usual.

Friday 17th Leaving Mr G—d to fulfill some appointments which we had made on the opposite side of the River for the two following dais I proceeded 20 miles up the Ohio to Alexandria.

Saturday 18 I preached at the last mentioned place to 7 persons.

Sabath 19 Preached to about 100 People—Again in the evening to 50 or 60. My Audiences seemed attentive & solemn. At this time I also baptised two children William & Ruth son & daughter of Wm. Russel & wife of this place.

Monday 20 Preached again at the same place to about 15 persons who seemed very serious some of them shed tears.

In this town which stands on the bank of the Ohio immediately below the mouth of Sciota there are very fiew who are even nominal presbyterians & fiewer still who have ever enjoyed comunion in the church. A few families in the town & vicinity however seem desireous to enjoy the public means of Grace. . . .

Sabath 3rd. I preached at Sqr. Henry's to about 50 people who (except a fiew young people) appeared solemn untill they were dismissed after which near or quite half of them seemed prepared for trifling & mirth I preached again this evening at Mr Jas Henry's 3 miles from the

Sqrs to 15 people who appeared very serious

Monday 4th I proceeded 5 miles across a mountain which divides Chenoth's fork from main Sunfish to Mr Bristols where I expected to preach but on my arrival found that the person who had been entrusted with my appointment had neglected to give notice to the neighbourhood It was an excessively rainy day & most of the people of this vicinity were collected to assist one of their neighbours husk his corn I therefore appointed to preach the next day at Mr Alexr Crosses. . . .

During the above rout I made it a stated rule to converse with the families where I lodged or called in for an hour or two on the subject of religion. On some occasions our conversation was agreable I would humbly trust profitable but too generally thro the ignorance or want of relish [?] in the people & my own unskilfullness in this important duty I had but little ground to hope that any good fruit would arrise. (W. Williamson, "Journal," in *Journal P.H.S.*, XXVII, 231.)

10. "To Moralize and Civilize the Indians"

Rev. Gideon Blackburn has been called the "Daniel Boone of the pulpit." In 1803, after ten years as a frontier preacher in Tennessee, he was appointed by the Standing Committee to be its first missionary to the Cherokee Indians. A school was opened at Hiwassee and soon had fifty pupils enrolled. The following rules were drawn up by Blackburn for the schoolmaster. They were published in Glad Tidings, *one of the earliest American missionary magazines.*

Instructions given by the Rev. Gideon Blackburn, Missionary to the Cherokees, to the master of the school instituted for the education of their children.

1. The teacher will always keep in view that the object of the Institution is to moralize and civilize the Indians, as well as to teach them the Rudiments of the English Language; and therefore his conduct in all cases will be such as will tend to those ends.

2. Each morning, in the presence of the scholars, he will begin the exercises of the day, by singing a few verses of an hymn, and by addressing a prayer to the Deity; and in the evening will close the school in the same manner:—taking opportunities, at as early a period as possible, to teach the pupils the design of this conduct, and of impressing their minds with the propriety of silence, solemnity, and composure, during the exercises.

3. The sabbath will always be carefully spent in religious duties; and as soon as the scholars can understand the nature of the case, they must

be catechised on the first principles of religion; and as their capacity encreases, advanced towards the knowledge of religion in general.

On those days, should any *of the Nation* visit the teacher, he will carefully avoid conversations on worldly topics, and in a family way introduce things relative to God &c. and the first principles of religion and morality; always retaining a grave and solemn manner during such conversation, in order to impress the hearers with the importance of those subjects.

4. In all interviews with the Indians, the teacher will take care to shew a respectful attention to them, that they may see, that as men, they are viewed as his equals; and that superior instruction does not make men proud, but more humble and polite.

5. He will carefully avoid adopting their manners and habits, and studiously keep up the characteristic of superior civilization. Thus he will lead them into our customs.

6. In the government of the school all severity will be avoided, at least until the scholars are brought to love their new employ; but ingenious penalties and well chosen inducements must be adopted. In the whole business care will be taken to shew disapprobation of vice.

7. In the hours of amusement, the master will do well to direct them in such exercises and plays, as are practised among the white people; thereby eventually to change the diversions of the nation.

8. The teacher will, in all cases, avoid entering into the disputes of the nation, or becoming a party in their politics; and thus maintain his influence with the whole.

9. He must use his best endeavors to form a vocabulary of the language of the nation.

10. Collect as much as possible, from the best attested facts, an history of the nation.

11. Keep a record of the scholars names; exhibiting carefully, every month, the progress of each, and marking those who especially excel. (*Glad Tidings*, 1804, 39–40.)

11. Vaccination

In 1803 the first step in medical missions was authorized by the General Assembly. Dr. Benjamin Rush of Philadelphia, a Presbyterian, was active in promoting this movement.

A letter was received from certain citizens of Philadelphia, styling themselves, "Friends of Humanity," accompanied with two hundred copies of a publication on the vaccine disease, requesting that the Assembly will take measures to have the same distributed among the people for their information on the subject; and to hasten that expected and desirable event, the total extinction of that loathsome and fatal disease, the small-pox. Fifty additional copies of the same publication, accompanied with a few copies of Dr. Jenner's Instructions on the practice of vaccine inoculation, were also received from the same benevolent persons, with a request that they may be sent by the missionaries from this Assembly to the frontiers of the country, and distributed for the caution and direction of those who have less opportunity of obtaining medical aid and advice, on the subject of vaccine inoculation.

The present was thankfully accepted by the Assembly, who feeling perfectly disposed to co-operate with those friends of humanity, distributed the two hundred copies aforesaid among the members, to be used at their discretion for promoting the end in view. The fifty copies, with the directions accompanying them, were transmitted to the Standing Committee of Missions, to the intent that they may be employed for the purposes aforesaid. (*Minutes of the G. A.*, 1803, 277.)

12. The Western Missionary Society

It has been said that the organization of the Western Missionary Society by the Synod of Pittsburgh in 1802 "began a new era in the missionary life of the Church." Missions were no longer a voluntary project but the main business of the Church. The position of the Society at the gateway of the West also increased the effectiveness of denominational missions.

The Synod of Pittsburgh, at their first annual meeting, in Pittsburgh, on the last Wednesday of September, 1802, appointed the Rev. Messrs. Thomas Hughs, Elisha M'Curdy, Joseph Badger, and James Edgar, Elder, a committee to digest a plan for the transaction of Missionary Business: whose Report, with amendments, was adopted as follows:

I. The Synod of Pittsburgh shall be styled "THE WESTERN MISSIONARY SOCIETY."

II. The object of the Missionary Society is, to diffuse the knowledge of the Gospel, among the inhabitants of the new settlements, the Indian tribes, and, if need be, among some of the interior inhabitants, where they are not able to support the Gospel.

III. The Society shall annually appoint a Board of Trust, consisting of seven members, a majority of whom shall be a quorum, whose duty it shall be to transact all Missionary business which may occur, necessary to be done between the annual meetings of the Society; which Board shall meet quarterly.

IV. It is required of the Trustees, that they employ no characters as Missionaries, except those who give credible evidence of being the subjects of special grace, and of that Christian zeal, wisdom, information, and experience in ministerial labours; able to do the work of Evangelists, in the most self-denying circumstances.

V. The Board of Trust shall have authority, to draw money from the Treasury, to pay Missionaries whom they have appointed. It is expected also, that the Board of Trust will give direction to the Missionaries how long they shall be out, and where their field of mission shall be.

VI. The Board of Trust are required to lay before the Society, at their annual meetings, in fair records, all their proceedings, together with the Journals of the Missionaries; and, if it can be, have the Missionaries to attend.

VII. That the Society engage a suitable person annually, to preach a Missionary Sermon, on the Thursday next after the opening of the Synod; at which a collection shall be made for the support of Missionaries. (*The Western Missionary Magazine*, Washington, Pa., 1803, I, 10.)

13. The Kentucky Revival

Beginning about 1797 and continuing for many years, the frontier churches of Kentucky and Tennessee were the scene of a spectacular revival of religion. Thousands of people gathered for "camp meetings." The following are eyewitness accounts of the great emotional excitement that prevailed.

A. Camp Meetings

And here I would assure the reader, that he is not to imagine a camp-meeting such as, perhaps he has witnessed in modern times—reduced to some degree of order and regularity, by specific rules and regulations. Such were not the ancient meetings of this description; where every man did after the sight of his own eyes. Let him imagine a countless multitude of all descriptions of society, say five, ten, or even twenty thousand, collected together, in one of the beautiful groves of Kentucky, with its "boundless contiguity of shade." Let him imagine a platform, or stand for the clergy, elevated some five or six feet, around which is crowded, to a certain distance, the devout and orderly worshippers; and beyond, as far as the eye can extend, the disorderly and dissipated. . . . The clergyman rises and introduces the solemn service; takes a text as a motto; commences a vociferous and passionate address . . . not to the understanding (for this would be formality), but to the passions; and he has spoken but a few sentences, until you see a moving in the multitude, which very soon rises to a general agitation, like a calm ocean agitated into waves by a storm. The process was briefly this: an individual to your right (may be a converted or unconverted person) is taken with the exercise, of which you were notified by a shriek; there is an immediate rush to that place; a circle collects around the individual, and commence singing, and then praying, and then exhorting. Another is seized to your left, another in front, which soon spreads over the whole extent of the congregation, in all of which the same ceremony is performed, as in the first case; so that the congregation is now divided into a number of separate circles, in which some are singing, some praying, and some exhorting at the same time; and many constantly passing and repassing, from cluster to cluster. By this time the speaker has closed his harangue, either because his voice has been overcome by the uproar, or perhaps the principal work has been effected; and all that is now necessary, is that it should be carried on by the people. The clergy now leave the stand, and spread over the congregation, to converse with the exercised, and exhort, as occasion may offer. This scene was exhibited, day and night, without intermission, as long as the meeting lasted. There was no regular intermission, for eating and sleeping; we must, therefore, add these as going on together with religious service. It was the declaration of some of the clergy, and perhaps believed, that the millenium had now commenced. (R. Stuart, "Reminiscences" (1837), reprinted in *Journal, P.H.S.*, XXIII, 170 ff.)

B. The Jerks

The Rev. John P. Campbell having declined the appointment given him to ride two months, in the bounds of Cumberland Presbytery: on motion, made by Mr. Campbell, the synod of Kentucky unanimously agreed to appoint me as a missionary to go the abovementioned route.

Sat. Nov. 2, 1805. I went to the Beach meeting house, where a meeting was appointed by the Presbyterians and Methodists, called in this country, the union meeting. There I heard a sermon delivered by a Mr. N——, who has lately been licensed by the Cumberland Presbytery, and is said to be a man of learning. There was nothing very remarkable in his sermon, except his pressing exhortations to the people to pray out——shout——dance, &c. in time of divine worship. He told them to shout——pray aloud, or do whatever duty they felt an impression to do. Said he, "I believe it will not offend God, and I am sure it will not offend me." The people, though prior to this seemingly careless and inattentive, were roused to action——shouted——prayed aloud ——exhorted and jerked, till near the setting of the sun.

I am well aware, that it is impossible to describe an assembly thus agitated, so as to give those who have never seen the like, a just and adequate idea of it. I would just observe, that though I had been accustomed to seeing strong and indescribable bodily agitations, in the upper counties of Kentucky, and had frequently seen the jerks, yet all this observation and experience, did not prepare my mind to behold, without trepidation and horror, the awful scenes now exhibited before me. The jerks were by far the most violent and shocking I had ever seen. The heads of the jerking patients flew, with wondrous quickness, from side to side, in various directions, and their necks doubled like a flail in the hands of a thresher. Their faces were distorted and black, as if they were strangling, and their eyes seemed to flash horror and distraction. Numbers of them roared out in sounds the most wild and terrific. I had heard the howling of wild beasts, and the tremendous roar of the lion, but I can say, without hyperbole, that those were gentle accents compared to some I heard in this assembly. The people camped in waggons and tents around the stand. I retired to the Rev. William M'Gee's. The people who lodged here appeared engaged in singing, conversing, leaping and shouting. They appeared much like a drinking party when heard from the other room; but when I drew nigh, found their language and rejoicings were of a religious kind.

Sabbath, Nov. 3. Preached on 1 Cor. 13, 13, last clause. The audience was large, very attentive, and a solemnity seemed to reign in almost every countenance, especially during the application. I heard that an infidel being convicted, exclaimed—"Where did that man come from" —fell on his knees and cried for mercy. Mr. M'Kindre, a methodist elder, preached after me: then the ordinance was administered to a large number of communicants, many of whom appeared deeply affected— some shouted—some wept—some leapt—and some danced and jerked, and jerked and danced a long time after they rose from table. Afterwards the people were dismissed. I retired to Mr. M'Gee's, with whom I conversed about the conduct of the Cumberland Presbytery, in licensing young men who were illiterate and tainted with Arminianism. (John Lyle, "Narrative of a Mission," *The General Assembly's Missionary Magazine,* 1807, 46–47.)

C. The Dancing Exercise

Another common exercise was dancing, which was performed by a gentle and not ungraceful motion, but with very little variety in the steps. During the administration of the Lord's Supper, in the presence of the Synod of Virginia, we witnessed a young woman performing this exercise for the space of twenty minutes or half an hour. The pew in which she was sitting was cleared, and she danced from one end to another; her eyes were shut and her countenance calm. When the dancing terminated, she fell, and seemed to be agitated with more violent emotions. We saw another who had, what was termed, "the jumping exercise"; which resembled that of the jumpers in whales. It was truly wonderful to observe the violence of the impetus with which she was borne upward from the ground; it required united strength of three or four of her companions to confine her down. (*The Biblical Repertory and Theological Review*, 1834, Vol. 6, 349.)

14. The Coming of Finis Ewing

A result of the Kentucky Revival was an increased number of congregations and a growing demand for more ministers. In 1801 the Transylvania Presbytery met this situation by authorizing four men, who were deeply religious, but without education, to exhort and catechize in vacant congregations. The following narrative tells of the coming of one of these men, and what it meant to the backwoodsmen. Ewing later became one of the founders of the Cumberland Presbyterian Church.

We emigrated from Virginia in 1796, and settled where we now live, in 1797. Both my Sarah and I had been religiously raised and accustomed to read our Bible. Away from all our friends, and in this then solitary place, we felt that we needed an almighty Protector. We sought the one thing needful as for goodly pearls. In 1800, we trust we both embraced that holy religion which has been our guide and comfort up to the present hour. The country was filling up rapidly; but there was no one to break to us the bread of life. O, how we did long to hear the blessed gospel preached! We joined with David Beaty and Henry Anderson in a petition, praying the Transylvania Presbytery to send us a preacher. We were rejoicing in hope, but hungering for the word of God. We were Presbyterians, so far as we understood ourselves, and wanted to cast our lot with that people among whom God was carrying on his glorious work. The field was wide, the harvest plenteous, and the laborers few: a preacher could not come to us. We wept, we mourned, we prayed; but we could take no denial. We petitioned again without success. Still we believed God would hear and help us. We could not be discouraged, seeing that God could, in answer to our prayers, incline the Presbyters to favor us, if only a little. No mortal man can conceive our anxieties, unless he has been placed in a like situation. We could hear of other places within ten, twenty, and thirty miles, where the people, like us, were petitioning for a preacher: some of them had attended the great meetings in Kentucky, or higher up in Tennessee, and returned glorifying God. We asked, would not a God of love take care of his own cause, and feed his own flock, however feeble, few, or scattered abroad? We called to mind his precious promises, and said, he surely will. He is a God of truth, a righteous Sovereign, and has all power. With this we were comforted, and began confidently to look forward to the blessed day, when we should hear the gospel's joyful sound.

There are two periods of my life which I never can forget, while I remember any thing: one is, when I found the Lord precious; the other is, when in answer to all our prayers, he sent his faithful servant to minister to our spiritual necessities. I often call to mind, as if it were but yesterday, the evening when a traveler as I supposed, an entire stranger, rode up to my log cabin. This house built of rock, was not here then. His eyes were red with weeping; and the tears seemed scarcely dried on his cheeks. He inquired for James Hutchinson. On being informed that I was the man, he seemed overjoyed. He said, "I have so long traveled this Indian path without seeing a house, that I seriously feared it would be my lot to lie out this night, and take my chance with the wolves. I have cried and prayed to the Lord, as my helper; and now after sunset, faint, weary, and disconsolate, he has brought me to this hospitable home."

I was filled with surprise and joy. I saw he was a man of genteel appearance, prepossessing manners; and better still, his language savored of grace and piety. I had seen but few religious persons since I professed; and I greatly rejoiced, that a pious traveler had done me the favor to come and spend a night with me at my cabin in this wilderness. A little further conversation convinced me, that the supposed traveler was indeed a very pious man. He soon took occasion to let me know his business in these parts, and that his name was Finis Ewing. We had heard of him. I saw at once that he was the young preacher, sent by Transylvania Presbytery to instruct us in righteousness, and feed spiritually the few poor sheep, straying in the wilderness without a shepherd. Sarah! Sarah! I called. She was out, preparing supper. Stepping to the door, I said, the preacher has come! Sarah came in, shouting; while I was crying for joy. God had answered our prayers, and sent us a preacher!

When we had become a little composed, Mr. Ewing modestly observed, "Do not mistake me, my friends: I am not a preacher, but have been sent in the place of one. I am authorized publicly to exhort, expound the scriptures, and, according to my ability, give all needful instructions, without the formalities of a sermon." We cared but little for the formalities of a sermon. Instruction was what we wanted. Being mere babes in Christ, we wanted some one to expound unto us the way of God more perfectly. And the more we conversed with this good man, the more we admired his spirit of humility, strength of mind, and knowledge of divine things. We were soon convinced that he had grace and gifts to be all to us, and do every thing for us that a regular preacher could.

We had long felt that we were in the midst of a people who were living without hope and without God in the world, actually perishing for the lack of knowledge. Without the gospel, without schools and almost without a Sabbath, we shuddered at the thought of raising our children in such a society. The new comers were honest, industrious, and friendly; but most of them seemed as little regardful of religion and its duties as the heathen. We needed schools for the young, and the gospel for all. Hence we had petitioned Presbytery and prayed to God. Our prayers were now answered. We felt we never could be grateful enough to our heavenly Father, nor do enough for this his servant, who had left friends, family, and home, to show unto us the way of salvation.

Mr. Ewing arrived on Thursday night. I mounted my horse on Friday morning, and spent nearly two days in giving circulation to an appointment for meeting, on the ensuing Sabbath, at the house of David Beaty. I rode through the settlements on Cumberland and Red rivers, and the region about Claresville. Others also exerted themselves to good effect, Saints and sinners appeared to take great interest, since preaching, especially by a Presbyterian, was a novel occurrence. Many persons had never attended meeting, or heard a sermon, since they came to the country.

On arriving at the place of meeting, Mr. Ewing was astonished at the size of his congregation. ("Narrative of James Hutchinson, Esq.," in F. R. Cossitt, *The Life and Times of Rev. Finis Ewing*, Louisville, Ky., 1833, 70 ff.)

15. The Cumberland Presbyterian Church

To meet the growing demand for ministers, the Cumberland Presbytery in 1802–1804 relaxed the educational requirements for ordination and ordained Finis Ewing and others. When censured by the Synod of Kentucky, the majority of the presbytery formed themselves into an unofficial council, and in 1810 when efforts at reconciliation had failed, they constituted themselves into an independent Cumberland Presbytery. Within a few years this frontier Church had expanded into a Synod. In 1906 they finally reunited with the Presbyterian Church U.S.A., after a century of magnificent missionary expansion. The following is the minute of the organization of the separate presbytery. (The records of the Synod of Kentucky and of the earlier Cumberland Presbytery may be found in W. W. Sweet, Religion on the American Frontier, *Vol. 2.*)

In Dixon county Tennessee State, at the Rev. Samuel M'Adow's this 4th day of February, 1810.

We Samuel M'Adow, Finis Ewing, and Samuel King, regularly ordained ministers, in the presbyterian church against whom, no charge, either of immorality, or Heresy has ever been exhibited, before any of the church Judicatures. Having waited in vain more than four years, in the mean time, petitioning the general assembly for a redress of grievances, and a restoration of our violated rights, have, and do hereby agree, and determine, to constitute into a presbytery, known by the name of the Cumberland presbytery. On the following conditions (to wit) all candidates for the ministry, who may hereafter be licensed by this presbytery; and all the licentiates, or probationers who may hereafter be ordained by this presbytery; shall be required before such licensure, and ordination, to receive, and adopt the confession and discipline of the Presbyterian church, except the idea of fatality, that seems to be taught under the mysterious doctrine of predestination. It is to be understood, however, that such as can clearly receive the confession, without an exception, shall not be required to make any. Moreover, all licentiates, before they are set apart to the whole work of the ministry (or ordained) shall be required to undergo an examination, on English Grammar, Geography, Astronomy, natural, & moral philosophy, and church history. The presbytery may also require an examination on all, or any part of, the above branches of literature, before licensure if they deem it expedient. (*A Circular Letter Addressed to the Societies and Brethren of the Presbyterian Church Re-*

cently Under the Care of the Council by the late Cumberland Presbytery . . . , Russellville, Ky. Printed by Matthew Duncan, at the office of the Farmer's Friend, 1810.)

16. "A Nursery of Vital Piety"

The answer of the General Assembly to the tendency to relax educational requirements for the ministry was the establishment of Princeton Seminary in 1811. Henceforth, the Princeton professors exerted an immense influence in molding the minds of the clergy. The following rules indicate the high academic and moral standards required of candidates for the ministry. They also explain why Presbyterianism lost out to Churches with less stringent requirements for ordination.

Article IV

Sect. 1. Every student, at the close of his course, must have made the following attainments, viz. He must be well skilled in the original languages of the Holy Scriptures. He must be able to explain the principal difficulties which arise in the perusal of the Scriptures, either from erroneous translations, apparent inconsistencies, real obscurities, or objections arising from history, reason, or argument. He must be versed in Jewish and Christian antiquities, which serve to explain and illustrate Scripture. He must have an acquaintance with ancient geography, and with oriental customs, which throw light on the sacred records.—Thus he will have laid the foundation for becoming a sound biblical critic.

He must have read and digested the principal arguments and writings relative to what has been called the deistical controversy.—Thus will he be qualified to become a defender of the Christian faith.

He must be able to support the doctrines of the Confession of Faith and Catechisms, by a ready, pertinent, and abundant quotation of Scripture texts for that purpose.

He must have studied, carefully and correctly, Natural, Didactic, Polemic, and Casuistic Theology. He must have a considerable acquaintance with the history of the Christian Church.—Thus he will be preparing to become an able and sound divine and casuist.

He must have read a considerable number of the best practical writers on the subject of religion. He must have learned to compose with correctness and readiness in his own language, and to deliver what he has composed to others in a natural and acceptable manner. He must be well acquainted with the several parts, and the proper structure of popular lectures and sermons. He must have composed at least two lectures and four popular sermons, that shall have been approved by the professors. He must have carefully studied the duties of the pastoral care.—Thus he will be prepared to become a useful preacher, and a faithful pastor.

He must have studied attentively the form of Church Government authorized by the Scriptures, and the administration of it as it has taken place in Protestant Churches.—Thus he will be qualified to exercise discipline, and to take part in the government of the Church in all its judicatories.

Sect. 2. The period of continuance in the Theological Seminary shall, in no case, be less than three years, previously to an examination for a certificate of approbation. . . .

Sect. 3. . . . The examination shall be conducted by the professors, in the presence of the board of directors, or a committee of them; and if it be passed to the satisfaction of the directors, they who so pass it, shall receive a certificate of the same, signed by the professors, with which they shall be remitted to their several presbyteries, to be disposed of as such presbyteries shall direct. Those who do not pass a satisfactory examination shall remain a longer space in the Seminary. . . .

Article V

Sect. 1. It is expected that every student in the Theological Seminary will spend a portion of time every morning and evening in devout meditation, and self-recollection and examination; in reading the holy Scriptures, solely with a view to a personal and practical application of the passage read, to his own heart, character, and circumstances; and in humble fervent prayer and praise to God in secret.

The whole of every Lord's day is to be devoted to devotional exercises, either of a social or secret kind. Intellectual pursuits, not immediately connected with devotion or the religion of the heart, are on that day to be forborne. The books to be read are to be of a practical nature. The conversations had with each other are to be chiefly on religious subjects. Associations for prayer and praise, and for religious conference, calculated to promote a growth in grace, are also proper for this day; subject to such regulations as the professors and directors may see proper to prescribe. It is wished and recommended, that each student should ordinarily set apart one day in a month for special prayer and self-examination in secret, and also that he should, on suitable occasions, attend to the duty of fasting.

Sect. 2. If any student shall exhibit, in his general deportment, a levity or indifference in regard to practical religion, though it do not amount to any overt act of irreligion or immorality, it shall be the duty of the professor who may observe it, to admonish him tenderly and faithfully in private, and endeavour to engage him to a more holy temper, and a more exemplary deportment.

Sect. 3. If a student, after due admonition, persist in a system of conduct not exemplary in regard to religion, he shall be dismissed from the Seminary.

Sect. 4. The professors are particularly charged, by all the proper means in their power, to encourage, cherish, and promote devotion and personal piety among their pupils, by warning and guarding them, on the one hand, against formality and indifference, and on the other, against ostentation and enthusiasm; by inculcating practical religion in their lectures and recitations; by taking suitable occasions to converse with their pupils privately on this interesting subject; and by all other means, incapable of being minutely specified, by which they may foster true experimental religion, and unreserved devotedness to God. (*Extracts from the Minutes of the General Assembly*, 1811, 339–349.)

CHAPTER

5

THE AGE OF BENEVOLENCE
1812–1828

1. The Mississippi Valley

In American political history the years following the War of 1812 are often called "The Era of Good Feelings." Among the churches this national tendency found expression in co-operative, benevolent enterprises on a scale hitherto unknown. Interdenominational societies were organized to distribute Bibles and tracts, to found Sunday schools, to care for the Negroes, and to send out missionaries. Among those who were most active in promoting interest in this "Benevolent Empire" was Samuel J. Mills, who as a student at Williams College had taken part in the famous "Haystack" prayer meeting which marks the beginning of the modern American foreign missionary movement. The passages below are selected from Mills's report of a journey to the Mississippi Valley in 1814–1815. Written as letters and later collected and published, they aroused tremendous interest in Western missions. Originally a Congregationalist, Mills was ordained in the Presbyterian Church. His traveling companion, Rev. Daniel Smith, was also Presbyterian.

The western settlements in this Territory [Illinois] are separated from the eastern by a wilderness of 100 miles. They lie in a country highly interesting, considered as missionary ground. The American Bottom is an extensive tract of alluvial soil on the bank of the Mississippi, 80 miles in length, and about 5 in breadth. This land is endowed with a surprising and an exhaustless fertility. It is capable of supporting, and is doubtless destined to receive an immense population. The high lands back are also extremely fertile. Kaskaskias is the key to all this country: and must therefore become a place of much importance, although at present it does not greatly flourish. It contains between 80 and 100 families, two thirds French Catholics. The people of this place are very anxious to obtain a Presbyterian clergyman. Gov. Edwards assured us, that a preacher of popular talents would receive a salary of $1000, per annum, for preaching a part of the time, and instructing a small school. By giving another portion of his services to the people of St. Genevieve he might obtain an addition of 2 or 300 dollars. Six miles from Kaskaskias there is an Associate Reformed congregation of 40 families. Besides this we did not hear of a single organized society of any denomination in the county, nor of an individual Baptist or Methodist preacher. The situation of the two upper counties is in this respect somewhat different. Baptist and Methodist preachers are considerably numerous; and a majority of the heads of families, as we were informed by Gov. Edwards and others, are professors of religion. A Methodist minister told us that these professors were almost all of them educated Presbyterians. And they would have been so still, said he, had they not been neglected by their eastern brethren. Now they are Baptists and Methodists. How many of them could be restored to the Presbyterian connexion by a prudent and pious missionary, it is impossible to say. In all this Territory there is not a single Presbyterian preacher. And that is not all: when we arrived there we learnt that very considerable districts had never before seen one. Already have the interests of orthodoxy and of vital godliness suffered an irretrievable loss. And they must suffer more and more, until missionaries are employed and sent to erect the standard of the truth, and establish the institutions of the Gospel. . . .

It seems desirable that missionaries in this country should pay particular attention to the towns and villages. They are much more destitute of religious privileges than the back settlements. The Baptist and Methodist preachers of this country find but little encouragement to visit them. The inhabitants of the towns having been long freed from the restraints of religion, have become much more vitiated in their morals, than those of the country. The character of Shawanee-town we have mentioned, not as in this respect singular; but as a specimen of almost all of them. Yet in these places there are many friends of good order and religion, who would hold up the hands of a respectable and pious minister. In these places we behold the germs of future cities. The village, that now contains nothing but log cabins, will soon become the dwelling place of thousands. And those thousands may all be favourably affected by the early establishment of religious institutions there. . . .

Natchez, Mississippi Ter. Feb. 6, 1815.

Dear Sir,—There are no very considerable villages, between this place and the falls of the Ohio, a distance of more than twelve hundred miles. The banks of the Ohio and Mississippi are but partially settled. In descending these rivers, we have passed but one settlement, in which the word and ordinances of the gospel are statedly administered, by a Presbyterian clergyman. Baptist and Methodist preachers are to be met with occasionally. The *former*, in many instances, do not inculcate upon their hearers the importance of observing the Sabbath day as holy time. Neither do they enjoin upon parents the duty of religiously educating their children. The belief of the *latter* is well known. The religious sentiments of the inhabitants are very incorrect; and great stupidity, as it respects a concern for the salvation of the soul, appears generally to prevail. A reason, which answers in part for this inattention is obvious, *the people perish for lack of knowledge.*

Not only are the inhabitants destitute in a great measure of the word preached in its simplicity and purity, but it is a fact much to be lamented, that but comparatively few families are supplied with the Bible. Very many, who desire to possess such a treasure, know not how to obtain it. Others there are, who would receive the Bible as a gift, and return their thanks for it; who, unless supplied in this way, would probably spend their lives without reading a chapter, or scarcely knowing that there is such a book extant. It would be a labour indeed, to ascertain precisely the number of Bibles wanted in a State or Territory, that every destitute family might be supplied. We can assert with safety, that but comparatively few are possessed of them. . . .

We had many applications for the sacred Scriptures, with which we could not comply. Some of the people asserted, that they never had an opportunity to purchase the Bible at any price; though they had been long anxious to obtain it. Others were evidently too poor to furnish themselves without much inconvenience. The Bible was received by many, to whom it was presented, with an eagerness, which induced us to believe, that it would prove "a lamp to their feet, and a light to their path." (S. J. Mills and Daniel Smith, *Report of a Missionary Journey Through that Part of the United States which Lies West of the Allegany Mountains,* Andover, 1815, 17, 21, 25.)

2. The Board of Missions

To meet the spiritual needs of the West, and to fulfill more effectively its role as a national Church, the General Assembly in 1816 created the Board of Missions with authority to extend the work of the Church. The history of this first Board of the Church has been written by Clifford M. Drury in Presbyterian Panorama, *1952.*

The committee appointed to consider whether the missionary business cannot be carried on with more efficacy, and to greater extent, reported, and their report being amended, was adopted, and is as follows, viz:

(a) The committee rejoice in prospect of a competent supply of the word of God to the poor and destitute in our country, by means of Bible societies. The numbers and resources of these institutions are every day increasing, so that, at no very remote period, it is hoped that the sun of revelation will shine on every dark corner of our land, and irradiate every dwelling however obscure. The committee, however, instead of regarding this as a reason for relaxing missionary efforts, are persuaded that its proper effect is to infuse new life and vigour into the missionary cause.

In proportion as the word of God is known and appreciated, will the preachers of the word, in its simplicity and purity, be effectual: in proportion as the Bible is diffused, will missionaries be successful in organizing Churches.

(b) That there is a wide extent of country destitute of the ordinary means of grace, is too well known to be mentioned in this place. The present demand for missionary labours very far exceeds the ability of supply, and the population of the country is increasing with such rapidity, that, were every place now vacant completely supplied with the regular ministrations of the gospel, after the lapse of a year there would probably be in the nation four hundred thousand souls requiring the labours of a competent number of religious instructors. When, then, there are such multitudes at this moment who rarely, if ever, hear the gospel preached, and such mighty additions are made every year to our numbers; when, too, great multitudes, sensible of their wants, are addressing their importunate cries to us for missionaries, the cry for help of souls ready to perish, it appears to your committee, that God and our brethren require of us much more than we have heretofore rendered. We are longing and praying for the coming of the day of glory, and perhaps many of us hope to see it. But we have no right to calculate on miraculous interpositions, and without a miracle, century after century must elapse before the earth can be filled with the knowledge of God. All that the Christian world is now doing with united effort, if continued without intermission for one thousand years, would barely serve to fill the world with Bibles and missionaries. Yet we are not to despair. God, in his adorable providence, seems to have changed, in these latter times, the scale on which he had for ages conducted the affairs of his government. Changes which formerly were the work of years, are now produced in a day. Magnificent and astonishing events have passed so often before the eyes of men of the present age, that their minds have acquired a tone and vigour which prompt them to undertake and accomplish great things. We ourselves witness every day the wonderful effects of combined counsels and exertions, both in the moral and political world. . . .

(d) For the purpose of enlarging the sphere of our missionary operations then, and infusing new vigour into the cause, your committee would respectfully recommend a change of the style, and enlargement of the powers of the Standing Committee of Missions. If, instead of continuing to this body the character of a committee bound in all cases to act according to the instructions of the General Assembly, and under the necessity of receiving its sanction to give validity to all the measures which it may propose, the Committee of Missions were erected into a Board, with full powers to transact all the business of the missionary cause, only requiring the Board to report annually to the General Assembly, it would then be able to carry on the missionary business with all the vigour and unity of design that would be found in a society originated for that purpose, and at the same time would enjoy all the benefit that the counsel and advice of the General Assembly could afford.

With these views of the subject, it is respectfully recommended,

1. That the style of the Committee be changed for that of "The Board of Missions, acting under the authority of the General Assembly of the Presbyterian Church in the United States." . . .

3. That in addition to the powers already granted to the Committee of Missions, the Board of Missions be authorized to appoint missionaries whenever they may deem it proper; to make such advances to missionaries as may be judged necessary, and to pay balances due to missionaries who have fulfilled their missions, whenever in their judgment the particular circumstances of the missionaries may require it.

4. That the Board be authorized and directed to take measures for establishing throughout our Churches auxiliary missionary societies; and that the General Assembly recommend to their people the establishment of such societies, to aid the funds, and extend the operations of the Boards. (*Minutes of the G.A.*, 1816, 632.)

3. The Board of Education and Four Hundred Vacant Congregations

Education societies for assisting "indigent and pious young men in acquiring an education" were a popular method of increasing the sup-

ply of ministers. The Presbyterian Education Society, organized in New York in 1818, was ready to help all qualified candidates regardless of their denomination. Others felt that only Presbyterians should receive aid. In an effort to "systematize and unite" these voluntary efforts, the General Assembly in 1819 established "a general Board of Education." The following is a part of the first publication of the Board.

Dearly Beloved Brethren,

It is on no ordinary subject, or ordinary occasion, that we find it our duty now to address you. The subject is, *the ministry of the gospel,* one of the most important institutions of our Lord and Saviour Jesus Christ; the occasion, the promulgation of *a plan devised by the Supreme Judicature of our Church* to provide, so far as their agency is concerned, for the preservation, extension and efficiency of this institution. On such a subject and occasion, it seems to us that we might *claim* your attention; "yet, for love's sake, we rather beseech you" to regard our statement and suggestions; to regard them with great seriousness and care, as what, in the discharge of a sacred trust, we are bound to lay before you. . . .

Know then, dearly beloved brethren, that we have at present, within the bounds of our church, more than four hundred vacant congregations, and that such congregations, in consequence of the rapid settlements on our frontiers, to say nothing of the vacancies made by the deaths of ministers, is fast increasing every year. There are, beside, large missionary regions, crying to us in the most moving language, to relieve them from a famine of the word of life. Now, for the supply of existing vacancies and missionary demands from our brethren on the frontiers, we want, at the present hour, beyond the number which we have, or know how to obtain, at least six hundred well qualified ministers of the gospel. Many more might be profitably employed within our bounds; but these are necessary to relieve pressing wants. . . .

Let every christian make it daily the subject of his earnest prayer, and all assemblies for social worship the subject of their united supplications, that God would graciously and effectually interpose to save his people from perishing for lack of spiritual knowledge: That he would pour out his Spirit and revive religion in our churches, so that, among other blessings attending such revivals, a host of precious youth may become the subjects of the renewing grace of God, and thus be prepared to offer themselves to the Lord for his service in the ministry of the gospel. Pray that they may be disposed to make this offering, and that their parents and guardians may not hinder, but encourage them to do it. Pray, brethren, that we may all feel as we ought to feel, and that we may act as we are called to act in this time of the church's necessity. . . . Let the execution of this plan be viewed, as it may justly claim to be viewed, as *a matter of fundamental importance* to the cause of Christ:—Not as on a footing with a hundred other good and benevolent plans, which are claiming, and rightfully demanding a portion of attention; but as demanding a preference to them all; as, in a word, of more immediate and pressing importance, than any one effort beside, for the propagation of the gospel.

Viewing it thus, let every Presbytery form a Board of Education, auxiliary to this Board; let other auxiliary societies in prosecution of the same great object be formed, wherever it may be practicable; and let every individual Christian resolve to do all in his power to give effect to this plan.

Let the poor contribute their mites, and the rich a proper part of their abundance. Let our pious and benevolent women, both young and old, who have acted so nobly in other instances, give us their important aid;—and let even children and babes contribute to it. Let us thus make one great and united effort, with humble faith and hope in God that his blessing may attend us:—and notwithstanding every discouragement and all opposition, we shall be successful. . . .

God will indeed preserve his own church, and accomplish his own glorious purposes in relation to his chosen people; but let it never be forgotten, that the dispensation of his grace is conducted on principles that require the use of established means, and invite and claim our co-operation in the great work of saving immortal souls and of extending the limits of the Saviour's kingdom; . . . anticipating that day, when the Judge of quick and dead, who will notice visits paid to his sick and food given to his hungry saints, shall distinguish with peculiar approbation that christian benevolence, which is employed in furnishing supplies to immortal beings who are perishing with want of the bread and water of life.

ROBERT RALSTON, PRESIDENT.

July, 1819.

(*The Address of the Board of Education . . . to the Presbyteries, Ministers, Churches, People, Under the Care of the Assembly*, Philadelphia, 1819, 13 ff.)

4. A Female Cent Society

Cent societies mark the beginnings of women's work in the Church. Many of the great benevolent enterprises of the day were supported in this humble way.

A society of this denomination (Presbyterian) has lately been organized in this town. A constitution has been adopted and subscribed by above twenty females, and there is reason to hope that the number will be considerably augmented. Agreeably to the constitution, the Society is to consist of females only . . . and they are to be such as sustain a religious or moral character. Those who become members are required to pay one dollar, in advance, and one cent a day through the year, to be discharged quarterly. The funds are to be distributed in the following manner: one fourth is to be sent to the professors of the Theological Seminary at Princeton, and one fourth to the Theological Seminary at New York (Auburn), to be applied to the use of such students in this state as have been received, as candidates for the ministry, by some Presbytery, and are preparing to attend either of the aforesaid seminaries, and for which they may require assistance. The remaining fourth is to be distributed in alms for the relief of the indigent and in procuring books for poor children who may attend Sunday-schools in this place. (*The Weekly Recorder*, Chillicothe, Ohio, April 17, 1816, reprinted in *Journal P.H.S.*, XXX, 219.)

5. The United Domestic Missionary Society

Dissatisfaction with the circuit-riding policy of the Board of Missions led to the formation of a new interdenominational society in 1822 for the purpose of aiding pastors and churches that were already established. From this society evolved the great American Home Missionary Society in 1826. New York Presbyterians were especially active in the U.D.M.S.

It will be difficult to impress upon the minds of those who are not already in some measure acquainted with the fact, an idea of the fearful obstacle which has been thrown in the way of the progress of the gospel, by the countenance which the system of itinerancy has obtained from the devout and zealous in our land. The ignorance, and in a few instances even the immorality of some who have dared to assume the guise of ministers of Christ, and thus fit themselves for the deepest perdition which the next world contains—have created prejudices against ministers and their message, which nothing can eradicate but the permanent system we would introduce. We are happy to report, this year, that this effort has followed in many cases. The missionary must locate himself, he must be known, he must be tried, he must win his way to general confidence—he does not deserve it if he cannot gain it; but once thus established, his light enlarges; he is no longer a lamp in a dark place; he becomes a star, and a little sun, in the region where the forest-trees are falling on every side, and the daylight of knowledge is exchanged for the darkness of atheism.

Nothing, also, but the system of our Society can cure the wide-spread evils of Sectarianism, with which it is vain to deny our land is infested. When preachers of various denominations perambulate the country, they each hinder the progress of the gospel, and gain not at all upon the number of the adherents of Christ's enemies. Your Committee make no pretensions to that excessive liberality which looks upon all sects as equally right—they are also far from that narrow-minded bigotry which asserts that all but our own are in all things wrong—with that rational preference for their own peculiar views of the Gospel, which is the right of those who can give a reason of the faith that is in them— they know that in essential views they accord with some other denominations of Christians, and they are glad when any of these locate themselves in a village, and fasten down their battering engines, and attack the strong works of sin. But they do deprecate that migratory species of warfare which scours the whole country, and gets a half dozen followers in each town, and leaves its force divided between some three or four sects, who apprehend alike the essential points of saving doctrine.

The evil grows out of our invaluable privilege of freedom in religion. But as all that is good, is by man readily perverted to the least wholesome ends, it is the aim of our Society, and the object we are happy to report, which we have attained in many instances in the last year, to beat down small as the dust those mountains of separation which man's sin and Satan's craft have created—the fire and the hammer, which are the word of God, have done it—sects have united to forward the coming of the Kingdom of heaven, and in the view of having a permanent minister of the sanctuary, they have come together to draw wood to build a house to the Lord, and to say of the topmost rafter when it was raised—"grace, grace unto it." (*Second Annual Report of the United Domestic Missionary Society,* New York, 1824, 21 ff.)

6. Indiana, 1825

The following is an example of the pleas for aid that were received by the United Domestic Missionary Society and were passed on by them to the public.

Since the first of last April I have constituted two new churches, and another brother of our Presbytery has constituted the same number. I have in the same time administered the sacrament in nine churches. Besides supplying my own congregation two sabbaths in the month, and my labours on my farm, (for I must do something at this or remove from these poor people,) I have in my missionary tours, travelled 1460 miles. I have examined near 30 persons for membership, eleven of whom were in my own congregation, and received about the same number by letter. The Rev. Mr. Bush, of your Presbytery, has received a call to settle at Indianapolis. If he should accept it, he and myself will be located in what is called the New Purchase, that immense tract of beautiful and fertile land bought of the Indians in the autumn of 1818, and which Congress have been surveying and selling since that time. Fifteen counties are now settled; and there are ten counties of the old purchase of the state nearer to me than is the nearest Presbyterian minister. Here then are twenty-five settled counties of a new country, and some of these counties are twenty-four miles square, some a little less, and probably some larger, and but two ministers. Now, sir, we have sixteen formed churches in these twenty-five counties, and a prospect of forming more the coming year. And every one of these churches would give to the extent of their ability, and some beyond their ability, to get a minister. But they don't know where to apply. Why? Because all they could raise would come short, and with numbers far short of 400 dollars a year; upon which sum paid, a minister can get along pretty well in this state. And they do not know any kind society who will help them, and encourage them to help themselves. (*Third Annual Report of the United Domestic Missionary Society, 1825, 52.*)

7. An Indian Mission in Michigan

The condition of the Indians and their shameful treatment by the white man may be traced in the voluminous correspondence of the missionaries sent among them by the various "foreign" boards and societies. (See also Harold S. Faust, The American Indian in Tragedy and Triumph, *P.H.S., 1945.) In the selection below, Mrs. Amanda Ferry writes to her family about the Indians of northern Michigan.*

Jan. 1st, [1824]

This is the commencement of a new year in Mackinac. I have *been* loaded with good wishes, such as they are. I had long been anticipating the day with delight, as a day of leisure, in which I might have opportunity to talk with my past hours—for the children had permission to spend the day with their parents and friends. All but two had places for such visits. The evening previous Mr. F. had remarked, that I must have New Year cakes in readiness, as I might have visitors in the morning. When morning came, in rushed the children to wish us a Happy New Year. Soon the whole family came for a morning salute. And now I supposed I might breathe fresh air, and have the remaining day to myself, as the children all arrayed in their new suits went forth for their visit. But we did not long enjoy our dignified silence. I assure you—Julia and I had been left entirely alone. Children of every description came flocking in, that I might not only share their good wishes (and kisses) but they wished very much to know what kind of cakes Madam Ferry could make. Next came Squaws without number, some sober, some not. Among them a blind woman, who insisted in moving her hand all over my face, when six kisses did I receive from her black lips before she released me. Next an Indian and his squaw, both so drunk they could not stand upright. But I kept at a distance from these filthy creatures, politely supplying them with cakes. Not hesitating to refuse them whiskey. They not getting whiskey, soon bade me good morning. While, later, preparing dinner, to our astonishment six of our children returned, and before supper they were all here but two!

March 9th, 1824

. . . For the almost perfect health of our family, I think it worthy of notice, scarcely one of our number has lost a meal from sickness. I find I am daily becoming more attached to them. They come to me with all their troubles, as much as any children to a mother, even when their own parents are in the building. . . . Recently I rode to Bois Blanc with Mr. Ferry, we took with us our little Thomas Shepard to visit his mother. He was unwilling to go until Mr. Ferry assured him that he should not be left. Owing to depth of snow in the woods, and finding only a footpath, I stopped at the first wigwam, for there is not an English or American family on the Island. The man was a Spaniard by birth, the woman a squaw apparently between 60 and 70 years old. It was a scene of wretchedness. She was standing at the door, her hair long and apparently never combed, was hanging in matted strings: her face and hands were incrusted in dirt. Her dress was a gown made very much in shape of a Quaker coat united before with a large pewter button, her skirt of very much defaced and worn broadcloth, made straight, extended from her waist to her knees, leggings of the same, and moccasins. For a moment I recoiled from entering, but there was no other way, so I bent and passed through a hole at top of the hut. There was a chain extending from a pole near the top, to receive a large tin pail, probably the only cooking kettle they possessed: there was no furniture, neither chair, stool, table, bed or anything to fix their fire, but a birch pole. A tin dipper with a wooden ladle and an Indian knife the only articles to be seen, either for eating or drinking. In the shape of eatables, a small bag of corn, and about a pound and a half of salt pork stood on one corner by a mat, for purposes of seasoning. By this time you may like to know where I sat while waiting for Mr. F.'s return. At one side of the hut there were some poles, over which some hemlock boughs were thrown. This formed a bed, or a seat for the old people,— or for any one who came in. The side opposite to this seemed to belong to a grandchild of the old squaw, and the three boys, for while I remained I observed them always standing in that place, when coming in, and the hollow of the ground, indicated, by size and shape, that it was their usual resting-place. When Mr. Ferry returned, he obtained consent to take the girl home with us. Immediately after our arrival she was given a thorough scrubbing in strong soap suds, was then dressed in suitable clothing, which so changed her appearance that after a few days acquaintance we presumed to give her the name of Sarah Barrett. . . .

June 10, 1824

This (day) we have attended to distributing premiums in the Sabbath School. A very interesting time. Many came to witness it. After the premiums, awards were given for punctual attendance, and for good behaviour. Nearly all received something, for, on looking around most of those who must be conscious of deserving to be passed by, were absent. One in my class who commenced in January last, received a premium with the remark from Mr. Ferry that she had been the best scholar he ever knew. She is not yet four years old, and since that time has repeated to me 59 verses from the book of Hymns for Infant Minds, and can only read in words of three syllables. She will now take her book, turn to each Hymn, and repeat every word with as much propriety and deliberation as a person of 20 years, and with the same readiness as though it was but yesterday she had committed them. When she takes any other book she cannot tell whether it is or not, right side up. She is the youngest daughter of Mrs. Stuart, named Katherine. She makes me very many visits. Two half Indians received the premiums of their class, one a New Testament, the other, younger, a valuable book. Yesterday, we had a visit from a young man who is on his way to St. Josephs to join Rev. Mr. McClay who is engaged in a mission there, employed by the Baptist Board. The interview with this devoted Christian was truly refreshing.

Aug. 23, 1824

When you want to see me just look into the kitchen from four or five in the morning till eight or nine at night, wait a few minutes and you will hear my step from the dining room, or cellar, or storeroom. I have a man cook to assist me, two boys when out of school to dress fish and vegetables, two girls to clear the tables, wash them, wash the dishes from them and keep the dining room clean. I take charge of six persons, make and mend their clothes, etc. Mr. Ferry, Mr. Gibson, myself, little Montague, and Samuel Anderson, son of Capt. Anderson, —Drummonds Island, who is four years old. He sleeps in my room and I dress and undress him. The first time I put him to bed, he immediately commenced his prayers, after repeating correctly the Lord's prayer and "Now I lay me" etc. He added "I pray God to make me a good boy. Amen." When I asked him who taught him to say his prayer he said "My mother." . . . But I have strangely digressed from my main subject. Everything pertaining to the cooking comes under my charge. Miss —— has charge of the girls of the school, in session, and when out, the charge of their clothing. Miss McFarland has immediate charge of ten more, and the mending of twenty-four, who are under the particular charge of Mr. Hudson and —— Bush. Two boys in their turns, make beds, clean their chambers, and schoolroom. Miss Osman has charge of the girls when out of school, and Miss Campbell, with the assistance of two girls and a boy each week, does the washing for the family. But, in our division, you see we have made no allowance for any to be called from labor to a sick-bed, and it seems impossible indeed that one could be spared. Yet we know not how soon this may develop, nor what God has in store for us. Thus far He has crowned our lives with loving kindness and tender mercy. At present every member of the family enjoys perfect health. A view of this at times, when seated at our meals affects me deeply. . . . Recently we received a box from Utica N. Y. valued at One Hundred and seventy odd dollars. If Ashfield people send another, ask them to remember all kinds of vegetable oils, herbs etc. such as catnip blossoms, tansy, motherwort, and thoroughwort, blossoms of sweet elder, garden seeds of all kinds, and the like. Father, I made a good dress of your present to me, and find it very comfortable at this season. It is the first one I have had since I left home,—except the one sister Shepard sent me. So you see I have not learned to be extravagant by being with extravagant people. But I should have had them if they were necessary. A very handsome one (dress pattern) came for me in the Utica box, and another in the Mission House box. I believe I was asleep about some things when I sent home last. Several of my charts, maps, etc. I had designed as keepsakes to my brothers. Several of my books, such as Rhetoric, Natural Philosophy, American History and many others are of no use to me here. . . .

Nov. 3, 1825

. . . Since writing Sister H. I have superintended making five and a half barrels of excellent soap, and, with the help of inexperienced girls, as the chief seamstress,—Without boasting, I will say they are all clad, or can be, on coming Sabbath, in their new clothes. Our little girls are much engaged in knitting. The yarn, supplied by charity, gave them forty pairs of socks to knit for the boys. If nothing extra prevents they will have knitted every yard of yarn before Spring. . . . Your dear brother unites with me in love to our dear Parents, and to you all. Mrs. Hudson is expecting to join us next Spring, after her winter in Cambridge and New York: and in that vicinity. A. W. F.

(*Letters of William Montague and Amanda White Ferry*, ed. by C. A. Anderson, *Journal P.H.S.*, XXV, 203 ff.)

8. Nineteenth Century Puritanism

The unbending morality of nineteenth century Presbyterians is reflected in the Pastoral Letter issued by the General Assembly in 1818. Not only is total abstinence recommended, but lotteries, once commonly used to raise benevolent funds, are condemned along with theaters and dancing. Throughout the century a ceaseless war was carried on to preserve the Sabbath. It was only in the twentieth century that the Presbyterian ethic relaxed.

A. Pastoral Letter

The first thing we shall notice is the crime of *Drunkenness*. This crime has at all times been a curse to our country, and has often made lamentable inroads upon our Church. We are convinced that it may be opposed more successfully by prevention than in any other way. When the character of drunkenness is fully formed, the unhappy victim is lost to those motives which ordinarily influence all other classes of men. In this state of things nothing but a miracle of divine grace can effect his reformation. The certain and acknowledged prospect of the wreck of his family, his fortune, and his character; and even of the ruin of his immortal soul, is not sufficient to arrest his course: and yet perhaps the same man may formerly have been in such a state of equilibrium or indecision upon this subject, that the smallest motives might have prevented the formation of a habit, which in its maturity has become so irresistible.—This consideration is certainly sufficient to justify an effort for saving our fellow men from the domination of so destructive a vice. For this purpose we earnestly recommend to the officers and members of our Church to abstain even from the common use of ardent spirits. . . .

But it is further our duty to testify, that all encouragement of lotteries, and purchasing of lottery tickets; all attendance on horse-racing, and betting on such, or on any other occasions; and all attempts of whatever kind to acquire gain without giving an equivalent, involve the Gambling principle, and participate in the guilt which attaches to that vice.

On the fashionable, though, as we believe, dangerous amusements, of *Theatrical Exhibitions* and *Dancing*, we deem it necessary to make a few observations. The Theatre we have always considered as a school of immorality. If any person wishes for honest conviction on this subject, let him attend to the character of that mass of matter, which is generally exhibited on the stage. We believe all will agree, that comedies at least, with a few exceptions, are of such a description, that a virtuous and modest person cannot attend the representation of them, without the most painful and embarrassing sensations. If indeed custom has familiarized the scene, and these painful sensations are no longer felt, it only proves that the person in question, has lost some of the best sensibilities of our nature; that the strongest safeguard of virtue has been taken down, and that the moral character has undergone a serious depreciation.

With respect to *Dancing*, we think it necessary to observe, that however plausible it may appear to some, it is perhaps not the less dangerous on account of that plausibility. It is not from those things which the world acknowledges to be most wrong, that the greatest danger is to be apprehended to religion, especially as it relates to the young. When the practice is carried to its highest extremes, all admit the consequences to be fatal; and why not then apprehend danger, even from its incipient stages. It is certainly, in all its stages, a fascinating and an infatuating practice. Let it once be introduced, and it is difficult to give it limits. It steals away our precious time, dissipates religious impressions, and hardens the heart. To guard you, beloved brethren, against its wiles and its fascinations, we earnestly recommend that you will consult that sobriety which the sacred pages require. We also trust, that you will attend with the meekness and docility becoming the christian character, to the admonitions on this subject of those whom you have chosen to watch for your souls. (*Minutes of the G.A.,* 1818, 54-56.)

B. THE SABBATH

Relative to receiving a person as a member of the Church, who is a proprietor in a line of stages, which carries the mail, and runs on Sabbath. . . .

Resolved, That it is the decided opinion of this Assembly that all attention to worldly concerns on the Lord's day, further than the works of necessity and mercy demand, is inconsistent both with the letter and spirit of the fourth commandment; and consequently all engagements in regard to secular occupations on the Lord's day, with a view to secure worldly advantages, are to be considered inconsistent with Christian character; and that those who are concerned in such engagements, ought not to be admitted into the communion of the Church while they continue in the same. (*Minutes of the G.A.,* 1819, 713.)

9. Sabbath Schools and Bible Classes

Although Sunday schools began to develop in the latter part of the eighteenth century, they were not officially recognized by the General Assembly until 1824. The following resolutions give an interesting outline of the contents of Christian education in 1816.

The committee to which was referred the overture from the Synod of New York and New Jersey, on forming classes of young people, for studying and reciting the Bible, reported; and their report, being read and amended, was adopted, viz:

Resolved, 1. That it be recommended, and it is hereby recommended earnestly, to the Ministers and Sessions which are in connection with the General Assembly, to pay especial attention to this subject, and provide, without delay, for the stated instruction of the children and youth in the sacred Scriptures within their respective congregations.

2. That although the particular manner of instruction and recitation in the congregations ought to be left to the discretion of their Ministers and Sessions respectively; yet as some degree of uniformity is desirable in a business of so much magnitude, it is recommended as the most effectual means of promoting the knowledge of the Holy Scriptures, that in all our churches, classes be formed of the youth, to recite the Scriptures in regular order; that the recitations, if convenient, be as often as once a week, and from two to five chapters appointed for each recitation. . . .

Resolved, 3. That the Presbyteries under the care of the Assembly be directed to take order on this subject; and they are hereby informed that this is not to come into the place of learning the Catechism of our Church, but to be added to it as an important branch of religious education. (*Minutes of the G.A.*, 1816, 627.)

10. A Deathbed Recovery

Rev. Gardiner Spring of New York was one of the most prominent Presbyterians of the nineteenth century. His reminiscences give a vivid picture of contemporary piety.

February 24th, 1819.—Still in this world of hope. In defiance of all sins of the past year, and a guilty life, I am permitted to see another birthday. I have been often surprised that I am suffered to live. Blessed be God, I am not afraid to die, and often more afraid to live. I am an abject sinner, and it will indeed be wonderful grace if I ever sit down with Christ at the Supper of the Lamb. That grace is my strong refuge; Calvary is my hiding-place. There is the munition of rocks. I hope in the grace and guardianship and faithfulness of that omnipotent Redeemer, to be kept from falling and presented faultless before the presence of his glory with exceeding joy. This text has often comforted me, when I have been afraid of trusting in the divine mercy: "The Lord taketh *pleasure* in them that fear him, in those that *hope in his mercy.*" It affords me unutterable pleasure to feel that I am not denied the privilege of laying my own soul beneath the droppings of the same blood I have for nine years recommended to my dying and guilty fellow-men.

Among the mercies I am bound to record, are the recovery of my dear wife from a very dangerous illness last June. . . .

My dear Susan's illness was most severe. After a most trying pregnancy, she was permitted to become the mother of a lovely daughter on the 29th of May, 1818. About ten days after her confinement, she began to decline. Incessant faintings left us with very little hope that she would survive more than a few days. I insert a sketch of some conversation with her here lest it should be lost. I remained at her bedside during the greater part of the time, and was much comforted by the happy state of her mind. On a Thursday morning, as I sat by her, I laid my head by hers and wept. She perceived it; and to anticipate any painful remarks my excitement might cause, I said, "Oh, my dear, I have confidence in God. *You have,* I trust." "I hope so," said she, "*I have all along considered it very doubtful whether I should re-*

cover from this sickness. Death appeared very near to me before my confinement; but I could not say I was willing to go and leave you all."

"But," said I, "if we are Christ's, we shall soon meet again." She replied, *"Yes, if I am Christ's; but that I cannot say."* She wept. I took her in my arms and held her up in the bed, observing, "This makes us feel like very little creatures." "Yes," said she, *"I feel fit for nothing but to be here in the hands of God."* I replied, "It is a precious privilege to be in the hands of God." She answered, with emphasis, *"IT IS."*

Soon after this, she said to me, *"Take care of these dear children; I cannot bear to leave them in the care of nobody better than a mother-in-law. I fear they will be neglected."* Here we wept.

The next day her danger was evidently increased. It became necessary to cover her body almost entirely with the most exciting stimulants, and the physicians began to despair of giving her any relief. I had previously told her I would watch every symptom, and give her the first intimations of her danger. On Friday evening I went to her bedside and sat down. She saw my solicitude, and I disclosed it by saying that we all feared she would never recover. She made no reply, but remained calm and unmoved. I could not but observe that her mind was very clear, and astonishingly calm. I said, "You hope you have been born again?" "Yes," said she, *"but I have always more doubts than hopes. But in my doubts I have seen nothing but grace to flee to. Christ has been my refuge, and is now, and I hope will be."* I said, "You have seen the sinfulness of your heart?" She answered, *"I have, and it is AWFULLY sinful. This has sometimes discouraged me, but there is enough in Christ to cleanse."*

I left her, and returned to her chamber after tea. The danger was hourly increasing, and I had resolved to bring it near. I told her plainly we thought she would die. She was aware of it, and said, *"My wish is that God would glorify himself by me."* I remarked, "It is a precious truth that God will glorify himself by such insignificant and vile creatures as we are." "Yes," said she, *"THAT has been my sweetest thought, that God would glorify himself in me and by me."* Here she seemed to hesitate, and added, *"unless it be some sweet views of the way of salvation by Christ."*

On Saturday morning no tokens for the better. I took the little babe, and said it was not improbable that this dear babe would live to see the Millennium. "This," said I, "is worth suffering for"; she added, *"yes, and dying for."*

She smiled when I gave her a view of Emerson's calculation as to the proximity of that glorious period, and spoke of the babe as born for such a season.

On Sabbath morning, no more hope and no less calmness. I enjoyed a very precious season of communion with her at the throne of grace, such as I hope never to forget. I thought it an anticipation of our everlasting fellowship in a brighter world. I read the 73d and 86th Psalms, in which she appeared to take much consolation. Before we prayed, I asked, "What shall we pray for?" *"Pray,"* said she, *"that I may be MEET for heaven; that I may be made HOLY. Everything else appears of little importance compared with this,—and for my dear children; they will need everything."*

Sabbath was a trying day; and towards evening, I saw that the physicians began to *hope*. She *lived*. After a tedious and long-continued debility, *she lives still*, the comfort of my heart, and more endeared through the severity of her trial, and the greatness of God's mercy. "His mercy endureth forever." (*Personal Reminiscences of the Life and Times of Gardiner Spring*, 1866, II, 68 ff.)

11. Manual Labor Schools

Educators in the late 1820's were enthusiastic about the new theory of combining studies with shop or farm work. Some of the hard-pressed Western colleges found that they could produce much of their fuel and provisions by means of student labor.

This is the peculiar principle of Manual Labour Colleges. We propose to direct the exertions of bodily power, which must be made in order to health, to *profitable use*. Instead of putting a youth to the ignoble service of beating the air, we put a hammer into his hand and teach him "to hit the nail on the head," instead of allowing him to shake the dice box, we instruct him in the art of shaking the saw. Instead of idly strolling over the fields, we teach him to turn up their soil with the plough, the spade, the hoe, and extract from the bosom of mother earth nourishment for his own. This is our simple principle. It is as old as nature, for it is her own plan. . . .

Upon the health of the student this system is calculated to operate a happy effect. Indeed to remedy an evil connected with and necessarily growing out of the old, lazy, monastic college system, has this been brought into operation. The feebleness of literary men is proverbial; and I may say, especially of the clerical corps. And the loss— the pecuniary loss, to the community, in educating men for—the active duties of life!—no, but for the grave, is immense. What multitudes, in all the learned professions, bring from the college classes into professional studies, the seeds of death? . . .

Now we are somewhat anxious, that the public should view this bearing of our working system of education, as its most important bearing. We have suffered in a misapprehension of this matter. An impression has gone forth, that the penny earned is the only penny in question: whilst the weight of the penny saved is never felt in the pocket. A student earns five or ten or fifteen dollars per quarter by his labor. This appears on his bill, and all men can read it. He saves five or ten thousand dollars worth of health; this does not appear on the bill, and men will not see it, though it be plainly visible on his countenance. He carries the receipt of it home; it beams from the rose on his cheek, it sparkles in the fire of his eye.—The fond parent reads it, it stirs emotions strong as nature in his kindling bosom, before he has time to examine the bill about money. But then, unfortunately, for manual labor schools, and for the public weal, there is no arithmetic by which the amount can appear on the leger, or the details be spread on the pages of the journal. All the algebra in his son's head, cannot compute the value of retained health. His arithmetic has not taught him to subtract from the value of a sound stomach the worth of a dispeptic's rennet bag, and to pass the balance to the credit of the manual labor school upon his father's leger. . . .

If, however, any man wishes perfect satisfaction on this point, let him visit Mount Lafayette, and there at the signal for work, he may read a hundred certificates of the health-preserving power of manual labor. (*Fellenberg or An Appeal to the Friends of Education on Behalf of Lafayette College*, 1835, probably by George Junkin, 9 ff.)

12. "A Plea for the West"

In his famous lecture, which captivated audiences throughout the East, Dr. Lyman Beecher of Lane Seminary, Cincinnati, dramatically coupled the financial needs of Western colleges with the patriot's pride in the vastness of the West and the nativist's dread of its domination by foreigners and Roman Catholics. The effect of such speeches on American nationalism is immeasurable.

The West is a young empire of mind, and power, and wealth, and free institutions, rushing up to a giant manhood, with a rapidity and a power never before witnessed below the sun. And if she carries with her the elements of her preservation, the experiment will be glorious—

the joy of the nation—the joy of the whole earth, as she rises in the majesty of her intelligence and benevolence, and enterprise, for the emancipation of the world.

It is equally clear, that the conflict which is to decide the destiny of the West, will be a conflict of institutions for the education of her sons, for purposes of superstition, or evangelical light; of despotism, or liberty. . . .

But how shall the requisite supply of teachers for the sons and daughters of the West be raised up? It can be accomplished by the instrumentality of a learned and pious ministry, educated at the West. . . . A land supplied with able and faithful ministers, will of course be filled with schools, academies, libraries, colleges, and all the apparatus for the perpetuity of republican institutions. It always has been so—it always will be. . . .

And yet what is done must be done quickly; for population will not wait, and commerce will not cast anchor, and manufactures will not shut off the steam nor shut down the gate, and agriculture, pushed by millions of freemen on their fertile soil, will not withhold her corrupting abundance.

We must educate! We must educate! or we must perish by our own prosperity. If we do not, short from the cradle to the grave will be our race. If in our haste to be rich and mighty, we outrun our literary and religious institutions, they will never overtake us; or only come up after the battle of liberty is fought and lost, as spoils to grace the victory, and as resources of inexorable despotism for the perpetuity of our bondage. . . .

When I first entered the West, its vastness overpowered me with the impression of its uncontrollable greatness, in which all human effort must be lost. But when I perceived the active intercourse between the great cities, like the rapid circulation of a giant's blood; and heard merchants speak of just stepping up to Pittsburgh—only six hundred miles—and back in a few days; and others just from New-Orleans, or St. Louis, or the Far West; and others going thither; and when I heard my ministerial brethren negotiating exchanges in the near neighborhood—only one hundred miles up or down the river—and going and returning on Saturday and Monday, and without trespassing on the Sabbath;—then did I perceive how God, who seeth the end from the beginning, had prepared the West to be mighty, and still wieldable, that the moral energy of his word and spirit might take it up as a very little thing.

This vast territory is occupied now by ten states and will soon be by twelve. Forty years since it contained only about one hundred and fifty thousand souls; while it now contains little short of five millions. At the close of this century, if no calamity intervenes, it will contain, probably, one hundred millions—a day which some of our children may live to see; and when fully peopled, may accommodate three hundred millions. It is half as large as all Europe, four times as large as the Atlantic states, and twenty times as large as New-England. Was there ever such a spectacle—such a field in which to plant the seeds of an immortal harvest!—so vast a ship, so richly laden with the world's treasures and riches, whose helm is offered to the guiding influence of early forming institutions. . . .

There is no danger that our agriculture and arts will not prosper: the danger is, that our intelligence and virtue will falter and fall back into a dark minded, vicious populace—a poor, uneducated reckless mass of infuriated animalism, to rush on resistless as the tornado, or to burn as if set on fire of hell. . . .

The great experiment is now making, and from its extent and rapid filling up is making in the West, whether the perpetuity of our republican institutions can be reconciled with universal suffrage. Without the education of the head and heart of the nation, they cannot be; and the question to be decided is, can the nation, or the vast balance power of it be so imbued with intelligence and virtue, as to bring out, in laws and their administration, a perpetual self-preserving energy? We know that the work is a vast one, and of great difficulty; and yet we believe it can be done. . . .

But the vast amount of uneducated population in our land already calls upon us loudly to set about the work of rearing every where the institutions requisite for universal education. . . .

Half a million of unprincipled, reckless voters, in the hands of demagogues, may, in our balanced elections, overrule all the property, and wisdom, and moral principle of the nation.

This danger from uneducated mind is augmenting daily by the rapid influx of foreign emigrants, the greater part unacquainted with our institutions, unaccustomed to self-government, inaccessible to education, and easily accessible to prepossession, and inveterate credulity, and intrigue, and easily embodied and wielded by sinister design. In the beginning this eruption of revolutionary Europe was not anticipated, and we opened our doors wide to the influx and naturalization of foreigners. But it is becoming a terrific inundation; it has increased upon our native population from five to thirty-seven per cent., and is every year advancing. It seeks, of course, to settle down upon the unoccupied territory of the West, and may at no distant day equal, and even out-number the native population. What is to be done to educate the millions which in twenty years Europe will pour out upon us? (Lyman Beecher, *A Plea for the West*, 2d ed., Cincinnati, 1835, 12 ff.)

13. Lane Seminary Students Revolt

In 1834 ninety-two students withdrew from Lane Theological Seminary, Cincinnati, because the trustees had forbidden them to discuss the slavery issue. Their defense of their right to freedom of discussion and of assembly (probably written by Theodore D. Weld) is an outstanding example of student writing. Most of the rebels continued their studies at the newly founded Oberlin Institute.

STATEMENT

The undersigned, recently members of Lane Seminary, having withdrawn from that Institution, desire to lay before the Christian public, the considerations which have influenced them; together with the circumstances which have mainly contributed to such a result.

Of those who have now severed their relationship with Lane Seminary, some attended its earliest recitations, and these, with a large number of the remainder, entered its first theological class in the fall of 1833.

The circumstances of our matriculation were peculiarly impressive. We were connected with an institution freighted with the spiritual interests of the West. We were numerous, without a precedent, in the beginnings of similar institutions. The Valley was our expected field; and we assembled here, that we might the more accurately learn its character, catch the spirit of its gigantic enterprise, grow up into its genius, appreciate its peculiar wants, and be thus qualified by practical skill, no less than by theological erudition, to wield the weapons of truth. . . .

We aimed, therefore, to make such a disposal of our influence, as would contribute to place Lane Seminary upon high moral ground, and thus greatly elevate the standard and augment the resources of ministerial efficiency.

As a primary step, we were led to adopt this principle, *that free discussion, with correspondent effort, is a DUTY, and of course a RIGHT.*

We proceeded upon this principle, without molestation, in our studies, at our recitations and lectures.

We applied it to missions, at home and abroad; and we *acted* immediately, through liberal contributions. We took up temperance. Discussion was needless, duty was plain, and we *acted*. With the Sunday school cause, we proceeded in like manner. Next moral reform came up. We examined it, in a series of adjourned meetings, light was elicited, principles were fixed, and *action* followed.

With the same spirit of free inquiry, we discussed the question of slavery. We prayed much, heard facts, weighed arguments, kept our temper, and after the most patient pondering, in which we were sustained by the excitement of sympathy, not of anger, we decided that slavery was a sin, and as such, ought to be immediately renounced. In this case, too, we *acted*. We organized an anti-slavery society, and published facts, arguments, remonstrances and appeals.

We threw ourselves into the neglected mass of colored population in the city of Cincinnati, and that we might heave it up to the light of the sun, established Sabbath, day and evening schools, lyceums, a circulating library, &c.; choosing rather to employ our *leisure hours* in offices of brotherhood to "the lame, the halt, and the blind," than to devote them to fashionable calls and ceremonial salutations. . . .

The ground of our secession from the Seminary, is, that free discussion and correspondent action have been prohibited *by law*. We are commanded to discontinue our anti-slavery society. We are prohibited from holding meetings among ourselves, and from making statements and communications at table or elsewhere, without permission. A committee of the board of trustees is set over us to exercise censorship, and vested with discretionary power to dismiss any student whenever they may deem it necessary so to do, without consultation with the faculty and without assigning reasons either to them, to the individual dismissed, or to the community.

These prohibitory enactments have driven us from our beloved institution. Sustaining relations to the church of Christ now rendered somewhat peculiar, duty to his cause demands from us an explicit statement of the grounds of our secession.

We believe free discussion to be the duty of every rational being. It is the acting out of the command *"Prove all things.".* . . . This duty of discussion and action is not confered by human authority, and we have no *license* to resign it upon entering into any association, literary or political. Free discussion being a duty is consequently a right, and as such, is inherent and inalienable. It is *our* right. It *was* before we entered Lane Seminary: privileges we might and did relinquish; advantages we might and did receive. But this *right* the institution "could neither give nor take away." Theological Institutions must of course recognize this immutable principle. Proscription of free discussion is sacrilege! It is boring out the eyes of the soul. It is the robbery of mind. It is the burial of truth. If Institutions cannot stand upon this broad footing, let them fall. Better, infinitely better, that the mob demolish every building or the incendiary wrap them in flames; and the young men be sent home to ask their fathers "what is truth?"— to question nature's million voices—her forests and her hoary mountains "what is truth?" than that our theological seminaries should become Bastilles, our theological students, thinkers by *permission,* and the right of free discussion tamed down into a soulless thing of gracious, condescending sufferance. But who can doubt the practicability of governing, especially *theological* students consistently with these principles. Authority is not nullified. Faculties have their legitimate powers still. It is theirs to inform their pupils that free discussion is a paramount duty, and a right, which the faculty have neither power nor inclination to take away.

It is theirs to *direct* the inquiries of their students; but they must have a care to direct them wholly by *principle.* If they find the students disposed to shrink from the practical results of their discussions, or to flee in panic when called ultraists, or to reverse their decision at the bidding of a mob, it is theirs, as faithful leaders, to inspire them with fresh courage and impel them forward. If a student should not submit to be directed *by* principle, it is conclusive evidence that he is not fit to search *after* principle; and in such case the faculty have unquestioned power to discipline or dismiss. . . .

Is this a time to lay our hands upon our mouths, when the ambassadors of Christ hold as merchandize, and sell for filthy lucre, the members of his own body; and, with the price of blood in their hands, still break the sacramental bread? When the shepherds of God's flock, instead of carrying his lambs in their arms, tear them from the fold, and hurl them to be rent by wolves—and yet are caressed by the church, accounted faithful shepherds and worthy of all honor? No!—with heart, and soul, and mind, and strength, we answer, No! We cannot betray inviolable trusts; we will not shout hosanna in the train of arbitrary power, nor plot treason against humanity, nor apostatize from God. No! God forbid that we should abandon a cause that strikes its roots so deep into the soil of human interests, and human rights, and throws its branches upward and abroad, so high and wide into the sunlight of human hopes, and human well-being. (*A Statement of the Reasons which Induced the Students of Lane Seminary to Dissolve their Connection with that Institution,* Cincinnati, 1834, 1-6, 16-17.)

CHAPTER

6

OLD SCHOOL—NEW SCHOOL
1829–1838

1. Albert Barnes: "The Way of Salvation"

The co-operative spirit of the first quarter of the nineteenth century was replaced in the second quarter by a self-conscious and often bitter denominationalism. The new era was initiated by a series of heresy trials involving the modifications of the older Calvinism by the so-called New School theologians. At the center of this storm was Albert Barnes, whose "Way of Salvation" was declared by the Old School majority in the Presbytery of Philadelphia to be both "highly objectionable" and "erroneous"! The portions of the sermon below will serve to indicate the best type of preaching, as well as the doctrinal astuteness, of the times.

The Way of Salvation

Titus, iii, 4,5,6,7.

All men have some scheme of salvation. Except the very few cases where individuals are thrown into a state of despair, there are none who do not expect to be happy beyond the grave. The proof of this is found in the composure with which most men look at eternity; and in their indifference when warned of a coming judgment. It requires the utmost strength of human hardihood, when a criminal looks without trembling of limbs on the gibbet where he is soon to be executed; and we infer, that there is no hardihood so great, no courage so strong, as to look upon eternal sorrow with a belief that it will be *ours,* and be unmoved. When we see, therefore, so many unconcerned about their eternal state; so many professing to believe that they are exposed to endless suffering, and still unanxious about it; the fair conclusion is, that not one syllable of the book that teaches that is truly believed. It is not, cannot be, human nature, to believe this, and still sit in indifference. Every man, therefore, has some secret scheme by which he expects to be saved. Yet it is perfectly clear that there can be but one scheme of salvation that is true. . . .

The full benefit of this atonement is offered to all men. In perfect sincerity God makes the offer. He has commissioned his servants to go and preach the gospel—that is, the good news that salvation is provided for them—to every creature. . . .

I assume the free and full offer of the Gospel to all men, to be one of those cardinal points of the system by which I *gauge* all my other views of truth. It is, in my view, a corner-stone of the whole edifice; that which makes it so glorious to God, and so full of good-will to men. I hold no doctrines—and by the grace of God never can hold any— which will be in *my* views inconsistent with the free and full offer of the Gospel to all men; or which will bind my hands, or palsy my tongue, or freeze my heart, when I stand before sinners to tell them of a dying Saviour. I stand as the messenger of God, with the assurance, that all that *will* may be saved; that the atonement was full and free; and that if any perish, it will be because they choose to die, and not because they are straitened in God. I have no fellow-feeling for any other Gospel; I have no right hand of fellowship to extend to any scheme that does not say that GOD sincerely offers all the bliss of heaven to every guilty wandering child of Adam,—be he a Caffrarian, a Hindoo, a man of China, or a Laplander;—a beggar or a king, a rich man, a learned man, a moral man, or an abandoned wretch of Christian climes. . . .

If the last point which I suggested be true, that all are disposed to reject the scheme, then it would seem to follow, that if any are saved, it will be by the special agency of God. To accomplish this, it is supposed he has sent down his Holy Spirit into the world. In the discharge of his great official work, he arrests the attention of heedless sinners. He does it by applying the preached gospel,—by leading the thoughts in a proper manner in the dispensations of his Providence,—by blessing the example and conversation of parents, brothers, and friends, or by a secret, silent influence, known only to the individual, drawing the thoughts along to eternity, producing distaste to the ways and wages of sin, and a panting and breathing of the soul for enjoyments suited to its nature. The effect of this operation of the Spirit is not to produce inactivity or slumber. It is not compulsion. No man is compelled, against his will, to be saved. The work of salvation, and the work of damnation, are the two most deliberate and solemn acts *of choosing*, that mortal man ever performs. . . .

No man has a right to conclude that *he* is shut out from salvation, except *by the fact*. If he loves sin, and will not repent and believe the gospel, he has no evidence that he will be saved; and if he persist in this course, he will be among the reprobate and be damned, by his own choice. If *he* should repent and believe, he would be saved, and be among the elect, and give the glory to God. . . .

It is no part of this scheme, as you will see, that God made men on purpose to damn them. No man, from the beginning of the world, to my knowledge, has ever professed to maintain that opinion. It is certainly not the sentiment of the Bible, and no man has any right to charge it on any system of religion; and I do not deem it too serious to say, is guilty of gross slander if he does it. God made men to glorify himself in their holiness and felicity; and has made provision for their salvation, and if they do not choose to be saved—if they choose to hate him, and rebel, and go to perdition, and HE does not choose to save them against their will, they cannot blame *him* for their self-chosen condemnation. . . . The Christian scheme, then, claims that God, by his spirit, renews all that will be saved. . . .

3rd. From this subject, we see what excludes men from heaven. It is not a want of fulness, and freeness, in the plan of mercy. It is not that God is unwilling to save the sinner. It is simply because *you will not be saved*. You choose your own pride, your own vanity, your own lust, your own course in life,—the path that leads to hell. . . . Who will be to blame, if you are lost,—if others are taken, and you are left? Will God? Will Christians? Will ministers? Will parents? Will friends? or will you yourselves? Let conscience answer. Go home this day, impenitent sinner, if God spares a rebel like you to get home—go home and reflect, that if you pass through this revival unmoved; if you resist all the appeals that are made to you, from day to day, and week to week, the probability is, that you will be damned, and the certainty is, that *you* only will be to blame if you are. I do not say that you will *certainly* be *lost,* I say that a most fearful probability "thunders perdition on your guilty path." What *should* move you hereafter, if you are not now moved? What more can be done for you than has been done? You have been warned, entreated, impressed. You *know* your duty, and your doom, if you do it not. You are in the hands of a Sovereign God. There I leave you. I have no other power than to spread out the scheme of mercy—to entreat you by the love of Jesus, and the mercy of God, and the value of your soul, to embrace the offer of life; and if you *will perish,* I must sit down and weep as I see you glide to the lake of death. Yet I cannot see you take that dread plunge—see you die, die for ever, without once more assuring you that the offer of the gospel is freely made to you. While you linger this side the fatal verge, that shall close life, and hope, and happiness, I would once more lift up my voice and say, See, sinner, see a God of love. He comes to you. He fills the heaven, the skies, the earth. Hear his voice as it breaks on the stillness of this house. Listen to the accents of the ever-living God—"As I live I have no pleasure in the death of the wicked, but rather that he turn and live: turn ye, turn ye, for why will ye die?" In the hands of that present God, the benignant Father, whose mercy breathes from every page of this book, I leave you. To him I commend you, with the deep feeling in my own bosom, that you are in his hands; that you are solemnly bound to repent *to-day*, and believe the gospel, and that if you perish, you only will be to blame. I feel, and know, that for not repenting, you have no excuse and that God will forever hold you guilty.

I also feel and know, that God is under no obligation to save you. That if you die, he will be guiltless. That if you are saved, it will be by his sovereign mercy—in such a way, that he only will have the praise; and that the great secret, whether you will live or die, is lodged in his bosom, and that no mortal can compel or control him. That he holds over you the sceptre of life, or the sword of death; and that if you die, all creation will bow and say Amen, and Amen. (A. Barnes, *The Way of Salvation, A Sermon, Delivered at Morristown, New-Jersey, February 8, 1829*, 7th ed., New York, 1836, 11 ff.)

2. The Western Foreign Missionary Society

Until 1831 Presbyterian concern for world missions had found expression through interdenominational societies, especially the American Board of Commissioners for Foreign Missions. The stiffening denominationalism of the 1830's led the Synod of Pittsburgh to expand its Western Missionary Society (see Ch. 4, art. 12) so as to include foreign work. In holding that missionary effort is not a voluntary matter, but is obligatory on all church members, the synod was far in advance of the Church. In 1838 the W.F.M.S. became the Assembly's Board of Foreign Missions.

It is a fact which the members of the Presbyterian Church, in common with some other branches of Christ's visible empire, recognize with joy and gratitude to God, that the indications of Prophecy and the signs of the times, call upon all who love our Lord Jesus Christ, in sincerity, of every denomination, and of every clime, to employ redoubled exertions, to extend the glorious gospel in the earth, and especially to those, who are enveloped in pagan and anti-christian darkness. . . .

Still, however, much remains to be done. The resources of large districts of the Presbyterian Church, are slumbering in inaction, and experience for a few years past, has demonstrated the fact, that they cannot be fully drawn forth, by a society so remote as the American Board, or by any that does not involve an ecclesiastical organization comporting with the honest predilections of many of our people.— No judicatory of the Presbyterian Church, it is believed, can act at this time on this subject, with as much propriety and prospect of unanimity as this; and from various considerations, which it is unnecessary to specify, it is also believed that no position on the continent is so favorable as this, for undertaking the institution of a society, which shall bring up the forces of the Presbyterian Church, in the Middle and Western States, to this great and blessed work.

Without any feeling of unkindness to any existing Board, *here*, in these western regions, of this large and opulent republic, the friends of the perishing heathen, can lift up a banner intended for *other* benefactors, and *other* ardent aspirants after missionery toils and labors, than any institution has yet numbered, and from hence a stream of benevolence can roll, which shall meet and commingle with those of distant places, and the friends of God, even, *here*, supply its demands, without coming in unhappy conflict, with any other society whatever. Disclaiming all party feelings, therefore, and listening to that voice from the Mediatorial throne, which seems to say, "Arise and be doing—collect my scattered soldiers, and display my banner, for the day of Salvation is opening on the world!" This Synod, trusting in the aid and guidance of the God of Missions.

Resolved, 1st. That it is expedient forthwith to establish a Society or Board for Foreign Missions, on such a plan as will admit of the cooperation of such parts of the Presbyterian church as may think proper to unite with it, in this great and important concern.

Resolved, 2d. That for the purposes above specified, the following be adopted as the Constitution of the contemplated Society, viz:

Constitution of the Western Foreign Missionary Society of the United States

ART. I. This Society shall be composed of the ministers, sessions and churches of the Synod of Pittsburgh, together with those of any other Synod or Synods, Presbytery or Presbyteries, that may hereafter formally unite with them, and shall be known by the name of the

Western Foreign Missionary Society of the U.S.

II. The objects of the Society shall be to aid in fulfilling the last great command of the glorified Redeemer, by conveying the gospel to whatever parts of the heathen and anti-christian world the providence of God may enable this Society to extend its evangelical exertions. (*Records of the Synod of Pittsburgh,* Oct. 24, 1831, 348 f.)

3. The Act and Testimony Convention

Among other sources of friction between Old and New School factions was the rivalry between the Boards of the Church and the great voluntary and interdenominational American Home Missionary Society and the American Education Society. In 1835 a pre-Assembly meeting of Old School men prepared the following "Act and Testimony" concerning the alarming conditions in Zion. The first three grievances had to do with matters of Church order.

IV. Nearly allied to this is our Fourth item of grievance, viz: The existence and operation within our Church of a missionary society in no sense amenable to her ecclesiastical jurisdiction. And here you will bear with us, first, in pointing out the connection with the preceding. If Presbyteries do exist, on the avowed principle of diversity in doctrinal opinion and feeling, and have the power of licensing and ordaining (in many instances *sine titulo*) men of their own creeds, then a missionary institution seems requisite to send such licentiates and Ministers into the field. Such an institution does exist, bound by its own rules to sustain missionaries, irrespective of their adherence to or rejection of the doctrinal standards of our Church. This institution operates largely in our congregations; first, by sweeping away from our own Board the funds which, by the laws of all social order, ought to come into the treasury of the body, to which its possessors belong; and secondly, by throwing into our Presbyteries, brethren who, in many instances, have never adopted the standards of our Church at all, and in more, who have only adopted them "for substance of doctrine"; that is, just as much of them as suits their own views. Thus a separate moneyed interest is created and kept up in the bosom of the same Christian community. The Assembly's own Board of Missions, created by herself, governed by herself, and amenable to herself, finds a great and powerful rival in her own house, with whom she comes in perpetual collision. And rival agents meet on the same field, and frequently those of our own Church are foiled in their efforts by the improper interference and influence of an institution which owns no allegiance to us, and feels no obligation to our Courts. . . .

V. Your attention is now invited to another part of the same system. Before youth looking forward to the gospel ministry can be properly licensed and sent forth, they must be educated: and efforts have been already made in this cause worthy of high commendation. . . .

Now the question before us is, to whom shall this most sacred and solemn duty be entrusted by the Church? Shall she do it herself, with her own hands? or shall she throw it into the hands of a body, self-created, and in no sense amenable to her ecclesiastical tribunals? a body which may change in half a generation, and train her sons to her own destruction? This is the question we would press upon your consideration: and we would most respectfully suggest, that no Church can be safe—safe in her doctrinal standards—safe in her ecclesiastical polity—safe in her financial operations—safe in the independence of her ministry, if that ministry are dependent upon an independent foreign body; and especially, if their houses and lands, their libraries and furniture, are under bonds. Without any impeachment of motives, or imputation of extraordinary weakness, we beg leave to repeat, "a gift blindeth the eyes," and to refer to the course of remark under the preceding item. (S. J. Baird, *Assembly's Digest*, rev. ed., 1855, 688–689.)

4. "This Presbytery Are Not Connected with the Assembly's Board"

New School "errors" were particularly prevalent in the areas of New York and Ohio where the Plan of Union (Ch. 4, art. 6) had been effective. The following reply to a request by the Board of Education illustrates the type of insubordination and lack of discipline which led the Old School to attack the whole plan of co-operation with Congregationalists.

Genoa   April 15, 1836

Dear Sir,

Yours of March 1st calling for a report from the Presbytery of Cayuga of their doings in relation to the education of men for the ministry was laid before the Presbytery the present week, and they have directed me to say in reply "that this Presbytery are not connected either directly or indirectly with the Assembly's Board of Education, but with the Presby. Ed. Society, and that the amount of contributions from our churches can be ascertained from the Annual Report of said Society." While we cherish none other than the kindest feelings towards the Assembly's Board, and desire their success in increasing the number of able and devoted ministers of Christ, and are laboring to accomplish the same great and good object, yet we prefer our present connection with the P.E.S. [Presbyterian Education Society].

Yours sincerely
Seth Smith
(Manuscript letter in P.H.S.)

5. "Testimony and Memorial," 1837

All the protests and grievances of previous years were summed up in the "Testimony and Memorial" of the Old School, pre-Assembly convention of 1837. Attention was centered on the New School errors in Church order, doctrine (see art. 10 below), and discipline, all of which were traced to the "unnatural intermixture" of Presbyterianism and Congregationalism. The remedy for these evils proposed by the convention was the abrogation of the Plan of Union, on the ground that it was unconstitutional (see art. 6, part A below). This Memorial sums up better than any other document the case of the Old School, and it was the basis of the subsequent actions in the Assembly that split the Church.

In Relation to Church Order

Among the departures from sound Presbyterian order, against which we feel called on to testify, as marking the times, are the following:

1. The formation of Presbyteries without defined and reasonable limits, or Presbyteries, covering the same territory, and especially such a formation founded on doctrinal repulsions or affinities; thus introducing schism into the very vital of the body.

2. The refusal of Presbyteries, when requested by any of their members, to examine all applicants for admission into them, as to their soundness in the faith, or touching any other matter connected with a fair Presbyterial standing; thus concealing and conniving at error, in the very strong-hold of truth.

3. The licensing of persons to preach the gospel, and the ordaining to the office of the ministry such as not only accept of our standards merely for substance of doctrine, and others who are unfit and ought to be excluded for want of qualification—but of many even who openly deny fundamental principles of truth, and preach and publish radical errors, as already set forth.

4. The formation of a great multitude and variety of creeds which are often incomplete, false, and contradictory of each other, and of

our Confession of Faith and the Bible; but which even if true are needless. . . .

5. The needless ordination of a multitude of men to the office of Evangelist, and the consequent tendency to a general neglect of the pastoral office; frequent and hurtful changes of pastoral relations; to the multiplication of spurious excitements, and the consequent spread of heresy and fanaticism, thus weakening and bringing into contempt the ordinary and stated agents and means, for the conversion of sinners, and the edification of the body of Christ.

6. The disuse of the office of Ruling Elder in portions of the Church, and the consequent growth of practices and principles entirely foreign to our system; thus depriving the pastors of needful assistants in discipline, the people of proper guides in Christ, and the Churches of suitable representatives in the ecclesiastical tribunals.

7. The electing and ordaining Ruling Elders, with the express understanding that they are to serve but for a limited time.

8. A progressive change in the system of Presbyterial representation in the General Assembly, which has been persisted in by those holding the ordinary majorities, and carried out into detail by those disposed to take undue advantage of existing opportunities, until the actual representation seldom exhibits the true state of the Church, and many questions of the deepest interest have been contrary to the fairly ascertained wishes of the majority of the Church and people in our communion; thus virtually subverting the essential principles of freedom, justice, and equality, on which our whole system rests.

9. The unlimited and irresponsible power, assumed by several associations of men under various names, to exercise authority and influence, direct and indirect, over Presbyters, as to their field of labour, place of residence, and mode of action in the difficult circumstances of our Church: thus actually throwing the control of affairs in large portions of the Church, and sometimes in the General Assembly itself, out of the hands of the Presbyteries into those of single individuals or small committees located at a distance.

10. The unconstitutional decisions and violent proceedings of several General Assemblies, and especially those of 1831, 2, 3, 4, and 6, directly or indirectly subverting some of the fundamental principles of Presbyterian government—effectually discountenancing discipline, if not rendering it impossible, and plainly conniving at and favouring, if not virtually affirming as true, the whole current of false doctrine which has been for years setting into our Church, thus making the Church itself a principal actor in its own dissolution and ruin.

In Relation to Discipline

With the woful departures from sound doctrine, which we have already pointed out, and the grievous declensions in Church order heretofore stated, has advanced step by step, the ruin of all sound discipline in large portions of our Church, until in some places our very name is becoming a public scandal, and the proceedings of persons and Churches connected with some of our Presbyteries, are hardly to be defended from the accusation of being blasphemous. Amongst other evils, of which this Convention and the Church have full proof, we specify the following:

1. The impossibility of obtaining a plain and sufficient sentence against gross errors, either *in thesi,* or when found in books printed under the name of Presbyterian ministers, or when such ministers have been directly and personally charged.

2. The public countenance thus given to error, and the complete security in which our own members have preached and published in newspapers, pamphlets, periodicals, and books, things utterly subversive of our system of truth and order; while none thought it possible (except in a few, and they almost fruitless, attempts) that discipline could be exercised; and therefore none attempted it.

3. The disorderly and unseasonable meetings of the people, in which unauthorized and incompetent persons conducted worship in a manner shocking to public decency; females often leading in prayer in promiscuous assemblies, and sometimes in public instruction; the hasty admission to Church privileges, and the failure to exercise any wholesome discipline over those who subsequently fall into sin, even of a public and scandalous kind; and by these and other disorders, grieving and alienating the pious members of our Churches, and so filling many of them with rash, ignorant, and unconverted persons, as gradually to destroy all visible distinction between the Church and the world.

4. While many of our ministers have propagated error with great zeal, and disturbed the Church with irregular and disorderly conduct; some have entirely given up the stated preaching of the Gospel, others have turned aside to secular pursuits, and others still while nominally engaged in some part of Christian effort, have embarked in the wild and extravagant speculations which have so remarkably signalized the times; thus tending to secularize and disorganize the very ministry of reconciliation.

5. The formation in the bosom of our Churches, and ecclesiastical bodies, of parties ranged against each other, on personal, doctrinal, and

other questions; strifes and divisions amongst our people—bitter contentions amongst many of our ministers: a general weakening of mutual confidence and affection; and, in some cases, a resort to measures of violence, duplicity, and injustice, totally inconsistent with the Christian name.

Method of Reform

Such being the state of things in the Presbyterian Church, we believe that the time is fully come, for the adoption of some measures, which shall speedily furnish relief from the evils already referred to. . . . In a word, it needs but a glance at the general character, the personal affinities, and the geographical relations of those who are antagonists in the present contest—to be satisfied that our present evils have not originated within, but have been brought from without—and are, in a great degree, the consequences of an unnatural intermixture of two systems of ecclesiastical action—which are in many respects entirely opposite in their nature and operation. . . . (S. J. Baird, *Assembly's Digest*, rev. ed., 1855, 712–715.)

6. The Exscinding Acts

Finding themselves in a majority in the Assembly of 1837, the Old School party proceeded to (a) abrogate the Plan of Union; (b) disown the synods formed under the plan; (c) sever connections with the interdenominational societies. As a result of these acts the Church was split into two parts in 1838.

A. Abrogation of the Plan of Union

The report was read and adopted, in part, as follows, viz:

In regard to the relation existing between the Presbyterian and Congregational Churches, the committee recommend the adoption of the following resolutions:

1. That between these two branches of the American Church, there ought, in the judgment of this Assembly, to be maintained sentiments of mutual respect and esteem, and for that purpose no reasonable efforts should be omitted to preserve a perfectly good understanding between these branches of the Church of Christ.

2. That it is expedient to continue the plan of friendly intercourse, between this Church and the Congregational Churches of New England, as it now exists.

3. But as the "Plan of Union" adopted for the new settlements, in 1801, was originally an unconstitutional act on the part of that Assem-

bly—these important standing rules having never been submitted to the Presbyteries—and as they were totally destitute of authority as proceeding from the General Association of Connecticut, which is invested with no power to legislate in such cases, and especially to enact laws to regulate Churches not within her limits; and as much confusion and irregularity have arisen from this unnatural and unconstitutional system of union, therefore, it is resolved, that the Act of the Assembly of 1801, entitled, a "Plan of Union," be, and the same is hereby abrogated. (Yeas, 143. Nays, 110.) (*Minutes of the G.A.,* 1837, 419, 431.)

B. THE DISOWNING ACTS

Resolved, That, by the operation of the abrogation of the Plan of Union of 1801, the Synod of the Western Reserve is, and is hereby declared, to be no longer a part of the Presbyterian Church in the United States of America. (Yeas 132, Nays 105.)

Be it resolved, by the General Assembly of the Presbyterian Church in the United States of America,

1. That in consequence of the abrogation by this Assembly of the Plan of Union of 1801, between it and the General Association of Connecticut, as utterly unconstitutional, and therefore null and void from the beginning, the Synods of Utica, Geneva, and Genesee, which were formed and attached to this body under and in execution of said "Plan of Union," be, and are hereby, declared to be out of the ecclesiastical connection of the Presbyterian Church of the United States of America, and that they are not in form or in fact an integral portion of said Church. (Yeas 115, Nays 88, *non liquet,* 1.) . . .

3. That the General Assembly has no intention, by these resolutions, or by that passed in the case of the Synod of the Western Reserve, to affect in any way the ministerial standing of any members of either of said Synods; nor to disturb the pastoral relation in any Church; nor to interfere with the duties or relations of private Christians in their respective Congregations; but only to declare and determine according to the truth and necessity of the case, and by virtue of the full authority existing in it for that purpose, the relation of all said Synods, and all their constituent parts to this body, and to the Presbyterian Church in the United States.

4. That inasmuch as there are reported to be several Churches and Ministers, if not one or two Presbyteries, now in connection with one or more of said Synods, which are strictly Presbyterian in doctrine and order, be it, therefore, further resolved, that all such Churches and Ministers as wish to unite with us, are hereby directed to apply for

admission into those Presbyteries belonging to our connection which are most convenient to their respective locations; and that any such Presbytery as aforesaid, being strictly Presbyterian in doctrine and order, and now in connection with either of said Synods, as may desire to unite with us, are hereby directed to make application, with a full statement of their cases, to the next General Assembly, which will take proper order thereon. (Yeas 113, Nays 60.) (*Minutes of the G.A.*, 1837, 440, 444.)

C. Disowning the Voluntary Societies

Resolved, That while we desire that no body of Christian men of other denominations should be prevented from choosing their own plans of doing good—and while we claim no right to complain should they exceed us in energy and zeal—we believe that facts, too familiar to need repetition here, warrant us in affirming, that the organization and operations of the so-called American Home Missionary Society, and the American Education Society, and its branches, of whatever name, are exceedingly injurious to the peace and purity of the Presbyterian Church. We recommend, accordingly, that they should cease to operate within any of our Churches. (Yeas 124, Nays 86.) (*Minutes of the G.A.*, 1837, 442.)

7. "They Violate the Plainest Principles of Presbyterian Government"

The New Side interpretation of the events of 1837 is presented with great clarity in the following article. It will be noted that the author ties up the controversy in the Church with the general political and social unrest of the Jacksonian era, and contends that the whole Old Side movement is the attempt of a power-hungry minority to gain control of the General Assembly, contrary to the principles of both Presbyterianism and democracy.

The "Plan of Union for the new settlements," formed in 1801, has acquired an importance which entitles it to more notice. It has been used as a means of dividing the Presbyterian church. . . . For thirty-six years the undisputed operation of that plan multiplied and increased the churches and the means of religious instruction. It was really a plan of united missionary enterprise,—the first fruits of a liberal spirit, manifesting itself in the concerted action of two great sects;—the same spirit which, a little later, brought so many, of so many sects, together, on the great platform of united action in voluntary association, interchanging the hands of cordial fellowship, and laboring for united success in a common cause. Of these none came forward with a readier zeal, or labored with a more willing industry, than the Presbyterians, urged on by the often repeated recommendations of the General Assemblies. It is refreshing to look back and see all those great men, whose talents and piety have given so much honor to that church, rallying upon the principles which should always characterize American Presbyterians. . . .

I said it was a harmonious sect. It would have remained so, if its own principles had not been departed from;—but where has not discord been, within the last few years? All human opinions and conduct seem to have been marked by a singular agitation. Religion, morals, politics, learning, have all felt it, and have been disturbed by its malign influence. . . . The Presbyterian church did not escape this besom of destruction. Individuals began to agitate there, also, and soon gathered a party which took up, in quick succession, the creed, the order, —the infallibility of the church, as the "one idea" with which to work reform. *The creed*—all its words must be learned and carried by vote, as the essence of truth. "And they said unto him, say now Shibboleth, and he said Sibboleth. Then they took him and slew him." *Order*—a departure, no matter on what expediency, from the forms or usages of the church, must not, in any, the least matter, be tolerated. *Infallibility* —the church, in her organized and corporate capacity, is, by the appointment of God, the censor of the books, the supervisor of the conduct, the conductor of the education, the collector and distributor of the alms of all mankind. In the matter of doctrine came doubts and suspicions and jealousies, spending their force, at first, in cold looks and unbrotherly passing by on the other side. It was whispered in certain places that Mr. —— is unsound,—he has said so and so. Dr. —— thinks thus and thus. His principles certainly tend to this or that error. The hint, the shrug, the solemn shake of the head, the significant regret poisoned the minds of the church and of the presbytery. . . . They then addressed themselves to the love of the constitution and order of the church, with the same modest practical demand, that all should bow to their interpretations. The same waking up of excitement, which had been resorted to in the matter of doctrine, told with still more effect on this point. They seized upon the assumption, that many of the churches in western New York, Ohio and Michigan, were formed on the plan of union,—were without ruling elders, and were Congregational or semi-congregational, in their government. The cry was raised, "the Congregationalists are trying to overthrow the constitution, and to substitute their own system in its place!" Every one knew that New England was Congregational, and the western part of our country was filled with citizens and clergymen of New England origin or descent. This gave a sort of foundation for the cry. "Look," said they, "at our opponents! were they not born Congregationalists? They are, of course, attached to the form of its government still.—We are the only true Presbyterians. Look at the men whom we could not overthrow.—They are New England men!—Look, who defended,—New England men!—Look at the majorities in the Assembly,—New England men—Congregationalists! Look at the West. Many churches there have no elders, no regular Presbyterian organization. And the graduates of the schools and seminaries of New England are now flocking thither to take charge of them! Our Zion is in danger; and when it is too late, the friends of good order—born Presbyterians,—will be but a handful;—we shall be driven from the church, or humbled and degraded in it!" Allegations so absurd and unsupported by proof were seldom noticed or denied by those against whom they were made, and that was made "confirmation strong, as proof from Holy Writ," of their truth. A portion of the church was fearfully excited and honestly alarmed;—but even yet the friends of union and peace were a majority. The General Assembly and the constitution were still bonds of union.—Then came a new rally, on the grounds both of doctrine and of order; and Congregationalism, and Pelagianism, and Taylorism, were rung, in discord and in unison, without specific charges, till there could be no peace. A foreign mission board was proposed to be appointed by the General Assembly. This was opposed by the friends of united and concentrated effort, as unnecessary, while the American Board located at Boston was so well performing that duty. This was another fact, to show the progress of Congregationalism! And the American Home Missionary Society, which had done more to extend the Presbyterian church permanently, than all other organizations was, without proof, charged with possessing the power and the purpose to subvert its constitution, simply because its happy plan of calling out and aiding effort had given it an almost miraculous growth and extension, and many, perhaps most, of those who had been its beneficiaries, voted against the disunionists; and its secretary had never ceased to contend for the integrity of the church.

Hereupon, suddenly, the American Home Missionary Society, the American Board of Commissioners for Foreign Missions, the American Education Society, (and later, the American Tract Society, and the American Sunday School Union, etc.) during their whole previous existence, the favorites of the Presbyterian church, were discovered to be, not the church in her organized and social capacity, but mere voluntary societies, and wholly unauthorized to spread the gospel. . . .

It was soon evident that party measures, of the strongest character, were to be adopted without mitigation, and that schism and disunion were to be thoroughly carried out, without delay, and in such a manner that the party could not be put in a minority, by the strong conservative sense of the church, which they feared would manifest itself in the next Assembly. The first use of their present power was to perpetuate it, and to secure the control over every man's standing in the church. They seemed desirous of driving the minority to immediate secession. A list of heresies was drawn up, apparently with a view to personal accusations, but the proceeding by accusation was liable to the great objection, that it gave the accused a trial, and an opportunity to prove his innocence, and the right of appeal, all which would take time, and might end in an acquittal. In the words of the Assembly "to have done it by personal process would have been impossible, and, if possible, tedious, agitating and troublesome." It was accordingly abandoned.

They then determined upon excision, by means of the plan of union. It was said "where is the local habitation of the liberal party? The region in which the plan of union has operated. Deduct the ministers of that region, from the party, and the residue may almost be counted on the fingers." It was supposed that important consequences would follow the abrogation of that plan, and it was abrogated. . . .

A threat, said to have been made by a prominent member of the committee, was then acted upon without delay, and resolutions were introduced, and urged through the house, cutting off from the church, without hearing or trial, or notice, by a summary edict, the synods of the Western Reserve, Utica, Geneva and Genesee, embracing about five hundred ministers and sixty thousand communicants, entitled to about sixty (more than one fifth of the whole number,) representatives in the General Assembly. . . .

It was, in effect, declared that all in those regions,—men, women and children, clergy and laity,—were excluded from the church. As a first act, on this construction, they excluded from the Assembly the sitting representatives from the presbyteries in the same regions, and put the clerks of the Assembly under a pledge, not to receive or enroll the commissions of delegates from the presbyteries, in any future General Assemblies. If these proceedings had been legal, or had been submitted to, the end was answered. The majority had perpetuated their power. But such proceedings, under the circumstances, could have no validity. They violated the plainest general principles of Presbyterian government, and the express provisions of the constitution, by disposing of individual rights, without the intervention of the primary courts, and, at the same time, destroying the right of appeal. The grand view of the proceedings, however, was the violation of one of those eternal principles of natural justice, which are superior to all positive enactments. That no one should be deprived of his right, or be punished, without an opportunity of being heard in his own defence, is a principle stamped by the hand of God upon the common understanding of mankind. It has been incorporated in all the codes of all nations, and, in the constitution of the Presbyterian church, it regulates all judicial proceedings. This principle was trodden under foot at every step of these proceedings. There was no pretence of a hearing, or even of notice. The synods and their whole constituency, ministers and church-members, were swept away by the same unforeseen decree, confounding the innocent with the guilty, and condemning all unheard. Wonderful proceedings, indeed!—for they were the work of a chosen deliberative Assembly!—for they were the work of a religious Assembly, an ecclesiastical court!—for the sufferers were their brethren! and the cause of Christ, dearer than all! (*The American Biblical Repository,* 1839, 2d series, I, 479 ff., 491 ff.)

8. "Congregationalists Are Not Presbyterians"

The Old School position is presented in the following report of the great debate on the exclusion of the Western Reserve Synod in the General Assembly of 1837.

Debate

On the other hand, the expediency of the measure is obvious from the following considerations. In the first place, these churches are in heart Congregational, why should they then be called Presbyterian? That they do really prefer Congregationalism, is plain from the fact that although it is twelve years since they were formed into a synod, you hear it stated by their own commissioners, that not one fourth of their number have adopted our form of government. Besides, it is generally known, that it required very great exertion, on the part of those who do not belong to the synod, to prevent a general secession of these churches, and the adoption of Congregationalism in full. Is it not preposterous and unreasonable that men, who can with difficulty be kept from rejecting the mere shadow of Presbyterianism, should be still nominally connected with our church, for no other purpose than to exert an influence in our church courts to which they have no right? In the second place, there is abundant evidence that the greatest disorders prevail in these presbyteries in reference to our system. Mr. Breck, of the presbytery of Cleaveland, has stated on the floor, that he never saw any elders ordained; that he *believes* the ministers adopt the confession of faith. Mr. Torrance stated he saw two Congregational ministers received into that presbytery without the constitutional questions being put. Mr. Kingsbury, though having a certificate of ordination as a ruling elder, when asked if, at his ordination, he had adopted our confession of faith? declined answering the question. It must be remembered that this evidence is not adduced as the ground of decision in a judicial case, but as a motive for action in a legislative one. All that kind of evidence which produces moral certainty as to the state of things in that region of country, may very properly be adduced as an argument why we should dissolve our connexion with a body in which our system is openly disregarded. We presume there is not an individual on this floor, who is not perfectly satisfied that there are such frequent and serious departures from presbyterial order permitted within the bounds of this synod, as would justify its excision by judicial process. This surely is a strong argument for passing this resolution, which we believe expresses the exact truth, that they are not now and never have been a constitutional portion of our church; a resolution which, while it frees us from the evils and responsibilities of the connexion, inflicts no injury on them. It leaves them every thing but the right to administer over us a constitution to which the majority of them are entirely opposed. The departures from Presbyterianism in this region are not confined to matters of government; we have every evidence such a case admits of, that what we believe to be serious departures from our doctrinal standards, prevail throughout this synod. We know what is the theology of Oberlin Seminary; we know what opinions the commissioners from these presbyteries have, at various times, avowed on the floor of the Assembly; we know, and every one else knows, that new-school theology, be it good or bad, is the theology of this synod. We believe this theology, especially in its recent shape, is not only inconsistent with our standards, but in a high degree injurious to true religion. Shall we then, in violation of our constitution, and in disregard of our solemn obligations, continue to recognize as a member of this body, a synod, which we believe is not entitled to be so regarded, and which we are certain is lending all its influence to spread, through our whole denomination, a system of doctrines we believe to be erroneous and destructive?

We believe then this whole case to be exceedingly plain. The plan of union, on which the churches of this synod are in general formed, we believe to be unconstitutional, and that its abrogation severs the only tie by which they were connected with this body. We believe that the act by which this synod was organized is also unconstitutional and void, and that, from the nature of our system and the constitution of our church, it is the rightful prerogative of this house to pronounce these acts to be invalid, and that the necessary operation of this decision is to declare the churches of this synod not to be a constituent portion of the Presbyterian church. . . . We do no man injustice by declaring that congregationalists are not presbyterians, and have no right to take part in the government of the Presbyterian Church. (*The Biblical Repertory and Princeton Review*, 1837, 465–467.)

9. "Because They Dared to Oppose Southern Slavery"

While the official documents are noticeably silent on the question of slavery, there was a strong feeling among abolitionists that the Excinding Acts of 1837 were a deliberate attempt to weaken the antislavery forces in the Church. Although the author of the following review vehemently denies that Breckenridge and Plumer made the statements attributed to them by the press, he does not mention that the speeches were made in the pre-Assembly, Old Side convention. (See W. W. Sweet, Religion on the American Frontier, II, 1936, *New York, 122–123 n.*)

It is notorious that the great majority of the house, on either side, took little part in the debates, and conducted themselves in every respect as became Christians and gentlemen. . . . Yet this body is spoken of in the most opprobrious manner in the papers to which we have referred. The Boston Recorder says, "We could not, in good conscience towards God, nor in loving kindness to our readers, nor in justice to ourselves, give even an abstract of the proceedings of the body." The Alton Observer says, "With the close of its sessions closes the history of the General Assembly of the Presbyterian church in the United States of America. And alas! it may be said of that body, with perfect truth, that it died as the fool dieth. . . . The crisis of these heart-burnings has now arrived; the inflamed imposthume has suppurated, and the stench of its offensive matter has pervaded the whole land like a pestilential presence." The New York Evangelist publishes a letter, which it says comes from one of the leading ministers of Connecticut, who asks, "Was it not a presbyterian who publicly declared, a few years ago, that at every meeting of the General Assembly there was 'a jubilee in hell?' And what was the spirit which actuated the majority of the General Assembly at their late meeting? . . . Who can doubt, that one leading motive was the motive which actuated Satan when he fell from heaven —the love of superiority and power?" The Cincinnati Journal says, "All the forms of law, civil and ecclesiastical, have been set at naught. . . . The greatness of the enormity would render idle all the expressions of reproach." Even the presbytery of Cayuga allow themselves, in an official document, to use the following language, "Resolved, That all the ministers and the churches belonging to and under the care of this presbytery be, and hereby are, cautioned to beware of the insidious and seductive stratagems and efforts of the adherents of the majority in the late Assembly, who are endeavouring by false pretences, misrepresentations, and 'pastoral letters' (so called), to induce them to dissolve their ecclesiastical connexion," &c. This language is used in reference to the official documents of the General Assembly, and to a pastoral letter prepared by Dr. Baxter, Dr. Alexander, and Dr. Leland. The most laboured effort at misrepresentation has been made to produce the impression that the desire to protect slavery was the ruling motive of the majority. That this should be done by the abolition papers is not a matter of surprise. But that papers which have hitherto been of a different character, should take the same course, is not so easily accounted for. The Cincinnati Journal says, "We had no doubt, when the course of the General Assembly was manifested, and when the four synods were cut off, of the cause which was urging on that body to such extremes of violence. Our belief is confirmed by our correspondent. The question is not between the new and old school—is not in relation to doctrinal errors, but it is slavery and anti-slavery." This correspondent of the Journal, a member of the Assembly, under the date of June 6, writes, "The resolutions for excluding the synods of Utica, Geneva, and Genesee, were offered by R. J. Breckinridge of Baltimore, and sustained by himself and W. S. Plumer of Virginia. The speech of the latter gentleman was the most unfair and uncandid that I ever heard. It was designed to excite the south to vote as one man against those synods, because they had dared to oppose southern slavery." We have read one report of the speech here referred to, in the Presbyterian, which occupies several columns, and another still longer in the Evangelist, in neither of which have we discovered the least allusion to the subject of slavery. We have asked men of both parties who heard the speech delivered, and they unhesitatingly pronounce the statement untrue. The author of such a letter, if a church member, would, in this part of the church, be subjected to discipline. We have given but a specimen of the manner in which the Assembly and its doings are spoken of by the new school men and presses. . . .

The avowed, and we believe the real object, which the majority desired to attain, was to put an end to the contentions which had so long distracted the church, and to secure a faithful adherence to our doctrines and discipline. To accomplish this object, they determined, in the exercise of what they believed to be the constitutional authority of the Assembly, to separate from the Presbyterian church those who, having no constitutional right to a seat in its judicatories, were yet the main supporters of the prevalent errors and disorders. The fact was notorious that a large portion of our ecclesiastical courts were composed in great measure of congregationalists or their representatives. And it was no less notorious that these bodies formed the strength of the party which the majority have ever believed to be more or less hostile to the doctrines and discipline of our church. It presented itself, therefore, as the most feasible, the most just and proper method of attaining the great object of peace and purity in the church, to separate from it the congregational portion. This we believe the Assembly had a perfect right to do. The only question was, no doubt, the method of doing it. As to this point there was, no doubt, diversity of views, and very obviously a change of plan. The first step was the abrogation of the plan of union. (*The Biblical Repertory and Princeton Review,* 1837, 478 ff.)

10. The Auburn Declaration

New School leaders deeply resented the list of errors attributed to them by their Old School adversaries. At a strategy convention held at Auburn, N.Y., in the summer of 1837, therefore, they issued a declaration of their true beliefs on the controversial doctrines. This clear-cut statement helped to establish the orthodoxy of the New School, and paved the way for the reunion of 1869 (see Ch. 8, art. 10).

Report of the Committee on Doctrine

Whereas it is declared in the "Circular letter" of the late General Assembly of the Presbyterian Church "to all the churches of Jesus Christ," that "very serious" and "alarming" errors and disorders have long prevailed in the bounds of the exscinded synods and other portions of the Church, and as the late Assembly appears to have been influenced in deciding on the case of these synods, by these alleged errors and disorders, therefore

1. *Resolved,* That while we bear in mind that with the excitement of extensive revivals indiscretions are sometimes intermingled—and that in the attempt to avoid a ruinous practical Antinomianism, human obligation is sometimes urged in a manner that favors Arminian errors—yet, we are bound to declare, that such errors and irregularities have never been sanctioned by these synods or presbyteries—that the prejudice has in a great degree arisen from censorious and exaggerated statements, and from the conduct of persons not in connexion with the Presbyterian Church—that all such departures from the sound doctrine or order of the Presbyterian Church we solemnly disapprove, and when known, deem it our duty to correct by every constitutional method.

2. *Resolved,* That, as the declaration of the religious sentiments of the synods and presbyteries whom we represent, we cordially embrace the Confession of Faith of the Presbyterian Church, "as containing the system of doctrine taught in the holy Scriptures," as understood by the Church ever since the Adopting Act of 1729; viz., "And in case any minister of the Synod, or any candidate for the ministry, shall have any scruple with respect to any article or articles of said confession, he shall in time of making said declaration, declare his scruples to the Synod or Presbytery; who shall, notwithstanding, admit him to the exercise of the ministry within our bounds, and to ministerial communion, if the Synod or Presbytery shall judge his scruples *not essential* or necessary in *Doctrine, Worship,* or *Government."*

3. *Resolved,* That in accordance with the above declaration, and also to meet the charges contained in the before-mentioned Circular and other published documents of the late General Assembly, this convention cordially disapprove and condemn the list of errors condemned by the late General Assembly, and adopt, as the expression of their own sentiments, and as they believe, the prevalent sentiments of the churches of these synods on the points in question, the list of "true doctrines" adopted by the minority of the said Assembly in their "Protest" on this subject, as follows, viz.:

Errors and True Doctrine

FIRST ERROR. "That God would have prevented the existence of sin in our world, but was not able, without destroying the moral agency of man; or, that for aught that appears in the Bible to the contrary, sin is incidental to any wise moral system."

TRUE DOCTRINE. God permitted the introduction of sin, not because he was unable to prevent it, consistently with the moral freedom of his creatures, but for wise and benevolent reasons which he has not revealed.

SECOND ERROR. "That election to eternal life is founded on a foresight of faith and obedience."

TRUE DOCTRINE. Election to eternal life is not founded on a foresight of faith and obedience, but is a sovereign act of God's mercy, whereby, according to the counsel of his own will, he has chosen some to salvation; "yet so as thereby neither is violence offered to the will of the creatures, nor is the liberty or contingency of second causes taken away, but rather established;" nor does this gracious purpose ever take effect independently of faith and a holy life.

THIRD ERROR. "That we have no more to do with the first sin of Adam than with the sins of any other parent."

TRUE DOCTRINE. By a divine constitution, Adam was so the head and representative of the race, that, as a consequence of his transgression, all mankind become morally corrupt, and liable to death, temporal and eternal.

FOURTH ERROR. "That infants come into the world as free from moral defilement as was Adam when he was created."

TRUE DOCTRINE. Adam was created in the image of God, endowed with knowledge, righteousness, and true holiness. Infants come into the world, not only destitute of these, but with a nature inclined to evil and only evil.

FIFTH ERROR. "That infants sustain the same relation to the moral government of God, in this world, as brute animals, and that their sufferings and death are to be accounted for on the same principles as those of brutes, and not by any means to be considered as penal."

TRUE DOCTRINE. Brute animals sustain no such relation to the moral government of God as does the human family. Infants are a part of the human family; and their sufferings and death are to be accounted for on the ground of their being involved in the general moral ruin of the race induced by the apostacy.

SIXTH ERROR. "That there is no other original sin than the fact, that all the posterity of Adam, though by nature innocent, will always begin to sin when they begin to exercise moral agency; that original sin does not include a sinful bias of the human mind, and a just exposure to penal suffering; and that there is no evidence in Scripture, that infants, in order to salvation, do need redemption by the blood of

Christ, and regeneration by the Holy Ghost."

TRUE DOCTRINE. Original sin is a natural bias to evil, resulting from the first apostacy, leading invariably and certainly to actual transgression. And all infants, as well as adults, in order to be saved, need redemption by the blood of Christ, and regeneration by the Holy Ghost.

SEVENTH ERROR. "That the doctrine of imputation, whether of the guilt of Adam's sin, or of the righteousness of Christ, has no foundation in the Word of God, and is both unjust and absurd."

TRUE DOCTRINE. The sin of Adam is not imputed to his posterity in the sense of a literal transfer of personal qualities, acts, and demerit; but by reason of the sin of Adam, in his peculiar relation, the race are treated as if they had sinned. Nor is the righteousness of Christ imputed to his people in the sense of a literal transfer of personal qualities, acts, and merit; but by reason of his righteousness, in his peculiar relation, they are treated as if they were righteous.

EIGHTH ERROR. "That the sufferings and death of Christ were not truly vicarious and penal, but symbolical, governmental, and instructive only."

TRUE DOCTRINE. The sufferings and death of Christ were not symbolical, governmental, and instructive only, but were truly vicarious, i.e. a substitute for the punishment due to transgressors. And while Christ did not suffer the literal penalty of the law, involving remorse of conscience and the pains of hell, he did offer a sacrifice, which infinite wisdom saw to be a full equivalent. And by virtue of this atonement, overtures of mercy are sincerely made to the race, and salvation secured to all who believe.

NINTH ERROR. "That the impenitent sinner is by nature, and independently of the renewing influence or almighty energy of the Holy Spirit, in full possession of all the ability necessary to a full compliance with all the commands of God."

TRUE DOCTRINE. While sinners have all the faculties necessary to a perfect moral agency and a just accountability, such is their love of sin and opposition to God and his law, that, independently of the renewing influence or almighty energy of the Holy Spirit, they never will comply with the commands of God.

TENTH ERROR. "That Christ does not intercede for the elect until after their regeneration."

TRUE DOCTRINE. The intercession of Christ for the elect is previous as well as subsequent to their regeneration, as appears from the following Scripture, viz. "I pray not for the world, but for them which thou hast given me, for they are thine. Neither pray I for these alone, but for them also which shall believe on me through their word."

ELEVENTH ERROR. "That saving faith is not an effect of the operations of the Holy Spirit, but a mere rational belief of the truth or assent to the word of God."

TRUE DOCTRINE. Saving faith is an intelligent and cordial assent to the testimony of God concerning his Son, implying reliance on Christ alone for pardon and eternal life; and in all cases it is an effect of the special operations of the Holy Spirit.

TWELFTH ERROR. "That regeneration is the act of the sinner himself, and that it consists in change of his governing purpose, which he himself must produce, and which is the result, not of any direct influence of the Holy Spirit on the heart, but chiefly of a persuasive exhibition of the truth, analogous to the influence which one man exerts over the mind of another; or that regeneration is not an instantaneous act, but a progressive work."

TRUE DOCTRINE. Regeneration is a radical change of heart, produced by the special operations of the Holy Spirit, "determining the sinner to that which is good," and is in all cases instantaneous.

THIRTEENTH ERROR. "That God has done all that *he can do* for the salvation of all men, and that man himself must do the rest."

TRUE DOCTRINE. While repentance for sin and faith in Christ are indispensable to salvation, all who are saved are indebted from first to last to the grace and Spirit of God. And the reason that God does not save all, is not that he wants the *power* to do it, but that in his wisdom he does not see fit to exert that power further than he actually does.

FOURTEENTH ERROR. "That God cannot exert such influence on the minds of men, as shall make it certain that they will choose and act in a particular manner, without impairing their moral agency."

TRUE DOCTRINE. While the liberty of the will is not impaired, nor the established connexion betwixt means and end broken by any action of God on the mind, he can influence it according to his pleasure, and does effectually determine it to good in all cases of true conversion.

FIFTEENTH ERROR. "That the righteousness of Christ is not the sole ground of the sinner's acceptance with God; and that in no sense does the righteousness of Christ become ours."

TRUE DOCTRINE. All believers are justified, not on the ground of personal merit, but solely on the ground of the obedience and death, or, in other words, the righteousness of Christ. And while that righteousness does not become theirs, in the sense of a literal transfer of personal qualities and merit; yet, from respect to it, God can and does treat them as if they were righteous.

SIXTEENTH ERROR. "That the reason why some differ from others in regard to their reception of the Gospel is, that they make themselves to differ."

TRUE DOCTRINE. While all such as reject the Gospel of Christ do it, not by coercion but freely—and all who embrace it do it, not by coercion but freely—the reason why some differ from others is, that *God* has made them to differ.

In further illustration of the doctrines prevalent in these sections of the Church, the Convention declare that the authors whose exposition and defence of the articles of our faith are most approved and used in these synods—are President Edwards, Witherspoon, and Dwight—Dr. Smalley, and Andrew Fuller—and the Commentators, Henry Doddridge, and Scott. (*Minutes of the Auburn Convention, Held August 17, 1837, to Deliberate Upon the Doings of the Last General Assembly etc.*, Auburn, 1837.)

CHAPTER

7

PARALLEL EXPANSION
1839–1860

1. "Manifest Destiny"

From 1838 to 1869 there were two General Assemblies, each claiming to represent the Presbyterian Church U.S.A. In these years the westward movement of population presented unparalleled challenges to both Churches as they struggled to supply the new territories. To the popular idea of "Manifest Destiny" was added the vision of a Christian continent. Sermons and reports like the following helped both to create and to maintain national self-consciousness.

The developments of American statistics are the romance of political economy. It has been computed, in popular language, that the wave of population rolls westward at the rate of eighteen miles a year, sweeping away the wilderness by a living tide of active and increasing encroachment. Unless the enterprise of the vast heterogeneous West and South-west shall be sanctified by the power of religion, that section of country will become the calamity of our great republic.

With an adequate supply of right-minded, devoted ministers, the number of Presbyterian churches might, in the Providence of God, be speedily doubled. The Board of Missions have affirmed that they might advantageously locate one thousand missionaries, if they could find the men. But where are the men? *"The labourers are few."* (C. Van Rensselaer, in *Report of the Board of Education*, 1847, 8.)

The field then will be whatever the ambition of the people, (mad though it be,) and the inscrutable providence of God, shall make it. If it shall embrace the whole American Continent, by whatever means, it will be our duty to go forth and stud the land with the Institutions which we propose. And the people! They, too, are coming from every quarter of the globe. Scourged by famine or oppression from their own lands, or allured by the prospect of worldly gain, they are coming!—Irish, German, Swiss, French, Italians, Danes, Norwegians.—"Parthians, and Medes, and Alamites," and what not? They are coming! and we are yet to speak to them, in their own tongues, and educate them to speak "in our tongue, wherein we were born, the wonderful works of God."

If, then, we need such an organization *now* to supply the present demand, much more will it be needed to meet the demands of the New States that are yet to be formed, and filled with people, from the Mississippi to the shores of the Pacific. We began with perhaps *twenty millions* of people; but our work will not be done until we, in connexion with other concurrent instrumentalities, shall have supplied *five hundred millions* with these "trees of centuries," as our Secretary has aptly denominated them, and made them sufficiently numerous to enlighten and bless the people, in all their coming generations. (Absalom Peters, in *Report of the Society for the Promotion of Collegiate and Theological Education at the West*, 1847, 34.)

2. "The Star of Texas"

In the same year that the Republic of Texas was established, the Cumberland Presbyterian Church laid plans for a Presbytery of Texas. Missionary zeal and an urgent sense of moral responsibility, as well as their self-conscious Americanism, are revealed in the minutes of the first meeting of this new court.

1836. Nov. 14.

In the pursuance of a resolution of Mississippi Synod of the Cumberland Presbyterian Church in Session at Jackson, Mississippi, Nov. 14th A.D. 1836.

"Resolved, that so soon as there may be three or more ministers in the Province of Texas, that they Organize themselves in-to a Presbytery.

Rev. Sumner Bacon to be their first Moderator and their bounds to include the whole Province."

Wm. H. Wilkins, *Mod.*
H.H. Hill, *Clk.*

1837. Nov. 27.

In pursuance of the above Resolution Rev. Sumner Bacon from Louisiana—Mitchell Smith from Talledago, and Amos Roark from Hatcher Presbyteries—all ordained ministers of the Cumberland Presbyterian Church—Being present at the house of Sumner Bacon, San Augustine County, Republic of Texas. Nov. 27th, A.D. 1837—

The introductory sermon was preached by Rev. Sumner Bacon from Joel, 2nd Chapter & 1st verse.

Constituted by prayer.

Mitchell Smith was chosen clerk.

Resolved that this Presbytery be known by the name of "Texas Presbytery."

James Burke a ruling elder in the Presbyterian Church, being present, was invited and took a seat as a corresponding member. . . .

On motion, Resolved, that this Presbytery Constitute a Home missionary Society, for the purpose of supplying the Republic of Texas, with the ministry of the Gospel, by the Cumberland Presbyterian Church. . . .

Resolved, that this Presbytery recommend to the churches under her care, and to all that portion of the Christian Community over whom they may have influence, the observance of the 1st Monday evening in each month, as a monthly Concert of prayer, for the blessings of God on the cause of missions throughout the world.

Richard O. Watkins, (a resident of Nacodoches County) gave a relation of his experimental acquaintance with Religion; of his internal call & motives to the ministry: was received a Candidate under the care of this Presbytery and a text was assigned him, found in Heb. 2nd Chap. and 3rd verse, from which to prepare a written discourse, to be read at a future period of this session of Presbytery.

Presbytery adjourned to meet tomorrow morning at 8 o'clock—Concluded with prayer.

Nov. Wednesday 29th. . . .

Resolved, that this Presbytery regard the Christian Sabbath, as an inestimable blessing to mankind, and are deeply impressed with the belief that upon its strict observance, depends, not only, the vital interest of Godliness & pure morals, but also the temporal prosperity of the Community, and that it be strictly enjoined upon the members of the Churches under our care, and respectfully & affectionately recommended to the citizens of this Republic generally to pay special attention to the sanctification of this day—It is especially recommended to all the professed followers of the Lord Jesus Christ to abstain from traveling on the Sabbath, that being a mode of desecration, which from the frequency of its occurrence, in the U.S. has obtained the sad preeminence of being called the "Christian mode" & to which, from the peculiar situation of our Country, the religious in this Republic, as well as travellers from abroad are peculiarly liable.

Resolved, that the Pres. having entire confidence in the liberal spirit which has always characterized the various benevolent institutions of the U.S. denominated "American," & feeling though in a foreign land, all that sympathy for and attachment to the land of our *nativity,* which always exists in the heart of the true patriot; and recollecting also, that though under a foreign government, over which the "American Eagle" wafts not her protecting wings, that we are yet on American Soil, and desiring to reap a portion of that beneficial influence, which these societies have exerted, on other portions of this Continent, and which some of them have already exerted in our own Country would cordially invite the following voluntary Associations to extend their operations into this Republic; and that we recommend these Societies to the confidence & liberality of the churches under our care, as well as the friends of Religion generally, and cordially invite their agents to come amongst us, assuring them that in our branch of the Church they will find a warm Coadjutor. (viz.) "American Bible Society," "American Tract Society"—"American Sunday School Union"—"American Temperance Union"— "American Temperance Society"—"American Home Missionary Society"—"American bond [Board] of Commissioners for foreign Missions"—"American Colonization Society" and the "American Education Society."

Resolved, that this body, appreciating the importance of the influence of the periodical press upon the moral & religious interests of the community, and desiring to gain their countenance & support to every enterprise, calculated to exert a beneficial influence upon the moral Character of the Republic, have seen with pleasure the prospectus of a periodical to be called the "Star of Texas" and promise to exert our influence to extend its circulation should it be published; and in case of its failure, they would recommend the speedy establishment of a newspaper in Texas, the primary object of which shall be the promotion of morals & Religion—Said periodical to be conducted on the broad basis of our common Christianity, and devoted to the promulgation of the peculiarities of no particular Sect.

Resolved, that this body, being convinced of the propriety of connecting manual labor with literary pursuits, and believing that an institution of learning founded on this plan would be peculiarly adapted to the wants & circumstances of our infant Republic; and desiring to exert all our influence in favor of the diffusion of knowledge throughout the community would recommend the establishment of a seminary of learning, as soon as possible on the manual labor System, in our bounds. (*Minutes of Texas Presbytery, Journal P.H.S.,* XXXII, 53 ff.)

3. Covered Wagons

The settlement of Oregon is inseparably associated with the New School missionaries Dr. and Mrs. Marcus Whitman. Commissioned by the American Board of Commissioners for Foreign Missions in 1836, the Whitmans labored among the Oregon Indians until they were both murdered in 1847, thus providing the Church with its first martyrs. The whole subject has been carefully presented by C. L. Drury in his trilogy, Henry Harmon Spalding, Marcus Whitman, *and* Elkanah and Mary Walker. *In the following letter Mrs. Narcissa Whitman tells of her journey across the great plains with the wagon-train of the American Fur Company.*

PLATTE RIVER, JUST ABOVE THE FORKS,
June 3d, 1836.

Dear Sister Harriet and Brother Edward:—Friday eve, six o'clock. We have just encamped for the night near the bluffs over against the river. The bottoms are a soft, wet plain, and we were obliged to leave the river yesterday for the bluffs. The face of the country yesterday afternoon and today has been rolling sand bluffs, mostly barren, quite unlike what our eyes have been satiated with for weeks past. No timber nearer than the Platte, and the water tonight is very bad—got from a small ravine. We have usually had good water previous to this.

Our fuel for cooking since we left timber (no timber except on rivers) has been dried buffalo dung; we now find plenty of it and it answers a very good purpose, similar to the kind of coal used in Pennsylvania (suppose now Harriet will make up a face at this, but if she were here she would be glad to have her supper cooked at any rate in this scarce timber country).

The present time in our journey is a very important one. The hunter brought us buffalo meat yesterday for the first time. Buffalo were seen today but none have been taken. We have some for supper tonight. Husband is cooking it—no one of the company professes the art but himself. I expect it will be very good. Stop—I have so much to say to the children that I do not know in what part of my story to begin. I have very little time to write. I will first tell you what our company consists of. We are ten in number; five missionaries, three Indian boys and two young men employed to assist in packing animals.

Saturday, 4th. Good morning, H. and E. I wrote last night till supper;

after that it was so dark I could not see. I told you how many bipeds there was in our company last night; now for the quadrupeds: Fourteen horses, six mules and fifteen head of cattle. We milk four cows. We started with seventeen, but we have killed one calf, and the Fur Company, being out of provision, have taken one of our cows for beef. It is usually pinching times with the Company before they reach the buffalo. We have had a plenty because we made ample provision at Liberty. We purchased a barrel of flour and baked enough to last us, with killing a calf or two, until we reached the buffalo.

The Fur Company is large this year; we are really a moving village—nearly 400 animals, with ours, mostly mules, and 70 men. The Fur Company have seven wagons drawn by six mules each, heavily loaded, and one cart drawn by two mules, which carries a lame man, one of the proprietors of the Company. We have two wagons in our company. Mr. and Mrs. S., husband and myself ride in one, Mr. Gray and the baggage in the other. Our Indian boys drive the cows and Dulin the horses. Young Miles leads our forward horses, four in each team. Now E., if you want to see the camp in motion, look away ahead and see first the pilot and the captain, Fitzpatrick, just before him; next the pack animals, all mules, loaded with great packs; soon after you will see the wagons, and in the rear, our company. We all cover quite a space. The pack mules always string along one after the other just like Indians. . . .

I wish I could describe to you how we live so that you can realize it. Our manner of living is far preferable to any in the States. I never was so contented and happy before, neither have I enjoyed such health for years. In the morning as soon as the day breaks the first that we hear is the words, "Arise! Arise!"—then the mules set up such a noise as you never heard, which puts the whole camp in motion. We encamp in a large ring, baggage and men, tents and wagons on the outside, and all the animals except the cows, which are fastened to pickets, within the circle. This arrangement is to accommodate the guard, who stand regularly every night and day, also when we are in motion, to protect our animals from the approach of Indians, who would steal them. As I said, the mules' noise brings every man on his feet to loose them and turn them out to feed.

Now, H. and E., you must think it very hard to have to get up so early after sleeping on the soft ground, when you find it hard work to open your eyes at seven o'clock. Just think of me—every morning at the word, "Arise!" we all spring. While the horses are feeding we get breakfast in a hurry and eat it. By this time the words, "Catch up! Catch up," ring through the camp for moving. We are ready to start usually at six, travel till eleven, encamp, rest and feed, and start again about two; travel until six, or before, if we come to a good tavern, then encamp for the night.

Since we have been in the prairie we have done all our cooking. When we left Liberty we expected to take bread to last us part of the way, but could not get enough to carry us any distance. We found it awkward work to bake out of doors at first, but we have become so accustomed to it now we do it very easily.

Tell mother I am a very good housekeeper on the prairie. I wish she could just take a peep at us while we are sitting at our meals. Our table is the ground, our table-cloth is an Indian-rubber cloth used when it rains as a cloak; our dishes are made of tin—basins for teacups, iron spoons and plates, each of us, and several pans for milk to put our meat in when we wish to set it on the table. Each one carries his own knife in the scabbard, and it is always ready for use. When the table things are spread, after making our own forks of sticks and helping ourselves to chairs, we gather around the table. Husband always provides my seat, and in a way that you would laugh to see. It is the fashion of all this country to imitate the Turks. Messrs. Dunbar and Allis have supped with us, and they do the same. We take a blanket and lay down by the table, and those whose joints will let them follow the fashion; others take out some of the baggage (I suppose you know that there is no stones in this country; not a stone have I seen of any size on the prairie). For my part I fix myself as gracefully as I can, sometimes in a blanket, sometimes on a box, just as it is convenient. Let me assure you of this, we relish our food none the less for sitting on the ground while eating. We have tea and a plenty of milk, which is a luxury in this country. Our milk has assisted us very much in making our bread since we have been journeying. While the Fur Company has felt the want of food, our milk has been for great service to us; but it was considerable work for us to supply ten persons with bread three times a day. We are done using it now. What little flour we have left we shall preserve for thickening our broth, which is excellent. I never saw any thing like buffalo meat to satisfy hunger. We do not want any thing else with it. I have eaten three meals of it and it relishes well. Supper and breakfast we eat in our tent. We do not pitch it at noon. Have worship immediately after supper and breakfast.

Noon.–The face of the country today has been like that of yesterday. We are now about 30 miles above the forks, and leaving the bluffs for the river. We have seen wonders this forenoon. Herds of buffalo hove in sight; one, a bull, crossed our trail and ran upon the bluffs near the rear of the camp. We took the trouble to chase him so as to have a near view. Sister Spalding and myself got out of the wagon and ran upon the bluff to see him. This band was quite willing to gratify our curiosity, seeing it was the first. Several have been killed this forenoon. The Company keep a man out all the time to hunt for the camp. (*Transactions of the Twenty-First Annual Reunion of the Oregon Pioneer Association for 1893,* 1894, 104–107.)

4. The Oregon Trail

In 1843, Dr. Marcus Whitman, who had been East on mission business, led a large party of settlers over the Rocky Mountains to Oregon. More followed in 1844, and the future of the territory as an American outpost was assured. The arrival of the emigrants at the Indian mission is described below by Narcissa Whitman.

WAIILATPU, Oct. 9th, 1844.

Beloved and Honored Parents:—I have no answered letters on hand, either from dear father and mother or any of the family, yet I cannot refrain from writing every stated opportunity. The season has arrived when the emigrants are beginning to pass us on their way to the Willamette. Last season there were such a multitude of starving people passed us that quite drained us of all our provisions, except potatoes. Husband has been endeavoring this summer to cultivate so as to be able to impart without so much distressing ourselves. In addition to this, he has been obliged to build a mill, and to do it principally with his own hands, which has rendered it exceedingly laborious for him. In the meantime, I have endeavored to lighten his burden as much as possible in superintending the ingathering of the garden, etc. During this period, the Indians belonging to this station and the Nez Perces go to Forts Hall and Boise to meet the emigrants for the purpose of trading their wornout cattle for horses. Last week Tuesday, several young men arrived, the first of the party that brought us any definite intelligence concerning them (having nothing but Indian reports previous), among whom was a youth from Rushville formerly, of the name of Gilbert, one of husband's scholars.

Last Friday a family of eight arrived, including the grandmother, an aged woman, probably as old, or older than my mother. Several such persons have passed, both men and women, and I often think when I gaze upon them, shall I ever be permitted to look upon the face of my dear parents in this land?

25th—When I commenced this letter I intended to write a little every day, so as to give you a picture of our situation at this time. But it has been impossible. Now I must write as briefly as possible and send off my letter, or lose the opportunity. The emigration is late in getting into the country. It is now the last of October and they have just begun to arrive with their wagons. The Blue mountains are covered with snow, and many families, if not half of the party, are back in or beyond the mountains, and what is still worse, destitute of provisions and some of them of clothing. Many are sick, several with children born on the way. One family arrived here night before last, and the next morn a child was born; another is expected in the same condition.

Here we are, one family alone, a way mark, as it were, or center post, about which multitudes will or must gather this winter. And these we must feed and warm to the extent of our powers. Blessed be God that He has given us so abundantly of the fruit of the earth that we may impart to those who are thus famishing. Two preachers with large families are here and wish to stay for the winter, both Methodist. With all this upon our hands, besides our duties and labors for the Indians, can any one think we lack employment or have any time to be idle?

Mr. and Mrs. Littlejohn left us in September and have gone below to settle in the Willamette. We have been looking for associates this fall, but the Board could get none ready, but say, they will send next year. Am I ever to see any of my family among the tide of emigration that is flowing west?

We have employed a young man of the party to teach school, so that we hope to have both an English school and one for the natives. . . .

This country is destined to be filled, and we desire greatly to have good people come, and ministers and Christians, that it may be saved from being a sink of wickedness and prostitution. We need many houses to accommodate the families that will be obliged to winter here. All the house room that we have to spare is filled already. It is expected that there are more than five hundred souls back in the snow and mountains. Among the number is an orphan family of seven children, the youngest an infant born on the way, whose parents have both died since they left the States. Application has been made for us to take them, as they have not a relative in the company. What we shall do I cannot say; we cannot see them suffer, if the Lord casts them upon us. He will give us His grace and strength to do our duty to them.

I cannot write any more, I am so thronged and employed that I feel sometimes like being crazy, and my poor husband, if he had a hundred strings tied to him pulling in every direction, could not be any worse off.

Dear Parents, do pray earnestly for your children here, for their situation is one of great trial, as well as of responsibility.

Love from us both to you all. I am disappointed in not getting letters from some of the dear ones this fall, but so it must be and I submit.

Your affectionate daughter,
NARCISSA.

(*Transactions of the Twenty-First Annual Reunion of the Oregon Pioneer Association for 1893, 66–68.*)

5. The Missouri Frontier

A glimpse of the sod-house frontier is found in the diary of Timothy Hill, who went as a New School missionary to northeast Missouri in 1845.

Evening, preached at Mrs. ——'s schoolhouse, about 25 hearers. Read and attempted to sing "Whilst Thee I Seek." No one followed with me, and I became somewhat confused. Read another hymn, which I sang to Ortonville, with no better success than before. Addressed the people half an hour from Matt. 25: 19, with but little apparent interest, and little satisfaction to myself. Found my singing displeased the people much. "Queer preacher this, much like a Roman Catholic!" . . .

Arrived at Mr. ——'s about sunset. His house is a small, miserable cabin, with but one room, and a chimney the outside of which is made of turf from the prairie! The inside has a rude floor of oak plank. Its furniture was two beds, a closed cupboard, and a much larger looking glass than is often found anywhere in this country, together with the necessary articles for the most ordinary culinary purposes. This is the habitation of a minister; but he seemed contented and happy, and I would not wish to make him discontented. . . .

Slavery here is strong. It affects every nerve and fibre of society, and acts like a paralysis, and is a prime obstacle in the way of him who would labor for the good of this community. . . . There are as many slaves connected with the families of those connected with the churches here as there are members in those families; and not a single person (slave) that I have heard of can read the Bible; and there are not half a dozen that make any pretensions to piety. They are almost never called in to be present at family worship. . . . I have felt my heart alsink within me as I addressed the Throne of Grace with the family, when my thoughts wandered to that dark kitchen where the slave must remain. To him no Bible is opened; for him no prayer is heard. Very few attend preaching where I am, and I know of no way in which they are instructed. I do not know of a single master or mistress that ever teaches them any systematic, religious truth. Sad, sad is their condition, and I do not see a cloud as big as a man's hand that portends their emancipation. . . . I could not say a syllable in private to the slaves themselves without setting in motion a train of opposition which would soon drive me from the State. The masters are nearly as inaccessible as the slaves. They are sensitive and suspicious to a very great degree; and the simple fact that I am a "Yankee" arouses their suspicions at once. . . .

I have come to the conclusion to wait quietly and discharge every duty in my power until the close of the year, and then as quietly *leave this State,* and seek a field of labor in a State where the curse of Slavery is not found. . . .

Rode all day alone, for many miles across a prairie nearly at water level, and found myself at night at Centerville, a miserable, whisky-soaked place. While waiting at the store for information and direction to a place of entertainment for the night, I inquired in what county and what part of it I was, and was told "In the southest of Macon." "Yes," said a young man, "you are right—in the southest corner of hell!" Shocked at the expression, I accosted him: "Young man, you and I can easily get out of this place; but you are fast going to a hell from which there is no escape, and it becomes you not to trifle with Eternity." The effect was almost magical, for he slid off immediately, and a change was seen in the conduct of everyone around. They in the store came to the door, and looked earnestly at me, as if in doubt what sort of man could be here. (*Diary of Timothy Hill,* ed. by J. B. Hill, *Journal P.H.S.,* XXV, 8 ff.)

6. "We Are Pioneers": California, 1850

Both Old and New School missionaries were among the thousands of "forty-niners" who participated in the great California gold rush. On April 1, 1850, Rev. Albert Williams of the First Presbyterian Church of San Francisco (O.S.) published an eight-page magazine called The Watchman. *In it are the following extracts from the sermon delivered before the first meeting of the Presbytery of San Francisco by Rev. T. B. Hunt.*

We must all have been impressed with the energy of this people. We are astonished, not more at the rapidity with which they fill the land, than with the energy with which they set to work. How quick the step! How soon their plans are matured and in operation! How hasty the pass-word! How absorbed the thoughts! Towns spring up as if by magic; steamboats already ply our bay and rivers; civil organizations are taking place; a State constitution is already formed. Our senators and representatives will soon be heard in the halls of our national legislature. Everything commercial and civil seems destined to a rapid growth. For this there is capital—for there are men of intelligence. For all civil and temporary organizations and improvements there is an imperative necessity which men *feel*. Their interest, their safety, demand it. But their religious interests are the last things thought of.

In the whirl of busy life men have few thoughts of God and the future. With business men the struggle is for wealth. With professional men it is for both wealth and distinction. We have witnessed, with pain, the defection of Church members. We have, with fearful apprehension, seen how soon the sons of the pious, trained in the Sabbath-school and in the sanctuary, have here forgotten both the Sabbath and the house of God. We have been astonished at the boldness with which vice has stationed itself on our plazas and in our streets. Our hearts have sighed over the thoughtlessness and recklessness of young and old. Have we not felt, Oh, for a thousand tongues to preach the gospel! Have we not longed to be in every place where this rushing, busy, thoughtless population were concentrating, that we might cry aloud and spare not? Have we not seen enough to convince us that the ministry here must be one of great activity and devotedness? Who but ministers of the gospel must call the attention of this people to the education of youth? Whose voice will be heard in behalf of the suffering, the homeless, the poor and the ignorant, if our tongues are silent? Who will transmit religious intelligence? who will appeal to the heart of the nation? who will direct the first religious press, and lay the foundation of a religious literature on the Pacific, if our pens lie idle? And how shall we attract this people to the house of God—how cultivate habits of sacred remembrance and observance of the Lord's day—except we render our pulpit instructions both pleasing and useful. To whom may fathers and mothers, pastors and teachers, beyond the mountains, commit their sons, and the lambs of their flocks, and their beloved pupils, if not to us! And to whom, if not to us, shall the returning prodigal confess his sins—to whom, if not to us, look for guidance and a friend? . . .

In conclusion, brethren, let me call your attention to the *position we occupy.* We are *pioneers;* and not more certainly do the first settlers of the wilderness determine the location and the shape of the town, and the character of the population that will grow around them, than we, under the great Head of the Church, shall determine the character and fruitfulness of the vine we cultivate, and the branches we may transplant. The government we adopt will be transmitted to our successors. The discipline we enforce will be continued when we shall have ceased to keep the fold. The habits we may cultivate among our people will govern the devotions and the labors of those who come after them. We are laying the foundations on which others are to build. We are preparing ground where others are to sow and reap. . . . Brethren, let our own standard of closet, study, pulpit and pastoral duties be *high.* Let us be ourselves devoted christians, diligent students, earnest and instructive preachers, faithful pastors, and patrons and guardians of all that is good and useful. Thus let us endeavor to give character to the future ministry of our State. Secondly, let us train our churches to habits of devotion and beneficence—to pray, to act, to give. Let us endeavor to impress them with their obligation to *share with us* the responsibility of the present and the future. . . .

Brethren, many eyes are upon us. The outpost we now occupy will soon be an important centre. Commercial men know this, and the eyes of capitalists are upon every portion of the land. The attention of philanthropists and christians is also directed hither. While statesmen and men of the world are watching the progress of politics and commerce, the Church also waits with eagerness for the religious developments of this far-off land. Much do our brethren beyond the mountains *expect of us.* Let us not disappoint them. And eyes from *above,* too, are upon us. Oh! may there be perpetual joy in heaven over sinners converted, through our instrumentality, to God! (*The Watchman,* San Francisco, April 1, 1850, reprinted in *Journal P.H.S.,* XXIII, 73 ff.)

7. "Presbyterian Publications"

Presbyterians were rather slow in entering the publishing field. Many questioned the propriety of the Church going into business. In 1838, however, the Old School Assembly authorized a Board of Publication. The following plans for circulating "a choice selection of books" is a reminder of the part played by the religious press in the intellectual history of America.

The Presbyterian Board of Publication, under the care of the General Assembly, commenced its operations in the year 1840. The object contemplated in its establishment, was to furnish the church with a choice selection of books, which should at once prove interesting and instructive. . . .

While the press is pouring forth cheap publications, which only have a tendency to corrupt the morale of the community, and to ruin the principles of the youth of our land, it becomes the clear duty of every friend of the gospel to aid in the circulation of religious books. Here is an opportunity. Ministers, ruling elders, and private Christians, you are affectionately urged to co-operate in this good work. It will profit your own souls; it may be the means of saving your own families, and the souls of your neighbours.

Who can calculate the good that may be done by the perusual of a single good book? A whole family, a whole neighbourhood, has been made to feel the effects, not only in time, but in eternity. Will you then refuse to expend a little money, and devote a little labour, in giving circulation to these books? Will you not readily devote a portion of your time, as well as your money, in giving success to this enterprise? It is exceedingly desirable that in our growing country, every family should be provided with a few choice religious books, besides their Bibles. Let us all help to furnish them.

Be pleased to ponder these objects:—

1st. Every congregation should have a congregational library, which should be regularly supplied with every book the Board publishes.

2d. Besides this, every family in a congregation should have for their own use a few of the best works published by the Board, to which they can constantly recur.

3d. Every congregation should purchase a number of copies of such books as Baxter's Call, Baxter's Saint's Rest, Doddridge's Rise and Progress, Alleine's Alarm, Almost Christian &c. &c. to lend or give away to persons in their neighbourhood, who belong to no church, and feel no interest in religion.

4th. Presbyterians who are desirous of having the doctrines of their church well understood, especially when many enemies are studiously caricaturing and perverting them, should purchase a few books on this subject to lend and circulate.

Presbyterians are now called on to labour for the gospel as it is understood by their own church. It is certainly not unreasonable to expect that they will give their preference to Presbyterian institutions and Presbyterian publications.

To effect their object, the Board have employed travelling agents and colporteurs to carry the books to every congregation and to every family. The object of the agent will be to present the subject, and to use his efforts to enlist the co-operation of all zealous Christians in the great work. (*Plan for Circulating the Books of the Presbyterian Board of Publication*, n.d., 2.)

8. The Colporteur

The humble colporteur or book agent is one of the forgotten men of Presbyterian history. Many of them combined a simple and sincere evangelism with their sales talks, and reached Americans untouched by other religious agencies. The following narratives are from Indiana and Minnesota.

As I was passing from Prairieville to Whitewater, I overtook five lead teams returning from Milwaukie. The teamsters were sitting under a tree while their oxen were resting. I asked them if they wanted any religious books. "Have you no novels?" said they. "None," I replied; "I am a christian, and sell none but christian books." One of them bought Nelson's Cause and Cure of Infidelity, another the Spirit of Popery, and another Bean's Advice. "Well," said one, "now, boys, we'll have something to do besides play cards when we stop nights and Sundays." Said I, "do you play cards, friends?" "O, yes," they returned, "except him," pointing to one of their number, "he's a Cumberland, and is our preacher." "Have you a pack on hand?" "Yes." "Will you sell them?" "For books? Yes. What will you give for them?" Handing out Baxter's Call and Alleine's Alarm, I offered those for the pack, and we made the exchange. I then gave them a lecture on the folly of spending their time in this manner. They voluntarily promised never to own or use cards any more. I asked them if they had a fire, as that would be the quickest way of cooking the cards. As they had none, I took my knife and began cutting the pack into shreds, in which two of the party assisted me. After giving them some good advice I drove on and left them. (*Facts Illustrating the Necessity, Method and Results of Colportage*, n.p., n.d., 6.)

Many of the poor people that I call on in my travels in Blackford county (Indiana), say they would like to have some of my books, but they are out of money. Some days I have travelled and not sold a book. Many of them are new comers, and have built cabins in the woods, and are living in them without being daubed, with very little improvement, and entirely without any kind of books. In some of these poor cabins a colporteur meets the most hearty welcome. Many times I forget I am not in a palace. You may judge how it is, when I tell you that I have not been charged one night's lodging for one year. I might give you many things of interest. In travelling through M—— county, in the forepart of the summer, I called on a young Lutheran preacher. He said he was glad to see me, as he wished me to visit a small congregation out in the country. I had been with some of them. I visited every family, and found every one a praying family, and all bought of my books.

This little band of brothers, although they are surrounded with the most degraded people of all classes, kept up a prayer-meeting, and that in the country, every night, summer and winter, seed-time and harvest, and for some years continue to have three meetings every week. Often when I would get cold and lifeless, and feel almost as if I should leave the field, through the corruptness of my evil and deceitful heart, and the cold reception of infidelity and Universalism, I would, in this lifeless condition, go to some of these warm-hearted brethren, and in the morning go on my way rejoicing. I will give one instance: After staying with one of these families over-night, the man told me of an old man about sixty-five years old, a very hard case—an infidel, who had been raised a Presbyterian. He wished me to call on him. Had I gone the day before, I suppose he would have put me out of the house, but this morning I felt above the fear of man—I introduced myself as a Presbyterian colporteur. I showed him my books, told him the object of the Board in sending us out, and showed him our Catechism and new Hymn Book, and told him how many colporteurs were in the field, scattering the bread of life, and some of the success of our labours, and exhorted him to his duty, as he was getting old. It brought up his early training; he was melted down in view of his departure from the truth, and bought the Confession, Hymn Book, and Catechism. I spent a very interesting hour with him, and bade farewell till the judgment of the great day, when the result of our labours will be fully made known to an assembled world. This is one of many such cases. (*Fifteenth Annual Report of the Board of Publication of the Presbyterian Church in the United States of America,* 1853, 25.)

9. Public Worship

Contemporary trends in worship are revealed in the following resolutions of the General Assembly (O.S.), 1849.

Posture in Prayer

While the posture of standing in public prayer, and that of kneeling in private prayer, are indicated by examples in Scripture, and the general practice of the ancient Christian Church, the posture of sitting in public prayer is nowhere mentioned, and by no usage allowed; but on the contrary, was universally regarded by the early Church as heathenish and irreverent; and is still, even in the customs of modern and western nations, an attitude obviously wanting in the due expression of reverence: therefore this General Assembly resolve, that the practice in question be considered grievously improper, whenever the infirmities of the worshipper do not render it necessary; and that Ministers be required to reprove it with earnest and persevering admonition. (*Minutes of the G.A., O.S., 1849, 255.*)

ON READING SERMONS

Whereas, This General Assembly has reason to believe that the practice of reading sermons in the pulpit is on the increase amongst our Ministers; and being decidedly of opinion that it is not the most effective and acceptable method of preaching the gospel; therefore,

Resolved, That we do earnestly repeat the recommendation of the Assembly of 1841, that this practice be discontinued as far as practicable; and and affectionately exhort our younger Ministers and candidates for the ministry to adopt a different method, as more scriptural and effective, and more generally acceptable to God's people. (*Minutes of the G.A., O.S., 1849, 271.*)

10. General Education

In 1847, Cortland Van Rensselaer, the new Secretary of the Board of Education, presented to the Assembly (O.S.) a plan for a system of elementary and secondary education throughout the Church. The scheme was adopted, and by 1853 there were some one hundred and one primary schools and forty-six academies under the care of local sessions and of the Board. Van Rensselaer's dream was that parochial schools would solve the dual problem of increased secularization and a declining supply of candidates for the ministry. The scheme, however, was too costly, and after 1870 was abandoned by the Church. (See L. J. Sherrill, Presbyterian Parochial Schools, *New Haven, 1932.*)

The general tendency of things in this country is unquestionably to dishonour the religious element in the system of education under the patronage of the State. This sufficiently accounts for the growing dissatisfaction of Christians, in all parts of the country, with the whole plan of political supervision. A general system of education that shall be a Christian system appears to be a State impracticability.

The increasing abandonment of the State plan by various sects of Christians affords a proper occasion for the Presbyterian Church to reconsider her position in regard to the work of Education. The Papists with that church-worldly wisdom which is so pre-eminently theirs, have adopted the plan of educating their own children—and ours too, as far as they can. Their institutions of learning have all the efficiency of an independent religious organization. Papal colleges, seminaries, and Church schools of every kind are in active operation all over the country and especially at the west. If we would save the lambs of our flock from the St. Mary Christianity of the Man of Sin, our schools must engage our efforts and our prayers. The Episcopalians, with characteristic zeal, are also establishing large and small institutions on a denominational basis. Many of their churches have parochial schools, while Presbyterians scarcely know the meaning of the word. The Methodists, in addition to several denominational colleges, have academies in all their Conferences, and are in this respect setting an example of well-manned, popular Church institutions. Whilst other denominations are more and more defining their position in favour of Christian education under their own supervision, Presbyterians are reminded of their obligations to develop the resources of their own Church in this great cause.

Our denomination, in re-modelling its school system on the proposed basis, would be only *returning to the good old ways of its former history*. Presbyterian schools, in other times, were religious schools. Religion was much more extensively taught in them than it now is even in what are called "select schools." The education of the country was once in a great degree under our own care; or at least we had the care of our own children. But the encroachments of a false liberality have so far banished Presbyterian and evangelical influence, that the education of our children is now mixed up with the politics of the State and knows nothing of the religion of the Church. It has become so fashionable to be liberal that even "select schools" often dispense with evangelical truth in order to please all Christian denominations! It is high time for the Presbyterian Church to fall back upon her glorious old landmarks; and what we cannot now do for all, we must endeavour to do for ourselves in the matter of thorough Christian education.

But what is meant by a *parochial school?* The term is imported from abroad; and ought to have come in duty-free, instead of being subjected to the heavy State tax which now almost amounts to prohibition. The idea of a parochial or *primary Church school* would with us embrace in general the following particulars:

1. A school under the care of the Session of a Church; 2. Designed for children, say from five to ten or twelve years of age; 3. In which the usual branches of a sound elementary education are taught; 4. *With the addition of daily religious instruction from the Bible;* 5. Under the superintendence of a *Christian teacher.* The probability is that most of the teachers would be females, especially in the country schools.

In addition to these primary schools, others of a high order might be needed to supply the wants of some congregations. The completion of the system would demand academies under the care of Presbyteries, and colleges under the care of one or more Synods. . . .

Action of the General Assembly

Resolved, That this Assembly do hereby express their firm conviction that the interests of the Church and the glory of our Redeemer demand that immediate and strenuous exertions should be made, as far as practicable in every congregation, to establish within its bounds one or more primary schools, under the care of the Session of the church, in which, together with the usual branches of secular learning, the truths and duties of our holy religion shall be assiduously inculcated. (*Report of the Board of Education on Parochial Schools,* Philadelphia, 1847, 4 ff.)

11. A Presbyterian Parochial School

The following is the report of a Presbyterian parochial school in 1856.

We would hereby respectfully communicate a statement of the condition of the Parochial School under our care. The winter session closed yesterday, March 19th, and although the day was very stormy, the examination was well attended, and all the closing exercises highly interesting.

The following exhibits the number of scholars, and the branches taught during the session, viz.

Whole number in attendance,	45
Average attendance,	35
In English Grammar,	24
" Latin,	3
" Geography,	23
" Arithmetic,	35
" Modern History,	18
" Ancient History,	11

"	Mensuration,	6
"	Astronomy,	10
"	Algebra,	7
"	Assembly's Shorter Catechism,	35
"	Bible History,	35
"	Essays,	20
"	Elocution,	25
"	Defining Words,	20

The scholars have been more regular in their daily attendance than formerly, and as might reasonably be expected, have made very creditable progress in all their studies. Their general deportment has been good, and they seem also to appreciate their privileges, which may be observed in their keenness for learning, diligence, and love of the daily duties and exercises in the school-room.

As observed in former reports, the standard of education is low, but public attention is being turned to the work. This school operates as a normal school for the township, as it supplies the free schools with teachers. Nearly all these schools are opened each morning with reading a portion of Scripture, and close each day's exercises with singing a hymn.

The cry of sectarianism has not troubled us near so much as our fears. Instead of being assailed with the cry of sectarian school, as we expected, we are agreeably disappointed, and find the sect that was formerly spoken against, now treated with more consideration and respect.

We do not know that any of the scholars have been hopefully converted as yet, but we believe that if they are trained up in the way they should go, when they are old they will not depart from it.

From the beginning, we have had more or less of poor scholars in attendance, who are not able to pay their tuition. These, if worthy poor, we have not rejected, and will not, if we can give the teacher an adequate support, and meet the contingent expenses of the institution. And we trust that under the good providence that has brought us thus far, we will be able to report a better state of finances in time to come.

You will please accept this as our half year's report. All which is respectfully submitted. (*Report of Board of Education*, 1856, 22 f.)

12. "Hopeful Subjects of Divine Grace"

Presbyterian colleges were not only academic institutions but centers of recurring religious revivals. The whole Church watched and prayed for the seasons of spiritual awakening that led scores of young men into the ministry or mission field. The following is an account of a revival at Oglethorpe University, North Carolina.

The revival during the past winter afforded a most striking and encouraging instance of direct answer to prayer. It began on the night of the last Thursday of February, the day set apart for the annual concert for prayer, in behalf of colleges. After public services in the chapel during the day, the pious students appointed a special prayer meeting in one of the recitation rooms at night. To their wonder and delight, a large number of their fellow-students were present, who were not in the habit of attending such meetings.

There had been up to that hour no special indications of the presence of God's Spirit. At that meeting, however, whilst engaged in singing, prayer, and reading the Word, a powerful influence came down upon them, and the whole assembly was bathed in tears. Worldly professors were smitten with remorse; careless sinners were pricked to the heart; and one that had been sorrowing under conviction for sin, found hope in Christ. From that night, a series of daily religious meetings were kept up for weeks. They were arranged in such a way as not to interfere with any literary exercise, except occasionally an individual was so overwhelmed with a sense of sinfulness, that he asked and obtained permission from his professor to be absent from a few recitations of his class.

For several weeks, the hours of relaxation were generally employed by the students in meetings for prayer and religious conversation. The voice of prayer and praise could be heard in all directions by a passer by. The groves and secret places of retirement in the fields around the college, were vocal with humble petitions, and with their songs of Zion. A very large proportion of the non-professing students were hopeful subjects of Divine grace;—though the faculty have advised most of the students, as being young, to deliberate well, and, especially, to confer with their friends, at home, before making a public profession of religion.

When the session closed, such was the predominant influence of religion, that profanity and vice dared not to show their heads. A young man, suspected of vicious habits, was shunned as an improper associate, and the whole tone and character of the students were on the side of virtue and piety.

Of the senior class, consisting of fifteen, all but one professed a hope in Christ. Of these, a large majority have selected the Christian ministry as their chosen work. A spirit of self-consecration, and an interest in foreign missions, have been awakened, throughout the institution, which promise happy results. (*Thirty-third Annual Report of the Board of Education*, 1852, 23.)

13. "New Themes for the Protestant Clergy"

In 1852 the Old School Presbyterian Magazine, *reviewing* New Themes for the Protestant Clergy, *exclaimed, "We deeply regret that any Protestant Church should have the credit for such a volume." Time, however, has shown that Stephen Colwell, a Presbyterian elder, was one of the first to see the religious implications of the new American industrialism, and was thus a pioneer of the social gospel.*

It is plain that the institutions of this world, political, social, commercial, and industrial, we had almost said religious, partake little of the spirit of Christ; and yet his ministers and disciples are its most noted and uncompromising defenders. Is it because these ministers and disciples are so well treated by the world, that they are in such strict league with it, and are so prompt to take its part? All over Christendom, masses of men, long oppressed, are rising clamorous for relief, and a better condition. Light from Christianity has broken upon the night of their ignorance and helplessness, and they know that they are entitled to something better in the world's portion than has been allotted them. But the whole truth has not been told them, and their notions of remedy are wild and impracticable. This great movement should be met by Christians with rejoicing that light is at length penetrating such a dark mass of ignorance; and they should hasten to hold up to them the precepts of Christ, as meeting their entire case, and providing a complete remedy for all their grievances. But how is it that the outcries of these masses who have been hitherto strangers to the voice of Christian kindness, are now met by both Romanist and Protestant with a stern frown of rebuke and rejection?

Christ is not preached to these poor, suffering millions, as all-sufficient for them; much less do they anywhere behold any Christian movement in their behalf, which might at once explain to them their errors and show them their remedy. They are not sought for in the lanes and highways, and invited, nay, compelled, to come into the feast of life; but they are rudely driven from the door as they present themselves, and are told that there is no room, no remedy, no alleviation; that the laws of property and the arrangements of society utterly forbid any amelioration of their sad condition. Thus it is that religion purchases her peace with this present world, by sustaining its institutions; thus it is that Christ is denied, to purchase a liberal provision for his ministers; thus it is that, whilst these ministers assume the office of denouncing this world, its maxims, its follies, its oppressions, its greediness of gain; they deny that privilege to those who are enduring the bitterest lot that can befall humanity. Christ did not so: He went first to the poor, and administered succour and comfort to them; and that such is the chief duty of his disciples now is as clear as the words of inspiration can make it. If Christ were to appear again on a mission to earth, he would go again to the multitudes; he would be seen again in the abodes of the poor; he would again claim no resting-place for his head; he would again repeat his words of solace to the lowly, and his works of mercy to the suffering. He would find little time for Protestant observances, and little occasion for their temples. His ministry would conform to his precepts; and many who repeat "Lord, Lord!" and claim to be his special and favourite disciples, would find themselves objects of his sternest indignation and most withering rebukes. The race of Pharisees and priests and false teachers is not extinct; they would again treat their Master with contempt and scorn, or utter neglect, if his associations were among the poor and lowly.

What, then, is to be done? No violent revolution is required. No despot is to be hunted from his place; no blood is to be shed; no legislation is indispensable; no new sect in religion or philosophy need be formed, nor in the first instance, need any one desert the position in which Providence has placed him. What is required is, that ever one who is, or who believes himself to be, a true disciple of Christ, should at once resolve so far as in his power, and so far as he might be favoured with divine aid, to live in this world according to the teachings of his Master. As soon as the Great law of doing to others as we would others should do to us begins to be exemplified, the reign of wrong, and injury, and extreme suffering will come rapidly to an end. Instead of one Howard, one Mrs. Fry, and one Miss Dix in a century, we should have thousands upon thousands, in every department of charity. When we look at what these three individuals have accomplished, what might we not expect from millions labouring with united strength and intellect in the great work of human welfare?

As soon as the law of charity is fulfilled on an extensive scale, in all its Christian beauty and loveliness, the world will pause to admire and believe and imitate. The apostles as well as their great Master mingled their preaching with incessant care of the poor and the suffering; it should be so now. Christians may not fold their arms, and be inactive, because there is an almshouse, a poorhouse, or a benevolent society. There should be no suffering within the reach of any Christian that he can relieve or alleviate, without making the attempt. It is not Christianity to attend weekly in the stately church and well-cushioned pew, to hear expositions of difficult passages of Scripture, while there is an utter failure to perform duties which are so plainly enjoined that the dullest intellect can comprehend. Nor does the most punctual attendance upon the Sunday-school, or upon lectures or weekly meetings for prayer, make up for neglect of the higher duties of charity. If the preacher and people in our rich and well-ordered congregations were, in the midst of the gravest sermon, suddenly visited from on high with a deep and adequate conception of their transgressions of the law of charity, and of the duties which they owe to those who are outside of the church; if they were made to realize the great contrast between their condition and that of those who were abroad and around them, their seats would in a moment become insupportable, and they would rush in a mass, preacher and people, from their splendid edifice, to the courts and alleys and cellars, to the abodes of destitution, ignorance, crime, and suffering. They would carry succour for present wants; and *all* would become teachers of the way of life. In vain do we preach, and in vain do we teach, unless we carry obedience to what we do understand, into our lives; our progress in knowledge of divine things must be limited by our actual progress in the practical duties of Christianity.

No people can ever fully comprehend Christianity but those who comply with its requisitions; and of course the world can never appreciate it until its laws of love are shown by example. This distinguishing feature of Christianity is that which Christians have most slighted. More attention has been given in our churches and Sunday-schools to Jewish manners, customs, ceremonies—to the ornaments of the tabernacle and temple—to breastplates and phylacteries, than to the obligations of brotherly kindness. There are fountains of tenderness in every human bosom; they are not taught to gush forth and flow in streams which no harshness of this world can ever check: there are chords of love in every breast; these are not taught to respond to every appeal for sympathy and succour. (*New Themes for the Protestant Clergy*, Philadelphia, 1852.)

14. "Our Duty to the Immigrants"

The problems presented by the foreign-speaking population also provided a new theme for Protestant preachers. The following extract is from a sermon by Dr. Scott of New Orleans—one of the gateways of the West.

One of the effects of the recent revolutions of Europe has been to unfetter the press. And as knowledge is imparted to the people through a free press, so will they gain information concerning this country and about their own rights; and in the same degree a majority of them will grow stronger in their aversion to their oppressors, and in the desire of finding a home in America. Our duty to immigrants does not properly come within my present purpose, but I cannot forbear to say that it comprehends the three following things:

First—To receive them kindly. The earth is the Lord's and the fulness thereof. The Almighty has not given this earth to a few families of any one nation and to their descendants only. He has not *patented* out this glorious land to any royal lines. He has made it the asylum of the oppressed from every clime—the homes of the brave. The ragged, the outcast, the starving, the ignorant, as well as the educated, the refined, and the wealthy, who seek a home amongst us, should be welcomed to our shores; and the country of their adoption should not be their stepmother, but fold them to her bosom as those born of her own vitals. Talk not to me of their unworthiness, nor of their vices. It is enough that they are wretched; it is enough that they are within reach of our sympathies. A *stranger, and you took me in*—is worth infinitely more than all the sagacity ever displayed in detecting impostors. I repeat it, then, our first duty is to receive them kindly—make them feel that we are a Christian people, and that we look upon them as men, made in the image of God, and heirs of a glorious immortality.

Secondly—We should provide for their immediate wants. I have not now time to amplify the way in which this should be done. Doubtless, however, poor foreigners, who are thrown into our large towns and cities, should be sent as soon as possible into the interior, where there is room enough and to spare, and where, in one twelvemonth after their arrival, they can all support themselves. They should be protected against the land-sharks who infest our wharves. They should, by means of cheap tracts and newspapers, be instructed in the nature of our climate and soil, and the way to get into the interior, and the way to make an independent living. I am not now speaking of religious or political tracts, but of tracts for the people on common subjects.

A House of Refuge, or an Asylum for the Poor, of all ages, is very much needed in this city. As our police is now administered, there is great cruelty and injustice in classing the poor with the convict. . . .

The foreign poor in our streets is not a tithe of what it will be in a few years; and the sooner and the more effectively some judicious mode of assisting them is devised by us, the better for them and for us. American pauperism is a term that happily has hitherto had no place in our history; but in our Atlantic towns, at least, it will soon call so loudly for relief, that legislators, and citizens, and property-holders, as well as philanthropists, will be obliged to attend to it.

Thirdly—We must educate the children of foreigners, and by every proper means seek to imbue them both old and young, with the spirit of Christ. The two great instruments by which this can be done, are public schools and domestic missions. These are the two great agencies intrusted to American philanthropists and Christians, by which to regenerate so much of the Old World as God in His providence may cast upon the bosom of the New. Of all secular agencies by which to do good to foreigners, there is nothing to compare to our Free Public School system; and if there was not a single native-born child benefited by our Public Schools, they should be fostered and upheld through every obstacle, for the sake of the child of the stranger within our gates, and for the sake of the orphan committed to the State by its Almighty Father. I do not mean that public schools should be for such only—by no means; they are and should be, open to all, rich and poor, native and foreign, but I mean that they are of the very first importance in view of immigrants to this country. It is there they begin to taste the sweets of liberty; it is there they begin to learn something of our blessed institutions, and to know how to enjoy them. (*The Home and Foreign Record*, Vol. III, 1852, 225–226.)

15. The United Presbyterian Church

In 1858, after twenty years of correspondence and conferences, the Associate Synod and the Associate Reformed Synod, both descended from Scottish Seceders, united to form the United Presbyterian Church of North America. The new Church took a strong position on the questions of slavery, close communion, and psalmody.

I. *We declare*, That God has not only in the Scriptures of the Old and New Testaments made a revelation of his will to man, as the only rule of faith and practice, but that these Scriptures, viewed as a revelation from God, are in every way the inspired word of God, and that this inspiration extends to the language, as well as to the sentiments which they express. . . .

XIII. *We declare*, That the law of God, as written upon the heart of man, and as set forth in the Scriptures of the Old and New Testaments, is supreme in its authority and obligations; and that where the commands of the Church or State are in conflict with the commands of this law, we are to obey God rather than man.

XIV. *We declare,* That slaveholding—that is, the holding of unoffending human beings in involuntary bondage, and considering and treating them as property, and subject to be bought and sold—is a violation of the law of God, and contrary both to the letter and spirit of Christianity.

XV. *We declare,* That all associations, whether formed for political or benevolent purposes, which impose upon their members an oath of secrecy, or an obligation to obey a code of unknown laws, are inconsistent with the genius and spirit of Christianity, and Church members ought not to have fellowship with such associations.

XVI. *We declare,* That the Church should not extend communion, in sealing ordinances, to those who refuse adherence to her profession, or subjection to her government and discipline, or who refuse to forsake a communion which is inconsistent with the profession that she makes; nor should communion in any ordinance of worship be held under such circumstances as would be inconsistent with the keeping of these ordinances pure and entire, or so as to give countenance to any corruption of the doctrines and institutions of Christ.

XVII. *We declare,* That public social covenanting is a moral duty, the observance of which is not required at stated times, but on extraordinary occasions, as the providence of God and the circumstances of the Church may indicate. It is seasonable in times of great danger to the Church—in times of exposure to backsliding—or in times of reformation, when the Church is returning to God from a state of backsliding. When the Church has entered into such covenant transactions, they continue to bind posterity faithfully to adhere to and prosecute the grand object for which such engagements have been entered into.

XVIII. *We declare,* That it is the will of God that the songs contained in the Book of Psalms be sung in his worship, both public and private, to the end of the world; and in singing God's praise, these songs should be employed to the exclusion of the devotional compositions of uninspired men. (R. E. Thompson, *A History of the Presbyterian Churches in the United States,* 1895, 374 ff.)

CHAPTER

8

THE IRREPRESSIBLE CONFLICT
1861–1869

1. Is Slaveholding a Sin?

As early as 1787 the Synod of New York and Philadelphia had recommended that slaveowners educate and prepare their slaves for freedom, and "use the most prudent measures . . . to procure eventually the final abolition of slavery in America." The Covenanters went much farther and in 1800 "enacted that no slaveholder should be allowed the communion of the Church." In 1811 the Associate Synod declared that "it is a moral evil to hold negroes or their children in perpetual slavery," and required all their members to stop buying or selling slaves. The General Assembly (1818) contented themselves with making the sale of slaves, without their consent, a ground for suspension. Strong feeling in North and South, however, led many local presbyteries to go much farther than the Assembly. The two conflicting pronouncements below appeared on the same day in The New York Evangelist.

Synod of Michigan, Oct. 2
Resolved, That this synod believe the buying, selling and owning of slaves in this country, to be A Sin Before God and man: that the system of American slavery is a great moral, political, physical and social evil, and ought to be *immediately* and universally abandoned—and that it is our duty, by the use of all kind and known means, and especially by cultivating a spirit of sympathy and prayer for the enslaved, and their masters, as well as of general moderation and wisdom in the dissemination of truth and light, to endeavor to hasten the happy day of universal emancipation.

Charleston Union Presbytery
Resolved, that in the opinion of this presbytery, the holding of slaves, so far from being a sin in the sight of God, is nowhere condemned in his Holy Word—that it is in accordance with the example, or consistent with the precepts of patriarchs, prophets and apostles; and that it is

compatible with the most fraternal regard to the best good of those servants whom God may have committed to our charge, and that, therefore, they who assume the contrary position, and lay it down as a fundamental principle in morals and religion, that all slaveholding is wrong, proceed upon false principles.

Resolved, that we deplore the evils incident to slavery, as we do the evils that may attend any and every condition of human society—that these evils may and ought to be mitigated and removed—and that every good man is bound to sustain all rational efforts to accomplish an object so desirable. (*New York Evangelist*, November 21, 1835, 258.)

2. "Domestic Slavery Is No Bar to Christian Communion"

Three positions may be distinguished on the slavery question—the abolitionists, the proslavery, and the so-called conservatives, who believed that the rightness or wrongness of slaveholding depended on the actual circumstances, and hoped for a gradual amelioration of the conditions in the South. This accounts for the reactionary deliverances of 1845 which were passed by the Assembly by a vote of 168 to 13. This remained the official position of the Old School until after the outbreak of the Civil War.

The question which is now unhappily agitating and dividing other branches of the church, and which is pressed upon the attention of the Assembly is, whether the holding of slaves is, under all circumstances, a heinous sin, calling for the discipline of the church.

The church of Christ is a spiritual body, whose jurisdiction extends only to the religious faith, and moral conduct of her members. She cannot legislate where Christ has not legislated, nor make terms of membership which he has not made. The question, therefore, which this Assembly is called upon to decide, is this: Do the Scriptures teach that the holding of slaves, without regard to circumstances, is a sin, the renunciation of which should be made a condition of membership in the church of Christ.

It is impossible to answer this question in the affirmative, without contradicting some of the plainest declarations of the word of God. That slavery existed in the days of Christ and his Apostles is an admitted fact. That they did not denounce the relationship itself as sinful, as inconsistent with Christianity; that slaveholders were admitted to membership in the churches organized by the Apostles; that whilst they were required to treat their slaves with kindness, and as rational, accountable, immortal beings, and if Christians, as brethren in the Lord, they were not commanded to emancipate them; that slaves were required to be "obedient to their masters according to the flesh, with fear and trembling, with singleness of heart as unto Christ," are facts which meet the eye of every reader of the New Testament. This Assembly cannot, therefore, denounce the holding of slaves as necessarily a heinous and scandalous sin, calculated to bring upon the Church the curse of God, without charging the Apostles of Christ with conniving at such sin, introducing into the Church such sinners, and thus bringing upon them the curse of the Almighty.

In so saying, however, the Assembly are not to be understood as denying that there is evil connected with slavery. Much less do they approve those defective and oppressive laws by which, in some of the States, it is regulated. Nor would they by any means countenance the traffic in slaves for the sake of gain; the separation of husbands and wives, parents and children, for the sake of "filthy lucre" or for the convenience of the master; or cruel treatment of slaves in any respect. Every Christian and philanthropist certainly should seek by all peaceable and lawful means the repeal of unjust and oppressive laws, and the amendment of such as are defective, so as to protect the slaves from cruel treatment by wicked men, and secure to them the right to receive religious instruction.

Nor is this Assembly to be understood as countenancing the idea that masters may regard their servants as *mere property*, and not as human beings, rational, accountable, immortal. The Scriptures prescribe not only the duties of servants, but of masters also, warning the latter to discharge those duties, "knowing that their Master is in heaven, neither is there respect of persons with him."

The Assembly intend simply to say, that since Christ and his inspired Apostles did not make the holding of slaves a bar to communion, we, as a court of Christ, have no authority to do so; since they did not attempt to remove it from the Church by legislation, we have no authority to legislate on the subject. We feel constrained, further, to say, that however desirable it may be to ameliorate the condition of the slaves in the Southern and Western States, or to remove slavery from our country, these objects we are fully persuaded can never be secured by ecclesiastical legislation. Much less can they be attained by those indiscriminate denunciations against slave-holders, without regard to their character or circumstances, which have, to so great an extent, characterized the movements of modern abolitionists, which, so far from removing the evils complained of, tend only to perpetuate and aggravate them.

The Apostles of Christ sought to ameliorate the condition of slaves, not by denouncing and excommunicating their masters, but by teaching both masters and slaves the glorious doctrines of the gospel, and enjoining upon each the discharge of their relative duties. Thus only can the church of Christ, as such, now improve the condition of the slaves in our country.

As to the extent of the evils involved in slavery and the best methods of removing them, various opinions prevail, and neither Scriptures nor our constitution authorize this body to prescribe any particular course to be pursued by the churches under our care. The Assembly cannot but rejoice, however, to learn that the ministers and churches in the slave-holding States are awaking to a deeper sense of their obligation to extend to the slave population generally the means of grace, and many slave-holders not professedly religious favour this object. We earnestly exhort every believing master to remember that his Master is also in heaven, and in view of all the circumstances in which he is placed, to act in the spirit of the golden rule: "Whatsoever ye would that men should do to you, do ye even the same to them."

In view of the above stated principles and facts—

RESOLVED, 1st. That the General Assembly of the Presbyterian Church in the United States was originally organized, and has since continued the bond of union in the Church upon the conceded principle that the existence of domestic slavery, under the circumstances in which it is found in the southern portion of the country, is no bar to Christian communion.

2d. That the petitions that ask the Assembly to make the holding of slaves in itself a matter of discipline, do virtually require this judicatory to dissolve itself, and abandon the organization under which, by the Divine blessing, it has so long prospered. The tendency is evidently to separate the northern from the southern portion of the Church; a result which every good citizen must deplore as tending to the dissolution of the union of our beloved country, and which every enlightened Christian will oppose as bringing about a ruinous and unnecessary schism between brethren who maintain a common faith. (*Minutes of the G.A., O.S., 1845, 16.*)

3. "Such Doctrines and Practices Cannot Be Tolerated"

While abolitionism was much more prevalent in the New School churches, their General Assembly was able to side-step the issue until 1850. In that year they declared slaveholding (without mitigating circumstances) to be a breach of discipline. Some Southern sessions ob-

jected to this ruling and were upheld by the Presbytery of Lexington, South. Such a challenge to the authority of the General Assembly could not be overlooked. As a result of the sharp reprimand in the following Act of 1857, representatives of twenty-one Southern presbyteries severed their connection with the New School Assembly and organized the United Synod of the Presbyterian Church. This was the first division in the Presbyterian Church over the question of slavery.

In the year 1846, the General Assembly made a declaration on this subject, of which the following is the introductory paragraph:

"1. The system of slavery as it exists in these United States, viewed either in the laws of the several States which sanction it, or in its actual operation and results in society, is intrinsically an unrighteous and oppressive system, and is opposed to the prescriptions of the law of God, to the spirit and precepts of the Gospel, and to the best interests of humanity."

In 1849, the Assembly explicitly reaffirmed the sentiments expressed by the Assemblies of 1815, 1818, and 1846. In the year 1850, the General Assembly made the following declaration: "We exceedingly deplore the working of the whole system of slavery as it exists in our country and is interwoven with the political institutions of the slave-holding States, as fraught with many and great evils to the civil, political, and moral interests of those regions where it exists.

"The holding of our fellow-men in the condition of slavery, except in those cases where it is unavoidable by the laws of the State, the obligations of guardianship, or the demands of humanity, is an offence in the proper import of that term as used in the Book of Discipline, chap. i, sec. 3, and should be regarded and treated in the same manner as other offences."

Occupying the position in relation to this subject which the framers of our Constitution held at the first, and which our Church has always held, it is with deep grief that we now discover that a portion of the Church at the South has so far departed from the established doctrine of the Church in relation to slavery as to maintain that "it is an ordinance of God," and that the system of slavery existing in these United States is scriptural and right. Against this new doctrine we feel constrained to bear our solemn testimony. It is at war with the whole spirit and tenor of the Gospel of love and good-will, as well as abhorrent to the conscience of the Christian world. We can have no sympathy or fellowship with it; and we exhort all our people to eschew it as serious and pernicious error.

We are especially pained by the fact that the Presbytery of Lexington, South, have given official notice to us that a number of ministers and ruling elders, as well as many church-members, in their connection, hold slaves "from principle" and "of choice," "believing it to be according to the Bible right," and have, without any qualifying explanation, assumed the responsibility of sustaining such ministers, elders, and church-members in their position. We deem it our duty, in the exercise of our constitutional authority "to bear testimony against error in doctrine or immorality in practice in any church, Presbytery, or Synod," to disapprove and earnestly condemn the position which has been thus assumed by the Presbytery of Lexington, South, as one which is opposed to the established convictions of the Presbyterian Church, and must operate to mar its peace and seriously hinder its prosperity, as well as bring reproach on our holy religion; and we do hereby call on that Presbytery to review and rectify their position. Such doctrines and practice cannot be permanently tolerated in the Presbyterian Church. May they speedily melt away under the illuminating and mellowing influence of the Gospel and grace of God our Saviour!

We do not, indeed, pronounce a sentence of indiscriminate condemnation upon all our brethren who are unfortunately connected with the system of slavery. We tenderly sympathize with all those who deplore the evil, and are honestly doing all in their power for the present well-being of their slaves and for their complete emancipation. We would aid and not embarrass such brethren. And yet, in the language of the General Assembly of 1818, we would "earnestly warn them against unduly extending the plea of necessity, against making it a cover for the love and practice of slavery, or a pretence for not using efforts that are lawful and practicable to extinguish this evil."

In conclusion, the Assembly call the attention of the Publication Committee to this subject, and recommend the publication, in a convenient form, of the testimony of the Presbyterian Church touching this subject, at the earliest practicable period.

The vote upon its adoption was by yeas and nays.

Adopted: Yeas, 169; Nays, 26; *non liquet*, 2. (*Minutes of the G.A. N.S.*, 1857, 401–404.)

4. "To Conserve and to Perpetuate the Institution of Domestic Slavery"

The extreme proslavery position was dramatically presented to the nation in a Thanksgiving Day sermon delivered by Rev. Benjamin M. Palmer at the First Presbyterian Church, New Orleans, November 29,

1860. This sermon received wide circulation and served as a rally cry in both North and South. In 1861, Dr. Palmer was chosen to be the first Moderator of the Southern Assembly.

In determining our duty in this emergency, it is necessary that we should first ascertain the nature of the trust providentially committed to us. A nation often has a character as well-defined and intense as that of the individual. This depends, of course, upon a variety of causes, operating through a long period of time. It is due largely to the original traits which distinguish the stock from which it springs, and to the providential training which has formed its education. But, however derived, this individuality of character alone makes any people truly historic, competent to work out its specific mission, and to become a factor in the world's progress. The particular trust assigned to such a people becomes the pledge of Divine protection, and their fidelity to it determines the fate by which it is finally overtaken. What that trust is must be ascertained from the necessities of their position, the institutions which are the outgrowth of their principles, and the conflicts through which they preserve their identity and independence. If, then, the South is such a people, what, at this juncture, is their providential trust? I answer, that it is *to conserve and to perpetuate the institution of domestic slavery as now existing.* It is not necessary here to inquire whether this is precisely the best relation in which the hewer of wood and drawer of water can stand to his employer; although this proposition may perhaps be successfully sustained by those who choose to defend it. Still less are we required, dogmatically, to affirm that it will subsist through all time. . . .

Without, therefore, determining the question of duty for future generations, I simply say, that for us, as now situated, the duty is plain of conserving and transmitting the system of slavery, with the freest scope for its natural development and extension. Let us, my brethren, look our duty in the face. With this institution assigned to our keeping, what reply shall we make to those who say that its days are numbered? My own conviction is, that we should at once lift ourselves, intelligently to the highest moral ground, and proclaim to all the world that we hold this trust from God, and in its occupancy we are prepared to stand or fall as God may appoint. If the critical moment has arrived at which the great issue is joined, let us say that, in the sight of all perils, we will stand by our trust: and God be with the right!

The argument which enforces the solemnity of this providential trust is simple and condensed. It is bound upon us, then, by the *principle of self-preservation,* that "first law" which is continually asserting its supremacy over others. Need I pause to show how this system of servitude underlies and supports our material interests? That our wealth consists in our lands, and in the serfs who till them? That from the nature of our products they can only be cultivated by labor which must be controlled in order to be certain? That any other than a tropical race must faint and wither beneath a tropical sun? Need I pause to show how this system is interwoven with our entire social fabric? That these slaves form parts of our households, even as our children; and that, too, through a relationship recognized and sanctioned in the scriptures of God even as the other? Must I pause to show how it has fashioned our modes of life, and determined all our habits of thought and feeling, and moulded the very type of our civilization? How, then, can the hand of violence be laid upon it without involving our existence? The so-called free States of this country are working out the social problem under conditions peculiar to themselves. These conditions are sufficiently hard, and their success is too uncertain, to excite in us the least jealousy of their lot. With a teeming population, which the soil cannot support—with their wealth depending upon arts, created by artificial wants—with an eternal friction between the grades of their society—with their labor and their capital grinding against each other like the upper and nether millstones—with labor cheapened and displaced by new mechanical inventions, bursting more asunder the bonds of brotherhood; amid these intricate perils we have ever given them our sympathy and our prayers, and have never sought to weaken the foundations of their social order. God grant them complete success in the solution of all their perplexities! We, too, have our responsibilities and our trials; but they are all bound up in this one institution, which has been the object of such unrighteous assault through five and twenty years. If we are true to ourselves, we shall, at this critical juncture, stand by it, and work out our destiny.

This duty is bound upon us again *as the constituted guardians of the slaves themselves.* Our lot is not more implicated in theirs, than is their lot in ours; in our mutual relations we survive or perish together. The worst foes of the black race are those who have intermeddled on their behalf. We know better than others that every attribute of their character fits them for dependence and servitude. By nature, the most affectionate and loyal of all races beneath the sun, they are also the most helpless; and no calamity can befall them greater than the loss of that protection they enjoy under this patriarchal system. Indeed, the experiment has been grandly tried of precipitating them upon freedom, which they know not how to enjoy; and the dismal results are before us, in statistics that astonish the world. With the fairest portions of the earth in their possession, and with the advantage of a long discipline as cultivators of the soil, their constitutional indolence has converted the most beautiful islands of the sea into a howling waste. It is not too much to say, that if the South should, at this moment, surrender every slave, the wisdom of the entire world, united in solemn council, could not solve the question of their disposal. Their transportation to Africa, even if it were feasible, would be but the most refined cruelty; they must perish with starvation before they could have time to relapse into their primitive barbarism. Their residence here, in the presence of the vigorous Saxon race, would be but the signal for their rapid extermination before they had time to waste away through listlessness, filth, and vice. Freedom would be their doom; and equally from both they call upon us, their providential guardians, to be protected. I know this argument will be scoffed abroad as the hyprocritical cover thrown over our own cupidity and selfishness; but every Southern master knows its truth and feels its power. My servant, whether born in my house or bought with my money, stands to me in the relation of a child. Though providentially owing me service, which, providentially, I am bound to exact, he is, nevertheless, my brother and my friend; and I am to him a guardian and a father. He leans upon me for protection, for counsel, and for blessing; and so long as the relation continues, no power, but the power of almighty God, shall come between him and me. Were there no argument but this, it binds upon us the providential duty of preserving the relation that we may save him from a doom worse than death.

It is a duty which we owe, further, *to the civilized world.* It is a remarkable fact, that during these thirty years of unceasing warfare against slavery, and while a lying spirit has inflamed the world against us, that world has grown more and more dependent upon it for sustenance and wealth. Every tyro knows that all branches of industry fall back upon the soil. We must come, every one of us, to the bosom of this great mother for nourishment. In the happy partnership which has grown up in providence between the tribes of this confederacy, our industry has been concentrated upon agriculture. To the North we have cheerfully resigned all the profits arising from manufacture and commerce. Those profits they have, for the most part, fairly earned, and we have never begrudged them. We have sent them our sugar, and bought it back when refined; we have sent them our cotton, and brought it back when spun into thread or woven into cloth. Almost every article we use, from the shoe-latchet to the most elaborate and costly article of luxury, they have made and we have bought; and both sections have thriven by the partnership, as no people ever thrived before since the first shining of the sun. . . . Even beyond this—the enriching commerce which has built the splendid cities and marble palaces of England as well as of America, has been largely established upon the products of our soil; and the blooms upon Southern fields, gathered by black hands, have fed the spindles and looms of Manchester and Birmingham not less than of Lawrence and Lowell. Strike now a blow at this system of labor, and the world itself totters at the stroke. Shall we permit that blow to fall? Do we not owe it to civilized man to stand in the breach and stay the uplifted arm? If the blind Samson lays hold of the pillars which support the arch of the world's industry, how many more will be buried beneath its ruins than the lords of the Philistines? "Who knoweth whether we are not come to the kingdom for such a time as this?"

Last of all, in this great struggle, *we defend the cause of God and religion.* The Abolition spirit is undeniably atheistic. The demon which erected its throne upon the guillotine in the days of Robespierre and Marat, which abolished the Sabbath, and worshiped reason in the person of a harlot, yet survives to work other horrors, of which those of the French revolution are but the type. Among a people so generally religious as the American, a disguise must be worn; but it is the same old threadbare disguise of the advocacy of human rights. From a thousand Jacobin clubs here, as in France, the decree has gone forth which strikes at God by striking at all subordination and law. Availing itself of the morbid and misdirected sympathies of men, it has entrapped weak consciences in the meshes of its treachery; and now, at last, has seated its high-priest upon the throne, clad in the black garments of discord and schism, so symbolic of its ends. Under this specious cry of reform, it demands that every evil shall be corrected, or society become a wreck—the sun must be stricken from the heavens, if a spot is found on his disk. . . . This spirit of atheism, which knows no God who tolerates evil, no Bible which sanctions law, and no conscience that can be bound by oaths and covenants, has selected us for its victims, and slavery for its issue. Its banner-cry rings out already upon the air—"Liberty, equality, fraternity," which, simply interpreted, mean bondage, confiscation and massacre. With its tricolor waving in the breeze, it waits to inaugurate its reign of terror. To the South the highest position is assigned, of defending, before all nations, the cause of all religion and of all truth. In this trust, we are resisting the power which wars against constitutions, and laws and compacts, against Sabbaths and sanctuaries, against the family, the State and the church; which blasphemously invades the prerogatives of God, and rebukes the Most High for the errors of his administration, which, if it cannot snatch the reins of empire from his grasp, will lay the universe in ruins at his feet. Is it possible that we shall decline the onset?

This argument, then, which sweeps over the entire circle of our relations, touches the four cardinal points of duty *to ourselves, to our slaves, to the world, and to almighty God*. It establishes the nature and solemnity of our present trust to *preserve and transmit our existing system of domestic servitude, with the right, unchanged by man, to go and root itself wherever Providence and nature may carry it*. This trust we will discharge in the face of the worst possible peril. Though war be the aggregation of all evils, yet, should the madness of the hour appeal to the arbitration of the sword, we will not shrink even from the baptism of fire. If modern crusaders stand in serried ranks upon some plain of Esdraelon, there shall we be in defense of our trust. Not till the last man has fallen behind the last rampart, shall it drop from our hands; and then only in surrender to the God who gave it. (B. M. Palmer, *Thanksgiving Sermon Delivered at the First Presbyterian Church, New Orleans, On Thursday, December 29, 1860*, New York, 1861, 6–13.)

5. "The Life of the Unhappy Victim of This Atrocious Tyranny"

Rev. Henry J. Van Dyke represented the large element in the Old School who hoped that by patience and reasonableness a complete break with the South might be avoided. For this conciliatory policy he was severely criticized by the abolitionists, as may be seen in the following attack on him by a neighboring minister in New York.

There has been no misrepresentation, however; the man is yet to be born who can paint slavery in its true colors; the word is yet to be coined which expresses the combination of wickedness which constitutes its essence. Could it rise in all its dreadful lineaments before the eyes of the civilized world to-night, its doom would be sealed before to-morrow's dawn. Mr. Van Dyke talks about Christian families in the South, in which the slaves are well fed, well clothed, and kindly treated. Suppose it granted—How many, I ask, of these millions of slaves are in the family of the master, or in any way connected with it? They toil during the day upon the plantation, under the eye of the overseer or underdriver; pass the night in cabins more or less comfortable, according to the ability or humanity of the owner, but always separated from the mansion, of course; they have no more connection with the master's family than his horses and mules—not a particle; and in ninety-nine cases out of a hundred, as little effort is made for their improvement. Talk about families! mockery of mockeries! Why, I have seen a slaveholder upon his horse, with his gun in his hand, followed by his dogs, out upon the hunt of a runaway slave! Fancy a father pursuing his son or daughter in that style! I have seen a slave-girl rise from the side of her mistress, and hobble across the floor, confined by fetters which clanked like those of a prisoner in his cell, to prevent her from flying to the woods, as she had formerly done, to escape the infernal tortures which that mistress inflicted upon her in outbreaks of passion. A mother might thus treat her daughter, but would it be tolerated? I have seen the face of a babe six months old streaming with blood, from a cut inflicted by the lash of the whip of an overseer, who, in his reckless haste, had aimed the blow at the nurse who held it in her arms; but I forbear; and yet Mr. Van Dyke dares to talk about misrepresentation, and asks us to send back the fugitive who is escaping from such service!

But let us look for a moment at ordinary slave life separated from these cruelties—I mean separated in imagination—for in reality they never are and can not be—they belong to the system; if you keep men slaves, you must treat them harshly; the relation is one of wrong inflicted upon the one side and received upon the other; it never can be harmonious. This is the apology I make for the southern people; they are no worse than others; they are not devils incarnate; the *system* makes them what they are, and compels these cruelties; they know it themselves, and in many instances deplore it. But let us look at this mode of existence apart from this cruelty. Go with me, then, to a Kentucky plantation. At early dawn you hear the horn of the overseer; as soon as it is possible to see, men, women, and children of sufficient age ready for work, march to the field, and work until breakfast. Breakfast consists of a large piece of corn-bread and fat meat—enough of both—with water to drink; dinner the same. I have sat by a poor fellow upon his log as he ate his unsavory meal; and when he said to me, "Don't you think we poor negroes have a hard time of it?" I felt that that was indeed a hard life; and as I looked to the blue heavens above, I wondered that the arm of the Almighty was not extended for their deliverance. Supper in the cabins, with some additions, provided the females are not too much fatigued to prepare it. Thus passes one weary day after another, in tiresome monotony, varied only by diversity of tasks, or such incidents as may be supposed to arise from such a life—no hope, no object in view, no stimulus but the fear of punishment; no possibility of improvement; hedged around on all sides by an iron necessity that permits no alleviation; yet, an immortal being, susceptible of all degrees of improvement and happiness, and painfully conscious of the injustice of the dreadful doom that oppresses and crushes him. Such is the life of the unhappy victim of this atrocious tyranny. (J. R. W. Sloane, *Review of Rev. Henry J. Van Dyke's Discourse on "The Character and Influence of Abolitionism,"* N.Y., 1861, 35–37.)

6. The Spring Resolutions

When the Old School Assembly met in May, 1861, ten Southern states had seceded and Confederate guns had already fired upon Fort Sumter. The slavery issue suddenly became secondary to preserving the Union. The following motion by Dr. Gardiner Spring was adopted after long debate, 156 to 66. The conservatives, led by the venerable Dr. Charles Hodge, protested that the General Assembly had no right to decide "to what government the allegiance of Presbyterians is due," nor "to make that decision a condition of membership in our Church." The protest, however, was overruled and the Southern presbyteries had little choice but to form their own General Assembly.

Gratefully acknowledging the distinguished bounty and care of Almighty God toward this favoured land, and also recognizing our obligations to submit to every ordinance of man for the Lord's sake, this General Assembly adopt the following resolutions:

Resolved, 1. That in view of the present agitated and unhappy condition of this country, the first day of July next be hereby set apart as a day of prayer throughout our bounds; and that on this day ministers and people are called on humbly to confess and bewail our national sins; to offer our thanks to the Father of light for his abundant and undeserved goodness towards us as a nation; to seek his guidance and blessing upon our rulers, and their counsels, as well as on the Congress of the United States about to assemble; and to implore him, in the name of Jesus Christ, the great High Priest of the Christian profession, to turn away his anger from us, and speedily restore to us the blessings of an honourable peace.

Resolved, 2. That this General Assembly, in the spirit of that Christian patriotism which the Scriptures enjoin, and which has always characterized this Church, do hereby acknowledge and declare our obligations to promote and perpetuate, so far as in us lies, the integrity of these United States, and to strengthen, uphold, and encourage, the

Federal Government in the exercise of all its functions under our noble Constitution: and to this Constitution in all its provisions, requirements, and principles, we profess our unabated loyalty.

And to avoid all misconception, the Assembly declare that by the terms "Federal Government," as here used, is not meant any particular administration, or the peculiar opinions of any particular party, but that central administration, which being at any time appointed and inaugurated according to the forms prescribed in the Constitution of the United States, is the visible representative of our national existence. (*Minutes of the G. A.,* 1861, 329.)

7. The Southern Address, 1861

On December 4, 1861, commissioners from forty-seven Southern presbyteries met at Augusta, Ga., and organized the General Assembly of the Presbyterian Church in the Confederate States of America. In a masterly open letter the new Church presented its reasons for separation and its position on slavery to the world. The author of the letter was probably Dr. James Thornwell of Columbia Seminary, South Carolina.

The General Assembly of the Presbyterian Church in the Confederate States of America, to all the Churches of Jesus Christ throughout the earth, greeting: Grace, mercy, and peace be multiplied upon you:

DEARLY BELOVED BRETHREN: It is probably known to you that the Presbyteries and Synods in the Confederate States, which were formerly in connection with the General Assembly of the Presbyterian Church in the United States of America, have renounced the jurisdiction of that body; and dissolved the ties which bound them ecclesiastically with their brethren of the North. This act of separation left them without any formal union among themselves. But as they were one in faith and order, and still adhered to their old standards, measures were promptly adopted for giving expression to their unity, by the organization of a Supreme Court, upon the model of the one whose authority they had just relinquished. . . .

1. . . . The first thing which roused our Presbyteries to look the question of separation seriously in the face, was the course of the Assembly in venturing to determine, as a Court of Jesus Christ, which it did by necessary implication, the true interpretation of the Constitution of the United States as to the kind of government it intended to form. A political theory was, to all intents and purposes, propounded, which made secession a crime, the seceding States rebellious, and the

citizens who obeyed them traitors. We say nothing here as to the righteousness or unrighteousness of these decrees. What we maintain is, that, whether right or wrong, the Church had no right to make them —she transcended her sphere, and usurped the duties of the State. The discussion of these questions, we are sorry to add, was in the spirit and temper of partizan declaimers. The Assembly, driven from its ancient moorings, was tossed to and fro by the waves of popular passion. Like Pilate, it obeyed the clamor of the multitude, and though acting in the name of Jesus, it kissed the sceptre and bowed the knee to the mandates of Northern phrenzy. The Church was converted into the forum, and the Assembly was henceforward to become the arena of sectional divisions and national animosities. . . . For the sake of peace, therefore, for Christian charity, for the honor of the Church, and for the glory of God, we have been constrained, as much as in us lies, to remove all occasion of offence. We have quietly separated, and we are grateful to God that, while leaving for the sake of peace, we leave it with the humble consciousness that we, ourselves, have never given occasion to break the peace. We have never confounded Caesar and Christ, and we have never mixed the issues of this world with the weighty matters that properly belong to us as citizens of the Kingdom of God.

2. . . . It is precisely because we love that Church as it was, and that Church as it should be, that we have resolved as far as in us lies, to realize its grand idea in the country, and under the Government where God has cast our lot. With the supreme control of ecclesiastical affairs in our hands, we may be able, in some competent measure, to consummate this result. In subjection to a foreign power, we could no more accomplish it than the Church in the United States could have been developed in dependence upon the Presbyterian Church of Scotland. The difficulty there would have been, not the distance of Edinburgh from New York, Philadelphia, or Charleston, but the difference in the manners, habits, customs, and ways of thinking, the social, civil, and political institutions of the people. These same difficulties exist in relation to the Confederate and United States, and render it eminently proper that the Church in each should be as separate and independent as the Governments.

In addition to this, there is one difference which so radically and fundamentally distinguishes the North and the South, that it is becoming every day more and more apparent that the religious, as well as the secular, interests of both will be more effectually promoted by a complete and lasting separation. The antagonism of Northern and Southern sentiment on the subject of slavery lies at the root of all the difficulties which have resulted in the dismemberment of the Federal Union, and involved us in the horrors of an unnatural war. The Presbyterian Church in the United States has been enabled by Divine grace to pursue, for the most part, an eminently conservative, because a thoroughly Scriptural, policy in relation to this delicate question. It has planted itself upon the Word of God, and utterly refused to make slaveholding a sin, or non-slaveholding a term of communion. But though both sections are agreed as to this general principle, it is not to be disguised that the North exercises a deep and settled antipathy to slavery itself, while the South is equally zealous in its defence. Recent events can have no other effect than to confirm the antipathy on the one hand and strengthen the attachment on the other. The Northern section of the Church stands in the awkward predicament of maintaining, in one breath, that slavery is an evil which ought to be abolished, and of asserting in the next, that it is not a sin to be visited by exclusion from communion of the saints. The consequence is, that it plays partly into the hands of abolitionists and partly into the hands of slaveholders, and weakens its influence with both. It occupies the position of a prevaricating witness whom neither party will trust. It would be better, therefore, for the moral power of the Northern section of the Church to get entirely quit of the subject. At the same time, it is intuitively obvious that the Southern section of the Church, while even partially under the control of those who are hostile to slavery, can never have free and unimpeded access to the slave population. Its ministers and elders will always be liable to some degree of suspicion. In the present circumstances, Northern alliance would be absolutely fatal. It would utterly preclude the Church from a wide and commanding field of usefulness. . . .

This is too dear a price to be paid for a nominal union. We cannot afford to give up these millions of souls and consign them, so far as our efforts are concerned, to hopeless perdition, for the sake of preserving an outward unity which, after all, is an empty shadow. If we would gird ourselves heartily and in earnest, for the work which God has set before us, we must have the control of our ecclesiastical affairs, and declare ourselves separate and independent.

And here we may venture to lay before the Christian world our views as a Church, upon the subject of slavery. We beg a candid hearing.

In the first place, we would have it distinctly understood that, in our ecclesiastical capacity, we are neither the friends nor the foes of slavery; that is to say, we have no commission either to propagate or abolish it. The policy of its existence or non-existence is a question which exclusively belongs to the State. We have no right, as a Church, to enjoin it as a duty, or to condemn it as a sin. Our business is with the duties which spring from the relation; the duties of the masters on the one hand, and of their slaves on the other. These duties we are to proclaim and enforce with spiritual sanctions. The social, civil, political problems connected with this great subject transcend our sphere, as God has not entrusted to his Church the organization of society, the construction of Government, nor the allotment of individuals to their various stations. The Church has as much right to preach to the monarchies of Europe, and the despotism of Asia, the doctrines of republican equality, as to preach to the Governments of the South the extirpation of slavery. This position is impregnable, unless it can be shown that slavery is a sin.

Others, if they please, may spend their time in declaiming on the tyranny of earthly masters; it will be our aim to resist the real tyrants which oppress the soul—Sin and Satan. These are the foes against whom we shall find it employment enough to wage a successful war. And to this holy war it is the purpose of our Church to devote itself with redoubled energy. We feel that the souls of our slaves are a solemn trust, and we shall strive to present them faultless and complete before the presence of God.

Indeed, as we contemplate their condition in the Southern States, and contrast it with that of their fathers before them, and that of their brethren in the present day in their native land, we cannot but accept it as a gracious Providence that they have been brought in such numbers to our shores, and redeemed from bondage of barbarism and sin. Slavery to them has certainly been over-ruled for the greatest good. It has been a link in the wondrous chain of Providence, through which many sons and daughters have been made heirs of the heavenly inheritance. The Providential result is, of course, no justification, if the thing is intrinsically wrong; but it is certainly a matter of devout thanksgiving, and no obscure intimation of the will and purpose of God, and of the consequent duty of the Church. We cannot forbear to say, however, that the general operation of the system is kindly and benevolent; it is a real and effective discipline, and without it we are profoundly persuaded that the African race in the midst of us can never be elevated in the scale of being. As long as that race, in its comparative degradation, co-exists, side by side, with the white, bondage is its normal condition.

As to the endless declamation about human rights, we have only to say that human rights are not a fixed, but a fluctuating quantity. Their sum is not the same in any two nations on the globe. The rights of Englishmen are one thing, the rights of Frenchmen another. There is a minimum without which a man cannot be responsible; there is a maximum which expresses the highest degree of civilization and of Christian culture. The education of the species consists in its ascent along this line. As you go up, the number of rights increases, but the number of individuals who possess them diminishes. As you come down the line, rights are diminished, but the individuals are multiplied. It is just the opposite of the predicamental scale of the logicians. There comprehension diminishes as you ascend and extension increases, and comprehension increases as you descend and extension diminishes. Now, when it is said that slavery is inconsistent with human rights, we crave to understand what point in this line is the slave conceived to occupy. There are, no doubt, many rights which belong to other men—to Englishmen, to Frenchmen, to his master, for example—which are denied to him. But is he fit to possess them? Has God qualified him to meet the responsibilities which their possession necessarily implies? His place in the scale is determined by his competency to fulfil its duties. There are other rights which he certainly possesses, without which he could neither be human nor accountable. Before slavery can be charged with doing him injustice, it must be shown that the minimum which falls to his lot at the bottom of the line is out of proportion to his capacity and culture—a thing which can never be done by abstract speculation. The truth is, the education of the human race for liberty and virtue, is a vast Providential scheme, and God assigns to every man, by a wise and holy decree, the precise place he is to occupy in the great moral school of humanity. The scholars are distributed into classes, according to their competency and progress. For God is in history.

To avoid the suspicion of a conscious weakness of our cause, when contemplated from the side of pure speculation, we may advert for a moment to those pretended intuitions which stamp the reprobation of humanity upon this ancient and hoary institution. We admit that there are primitive principles in morals which lie at the root of human consciousness. But the question is, how are we to distinguish them? The subjective feeling of certainty is no adequate criterion, as that is equally felt in reference to crotchets and hereditary prejudices. The very point is to know when this certainty indicates a primitive cognition, and when it does not. There must, therefore, be some eternal test, and whatever cannot abide that test has no authority as a primary truth. That test is an inward necessity of thought, which, in all minds at the proper stage of maturity, is absolutely universal. Whatever is universal is natural. We are willing that slavery should be tried by this standard. We are willing to abide by the testimony of the race, and if man, as man, has everywhere condemned it—if all human laws have prohibited it as crime—if it stands in the same category with malice, murder, and theft; then we are willing, in the name of humanity, to renounce it, and to renounce it forever. But what if the overwhelming majority of mankind have approved it? what if philosophers and statesmen have justified it, and the laws of all nations acknowledged it? what then becomes of these luminous intuitions? They are an *ignis fatuus,* mistaken for a star.

We have now, brethren, in a brief compass, for the nature of this address admits only of an outline, opened to you our whole hearts upon this delicate and vexed subject.

We have concealed nothing. We have sought to conciliate no sympathy by appeals to your charity. We have tried our cause by the word of God; and though protesting against its authority to judge in a question concerning the duty of the Church, we have not refused to appear at the tribunal of reason. Are we not right, in view of all the preceding considerations, in remitting the social, civil, and political problems connected with slavery to the State? Is it not a subject, save in the moral duties which spring from it, which lies beyond the province of the Church? Have we any right to make it an element in judging of Christian character? Are we not acting as Christ and his Apostles have acted before us? Is it not enough for us to pray and labor, in our lot, that all men may be saved, without meddling as a Church with the technical distinction of their civil life? We leave the matter with you. We offer you the right hand of fellowship. It is for you to accept it or reject it. We have done our duty. We can do no more. Truth is more precious than union, and if you cast us out as sinners, the breach of charity is not with us, as long as we walk according to the light of the written Word.

The ends which we propose to accomplish as a Church are the same as those which are proposed by every other church. To proclaim God's truth as a witness to the nations; to gather his elect from the four corners of the earth, and through the Word, Ministries, and Ordinances, to train them for eternal life, is the great business of His people. The only thing that will be at all peculiar to us, is the manner in which we shall attempt to discharge our duty. In almost every department of labor, except the pastoral care of congregations, it has been usual for the Church to resort to societies more or less closely connected with itself, and yet logically and really distinct.

It is our purpose to rely upon the regular organs of our government, and executive agencies directly and immediately responsible to them. We wish to make the Church not merely a superintendent, but an agent. We wish to develop the idea that the congregation of believers, as visibly organized, is the very society or corporation which is divinely called to do the work of the Lord. We shall, therefore, endeavor to do what has never yet been adequately done—bring out the energies of our Presbyterian system of government. From the Session to the Assembly we shall strive to enlist all our courts, as courts, in every department of Christian effort. We are not ashamed to confess that we are intensely Presbyterian. We embrace all other denominations in the arms of Christian fellowship and love, but our own scheme of government we humbly believe to be according to the pattern shown in the Mount, and, by God's grace, we propose to put its efficiency to the test.

Brethren, we have done. We have told you who we are, and what we are. We greet you in the ties of Christian brotherhood. We desire to cultivate peace and charity with all our fellow Christians throughout the world. We invite to ecclesiastical communion all who maintain our principles of faith and order. And now we commend you to God and the word of his grace. We devoutly pray that the whole Catholic Church may be afresh baptized with the Holy Ghost, and that she may speedily be stirred up to give the Lord no rest until he establish and make Jerusalem a praise in the earth. (R. E. Thompson, *A History of the Presbyterian Churches in the United States*, Appendix, XIX, 393–406.)

8. Reconstruction

At the conclusion of the war, the General Assembly (O.S.), like the U.S. Congress, devised its own scheme of ecclesiastical reconstruction. The following resolutions, making loyalty to the Union the test for Church membership and proposing to set up "scalawag" churches and presbyteries in the South, were deeply resented, not only in the South, but also by those Northerners who felt that such political tests were both unchristian and unconstitutional.

Whereas, During the existence of the great rebellion which has disturbed the peace and threatened the life of the nation, a large number of Presbyteries and Synods in the Southern States, whose names are on the roll of the General Assembly as constituent parts of this body, have organized an Assembly denominated "The General Assembly of the Confederate States of America," in order to render their aid in the attempt to establish, by means of the rebellion, a separate national existence, and "to conserve and perpetuate the system of slavery," therefore,

Resolved, 1. That this Assembly regards the civil rebellion for the perpetuation of negro slavery as a great crime, both against our National Government and against God, and the secession of those Presbyteries and Synods from the Presbyterian Church, under such circumstances and for such reasons, as unwarranted, schismatical, and unconstitutional.

Resolved, 2. That this Assembly does not intend to abandon the territory in which these churches are found, or to compromise the rights of any of the church courts, or ministers, ruling elders, and private members belonging to them, who are loyal to the government of the United States, and to the Presbyterian Church. On the contrary, this Assembly will recognize such loyal persons as constituting the churches, Presbyteries and Synods, in all the bounds of the schism, and will use earnest endeavours to restore and revive all such churches and church courts.

Resolved, 3. The Assembly hereby declares that it will recognize as the church, the members of any church within the bounds of the schism, who are loyal to the government of the United States of America, and whose views are in harmony with the doctrines of the Confession of Faith, and with the several testimonies of the Presbyterian Church on the subject of domestic slavery. And where any three ministers, who entertain the views above mentioned, belong to the same Presbytery, such ministers are hereby authorized and directed to continue their organization as a Presbytery; or any two such ministers are authorized to receive any minister of the same views, regularly dismissed to them, and thus continue their organizations with the churches above described in the same bounds, in connection with this Assembly. But if a sufficient number are not found in one Presbytery, they are authorized to unite with the loyal ministers and churches of one or more adjacent Presbyteries, retaining the name of one or both such united Presbyteries as shall be deemed expedient. A similar course is also authorized with regard to Synods.

Resolved, 4. In cases where there is not a sufficient number of loyal ministers and churches within a convenient district to form a Presbytery, such ministers are directed to supply churches and other places around them, as God may open the way, with the preaching of the gospel, and such churches are exhorted to use all diligence to secure the stated means of grace; and both ministers and churches are directed to report to the next General Assembly what has been done in these respects, that further order may be taken by the Assembly in the premises as the interests of Christ's cause may require.

Resolved, 5. The General Assembly furthermore give counsel to the Presbyteries and churches which may be revived and restored under the provisions of the above action, to treat with kindness ministers and churches or parts of churches, who are disloyal, or who are not in sympathy with the former deliverances of the General Assembly on the subject of slavery, and to inform such persons of their readiness to receive them into ecclesiastical fellowship, when they properly acknowledge and renounce their errors.

Resolved, 6. The Board of Domestic Missions is hereby authorized and requested to give special attention to the Southern field, in providing missionaries and appropriating pecuniary aid in order to carry into effect the measures contemplated in this Minute. And the Board is also authorized to employ any loyal minister whose residence may be in the South, as a missionary, provided he shall furnish satisfactory evidence of his fitness for the work, though circumstances may render it impracticable for him to obtain a Presbyterial recommendation. (*Minutes of the G. A., O.S., 1865, 560–561.*)

9. The Reunion of 1869

In 1869, after the upheavals of the recent conflict, the differences which had divided Old and New School Presbyterians in 1837 did not loom so large. The "abuses" and "errors" were forgotten as the commissioners of the two General Assemblies met at Pittsburgh and recognized one another as "sound and orthodox" and, joining arms, marched into a reunited Church. It will be noticed that the basis of union is simply the Bible as "the only infallible rule of faith and practice," and the Confession of Faith as systematizing this Biblical guidance. The Church thus returned to the broad foundations laid by the men of 1729 (see Ch. 1, art. 11).

A. Basis of Reunion

Believing that the interests of the Redeemer's kingdom would be promoted by the healing of our divisions, and that the two bodies bearing the same names, having the same Constitution, and each recognizing the other as a sound and orthodox body according to the principles of the Confession common to both, cannot be justified by any but the most imperative reasons in maintaining separate and, in some respects, rival organizations; we are now clearly of the opinion that the reunion of those bodies ought, as soon as the necessary steps can be taken, to be accomplished, upon the basis hereinafter set forth.

1. The Presbyterian Churches in the United States of America, namely, that whose General Assembly convened in the Brick Church in the city of New York, on the 20th day of May, 1869, and that whose General Assembly met in the Church of the Covenant in the said city on the same day, shall be reunited as one Church, under the name and style of the Presbyterian Church in the United States of America, possessing all the legal and corporate rights and powers pertaining to the Church previous to the division in 1838, and all the legal and corporate rights and powers which the separate churches now possess.

2. The reunion shall be effected on the doctrinal and ecclesiastical basis of our common standards; the Scriptures of the Old and New Testaments shall be acknowledged to be the inspired Word of God, and the only infallible rule of faith and practice; the Confession of Faith shall continue to be sincerely received and adopted as containing the system of doctrine taught in the Holy Scriptures; and the government and discipline of the Presbyterian Church in the United States shall be approved as containing the principles and rules of our polity.

B. Reunion in Pittsburgh, 1869

Besides the crowds who thronged the sidewalks and filled the doors and windows, the broad avenue was ajam with eager spectators. . . . The Iron City was electrified. . . . The hearts of the people were stirred. It was, indeed, a spectacle altogether novel. . . . . The parallel ranks, Old School and New School, on opposite sides of the avenue, two-and-two, arm-in-arm, moved along one block, when a halt was made.

The two Moderators who headed their respective columns, then approached each other, and grasped hands with a will. This was the signal for the Clerks, who followed, and then the pairs all through the ranks parted over, crossed over, and paired anew—the Old and the New, grasping each other, and amidst welcomes, thanksgivings, and tears, they locked arms and stood together in their reformed relations. (*Presbyterian Reunion: A Memorial Volume, 1837–1871*, New York, 1870, 275, 380.)

PART
III

RECENT PRESBYTERIANISM
1870–1956

CHAPTER

9

RECONCILED AND EXPANDING
1870–1886

1. "A Little Giant"—Sheldon Jackson

Home missions had been a principal motive of Presbyterian reunion in 1869. But with the completion of a transcontinental railroad in 1869, and the rapid thrust of population into the Far West, existing methods and resources of Presbyterian home missions were strained to the uttermost. In this emergency Sheldon Jackson (1834–1909) emerged as a brilliant and colorful improviser and pioneer. By indefatigible travel and correspondence he chose likely sites for new churches and then interested Eastern donors. After completing one career in the West (1858–1882), he entered upon a second in Alaska (in 1884).

For an outline of Presbyterian history since 1869, see L. A. Loetscher, A Brief History of the Presbyterians, 1938; and idem, in G. J. Slosser, ed., They Seek a Country, 1955, 251–265. The definitive history of Presbyterian home missions is C. M. Drury, Presbyterian Panorama, *1952.*

Denver, Colorado, 1877.

Rev. Henry Kendall, D.D.,
   Secretary of Home Missions,
     New York, N. Y.

My dear Dr. Kendall:

The transition from a mission tour off the coast of Alaska in a canoe to one over the Rocky Mountains on horseback was sudden and great. Reaching home from Alaska on a Wednesday night, the following Saturday morning I was off for the frontier stations over the range before the early snows should render the trails impassable.

Two hundred and fifty miles on the D & R. G. Railway, south along the base of the Mountains, then westward over the Sangre-de-Christo Range at an elevation of 9333 feet brought me to Alamosa on the Rio Grande Del Norte River.

The next morning I preached in the little Presbyterian Church of the

Strangers. Rev. Alex. M. Darley then took me into his buggy and drove 35 miles to Del Norte, arriving just as the bell was ringing for church. Hastily swallowing a cup of tea, I went to the Court Room and preached to a full house.

Getting up at 3 o'clock the next morning and taking the stage we were whirled at a rapid rate up the picturesque valley of the Rio Grande, through Waggon Wheel Gap, along the romantic mountain lake, San Miguel, until at an elevation of 1140 feet above tide water we were at the Head Springs of the Rio Grande upon the Continental Divide.

From thence the descent was rapid over a Corduroy road down Slumgullion Pass to Lake City. This thriving mining town is the Bishopric of Rev. Geo. M. Darley.

The church, parsonage and other surroundings attest his efficiency in the work.

This is the most prosperous church in the San Juan Mining district and so popular in Lake that other denominations have not been able to get a foot-hold.

Tuesday morning taking Rev. M. Darley, who is ever ready for any hard and dangerous trip for the church, we started on horseback to cross the range to Silverton, 35 or 40 miles distant. Turning up Hensen Creek and riding through scenery indescribably wild and grand, noon brought us to Capitol for dinner.

Re-saddling our horses, we pressed forward as rapidly as the high elevation would admit of. We were now higher than Mt. Washington. On and upward, until we were in the clouds—on to timber line, where two or three years ago, we anxiously waited to cross the range at two a.m., while the frozen crust of the snow would bear us. Still on over great fields of jagged rock. It was a second Mt. Washington on top of the first. And still our horses were painfully and slowly toiling upwards.

We pass a large field of perpetual snow and are on the summit of Engineer Pass, amid a vast wilderness of Peaks over 14000 feet high, that in their grand and awful desolation seem like the chaos of ruined worlds. The vastness of our surroundings is oppressive. No living thing is seen but the little conies that bark among the rocks. We seem the sole occupants of illimitable space. We give but a few moments to this sublime scene, as there is a hard ride before us and the afternoon is wearing away. Retightening the girths to our saddles, we commence the steep zig-zag descent. Down and down and down until there seems no bottom. Down to where Animas Forks Mining Camp is perched at timber line. Down over the paths of the avalanche that every winter claim their victims. It is the U. S. Post Mail route to death. Not a single season has passed since its establishment that one or more mail carriers with the mail lashed to their backs have not started out never to return alive, but to be overtaken and swept into Eternity by the swift terrible snow slide.

Down we go to Eureka, whose one long street is lined on either side by deserted log houses. Down past mines innumerable, where men delve for gold and silver amid great privations; where large numbers sacrifice early religion, training, integrity and manhood; and wrecked in fortunes and characters find premature graves. They swarm and burrow in the mountains by the thousands. When will the Church enable the Board of Home Missions to follow them with the sustaining strength and consolation of the gospel that far from home and kindred and moral restraint, they may be saved to their country, their friends, their church and Redeemer. Below Eureka the valley widens out and we gallop down into Howardsville and catch a passing glimpse of young men in the saloons; it may be the hope of a widowed mother, or the sons of Christian parents on the downward road to ruin. What else can Christian parents expect, when, by with-holding their means, they prevent the sending of Ministers to such communities.

Night is upon us, still we are galloping on and down, until late in the evening we reach the hotel at Silverton, so tired and sore and raw that it is with great pain and difficulty we are able to undress and get to bed. Early the next morning we are again in the saddle for we must make 50 miles and we do it. Just after sun down we reach Animas City and are warmly welcomed by Rev. W. C. Beebe and his church.

Mr. Beebe is bishop of a district as large as the state of Vermont. He had recently returned from a horse-back trip of 300 miles into the wilderness near the edge of Utah to marry a couple and preach in the regions beyond. Our cause at Animas is represented by a neat chapel, good congregation and an efficient minister.

The next day after calling on nearly all the families of the congregation in the village, we are again in the saddle on our return trip. Night found us enjoying the hospitality of the Hon. Judge Pinkerton. On his farm are several fine hot Springs that will some day be much visited.

At 6 o'clock the next morning we were again on the road. The forests were on fire in every direction. Set on fire by small bands of Utes. Two miles west of us they were destroying the fences and hay of a frontier settler. The Utes were on the war path and small bands were in the woods on either side of us. Even then couriers were flying through the country warning exposed settlers of their danger. Not meeting any of them, we rode on unconscious of our danger, and it was not until we reached our stopping place for the night that we heard of the outbreak. We rode 52 miles that day. The next morning it was judged best that Mr. Darley return to his family, while I continued on the trail to Ouray.

Reaching there everything was in a high state of excitement. The farmers outside of the village were hurridly bringing their families in for protection. Two companies of Militia had been organized, guns and amunition distributed—a rude barracade and earth works were being hastily thrown up, pickets were stationed outside and all kinds of rumors flying from mouth to mouth.

All the families of the congregation were visited and on Sabbath good audiences were at church considering the excited condition of the community.

Sabbath night the fitful gusts of wind accompanied with a driving rain, gave warning of the coming storm and anxiety lest the mountain passes should be blocked with snow.

Rising as soon as it was light, a glance at the range revealed it white with fresh snow. Getting an early breakfast I started out to cross the range. A few miles out and an unexpected difficulty presented itself. The forests had been on fire and in some places burnt out the timbers that supported the trail. The storm of the preceding night had also blown a good many trees across the track, some of them too large either to remove or get over. The only thing to be done was to throw off my wrappings and with my hands make a new trail around the obstructions. This consumed nearly all forenoon. At one place having forced my horse up the mountain side on some loose rocks, it started a land slide. The rocks slipping out from under his feet, he quietly lay down on his side and went down with the rest. When almost exhausted these difficulties were overcome and after that I made more rapid progress.

As I climbed upward the rain gave place to snow. Passing upward through the snow cloud at an elevation of 13000 feet I was above it and saw the snow storm raging below, while all around the great peaks were glistening in the sunshine. The wind that swept across the summit was too cold to allow of much tarrying, so hastening down the eastern side, by dusk I was safely housed at the parsonage at Lake City.

A day and night of staging and fourteen hours on the railroad brought me home in time to attend the fall meeting of the Presbytery of Colorado.

Very sincerely yours,
Sheldon Jackson

(Sheldon Jackson to Henry Kendall, 1877 [no month given] in Sheldon Jackson, "Correspondence—1856–1908," Vol. 7, 305–307, in P.H.S., Philadelphia.)

2. Help from the Ladies

While Sheldon Jackson and numerous less famous home missionaries were busy on the field, Henry Kendall and Cyrus Dickson, formerly of the New School and Old School, respectively, exercised executive leadership of the Board of Home Missions as cosecretaries.

With the growing strength of the feminist movement in the nineteenth century and with the heavy strain which migration to the Far West was placing on existing home missions resources, Presbyterian women organized to help. In 1870 a Woman's Foreign Missionary Society had been organized, and this was followed in 1879 by the organization of a Woman's Board of Home Missions. The document presented below over the names of Drs. Kendall and Dickson is frankly promotional and is a fair specimen of this type of literature.

BOARD OF HOME MISSIONS,
No. 23 Centre Street, New York

AN APPEAL TO CHRISTIAN WOMEN.

Great Enlargement of Home Missionary
Work in Utah, New Mexico and Alaska

Suitable Buildings for Chapels and School
Houses an Immediate Necessity

[1.] *Women began this Work.*

The first effort to evangelize the neglected and misguided populations in these distant Territories sprung from the fertile brain and warm hearts of Christian women. They were the first to make an effort in behalf of their own sex who were the devotees of the Papacy, or Mormonism, or belonging to the heathen tribes of Indians. Step by step have they gone forward, working through the Board of Home Missions, till now there are on this field, or under appointment, more than fifty Missionaries and teachers—twenty-four in Utah, twenty-three in New Mexico, and *five* in Alaska.

(2.) *A large share of the means necessary to carry on the work has been furnished by the women.*

As it was primarily a work for women and children, nearly every Missionary sent into the field having conducted or directed a school, it was appropriate and wise that the women should furnish a large part of the funds; this they have continued to do to the present time.

(3.) *We hope and expect that the women will furnish the necessary means for present work and its expected enlargement.*

Burdened as we are with other work, we trust them to furnish the funds for this new department; hence when the Board undertook the expansion of the work as it pressed on us in this new form, we saw in it an appropriate field for the labors and zeal and sacrifices of self-denying women, and we said:

"So far as may be practical, the financial support for this school-work shall be committed to the women of our church as their special trust, out of whose contributions, without drawing upon our regular Home Missionary Fund, shall be taken what, in our judgment, may be needed for this work."

In an appeal we made to you last winter we said:

"The Board appeals, with confidence to the women of the Presbyterian Church, for aid to undertake and carry on this department of the great work laid upon it by the General Assembly."

To our appeals you have responded promptly and generously. Your contributions, to a large extent, have supported the Missionaries and teachers.

Chapels and School Buildings

But we have reached a new phase of this work. Success always brings enlarged responsibility. Suitable buildings for the Missionaries and teachers have become a pressing and imperative necessity. And this work, in addition to all they have been doing before, we must also commit to the women of the church. Chapels and school-houses are essential to a prosperous beginning and to any permanent work of success. We lost much last year for want of such buildings, and we must continue to lose till the want is supplied.

Says one of our Missionaries in Utah:

"We have sixty in one Sunday School almost every Sabbath, and, but for the miserable little *hovel* in which we are obliged to hold our services, would have many more. But when I tell you we are obliged to hold our services at eight in the evening, in a little, low-roofed adobe hut, 12×24, and cut into two by a partition, each room *packed* full of desks and seats for children, and that the miserable rookery is full of vermin, that the rooms are so low and small that when the lamps are lighted the heat is fearful, you will understand why these people are not enthusiastic to attend these hot evenings."

Another says:

"The great lack is to get a building. There might just as well be a school of seventy-five scholars as of thirty-five. But the only building that could be obtained was a dwelling house, and that had to be given up last week.

"Already Mr. L. has paid out of his own pocket $315 during the year for rent and other necessary expenses of the school, thereby pinching himself in a way which grieved me to behold."

A Missionary in New Mexico speaking of his field, says:

"We do need a church building at both places very much indeed. At Ocaté we meet in a private room (though large), in a common dwelling, when the usual congregation get in it is so full that I wonder often how we endure it."

A Missionary and his family were sent to the Zuñi Indians in Western New Mexico last fall. No suitable building could be found for his family, or for school and church purposes. The consequent discomfort and exposure of the winter so broke down his health that he was compelled to leave the field in early Spring, and it is still feared that the seeds of fatal disease have been sown in his system.

With funds raised by the women of Rochester Presbytery and other parts of the country, we are putting up suitable buildings to furnish a better opportunity for successful missionary effort among the people. Past experience there has taught us that such buildings are indispensable.

The Missionaries and teachers in Alaska are also suffering greatly for suitable buildings. They have been allowed to preach the Gospel and open their schools in Government buildings, both at Sitka and Fort Wrangel. But this arrangement cannot be permanent.

These are only specimens of what is wanted at nearly every place in all these great Territories where we have preaching stations or schools. What we want is just what is furnished to the Freedmen at the South, namely, *a chapel which can be used for a school room during the week, and for Sabbath Schools and the worship of God on the Sabbath.*

But you may ask, why is not this appropriate work for the Church Erection Board? The reply is, that the Board is forbidden by its Rules or Charter to aid in the erection of a chapel where there is *no church organization.* But among the Mormons and Mexicans and Indians, we need the chapel and the school house for the purpose of *preparing the way* for church organization. We must begin at the foundation; we must teach the children, and preach to all, repentance towards God and faith in the Lord Jesus Christ. We must have a place to teach and preach in before we can find believers to organize into a church. This is the pressing demand of the hour.

Ladies' Societies have secured possession of valuable property in Santa Fé and Las Vegas, in New Mexico, and stock in various other buildings, some fully and some but partially paid for.

Such Societies have built Sanitariums and school-houses, and residences for Missionaries and teachers in foreign lands. And they have done well. We beg of you to undertake the same kind of work for your native land. We appeal to Ladies' Societies in single churches or Presbyteries to undertake, singly or by your combined efforts, to secure a building for school and church purposes at Taos—the Indian Pueblo of Jemez—or Ocaté, New Mexico; Springville, Brigham City, Manti, Ephraim or Logan, Utah; or for a home for girls at Fort Wrangel, or for a chapel there or at Sitka, the Capital of Alaska.

This work needs to be done at all these or other stations, and it will need to be done whenever we establish a preaching station, a Missionary or a school. And it needs to be done at once.

How sad it must be to turn such children back to their dark and heathen houses because there is no room to receive them! And how useless it is to send out the teacher or the Missionary unless we can furnish him a suitable place for labor.

We hope then all the women in our churches will enlarge their plans for Home work so as to embrace this feature of it. Organize for this purpose. Consult with other Societies and combine your energies. Take this matter to your pastors before they go to Presbytery or Synod; take it to your own hearts and set about the work; and chapels and schoolhouses here and there will spring up in these dark Territories that shall be centres of intellectual and spiritual light and culture for many years to come.

And since this crisis has been reached, though at this period of financial distress, who can doubt that God has laid it over on you, and that, in response to prayer and faith and love, He will make you abundantly able to do all that His Providence seems thus to open before you.

H. KENDALL,
CYRUS DICKSON, } *Secretaries.*

O.D. Eaton, *Treasurer.*

(Clipping from Board of Home Missions promotional literature, n.p., n.d., signed by H. Kendall and Cyrus Dickson, Secretaries, and O.D. Eaton, Treasurer, in Sheldon Jackson's Scrapbook, Vol. 55, 20-22.)

3. Sunday School Missions

In the race to win the new settlers in the West, Presbyterians were handicapped in competition by their ideal of settled congregations, each served by a fully trained minister. But the "Sabbath school missionary"—a kind of Presbyterian circuit rider who might be a layman—represented an informal and more elastic approach to the work. Rev. Joseph Brown, quoted below, started work as a Sabbath school missionary in Wisconsin in 1889, and in the next fifteen years traveled 256,916 miles, made 9,476 visits, and organized 91 Sabbath schools and 44 churches.

The following request has been addressed to me: "Will you state particulars as to the manner in which you seek to do your work as a Sabbath-School missionary?" It is a privilege to give the desired information.

I select a district of the country within my bounds. With my bag filled *with books, tracts, and papers,* and with umbrella in hand, I set out for the duties of the day. If my work lies in a district in which there is a settled minister, I generally walk two miles away from his field of labor. This I do that I may not work on ground in charge of another. By so doing I have never had unpleasant relations with any one.

Having reached what I regard as a proper field, I begin my work by calling at the different houses along my way. The amount of time spent in these houses varies, as I am regulated by the character of the reception given and by the prospect of doing good. In visiting a district for the first time, the people are strangers to me, and I have to introduce my way among them as best I can. In such case my work is, in fact, both a tour of discovery *and a species of fishing.* I go among the people to do them good, and in order to accomplish this prudence and tact are needed. As I step into the various homes, and they are various in many respects, I tell the occupants who I am and what is the purpose of my visit, and as I do so I generally extend a cheerful greeting, wishing them, in the most pleasant manner possible, a good-morning. This cheerful greeting seems, in most cases, to take the people by storm. This I judge from the cordial receptions generally accorded to me. After having been invited to come in and sit down, and having accepted, my talk begins and is carried on according to circumstances.

In every district there are some families *more in sympathy with good than others.* To find out such families is a matter of great importance to me in the prosecution of my work. Having found such, they become the objects of special attention. Conversation is held with them as to the needs of the people in relation to Sabbath-School work. After I have obtained the necessary information, and have excited some interest in the minds of those with whom I have conversed, generally a place and time are fixed for holding a meeting, and arrangements are made for conducting the service. At this meeting the importance of Sabbath-School work is pointed out in the most forcible manner possible, and at its close the judgment of those present is sought as to the propriety of establishing a school.

When an organization has been decided upon, which is generally the case, the different officers are selected by the people present and all necessary arrangements are made. Before all this can be perfected, however, it must be preceded by many long walks and frequent visitations. Success assured, a feeling of pleasure and satisfaction fills the mind of the Sabbath-School missionary.

When Sabbath-Schools are planted, are they left to themselves without the planter's care? Nay, verily. They are fostered by prayer, by sympathy, by revisitation, and by many helps, as each case may require and as means and opportunity are afforded. The Sabbath-School missionary has a love for the schools he plants; and the people, knowing this and knowing where he lives, are ever ready to let him know when help is needed. Such help is frequently asked for, and the missionary, with the means placed at his disposal by the Board, and by books and papers received from the friends of Sabbath-School missions, is always able to extend it. If wise and faithful, he so directs his gifts and labors as to nurture the good work begun. By use of the varied means at the disposal of the Sabbath-School missionary, a grand work is being done for Christ and the people.

By this Sabbath-School mission agency the Presbyterian Church has an instrument in her grasp by which the numerous and widespread settlers can be reached and evangelized. This attained, a moral and spiritual result will be reached that will bring honor to God and stability and prosperity to our beloved land. (J. Brown, *Sabbath-School Missions in Wisc.* Pres. Bd. Publ., 1904, 1–4. Used by permission.)

4. Evolution Attacked and Defended

Among the more important forces that were transforming the American cultural climate in the second half of the nineteenth century were the doctrine of evolution and Biblical criticism. Charles Darwin's The Origin of Species (1859) carried earlier genetic and evolutionary theories to new ground and marked an epoch. By the 1870's and 1880's many churchmen were discussing the relationship of the theory to the Bible, to ideas of God's creation and providence, to traditional conceptions of man's Fall and redemption. Rejection of the idea of fixed, unchanging truth, and "social Darwinism" with strong implications for laissez faire presently emerged also. Dr. Charles Hodge (1797–1878), venerable professor at Princeton Theological Seminary, rejected the Darwinian form of evolution because of what he felt to be its explicit denial of God's purposive control over the process. Dr. James McCosh (1811–1894), president of the College of New Jersey, accepted a very qualified evolution which acknowledged God's purposive control and which McCosh could harmonize with his own conservative view of the Bible. Some American clergymen—like Lyman Abbott, for example—went considerably farther with the doctrine than did Dr. McCosh. For further background see Bert Loewenberg, "Darwinism Comes to America, 1858–1900," in Mississippi Valley Historical Review, XXVIII *(1941), 339–368.*

A. Darwinism Rejected

Darwinism includes three distinct elements. First, evolution; or the assumption that all organic forms, vegetable and animal, have been evolved or developed from one, or a few, primordial living germs; second, that this evolution has been effected by natural selection, or the survival of the fittest; and third, and by far the most important and only distinctive element of his theory, that this natural selection is without design, being conducted by unintelligent physical causes. Neither the first nor the second of these elements constitute Darwinism; nor do the two combined. . . .

It is . . . neither evolution nor natural selection, which give Darwinism its peculiar character and importance. It is that Darwin rejects all teleology, or the doctrine of final causes. He denies design in any of the organisms in the vegetable or animal world. He teaches that the eye was formed without any purpose of producing an organ of vision.

Although evidence on this point has already been adduced, yet as it is often overlooked, at least in this country, so that many men speak favorably of Mr. Darwin's theory, who are no more Darwinians than they are Mussulmans; and as it is this feature of his system which brings it into conflict not only with Christianity, but with the fundamental principles of natural religion, it should be clearly established. The sources of proof on this point are,—1st. Mr. Darwin's own writings.

2d. The expositions of his theory given by its advocates. 3d. The character of the objections urged by its opponents.

The point to be proved is that it is the distinctive doctrine of Mr. Darwin, that species owe their origin, not to the original intention of the divine mind; not to special acts of creation calling new forms into existence at certain epochs; not to the constant and everywhere operative efficiency of God, guiding physical causes in the production of intended effects; but to the gradual accumulation of unintended variations of structure and instinct, securing some advantage to their subjects. . . .

By design is meant the intelligent and voluntary selection of an end, and the intelligent and voluntary choice, application, and control of means appropriate to the accomplishment of that end. That design, therefore, implies intelligence, is involved in its very nature. . . . But in thus denying design in nature, these writers array against themselves the intuitive perceptions and irresistible convictions of all mankind. . . .

The conclusion of the whole matter is, that the denial of design in nature is virtually the denial of God. Mr. Darwin's theory does deny all design in nature, therefore, his theory is virtually atheistical; his theory, not he himself. He believes in a Creator. But when that Creator, millions on millions of ages ago, did something,—called matter and a living germ into existence,—and then abandoned the universe to itself to be controlled by chance and necessity, without any purpose on his part as to the result, or any intervention or guidance, then He is virtually consigned, so far as we are concerned, to non-existence. . . . The denial of final causes is the formative idea of Darwin's theory, and therefore no teleologist can be a Darwinian. (Charles Hodge, *What Is Darwinism?* New York, 1874, 48 ff.)

B. A Qualified Evolution Accepted

Men of enlarged minds do now acknowledge that in the doctrine of universal causation, of God acting everywhere through second causes, there is nothing irreligious. On the contrary, the circumstance that God proceeds in a regular manner which can be anticipated, is evidently for the benefit of intelligent beings who can thus so far foresee the future and prepare for it and act upon it. But causation leads to development. If there be nothing irreligious in causation, as little is there impiety in the development which issues from it. It will be shown that development by causation is the plan by which God carries on his works, thus connecting the past with the present, and the present with the future. It was my privilege in my earliest published work to justify God's method of procedure by natural cause and natural law, as specially adapted to man's constitution. I reckon it as a like privilege in my declining life to be able to defend God's way of acting by development, which gives a consecutive unity to all nature, and as a stream from the throne of God flows through all time, widening and deepening till it covers the earth, as the waters do the sea, with the riches it carries. . . .

Like all creature action it will be found to have very stringent limitations. We may fix on some of these.

I. It cannot give an account of the origination of things. This is implied in its nature and its very name. Development takes place among materials already existing. Evolution is the derivation of one thing from another thing. But the mind does seek after an origin. . . .

II. It does not originate the power which works in development. That process shows us objects acting causally, but takes and gives no account either of the objects or the forces in them. . . .

III. Evolution of itself cannot give us the beneficent laws and special ends we see in nature. There is in force, considered in itself, neither good nor evil. It is as ready to work destruction as to promote the spread of happiness. . . .

There is need of a power above evolution to account for the beneficence of evolution. . . .

Geology clearly reveals that new products have appeared. There was a time when there was no organism and no life, no plant or animal. But at a set time organized matter appeared, say protoplasm. When there was no animated being I believe that there was no sensation, pleasant or painful, and it certainly cannot be proven that there was any feeling in the protoplasm or in the plant. As ages roll on we have creatures evidently feeling pleasure and liable to pain. Organisms both in the vegetable and animal form rise higher and higher, and animals become possessed of impulses which prompt them to act in a certain way. We have now powers higher than the mechanical, we have the vital, the sensitive, and the beginning of the psychical. . . . Finally, we have a moral nature discerning between good and evil, laying obligations upon us to promote the happiness, and as higher, the moral good of man, and pointing to a judgment-day. . . .

Was there Life in the original atom, or molecule formed of the atoms? If not, how did it come in when the first plant appeared? Was there sensation in the original molecule? If not, what brought it in when the first animal had a feeling of pleasure or of pain? Was there mind in the first molecule, say a power of perceiving an object out of itself? . . .

I am sure that when these things appear, there is something not previously in the atom or molecule. All sober thinkers of the day admit that there is no evidence whatever in experience or in reason to show that matter can produce mind; that mechanical action can gender mental action; that chemical action can manufacture consciousness; that electric action can reason, or organic structure rise to the idea of the good and the holy. I argue according to reason and experience that we must call in a power above the original physical forces to produce such phenomena. I may admit that a body may come out of another body by the powers with which the bodies are endowed; but I say that a sensitive, intelligent, moral discerning soul cannot proceed from the elements of matter. New powers have undoubtedly come in when consciousness and understanding and will begin to act. They may come according to laws not yet discovered, but they are the laws of the Supreme Lawgiver.

It will be argued by some that there must have been all along in the atoms a latent life, sensation, consciousness, and mind, with beneficence and capacity of choice, ready to be developed in the æons, some in thousands and some in millions of years. Those who deny that any new powers have appeared must resort to some such supposition. It may be allowed that this is a thing imaginable and possible, but there is not the semblance of a proof in its favor. . . .

The objects we are now looking at lie on the horizon of our vision and appear dim. We are constrained to call in a power to produce the effects, but whether it is to be regarded as natural or supernatural, we may not be able to say. God is working, but whether without or with secondary instrumentality we cannot determine. We may have come to a region where the difference between natural and supernatural disappears. . . .

Have we not, after all, the most satisfactory account of the process in the opening of our Scriptures? There is certainly a wonderful correspondence or parallelism between Genesis and geology, between the written record and the record in stone. . . .

More particularly the book of Genesis represents the work as proceeding by *days*, which in every part of Scripture is employed to denote epochs; thus in chap. ii. 4, it is said, "In the day that the Lord God made the earth and the heavens." Regarding the days as epochs, there is a very remarkable parallelism between the order in Genesis and the order in geology, quite as much so as that between the stages in embryology and that in paleontology pointed out by Von Baer. . . .

I cannot say how man's body was formed. But the Scriptures evidently speak truly when they declare that it was formed out of previously existing materials—out of the dust of the ground. They also declare that God "breathed into his nostrils the breath of life, and he became a living soul." As to his higher nature, it is said that he was made after the image of God. This must mean in knowledge of truth and in holiness. . . . In all this there is a new power not produced by mechanical or animal agency. (J. McCosh, *Development: What It Can Do and What It Cannot Do,* New York, 1883, 4 ff.)

5. Biblical Inerrancy

For late nineteenth century Presbyterians, theological problems created by cultural change came to focus in the question of the nature of the Bible's authority. The problem was in part a question as to what was the teaching of the Protestant Reformation concerning religious authority, and what was the value of the Protestant scholasticism that followed the Reformation. This debate foreshadowed the "fundamentalist-modernist" controversy of the 1920's and 1930's (see Ch. 11, arts. 7 and 9). For a treatment of the Presbyterian discussions in the light of this background, see L. A. Loetscher, The Broadening Church; A Study of Theological Issues in the Presbyterian Church Since 1869, *Philadelphia, 1954.*

The doctrine of the inerrancy of the original (and now lost) "autograph" manuscripts of the Bible, taught in the article below by Dr. A. A. Hodge (1823–1886) of Princeton Seminary and Dr. B. B. Warfield (1851–1921) of Western Seminary, was officially endorsed by the General Assembly in 1892 (see Ch. 10, art. 3) and was the chief basis of the suspension of Dr. Briggs (see Ch. 10, art. 4).

The writers of this article are sincerely convinced of the perfect soundness of the great Catholic doctrine of Biblical Inspiration *i.e.*, that the Scriptures not only contain, but ARE THE WORD OF GOD, and hence that all their elements and all their affirmations are absolutely errorless, and binding the faith and obedience of men. . . .

The historical faith of the Church has always been, that all the affirmations of Scripture of all kinds, whether of spiritual doctrine or duty, or of physical or historical fact, or of psychological or philosophical principle, are without any error, when the *ipsissima verba* of the original autographs are ascertained and interpreted in their natural and intended sense. . . .

Let . . . it be proved that each alleged discrepant statement certainly occurred in the original autograph of the sacred book in which it is said to be found. . . .

It is plain, however, that if the Scriptures do fail in truth in their statements of whatever kind, the doctrine of Inspiration which has been defended in this paper cannot stand. . . . A proved error in Scripture contradicts not only our doctrine, but the Scripture claims and, therefore, its inspiration in making those claims. . . .

We do not assert that the common text, but only that the original autographic text was inspired. No "error" can be asserted, therefore, which cannot be proved to have been aboriginal in the text. (A. A. Hodge and B. B. Warfield, "Inspiration," in *Presbyterian Review*, II, 1881, 237 ff.)

6. "Reaching the Masses"

Presbyterian and other periodical literature of the post-Civil War decades frequently discusses the Church's problem of "reaching the masses." Industrialization and accompanying urbanization were detaching the industrial worker from the church, and immigration was further increasing the number of the unchurched. The remedy commonly offered was revivalism and—a little later—the social gospel. Dr. A. T. Pierson (1837–1911), pastor of the Fort Street Presbyterian Church, Detroit, was less complacent and more self-critical than many in discussing the problem.

How often do we hear it said, that "the Gospel has *lost its hold* upon the masses!" Has it ever, in these days, *had hold* of them? . . .

To the heathen about us, we offer a dainty gloved hand or a fingertip, as though we feared that contact might contaminate; we do not identify ourselves with the want and woe that is beneath the very shadow of our church spires, and then we wonder at the indifference of the masses to the Gospel, and ask why it has lost its hold! . . .

Our Lord both preached to the people, and reached them: they formed the bulk of all His hearers and followers. Human nature has undergone and can undergo no radical change. If our Saviour's brief sojourn on earth had fallen in these days instead of those, the multitudes who do not come to our churches, and the problem of whose evangelization the Church seems unable to solve, would be found now, as then, thronging about Him. . . . Our profound conviction is, that if we, Christ's disciples, will not shut ourselves up in our gilded fanes, will not enshrine mammon, where we claim to enthrone God; if we will go and make ourselves saviours to the lost, one with, one of, the least and lowest; take hold of poverty and misery, want and woe, with an ungloved hand, through whose firm grasp may be felt the beat of a warm heart, we shall reach the "common people," as our Master did. . . .

There are not a few in the Church, both among her ministry and her membership, who yearn to make a fair and a faithful trial of a more simple, scriptural model of church organization and administration, uncontrolled by worldly minds or worldly maxims, with a severe simplicity of work and worship, with no attempt at worldly attractions, in choir or pulpit; where everything shall exalt God, fulfilling the literal intent of worship, viz: ascribing *worth* to God; where there shall be no salaried preacher, hired choir, or rented pew, and where the preaching of the Gospel and benevolent work shall be supported by the voluntary gifts cheerfully offered by consecrated hearts, rather than wrung by impassioned appeal from the unwilling and worldly-minded, and even the unconverted. (A. T. Pierson, in *Presbyterian Review*, I, 1880, 455 ff.)

7. Social and Cultural "Lawlessness"

Rapid social and cultural change created near panic in the minds of some during these years, driving them to resist change at every point. Dr. Samuel H. Kellogg, who was a leader in the premillennial movement which was making a vigorous appearance in various denominations in the 1870's, in his inaugural address at Western Seminary in Allegheny (now Pittsburgh), quoted below, classified ecclesiastical and cultural change with the recent railway strike as common manifestations of "lawlessness."

Since the startling and terrible events of last summer [i.e., the railway strike in July, 1877] in our own midst and elsewhere, many have anxiously speculated as to the causes and occasions of such a revelation of destructive lawlessness. . . .

To sum up, then, I believe that the one word, *anomia*, "lawlessness," as denoting the contemning or repudiation of divine law in all its various expressions, in the family, in society, in the state, and in the church, more precisely and comprehensively than any other term indicates the special and distinctive evil tendency of our times, and eminently of our own country. I believe that this spirit of *anomia*, instead of being a superficial affection of the body social, political, and ecclesiastical, more or less pervades the inmost heart of society with its baneful power. I believe that so far from being due to causes merely external and occasional, to be remedied by improved legislation and various apparatus of social and church reform, it has its radical cause deep in the prevailing speculative doubt and unbelief in the fundamental truths of theism. It is simply the natural result of a godless scientific philosophy, which, whether pantheistic, materialistic or agnostic, announces as the result of its investigations that it cannot find by miscroscope, or telescope, or chemical analysis, any personal God to whom men have to give account; and thereby takes away the ultimate ground of all responsibility to law of any kind, whether human or divine. (S. H. Kellogg, in *Charges and Addresses at the Inauguration of Rev. W. H. Jeffers, D.D., and Rev. S. H. Kellogg, D.D. . . . 1877*, Pittsburgh, 1878, 51, 54.)

8. The Church and Its Colleges

American Presbyterians had been interested in higher education from the early years of their organized life (see Ch. 2, arts. 1 and 10; Ch. 7, art. 10), and the early nineteenth century had seen expanded activity in this direction (see D. D. Tewksbury, The Founding of American Colleges and Universities Before the Civil War, New York, 1932).

During the Civil War the Church's interest in higher education temporarily declined because of financial difficulties and the growth of the state educational systems. Many Presbyterian academies and colleges closed during these years. The creation in 1883 of a special "Board of Aid for Colleges and Academies" marked the reviving and strengthening of the earlier interest. The General Assembly action creating this Board, quoted in part below, summarizes the Church's motives and objectives in higher education.

This movement in the interest of higher education first took form in the Assembly of 1877, in the appointment of a Committee "to consider the matter of enlarging the functions of the Board of Education," having in view "some plan which would result in the better endowment of our collegiate and theological institutions." The Committee was continued by the Assemblies of 1878, 1879, and 1880, and made their Report to the Assembly of 1881. . . .

To the same Assembly a report was submitted from the Standing Committee on Home Missions, recommending in substance, the appointment of "a permanent Committee on Education in the West," to have in charge the locating, assisting, and endowing of institutions of learning, "with special reference to the supply of missionaries and teachers for the frontier." Both these reports were finally referred by the Assembly of 1881 to a "special Committee on Education" to report to the next Assembly. . . .

Presbyterianism has special affinities for learning and the diffusion of knowledge. . . . Her doctrines are such that they require intelligence for their grasp and retention. . . .

So, too, the Presbyterian form of government suggests and necessitates education. It is representative, as is that of the republic. And under it, as under that of the republic, "the people is king." Widespread wisdom and knowledge are, therefore, vital to Presbyterian growth and perpetuity. . . .

The field that should have our prompt attention is west of Ohio—the vast sweep of country stretching from about the 85th degree of longitude to the Pacific. . . .

It is hardly possible, and it were hardly desirable, if possible, for our Church to establish a system of parochial schools. The State has come to have chief charge of our primary education, and though this education is essentially secular, it is pursued while the children are still under the constant influence of home and church and Sabbath-school. Many of the evils of secularization are thus happily counteracted.

But lying between this primary training and the strictly professional is the educational process to which, it is our profound conviction, the Presbyterian Church needs to give her immediate and most considerate attention. The academy and the college are the schools that we must plant and nurture. . . .

There character forms fast. As young men are, in moral bent and conformation when graduating, so as a rule they stay. . . .

The colleges that the Church should found and favor should therefore be:

1. Colleges that shall have as their chief aim education, with a view to the whole man. . . .

2. Colleges that shall be pervaded by a positive Christian atmosphere.

3. Colleges that shall make the Bible one of the text-books.

4. Colleges that shall have all their instruction in harmony with the Christian faith.

5. Colleges that shall influence decisions for life-work, so that the tendency shall be toward the ministry rather than away from it. Choice of profession is most frequently made in college. Secularism sets no currents toward the ministry. . . .

6. Colleges that shall be under our own denominational control. And this for two reasons:

a. Self-preservation. Other denominations are in the field pushing their way by institutions. . . .

b. Stewardship. . . . We are under obligation exactly proportionate to our wealth and numbers and intelligence to attend to this great trust. (*Minutes of the G. A.,* 1883, 582 ff.)

CHAPTER
10

RESISTANCE TO SOCIAL AND CULTURAL CHANGE
1887–1899

1. The Ideal of Christian Unity

Nineteenth century America witnessed increasing centralization of political and economic life. Similarly the American Churches, to make their missionary and promotional work more effective, strengthened their national organizations. This gave a heightened consciousness of the "Church" as a functioning organization. From about the second third of the nineteenth century important groups in European and American Protestantism were becoming more conscious of the Church as a mystical body. These tendencies, both practical and mystical, were by the 1880's and 1890's expressing themselves in a growing demand among Presbyterians for greater Christian unity, in spite of the conservatism which dominated the Church during this period. Dr. Charles A. Briggs (1841–1913), professor at Union Theological Seminary, was a leading spokesman for unity. His article excerpted below is notable in discerning the radical dynamism under the outward conservatism of American Christianity, and also in its "conservative" demand that Christian unity be built on a positive affirmation of the Christian heritage and not on a mere negative reduction to a "least common denominator" of the existing denominations.

Christian Union has become one of the burning questions of the day. Unity is a grand ideal of the Church of Christ. . . .

The ideal of the Church is visible unity, but the visible Church cannot entirely attain its ideal until its completion in Jesus Christ. . . .

The Christian Church has never altogether lost sight of its ideal, but it has endeavored to realize it in mistaken ways, and has thus erected barriers in the way of Christian Union and has occasioned the development of a number of variations. . . .

The first great barrier to Christian Union is the theory of *submission to a central ecclesiastical authority claiming divine right of government.*

RESISTANCE TO SOCIAL AND CULTURAL CHANGE 245

This is the great sin of the Roman Catholic Church. . . .

Another great barrier to the reunion of Christendom is *subscription to elaborate Creeds*. This is the great sin of the Lutheran and Reformed churches. . . .

The differences between the Lutherans, Calvinists, and Arminians have nothing to do with the essentials of Protestantism. . . .

The theological systems of the three great branches of Protestantism have been elaborated by *a priori* logic and by deduction from premises that are not sufficiently accurate and comprehensive. They have all of them departed a long distance from the Scriptures and the Creeds of the Reformation. . . .

The third great barrier to Christian Union is the insisting upon *uniformity of worship*. This is the special sin of the Church of England. . . .

The excellence of the Book of Common Prayer of the Church of England is generally recognized. But considerable alterations will need to be made in order to make it acceptable to American Christians in general; and there must be the recognition of the liberty of free prayer in a part of the service. . . .

On the other hand, those churches that have no prayer-books should overcome their prejudices against their use. . . .

The greatest difficulty remains in the celebration of the Sacraments. . . .

Traditionalism is another great barrier in the way of Christian Union. There are in human nature two forces which, like action and reaction, tend to keep everything in stability—the conservative and the progressive. Either of these apart is harmful. Their combination is a great excellence. . . .

In some respects the American churches are traditional and in other respects radical when compared with the churches of Europe. There is thus an internal inconsistency that will erelong produce great changes that may be little less than revolutionary. The practical side of Christianity will erelong overcome the traditionalism in doctrine and worship, and reconstruct on broader lines and in more comprehensive schemes; so that there will be better correspondence between the doctrines and worship and the real American Christian life. These traditions are those of foreign national Churches that grew up out of historical circumstances that have long past and that are no longer appropriate to the circumstances of a new age and a new continent. . . .

Theological progress is not in the direction of simplicity, but of variety and complicity. We cannot retreat in theological definition; we must advance in this scientific age. The Apostles' Creed represents the simple faith of the early Church; we cannot ignore Christian history and go back to that. The Ante-Nicene Church was crude in its theology; we cannot fall back on the Nicene Creed for a reunion of Christendom. The inheritance of the Truth is more precious than external Unity. . . .

Unity is to be attained by conserving all that is good in the past achievements of the Church, and by advancing to still higher attainments. . . . Such progress is possible only by research, discussion, and conflict. The more conflict the better. Battle for the truth is infinitely better than stagnation in error. Every error should be slain as soon as possible. . . .

Christian churches should go right on in the lines drawn by their own history and their own symbols; this will in the end lead to greater heights, on which there will be concord. . . .

The Evangelical Alliance has done a good work in the past, but it is a voluntary association of kindred spirits, and is in no sense a representative body. There can be no effective Alliance unless that Alliance represents the Churches that constitute it; in an assembly of delegates chosen for conference. The times are well-nigh ripe for such an Alliance of the Churches in America; and we may anticipate, at no very great distance in the future, that there will be such an Alliance for the Christian world. (C. A. Briggs, "The Barriers to Christian Union," in *Presbyterian Review*, VIII, 1887, 445 ff.)

2. Creedal Revision Defeated

The increasing emphasis of nineteenth century culture on man's power and responsibility led many Presbyterians in Europe and America to attempt to revise, or to change the terms of subscription to, their doctrinal Standard, the Westminster Confession of Faith. This Confession, which had been drafted in the 1640's, was one of the most emphatic and detailed of the Calvinistic creeds in its teaching about God's sovereignty and about election. The issues were thoroughly discussed in the early 1890's, but actual revision for American Presbyterians did not come until 1903 (see Ch. 11, arts. 1, 10, and 11).

A. Dr. Van Dyke Advocates Revision

The opponents of the [revision] movement eulogize the Westminster Assembly and their work, insist that the Confession cannot be improved, charge upon the other side the desire to engraft private opinions and idiosyncrasies upon a public document, and seek to show that there would be no need of amendment even if the Confession were ever so full of faults, because the terms of subscription are so liberal. This last argument has been pushed to a dangerous extreme, at which conservatism and radicalism have joined hands in opposition to revision. The extreme conservative wants to keep the Confession just as it is, because he thinks it is as near perfection as any thing human can be. He has no hope of bettering it. The extreme radical wants to keep it unchanged, because *he* thinks that is the surest way to lay the whole thing on the shelf, and cause it to be regarded simply as a grand old historic monument of what that eminent body, the Westminster Assembly of Divines, believed. And so the conservative and the radical opponents of revision unite in eulogizing liberal terms of subscription. . . . We [i.e., "the friends of revision"] regard the Confession not simply as a historic monument, not simply a standard and test of ministerial orthodoxy, but as the banner of the whole church, the public declaration of *what Presbyterians believe*. What we complain of is not that the church is too strictly bound to her creeds; but that the creed does not with sufficient clearness express the faith of the church on certain specified points. To keep statements in our Confession which none of us believe is demoralizing to ourselves and a misrepresentation of our faith to the world. (H. J. Van Dyke, "Revision of the Confession of Faith," in *Presbyterian*, August 17, 1889.)

These two truths, God's *sovereignty* in the bestowal of his grace, and his *infinite love for all men,* are the hinges and turning points of all Christian theology. The *anti-*Calvinist decries the first. The *hyper-*Calvinist or Supralapsarian decries the second, holding that God creates some men on purpose to damn them, for his glory. The true Calvinist believes both and insists that they are consistent. It is upon the union of these two truths that the strength and beauty of our theology depends. The ultimate and dominant reason why I advocate the revision of the Westminster Confession is that it does not state these two truths in their relations and harmony. It is full of God's sovereignty in the choice of the elect, and overflows with the declaration of his special love for them, all of which I devoutly believe. But it contains no summary of those Scriptures, and of those acts and words of God in Christ, which explicitly teach that he is the Saviour of all men, and not willing that any should perish, but that all should come to repentance. In former articles I have stated the proposition thus: Our Confession does not contain one declaration of God's infinite love to men, nor one declaration that Christ's sacrifice for sin is sufficient for all, adapted to all, and offered to all. This statement . . . does not say that the Confession *denies*, or even that it contains no *implication* of God's infinite love to all men, but that the Confession contains no *declaration* of this great truth. (H. J. Van Dyke, "God's Infinite Love to Men," in *Presbyterian*, October 5, 1889.)

B. Dr. Patton Opposes Revision

It looks now as though conservative men would need all their strength in order to keep the Church from throwing the Confession overboard altogether. . . . Whether we desire it or not, we cannot avoid facing the question whether there is any future for the Presbyterian Church. It is the demand for Christian unity; it is the anti-confessional drift; it is the growing spirit of comprehension that is giving momentum to the movement for a moderate revision. The smaller question [i.e., revision] is only a form in which the larger question happens to be presenting itself. . . . The real question in the minds of some of our leading men is whether the denominations have not outlived their usefulness. . . .

It would be easier to make a new creed than to pare the old one down to the size that would suit the Comprehensionists. . . .

If, then, in the interests of Comprehension the work of revision is to go, where will it stop? Shall we strike out everything but what is common to evangelical Christians? That seems to be a feasible thing. But is anybody prepared to state the *consensus* of evangelical doctrine? Any one who attempts it will find it a hard thing to do. Will you widen your doctrinal area until the profession of Christian faith becomes the only condition of ministerial fellowship? Will you accept, for instance, the Apostles' Creed as your ecclesiastical symbol? That is a good one, but in what sense will you have it accepted? (F. L. Patton, *The Revision of the Confession of Faith*, read before Presbyterian Social Union, New York, December 2, 1889, 13 f.)

C. Dr. Briggs Advocates a New Creed

The terms of subscription are the real difficulty in the situation. . . . We venture to say that the terms of subscription are the key to the history of the American Presbyterian Church, and in some respects of the history of British Christianity since the Reformation. . . .

The first step in revision, therefore, should be to revise the terms of subscription and make them definite, so that the subscriber would know that he was subscribing to the essential and necessary articles of the Westminster system. The second step should then be to define what these essential and necessary articles are. This may be done in the new creed. The new creed should (1) set forth the essential and necessary articles of the Confession, and omit all unessential and unnecessary articles; (2) give adequate expression to those doctrines that have risen into prominence since the Westminster Confession was composed. The new creed would thus be of the nature of a declaratory act in the form of a devotional and a congregational creed. . . .

In our opinion it would be best not to touch the Westminster Confession, but to give our strength to the construction of a new creed. (Charles A. Briggs, "Revision of the Westminster Confession," in *Andover Review*, XIII, January–June, 1890, 65 ff.)

D. Report on the Revision Amendments

All the Overtures on Revision having failed of receiving this constitutional two-thirds majority, *i.e.*, 147 votes, no legislative action upon them by the General Assembly is possible under the Constitution. (*Minutes of the G. A.*, 1893, 198.)

3. The Assembly Affirms the Inerrancy of the Bible

Meeting in Portland, Oregon, in 1892, the General Assembly, in agreement with the Hodge-Warfield article (see Ch. 9, art. 5, q.v. also for editorial comment) declared Biblical inerrancy to be the official doctrine of the Church, but this position was tacitly abandoned in the twentieth century (see editorial comment on Ch. 11, arts. 7 and 9).

A. The Assembly's "Portland Deliverance" Affirms Inerrancy

The General Assembly would remind all under its care that it is a fundamental doctrine that the Old and New Testaments are the inspired and infallible Word of God. Our Church holds that the inspired Word, as it came from God, is without error. The assertion of the contrary cannot but shake the confidence of the people in the sacred Books. All who enter office in our Church solemnly profess to receive them as the only infallible rule of faith and practice. If they change their belief on this point, Christian honor demands that they should withdraw from our ministry. They have no right to use the pulpit or the chair of the professor for the dissemination of their errors until they are dealt with by the slow process of discipline. But if any do so act, their Presbyteries should speedily interpose, and deal with them for violation of ordination vows. The vow taken at the beginning is obligatory until the party taking it is honorably and properly released. The General Assembly enjoins upon all ministers, elders and Presbyteries, to be faithful to the duty here imposed. (*Minutes of the G. A.*, 1892, 179–180.)

B. The Assembly Restates the "Portland Deliverance"

This General Assembly reaffirms the doctrine of the deliverance of the Assembly of 1892, touching the inspiration of the Holy Scripture, viz., That the original Scriptures of the Old and New Testaments, being immediately inspired of God, were without error, and in so doing declares that the said deliverance enunciates no new doctrine and imposes no new test of orthodoxy, but interprets and gives expression to what has always been the belief of the Church taught in the Westminster Confession of Faith. (*Minutes of the G. A.*, 1893, 163.)

C. Eighty-seven Protest Inerrancy

The undersigned enter respectful and earnest protest against the action of this Assembly, which declares the inerrancy of the original autographs of Scripture to be the faith of the Church. We protest against this action.

1. Because it is insisting upon a certain theory of inspiration, when our Standards have hitherto only emphasized the fact of inspiration. So far as the original manuscript came from God, undoubtedly it was without error. But we have no means of determining how far God controlled the penmen in transcribing from documents in matters purely circumstantial.

2. Because it is dogmatizing on a matter of which, necessarily, we can have no positive knowledge.

3. Because it is insisting upon an interpretation of our Standards which they never have borne, and which, on their face, is impossible. No man in subscribing to his belief in the Scriptures as the Word of God, and the only infallible rule of faith and practice, has his mind on the original autographs.

4. Because it is setting up an imaginary Bible as a test of orthodoxy. If an inerrant original Bible is vital to faith, we cannot escape the conclusion that an inerrant present Bible is vital to faith.

5. Because it is disparaging the Bible we have, and endangering its authority under the pressure of a prevalent hostile criticism. It seems like flying for shelter to an original autograph, when the Bible we have in our hands to-day is our impregnable defense.

Believing these present Scriptures to be "The very Word of God" and "immediately inspired by God," "kept pure in all ages" and "our only infallible rule of faith and practice," notwithstanding some apparent discrepancies in matters purely circumstantial, we earnestly protest against the imposing of this new interpretation of our Standards upon the Church, to bind men's consciences by enforced subscription to its terms. (*Minutes of the G. A.*, 1893, 167–168.)

4. The Briggs Heresy Case

Dr. Charles A. Briggs (1841–1913), the Presbyterian Church's leading contender for Biblical criticism and for a new and simpler creed, and conspicuous advocate of Church union (see Ch. 10, arts. 1 and 2), was prosecuted for heresy as a result of the inaugural address which he delivered in 1891, on the occasion of being transferred to the new chair of Biblical theology in Union Theological Seminary, New York.

A. DR. BRIGGS'S INAUGURAL ADDRESS (JANUARY 20, 1891) Protestant Christianity builds its faith and life on the divine authority contained in the Scriptures, and too often depreciates the Church and the Reason. Spurgeon is an example of the average modern Evangelical, who holds the Protestant position, and assails the Church and Reason in the interest of the authority of Scripture. But the average opinion of the Christian world would not assign him a higher place in the kingdom of God than Martineau or Newman. . . .

The first barrier that obstructs the way to the Bible is *superstition*. . . . Superstition is no less superstition if it take the form of *Bibliolatry*. . . .

The second barrier, keeping men from the Bible, is the dogma of *verbal inspiration*. . . . No such claim is found in the Bible itself, or in any of the creeds of Christendom. . . .

The third barrier is the *authenticity of the Scriptures*. The only authenticity we are concerned about in seeking for the divine authority of the Scriptures is *divine authenticity*, and yet many theologians have insisted that we must prove that the Scriptures were written by or under the superintendence of prophets and apostles. . . . It may be regarded as the certain result of the science of the Higher Criticism that Moses did not write the Pentateuch . . . ; Isaiah did not write half the book that bears his name. . . .

The fourth barrier set up by theologians to keep men away from the Bible is the dogma of the inerrancy of Scripture. . . . I shall venture to affirm that, so far as I can see, there are errors in the Scriptures that no one has been able to explain away; and the theory that they were not in the original text is sheer assumption, upon which no mind can rest with certainty. . . . The Bible itself nowhere makes this claim. The creeds of the Church nowhere sanction it. . . .

The fifth obstruction to the Bible has been thrown up in front of modern science. It is the claim that the *miracles* disturb, or violate, the laws of nature and the harmony of the universe. . . .

Another barrier to the Bible has been the interpretation put upon *Predictive Prophecy*, making it a sort of history before the time, and looking anxiously for the fulfilment of the details of Biblical prediction. Kuenen has shown that if we insist upon the fulfilment of the details of the predictive prophecy of the Old Testament, many of these predictions have been reversed by history; and the great body of the Messianic prediction has not only never been fulfilled, but cannot now be fulfilled, for the reason that its own time has passed forever. . . .

There is no authority in the Scriptures, or in the Creeds of Christendom, for the doctrine of immediate sanctification at death. The only sanctification known to experience, to Christian orthodoxy, and to the Bible, is progressive sanctification. Progressive sanctification after death, is the doctrine of the Bible and the Church. . . .

Biblical Ethics presents us an advancing system of morals—God showing His holy face and character and the sublime precepts of morality as men were able to hear them. . . .

The ancient worthies, Noah and Abraham, Jacob and Judah, David and Solomon, were in a low stage of moral advancement. . . .

The Messiah is the culmination of the Old Testament. He is the pivot of History. . . .

Sometimes the deity of Christ has been so exalted that men have forgotten His humanity. Then others have been so absorbed in the wonders of His humanity that they have not seen His divinity. Then the complex nature, the union of the human and divine in the Theanthropos,—the profoundest minds of the Christian centuries have thought upon it and unfolded some of its glories, but it is still like the very heavens for heights of mystery and glory. . . .

I have not departed in any respect from the orthodox teaching of the Christian Church as set forth in its official creeds. . . .

Let us cut down everything that is dead and harmful, every kind of dead orthodoxy, every species of effete ecclesiasticism, all merely formal morality, all those dry and brittle fences that constitute denominationalism, and are the barriers of Church Unity. Let us burn up every form of false doctrine, false religion, and false practice. Let us remove every incumbrance out of the way for a new life; the life of God is moving throughout Christendom, and the spring-time of a new age is about to come upon us. (C. A. Briggs, "The Inaugural Address," in *The Edward Robinson Chair of Biblical Theology in the Union Theological Seminary New York,* New York, 1891, 28 ff.)

B. Judgment Pronounced

This General Assembly of the Presbyterian Church in the United States of America, sitting as a judicatory in this cause on appeal, does hereby suspend Charles A. Briggs, the said appellee, from the office of a minister in the Presbyterian Church in the United States of America, until such time as he shall give satisfactory evidence of repentance to the General Assembly of the Presbyterian Church in the United States of America, for the violation by him of the said ordination vow as herein and heretofore found. (*Minutes of the G.A.,* 1893, 165.)

5. "A Plea for Peace and Work"

In the decades when Charles Peirce and William James were developing the philosophy of pragmatism, Presbyterians of nearly every theological type were moving toward a more pragmatic conception of the Church, which said in effect that controversy about the Church's beliefs must not obstruct the Church's diversified and expanding activities. The "Plea," given in full below, is in its method of argument a notable expression of this pragmatic attitude. In its purpose the "Plea" was a protest against the preceding Assembly's affirmation of the inerrancy of the Bible (see Ch. 10, art. 3) and foreshadowed in part the Auburn Affirmation of 1924 (see Ch. 11, art. 9).

To those who are actively engaged in the Ministry of Christ, the chief interest and the first duty is the bringing of the simple Gospel home to the hearts and lives of men.

This is the great work of the Church to which everything else must give way. She can only win the favor of God and the love of men by single-hearted devotion to the task of preaching and practicing plain Christianity.

As Ministers of Jesus Christ, and working Pastors in the Presbyterian Church, we are filled with the gravest fears lest the usefulness of the Church should be hindered, her peace disturbed, and her honor diminished by the prevalence of theological controversy and strife over doctrines which are not essential.

We remember that there have been two sad periods in the history of our church in which this has happened. We remember that our Church has been twice rent asunder by issues which have been recognized shortly afterwards as unnecessary. We dread the possibility of having such a painful experience repeated in our own times. We are persuaded that the great body of the Church, laymen and ministers, have little sympathy with the extremes of dogmatic conflict, and are already weary of the strife of tongues, and are longing for peace and united work. We feel that we do not speak for ourselves alone, but for the great multitude who hold the same conviction in regard to the first duty and main work of the Church, while representing at the same time many different shades of theological opinion.

It is in this spirit that we join our voices in a plain, straightforward fraternal expression of the desire for harmony and united devotion to practical work. For this reason we deprecate any and every attempt to impose new tests of orthodoxy, or to restrict the liberty hitherto enjoyed by those who sincerely subscribe to the essential and necessary articles of the Presbyterian Church. Especially would we deplore any hasty addition by informal resolution or by judicial decision, to the confessional statement of the doctrine of Holy Scripture. We hold firmly to the teaching of the first chapter of "The Confession of Faith," and to the Holy Scriptures as the Word of God, the only infallible rule of faith and practice. We do not express any individual opinion in regard to the theory of the inerrancy of the original autographs of Scripture in matters which are not essential to religion, but differing as we may in regard to the abstract truth of that theory, we protest unitedly and firmly against making assent to it a test of Christian faith or of good standing in the Presbyterian ministry.

In the interests of Christian liberty, in the interests of peace and unity, in the interests of missionary enthusiasm and progress, we take this position clearly and firmly, and we cordially invite all who agree with us, to coöperate in maintaining these principles, believing that the end of the Commandment is love out of a pure heart, and a good conscience, and a faith unfeigned; and that the surest defence of the truth is its unfaltering proclamation. (*A Plea for Peace and Work*, n.p., February 17, 1893. A copy is in Box No. 174, Henry van Dyke Papers, Princeton University Library. Signed by 235.)

6. The Reform of Worship

A striking characteristic of the nineteenth century, as part of the reviving churchliness of the time, was a quickened interest in liturgical worship in the Roman, Lutheran, Reformed, and Anglican Churches of the world. American Presbyterian worship under the influence of Puritanism, the frontier, and revivalism had by mid-nineteenth century moved from "purity" to outright slovenliness. As early as 1855 C. W. Baird, in his book Eutaxia, *had called the attention of Presbyterians to almost forgotten liturgical aspects of their heritage. Dr. Briggs also did, as quoted below. The Church Service Society, led by Dr. Henry van Dyke, pastor of the Brick Church, New York, was much influenced by similar developments among Scottish Presbyterians. An informing introductory study on Reformed worship is W. D. Maxwell,* An Outline of Christian Worship, London, 1936.

A. Decline of Presbyterian Worship Lamented

The tendency in the Presbyterian Church has been from bad to worse [i.e., *in re* worship] since the Westminster Assembly. One may trace this descent by comparing the Directory of Worship in its successive revisions with the worship of Presbyterian congregations in our day. The American Presbyterian churches are drifting toward an uncertain future. It is high time that the General Assembly should take the Directory for Worship in hand. I do not hesitate to state that the public worship in many of our Presbyterian churches is so different from the Directory, that our Presbyterian fathers could not recognize it as Presbyterian, and that in many respects the American Episcopal churches are more conformed to the Westminster ideal than their Presbyterian neighbors. . . .

A great reform is needed in Presbyterian prayers. I doubt whether much can be accomplished in this direction without a partial and voluntary Liturgy. (C. A. Briggs, "Presbyterian Worship," in *New York Evangelist*, April 12, 1888, 2.)

B. The Church Service Society

I. The Church Service Society of the Presbyterian Church in the U.S.A. stands upon the basis of that doctrine of the Church, the Ministry, and the Sacraments, which is set forth in the Westminster standards. . . .

II. The Society proposes as its first object an inquiry into the present conduct of public worship in The Presbyterian Church, and the various orders of worship in actual use.

III. The Society proposes to study the modes of worship which have been in use in those Churches known as the Reformed, of which we are one; and thus to recognize the importance of this branch of historical theology, to make its lessons clear to the mind of the Church, and to strengthen in our services the links which bind us to historic Christianity.

IV. The Society aims to follow this study of the present conduct and past history of the worship of the Church by doing such work in the preparation of forms of service in an orderly worship as may help to guard against the contrary evils of confusion and ritualism, and promote reverence and beauty in the worship of God in His holy House, unity and the spirit of common praise and prayer among the people. ("Statement of Principles" of the Church Service Society, in *The Church Service Society of the Presbyterian Church in the U.S.A.*, n.p., n.d. [1897]. A copy is in the Henry van Dyke Papers, Presbyterian Historical Society, Philadelphia.)

When the returns from the responding pastors came to be studied by the Committee, it became apparent that the variety in the Orders of Service at present observed in the churches is so extreme that it was impossible to classify them as variations around a particular norm, or even to gather them into groups having generic likeness. (Report on an Inquiry in *Church Service Society Papers, No. 1, The Report of an Inquiry into the Present Conduct of Public Worship*, n.p., 1899. A copy is in the Presbyterian Historical Society, Philadelphia.)

7. The New Immigration

The "new" immigration, in which immigrants of Roman Catholic and Jewish background from southern and western Europe began to predominate in the middle 1880's, alarmed "Nordic" Protestant Americans. Efforts to win them to the Protestant faith, though sincere, were greatly handicapped by the psychological and sociological barriers, reflected in the quotations below, which existed for both Protestant and immigrant.

Never in the history of the country, has the tide of immigration reached the rate of the past few months. . . . Hundreds and thousands of them are paupers and criminals sent to us by communities and local governments in Europe. . . . Do we incur any risk in receiving them into our bosom? The question is simply this . . . whether this Christian civilization of ours shall absorb and assimilate these multitudes that are pouring in upon us, in constantly increasing streams, or whether they shall absorb and assimilate us! (*Minutes of the G.A.*, 1883, p. 599.)

Our foreign population. . . . The increase of this element of our population, especially in the great Central West, is something appalling. . . . What is to be done with these people? . . . Will they become American, or shall we become European? The emigrants that we see crowding all these Western railway trains, carrying their blankets and their bundles, with a dozen children in every family, these are the men and women who in a few years are to have wealth and influence, and are to determine largely our social and moral conditions. There are tremendous perils in this state of things. Within the last thirty days there have been outbursts of anarchy, bloody collisions of law with Socialistic elements of the worst type [i.e., the "Haymarket riot" in Chicago, May 4, 1886]. The whole land has been roused and brought into actual contact with some of the portentous facts of our foreign emigration. People can see, in the light of these recent outbreaks, that some of our foreign population are bitterly hostile to the best interests of man. It is absolutely certain that these people of foreign birth and alien habits must have the Gospel of Christ, or else they will be only an ever present source of danger to our civilization. (*Minutes of the G.A.,* 1886, 42.)

(a) *The National Peril.*—We believe our country was founded for great providential ends. We delight to contemplate the work of God in preparing the nations by long training for the development of civil and religious liberty, which the few choice specimens sifted out of these nations, by the sieve of the persecutor and the oppressor, planted as a seed in the western world. We believe that our national institutions are the fruit of the ripest and holiest thought. . . . But this national life, and the purpose of God in it, are threatened by the introduction of millions of people, whose sole education has been under conditions diametrically opposed to those which subsist here. . . .

(b) *The Moral Peril.*—It is not the number but the quality of the people that gives strength to a nation. . . . The duty of the Church seems imperative, to take hold at once of this work, and to meet the immigrant with the helpfulness and blessedness of the Gospel.

(c) *The Religious Peril.*—It is not only that our Protestant Christianity is threatened by the great influx of Romanism, but rather that religion itself is endangered. . . . East and West, churches, once prosperous, have been closed and sold because the American element has been crowded out. . . .

The work is evangelization. . . . To do this, the first essential is to secure the love and confidence of the immigrant. (*Minutes of the G.A.,* 1889, 41–42, 44.)

8. Wanted: "Christian Sociology"

Individualism was fostered by many powerful forces in nineteenth century America, such as the frontier, laissez-faire economics, and many aspects of the conception of freedom. In American Christianity, with its traditions of Puritanism and of revivalism, and with its greatly weakened conception of the Church, individualism was peculiarly strong. But rapid industrialization in the last decades of the nineteenth century, bringing with it economic interdependence, tended to make the old individualism ineffective. The problem for Christian leaders was where to find within Christianity an integrating principle to meet the new interdependence. The so-called "social gospel" which arose to meet this need sought the cohesive principle in the Kingdom of God (i.e., the community of the ethically earnest) rather than in the Church (i.e., the community of the redeemed). By the 1880's and 1890's leaders like Dr. Thompson were sounding a social note, but it was not until the twentieth century that denominations as such—the Presbyterian among the earliest of them—began to endorse the new social ideas and techniques (see Ch. 11, art. 3). Dr. Robert E. Thompson (1844–1924), quoted below, was a Presbyterian minister and professor of political economy at the University of Pennsylvania (1874–1892) and president of Central High School, Philadelphia (1894–1920). For the social gospel, see C. H. Hopkins, The Rise of the Social Gospel in American Protestantism 1865–1915, *New Haven, 1940.*

We have come to the end of a great era of mere individualism in religion, in politics, in economics. John Wesley, Adam Smith, and Jean Jacques Rousseau were the prophets of that age, working on parallel lines for the same great end,—the recognition of the worth of the individual man as distinct from social bodies and corporations of whatever kind. That movement did vast good. It has left us a harvest of priceless results. But it always was an exaggeration,—a presentation of half a truth as though it were the whole truth. Like all exaggerations it has produced an equal reaction, and we now are in the rebound of the movement.

The social side of religion, of politics, of economics, is becoming the more prominent. We find men laboring again in very different fields and with no consciousness of a common end,—men like John Henry Newman, Karl Marx, and Otto von Bismarck,—for the introduction of a new era. The present truth,—as our fathers called it,—the truth demanded by the needs and the cravings of to-day, is the proclamation of the kingdom of God,—the revelation of God to men in social relations and social duties,—the presence of God in the perplexities, the problems, even the convulsions, of society. . . .

Of course there is danger—nay, there is certainty—of exaggeration. We see that all around us already. We see it in the weaker brethren, who are carried most easily off their balance by popular tendencies of any kind, and who talk sometimes as though men were to be regenerated by clean homes and fresh air, or as if the gospel had been superseded by political economy. In this Darwinian age, when everything is made to depend on environment, it must needs be that such offenses come. . . .

Gentlemen, your proper work as ambassadors for God, pleading with men to be reconciled to him, is the greatest of social tasks. Nothing can compare with that in lasting importance. Only let that be done with due regard to the work of Christ as the gatherer of our scattered humanity out of the isolation of sin into right human relations with each other. Preach the gospel, but preach no truncated gospel. Preach the Christ who died to save sinners; but preach him also as turning the hearts of the fathers to the children, of the ruled to the rulers, of the rich to the poor, and the poor to the rich, that he may gather into one grand fellowship all that are in heaven and all that are upon the earth. . . .

In pleading for this recognition of a social side to the gospel, I am asking you to establish yourselves more firmly on the ground occupied by the Protestant Reformers generally, and especially by the founders of our Reformed Church. Calvinism in its heroic days was a social as well as a theological faith. It was theocratic to the core. And let us not misunderstand that word "theocratic." Theocracy, the rule of God in all human affairs, has been too often confounded with hierocracy, the rule of a priesthood or a clergy. No men ever hated hierocracy with more vehemence than did our fathers, because they regarded it as the great enemy of theocracy, the rule of God. It was their faith in his direct rule over all human spirits and all social relations, which made them the strong men they were, and weighted them—as Emerson says of them—with the weight of the universe.

The sovereignty of God was to them no mere abstraction. It was the ground of all other sovereignty and of all authority. The divine will was the basis of all human relationship in family, state and church, as it was the basis of all righteousness in man and of all freedom in society. It was the calling and election of God which was drawing men into the life of affection in the Christian household, the life of righteousness in the Christian state, the life of human fellowship in the Christian church, out of a state utterly destitute of all good, a state of bondage to sin and darkness. . . .

Christian sociology differs from the agnostic sociology of our own time, as natural science pursued in the spirit of an Asa Gray or a Principal Forbes differs from the same science in the hands of a materialist such as Professor Haeckel, or an agnostic such as Professor Huxley. . . .

A Christian sociology is as important to us as any other part of our Christian philosophy. To rule God out of social development is to establish the absolute supremacy of the state over both church and family, to sanction the persecution of views held objectionable to state authority, and to suppress appeal to any higher law than the public opinion of the hour. It is indeed to exalt the spirit of the age to an absolute supremacy by denying the possibility of personal relation to the Spirit of all ages. It is to destroy our Christian liberty by elevating the will of the majority to absolute control. It is to resolve conscience into an evolution from non-moral forces, and to deprive it of right of protest against the society which is proclaimed as its creator, and therefore its master.

In fact, there is no line of attack upon the Christian position more insidious in its method and more disastrous in its practical results than this, and yet none on which Christians have been less active for either offense or defense. (R. E. Thompson, *De Civitate Dei. The Divine Order of Human Society*, Philadelphia, 1891, 8 ff.)

9. Cleaning Up City Hall

Among the greatest social problems accompanying rapid industrialization were those of the large cities, including immigrants whose assimilation was difficult (see Ch. 10, art. 7), and corruption in municipal government. Dr. Charles H. Parkhurst (1842–1933), pastor of the Madison Square Presbyterian Church, New York, on February 14, 1892, in the flaming sermon quoted in part below, charged collusion by the New York City government with crime and vice. His crusade succeeded when he presently collected evidence, and a committee of the state senate investigated conditions, and voters of the city elected a reform government.

Sermon

"Ye are the salt of the earth."—Matthew v.13.

That states illustratively the entire situation. It characterizes the world we live in; it defines the functions of the Christianity that has entered into the world, and it indicates by implication the stint which it devolves upon each Christian man and woman of us to help to perform. . . .

We are not thinking just now so much of the world at large as we are of the particular part of the world that it is our painful privilege to live in. . . .

Here is an immense city reaching out arms of evangelization to every quarter of the globe; and yet every step that we take looking to the moral betterment of this city has to be taken directly in the teeth of the damnable pack of administrative bloodhounds that are fattening themselves on the ethical flesh and blood of our citizenship.

We have a right to demand that the Mayor and those associated with him in administering the affairs of this municipality should not put obstructions in the path of our ameliorating endeavors; and they do. There is not a form under which the devil disguises himself that so perplexes us in our efforts, or so bewilders us in the devising of our schemes as the polluted harpies that, under the pretence of governing this city, are feeding day and night on its quivering vitals. They are a lying, perjured, rum-soaked, and libidinous lot. If we try to close up a house of prostitution or of assignation, we, in the guilelessness of our innocent imaginations, might have supposed that the arm of the city government that takes official cognizance of such matters, would like nothing so well as to watch daytimes and sit up nights for the purpose of bringing these dirty malefactors to their deserts. On the contrary, the arm of the city government that takes official cognizance of such matters evinces but a languid interest, shows no genius in ferreting out crime, prosecutes only when it has to, and has a mind so keenly judicial that almost no amount of evidence that can be heaped up is accepted as sufficient to warrant indictment. . . .

I should not be surprised to know that every building in this town in which gambling or prostitution or the illicit sale of liquor is carried on has immunity secured to it by a scale of police taxation that is as carefully graded and as thoroughly systematized as any that obtains in the assessment of personal property or real estate that is made for the purpose of meeting municipal, State, or Federal expenses current. The facts do not always get to the surface, but when they do they let in a great lot of light into the subterranean mysteries of this rum-besotted and Tammany-debauched town. . . .

The District-Attorney said to me in his own house four weeks ago that until after McGlory's establishment was raided he had no idea that institutions of so vile a character existed in this city. All we can say is that we must give the young man the benefit of the doubt. Such a case is truly affecting. Innocence like that in so wicked a town ought not to be allowed to go abroad after dark without an escort. . . .

We speak of these things because it is our business as the pastor of a

Christian church to speak of them. You know that we are not slow to insist upon keenness of spiritual discernment, or upon the reticent vigor of a life hid with Christ in God. Piety is the genius of the entire matter; but piety, when it fronts sin, has got to become grit. Salt is a concrete commodity, and requires to be rubbed into the very pores of decay. I scarcely ever move into the midst of the busier parts of this town without feeling in a pained way how little of actual touch there is between the life of the church and the life of the times. As we saw last Sabbath morning, we must have a consciousness of God, but the truth complementary to that is that we must have just as lively a consciousness of the world we are living in. . . .

Say all you please about the might of the Holy Ghost, every step in the history of an ameliorated civilization has cost just so much personal push. You and I have something to do about it. If we have a brain, or a heart, or a purse, and sit still and let things take their course, making no sign, uttering no protest, flinging ourselves into no endeavor, the times will eventually sit in judgment upon us, and they will damn us. Christianity is here for an object. The salt is here for a purpose. If your Christianity is not vigorous enough to help save this country and this city, it is not vigorous enough to do anything toward saving you. Reality is not worn out. The truth is not knock-kneed. The incisive edge of bare-bladed righteousness will still cut. Only it has got to be righteousness that is not afraid to stand up, move into the midst of iniquity and shake itself. The humanly incarnated principles of this Gospel were able in three centuries to change the moral complexion of the whole Roman Empire; and there is nothing the matter with the Christianity here except that the incarnations of it are lazy and cowardly, and think more of their personal comfort than they do of municipal decency, and more of their dollars than they do of a city that is governed by men who are not tricky and beastly. . . .

You see that these things do not go by arithmetic, nor by a show of hands. A man who is held in the grip of everlasting truth and is not afraid is a young army in himself. That is exactly what the Bible means when it says that one man shall chase a thousand. . . .

This is not bringing politics into the pulpit, politics as such. The particular political stripe of a municipal administration is no matter of our interest, and none of our business; but to strike at iniquity is a part of the business of the Church; indeed, it is the business of the Church. It is primarily what the Church is for, no matter in what connection that sin may find itself associated and intermixed. If it fall properly within the jurisdiction of this church to try to convert Third Avenue drunkards from their alcoholism, then certainly it is germane to the functions of this church to strike the sturdiest blows it is capable of at a municipal administration whose supreme mission it is to protect, foster, and propagate alcoholism. If it is proper for us to go around cleaning up after the devil, it is proper for us to fight the devil. . . .

There is no malice in this, any more than there would be if we were talking about cannibalism in the South Sea Islands; only that having to live in the midst of it, and having to pay taxes to help support it, and having nine-tenths of our Christian effort neutralized and paralyzed by the damnable pressure of it, naturally our thoughts are strained to a little snugger tension. . . .

The good Lord take the fog out of our eyes, the paralysis out of our nerves, and the limp out of our muscles, and the meanness out of our praise, show to us our duty, and reveal to us our superb opportunity, making of every man and woman among us a prophet, instinct with a longing so intense that we shall not be afraid, loving righteousness with a loyalty so impassioned that we shall feel the might of it and trust it, and our lives become this day enlisted in the maintenance of the right, and thus show that Almighty God is mightier than all the ranks of Satan that challenge His claims and dispute His blessed progress. (C. H. Parkhurst, sermon preached in Madison Square Presbyterian Church, February 14, 1892, in Parkhurst, *Our Fight with Tammany*, 1895, 8–25.)

10. The Church and American Imperialism

The early Puritan theocratic ideal of a "wilderness Zion" had become, by the early nineteenth century, a vision of America—and of the new American West in particular—as the hope of the world. Before the end of the nineteenth century, some, like Josiah Strong (in Our Country, *1885), and Captain Mahan in a more secularized version, had gone on to demand that Americans lead the "Anglo-Saxon" nations in forcing their blessings on a reluctant world. A change of opinion in this direction is discernible in the Presbyterian documents below within the short span of the Spanish-American War and its aftermath, but accompanied by protesting voices also, such as that of Dr. van Dyke.*

A. A Church Paper Warms to the Fray

The Senate by an almost unanimous vote last week expressed its sympathy with the Cubans as against Spain by favoring their recognition as belligerents. . . . But the resolutions go much further and urge the President to use his friendly offices in their behalf. At this point there will be difference of opinion as to the wisdom and expediency of the action taken. Intervention at the present juncture of affairs seems premature. . . . It becomes, then, our government to move slowly and carefully. . . . A big issue is before us, and it should be considered in all its far-reaching bearings before the country commits itself to its settlement. (*Presbyterian*, March 4, 1896, 29.)

Many of us thought the sword should have remained in the scabbard and peace should not have been disturbed, but the force of events has been too strong for peace loving conservatism. Now that the gauge of battle has been thrown down, there remains but one thing for Americans to do, and that is, to loyally support their government. . . .

Those who cry, "Remember the Maine!" in our judgment, make a great mistake, and place the war upon the low level of revenge, but those who, with our wise and judicious Chief Executive, base it upon humanitarian considerations, and keep these distinctly to the fore, give us something more worthy and noble for which to contend. . . .

It is even possible that the entire course of our nation's future will be changed. Foreign complications are possible. (*Presbyterian*, April 27, 1898.)

But now that the first crisis is over, what next? Support the brave men as quickly as possible. The nation owes it to them and itself that the results of such matchless heroism shall be preserved. It should not be deterred by the long abiding impression that we have no business to become mixed in European affairs. This is a wise political maxim, and in our young life it saved us from dangerous complications. But no maxim or mode of the past can corral the Providence of God, who is sovereign in battles and in the new policies they bring into existence. A war for humanity has no limitation, except humanity lines. Wherever there is suffering, it must be alleviated. If the helpless are being crushed in our neighbor's back yard, into it we must go, though the law regards it as the sacred precinct of his castle.

That we shall not interfere in European affairs is rather the dictate of policy than of right. If the interfering is from love of conquest, or from national pride, or from any other cause less doubtful than humanity, it ought to be that, in the end, we may extend the principles upon which our government rests. (*Presbyterian*, May 4, 1898.)

We talk of sixty and ninety days of war. This is the result of shallowness, or want of proper knowledge of history and of the laws of cause and effect. . . .

The signs are ominous that that war begun between Spain and the United States will involve the world. If this proves to be the case, it will be the first world war on record. The time may be at hand when the dream of an Armaggedon may become an actual fact. It is time, therefore, for us to cease talking of a short and decisive war between Spain and the United States. It may be a war which will fleck the globe with blood. (*Presbyterian,* May 18, 1898.)

We are compelled to the conviction that it is the divine destiny of the Anglo-Saxons to rule, and they will rule. . . .

Some nation must rule the world, if it is to grow greater and better, not in servitude, but beneficently. Who will do this? Russia, the only one who could aspire to the task by reason of her position, armies and multitudes, is only a fledgling in the business of ruling colonies, though she has absorbed vast territory and peoples in the East. . . .

Then again our religious force runs in the same channel with Great Britain. This is a prodigious power because it is moral and without bloodshed or oppression. It is the liberty of being well governed according to divine law summarized in love to God and our fellow men. The missionaries of England and the United States now are redeeming the nations to Christ. The greatest harmony of purpose and co-operation prevails. These are Christian nations and are doing more for the world's uplifting than any other, for religion with them is conquest for God, and their unity in mission work will compel us to interfere in the affairs of nations in the interest of humanity to give liberty and justice. It would in a moral aspect be cowardly to withdraw from any responsibility that God's providence has opened up before us. There are dangers in extension, but there are as great in moral repression. It seems to us God is saying at this moment, "Speak to the children of Israel that they go forward in all Christian purposes and activities, that war itself shall be utilized in the conquest for permanent peace." (*Presbyterian,* July 13, 1898, 4–5.)

B. The Assembly and the War

The Presbyterian Church has always stood for loyalty to the nation, and its sons have ever manifested their loyalty by deeds not words, and therefore, in view of the action taken at the patriotic meetings held on Saturday last, in which the members of this Assembly generally participated, this Assembly does not deem it necessary to take action at this time, further than to declare the loyalty of its members, and to voice its prayer, that our Chief Magistrate, his counselors, as well as our

Senators and Representatives, may be divinely guided in the solemn issues of the present hour, and that the blessing of God may rest upon our sailors and our soldiers, and that the result of this war may be the deliverance of the oppressed and the extension of Christ's kingdom. (*Minutes of the G. A.*, 1898, 119.)

In addition to fields [i.e., foreign missionary fields] already occupied, we cannot be deaf or blind to the startling providence of God which is just now opening up new and unexpected fields for Foreign Mission work. The peace-speaking guns of Admiral Dewey have opened the gates which henceforth make accessible not less than 12,000,000 of people who have for 300 years been fettered by bonds almost worse than those of heathenism, and oppressed by a tyrannical priesthood only equal in cruelty to that of the nation whose government has been a blight and blistering curse upon every people over whom her flag has floated. . . . We cannot ignore the fact that God has given into our hands—that is, into the hands of American Christians, the Philippine Islands, and thus opened a wide door and effectual to their populations, and has by the very guns of our battleships summoned us to go up and possess the land. (*Minutes of the G. A.*, 1898, 66.)

C. The Peril of Imperialism

Are the United States to continue as a peaceful republic, or are they to become a conquering empire? Is the result of the war with Spain to be the banishment of European tyranny from the Western Hemisphere, or is it to be the entanglement of the Western republic in the rivalries of European kingdoms? Have we set the Cubans free, or have we lost our own faith in freedom? . . .

The argument drawn from the supposed need of creating and fortifying new outlets for our trade has the most practical force. It is the unconscious desire of rivalling England in her colonial wealth and power that allures us to the untried path of conquest. . . .

We cannot compete with monarchies and empires in the game of land-grabbing and vassal ruling. We have not the machinery; and we cannot get it, except by breaking up our present system of government and building a new fabric out of the pieces. . . . To enter upon a career of colonial expansion with our present institutions is to court failure or to prepare for silent revolution. . . .

Is our success in treating the Chinese problem and the Negro problem so notorious that we must attempt to repeat it on a magnified scale eight thousand miles away? The rifle-shots that ring from Illinois and the Carolinas, announcing a bloody skirmish of races in the very heart of the republic—are these the joyous salutes that herald our advance to rule eight millions more of black and yellow people in the islands of the Pacific Ocean? . . .

Expansion means entanglement; entanglement means ultimate conflict. The great nations of Europe are encamped around the China Sea in arms. If we go in among them we must fight when they blow the trumpet. . . .

But the chief argument against the forcible extension of American sovereignty over the Philippines is that it certainly involves the surrender of our American birthright of glorious ideals. . . .

Anonymous patriots have written to warn me that it is a dangerous task to call for this discussion. . . . If the test of loyalty is to join in every thoughtless cry of the multitude, I decline it. I profess a higher loyalty—*allegiance to the flag, not for what it covers, but for what it means.* . . .

May it never advance save to bring liberty and self-government to all beneath its folds. May it never retreat save from a place where its presence would mean disloyalty to the American idea. . . .

God save the birthright of the one country on earth whose ideal is not to subjugate the world but to enlighten it. (H. van Dyke, *The American Birthright and the Philippine Pottage; A Sermon Preached on Thanksgiving Day, 1898,* New York., n.d., 4 ff.)

CHAPTER

11

ADJUSTMENT TO SOCIAL AND CULTURAL CHANGE
1900–1936

1. The Confession of Faith Revised

The issues involved in accomplishing revision of the Westminster Confession of Faith in 1903 were the same as in the unsuccessful revision attempt, 1888–1893 (see Ch. 10, art. 2). The most important changes made in 1903 were the addition of a "Declaratory Statement," given below, and of two chapters entitled "Of the Holy Spirit" and "Of the Love of God and Missions," which gave emphasis to God's love for all men. The United Presbyterian Church and the Southern Presbyterian Church took action of somewhat similar import (see arts. 10 and 11, below).

DECLARATORY STATEMENT

While the ordination vow of ministers, ruling elders, and deacons, as set forth in the Form of Government, requires the reception and adoption of the Confession of Faith only as containing the System of Doctrine taught in the Holy Scriptures, nevertheless, seeing that the desire has been formally expressed for a disavowal by the Church of certain inferences drawn from statements in the Confession of Faith, and also for a declaration of certain aspects of revealed truth which appear at the present time to call for more explicit statement, therefore the Presbyterian Church in the United States of America does authoritatively declare as follows:

First, With reference to Chapter III of the Confession of Faith: that concerning those who are saved in Christ, the doctrine of God's eternal decree is held in harmony with the doctrine of his love to all mankind, his gift of his Son to be the propitiation for the sins of the whole world, and his readiness to bestow his saving grace on all who seek it. That concerning those who perish, the doctrine of God's eternal decree is held in harmony with the doctrine that God desires not the death of any sinner, but has provided in Christ a salvation sufficient for all, adapted to all, and freely offered in the gospel to all; that men are fully responsible for their treatment of God's gracious offer; that his decree hinders no man from accepting that offer; and that no man is condemned except on the ground of his sin.

Second, With reference to Chapter X, Section 3, of the Confession of Faith, that it is not to be regarded as teaching that any who die in infancy are lost. We believe that all dying in infancy are included in the election of grace, and are regenerated and saved by Christ through the Spirit, who works when and where and how he pleases. (*The Constitution of the Presbyterian Church in the United States of America,* 1950, 125. Presbyterian General Assembly. Used by permission.)

2. The Church's Foreign Missions Program

Amid varying international developments, the foreign missionary activity of the Church continued to expand. Dr. Robert E. Speer (1867–1947), Secretary of the Presbyterian Board of Foreign Missions (1891–1937), was one of America's best-known and most effective champions of foreign missions.

The missions of our Church thus girdle the world. There is never an hour when our missionaries are not telling to some hearts the glad tidings of the Saviour. On every continent, save Europe, and among the adherents of every religion our representatives are at work; in North America, South America, Asia, Africa, and the Islands of the Sea; among Hindus, Mohammedans, Buddhists, Confucianists, Shintoists, Shamanists, Fetich worshipers, and degraded forms of Christianity. It has been estimated that nearly one hundred and fifty million people in the countries occupied by our missionaries have become the charge of our Church, and will hear the gospel from us or from no one. Shall we give it to them?

What right to the gospel have we which is not also a right of theirs? If the gospel is not for them, it is not for us. If it is worth anything to us, it is worth as much to them. Is not our Saviour the Saviour of the world? That is his desire and his prayer. And his will for us is that we should carry him to the world, should lift him up before the world, that, being lifted up, he may draw all men unto himself.

It is for this that the Church exists. In reading about her missions, we are not reading of any incidental or secondary enterprise. This is her chief business. If we are ignorant of what the Church is doing to evangelize the world, we are faithless to her. Those are her true children who know and love the story of her triumphs, who with eyes upon the uttermost parts of the earth, and hearts embracing all the peoples, pray ever sincerely, "Thy kingdom come, thy will be done on earth," and who toil for the fulfillment of their prayer. (Robert E. Speer, *Presbyterian Foreign Missions*, Philadelphia, 1901, 295–296.)

3. Labor Temple

Increasing industrialization evoked the social gospel in late nineteenth century America (see Ch. 10, art. 8). One of the first denominational bodies to act officially on the new social ideas was the Presbyterian Church, when in 1903 it organized the Workingmen's Department, which later became the Department of Church and Labor (see also Ch. 11, art. 6, below). Charles Stelzle (1869–1941), mechanic turned minister, was the vigorous leader of this work and of the Department's foremost project, Labor Temple in New York, which is described below in Stelzle's autobiography. (For more recent action of the Church in the area of industrial relations, see Ch. 12, art. 1.)

Lower New York is the arena in which the greatest battles of America's masses will be fought for some time to come. Here every social, economic, and religious problem of the day is being faced by the people of the tenements, without regard for precedents and untrammeled by tradition.

For many years working people had been pouring into this district, creating a congestion unparalleled in the history of the world. Yet as the people moved in, the Protestant churches steadily moved out, deserting them in spite of the fact that for generations the Church had been insisting that the Gospel which it preached was a universal Gospel; that it met the needs of all classes and conditions of men, and that it alone could solve the social problems of the times.

The churches thus practically confessed that they could live only when they followed the well-to-do to the uptown districts and to the suburbs; that only Socialism and Anarchism could thrive in the soil produced by congested tenement life. . . .

On the corner of Fourteenth Street and Second Avenue stood a brownstone church which had had a most glorious career. Its ministers through a half-century had rendered valiant service. But its membership had steadily moved out of the district, until a dozen or so years ago there was a mere handful left, only thirty or forty people to attend its Sunday service. . . .

It was not strange, therefore, that when the question of selling the property came up in about 1910 before the remnant of the congregation they felt justified in disposing of it for a considerable sum, and agreeing to combine with another Presbyterian church on the West Side of the city. Before the plan was consummated, however, I made a proposal to the officers of the church that they give me the use of the church building three nights in the week to conduct services in whatever way I thought best, but not without their entire approval; simply to see what could be done by a new method of attack.

After considering the proposal for some time, the officers voted that my plans be accepted, on condition that I pay the church five thousand dollars a year in addition to furnishing all the money for carrying on the work itself. Frankly, I was stunned, particularly as I had agreed to take on this work as an extra task. I was already responsible for three or four other enterprises. I realized, however, that it was because these men were simply tired out with the situation under which they had been working so long with complete failure, that they wished to absolve themselves of any further responsibility, financially or otherwise.

Then I submitted the same general proposal to the Church Extension Committee of the New York Presbytery, to whom I spoke even more strongly about the responsibility of the Church toward this downtown district. Finally, the Committee voted to purchase the property outright with part of two million dollars left by John L. Kennedy to the Board of Home Missions, with the understanding that I should conduct this work for two years as an experiment; that I was to have complete charge of every department of the work without interference by any committee or individual.

That was the happiest moment in my career as a minister. I was about to realize a dream which I had had since my machinist days—of organizing and conducting a church such as I felt would appeal to the average workingman. It was to be a real workingman's church in every particular. Avowedly it was to be run by workingmen, the men who actually lived in the community. So I called it the "Labor Temple," a name which as a religious enterprise became famous the world over even before I had completed my two years' experimentation. . . .

The Labor Temple bordered the most congested area in New York, although at one time it was one of the most fashionable districts in the city. Fourteenth Street was the dividing line between the masses living in the big tenements to the south and the more favored ones who could afford the greater exclusiveness of the club and the "private house." Less than two blocks away was Tammany Hall's great building, a beehive of political activity affecting not only every part of New York's life but that of the nation. Within a block was the great downtown amusement district of the people. . . .

The opening meeting, on a Sunday afternoon, was exclusively for men. To the amazement of everybody, three hundred and fifty turned out. They were all men of the neighborhood who had been especially invited by letter. We had secured their names and addresses from the polling list at the county clerk's office. With them the entire proposal was frankly talked out, and we urged upon them the importance of their backing it if it were to be a success. They responded enthusiastically. . . .

Meetings were held every night of the week, and practically every address was followed by an open forum discussion. For a month I listened to the severest arraignment of the Church that I had ever heard—and I had been listening to criticisms of the Church for many years in practically every industrial center in this country. When I felt that the criticisms were just, I frankly admitted it, but pointed out that the opening of this Labor Temple was an attempt to get at the actual facts, and that we were going to talk about the thing as friends, and altogether we were going to right as many wrongs as we could and that the whole thing was to be done in a thoroughly democratic fashion, without any patronage on either side.

It was interesting that the Labor Temple audience exhausted itself making criticisms of the Church, and the speakers never repeated their accusations. After every person had once delivered himself of the speech against the Church which rankled somewhere in his system, he never repeated it. When a stranger wandered in and began to berate the Church, the audience promptly came to the defense of the Church, because all that was old stuff; we had admitted it, and there was no need of our talking further about it. After the atmosphere was thus cleared, we got down to real business. . . .

The Labor Temple was by no means second to its neighboring movies in the number of features it offered. It ran a continous "bill" on Sundays, in addition to speeches and discussions every other night, and social reform clubs in lieu of church brotherhoods, besides other activities which got down to the every-day problems and life of the people in the neighborhood.

Sunday's events, from two-thirty till ten, ran as rapidly into one another and were as diversified as a radio program nowadays: children's hour, Bible class; organ recital; reading of a literary masterpiece; concert or lecture; and sermon. At five o'clock a carefully censored motion picture was shown. It was most effective to use the story of "Kelly the Cop," for example, who did a real man's job as a policeman, built up his

ADJUSTMENT TO SOCIAL AND CULTURAL CHANGE 273

home, and helped to make New York a better city, more so than to present the impossible characters which were shown in the average religious film. At six o'clock two hundred persons (Temple helpers, choir members, student workers, ushers, club leaders, Sunday-school teachers, the Temple staff, in addition to such friends as might wish to do so) sat down to a simple supper, and often there were brief inspirational addresses by prominent out-of-town guests or by those who were picked upon by the toastmaster—"roastmaster" he was sometimes called.

Meanwhile, the members of the choir were gathering. Promptly at seven, one hundred strong, they had taken their seats on the platform, but behind a screen upon which illustrated hymns and solos were thrown during the half-hour of music preceding the regular Sunday-night service. As the door of the main auditorium was almost upon the street, passers-by, seeing the songs upon the screen, came in. At eight o'clock the hall was always packed.

I had carefully studied the methods of motion-picture houses and vaudeville theaters to discover means for introducing life and snappiness into the program. One of the things which I observed was that no time was lost between the acts. I realized that the most perilous moment for our service was at the transition point from the screen and song service to the regular meeting. Therefore it was contrived that almost at the snap of the finger the curtain was pulled to one side, the lights were turned up, and the choir burst forth into an inspiring song. I was on my feet before the choir had finished the song, and with a studied gesture—differing according to the occasion and the audience—I prevented a pell-mell movement toward the big front door. We rarely lost more than a dozen of our audience.

The Sunday-night meeting was like a normal church service in the sense that the same sort of things were done—but they were done decidedly differently. It was designed to inject more life and "pep" in the actions of the participants. This was true even of the audience, which was always an unusual one. There was an expectancy about the people which was exhilarating to the speaker. But this spirit also carried with it the possibility that if the audience were disappointed, it might suddenly leave him—and the big double door in the rear of the auditorium was on a level with the street! The audiences never behaved the same except that they always applauded the prayers; that was their way of saying "Amen." The songs and the Scripture and the prayer were exactly the same as in the average church. The sermon was thoroughly evangelical, a straight appeal to the hearts of men. They were the same sermons precisely that I had used in old St. Louis in the big tent, or in the big hall at the mission. I rarely had time to prepare new sermons. There was no forum discussion on Sunday night, although we had our biggest audiences at that time.

I have always felt that Sunday night between nine and ten is the zero hour in a big city. Perhaps more young people go wrong during that hour than almost any other. Not young people only, but older people as well—those without homes, without definite occupations, without something to grip them. So from nine to ten was motion-picture hour at the Temple. We kept our very best pictures for then, for we felt that if we could hold our audience for another hour it would go a long way toward the right closing of the day. It was interesting, however, that, in spite of every effort put into the motion-picture program, we always had more people at the preaching service between eight and nine than we had during the motion-picture hour which followed it. That simply verified a fact which I had long known, that there is no appeal to the human heart which is quite so strong as that of religion if it is presented to the people in a thoroughly human fashion, and if you can get it over to them. . . .

In all the discussion regarding the Labor Temple and the purpose for which it was organized, I wish to keep to the forefront the major fact that it was started not primarily to serve as a lecture or social center, but as a demonstration of what the Church can do in building up the whole life of the people, with special emphasis upon their spiritual welfare. (Charles Stelzle, *A Son of the Bowery; The Life Story of an East Side American*, 117 ff. George H. Doran Co., 1926. Used by permission.)

4. The Book of Common Worship

Reflecting the reviving churchliness of the times, some Presbyterians in the nineteenth century had urged a recovery of the Church's liturgical heritage (see Ch. 10, art. 6). What was then purely private exhortation received a degree of official encouragement by the preparation, under the auspices of the General Assembly, of The Book of Common Worship. *It was published in 1906, revised slightly in 1932, and more extensively in 1946.*

Resolved, 1. That a Committee of eleven be appointed by the Moderator, in conference with the Editorial Committee of the Board of Publication, to take into consideration and if possible to prepare, in harmony with the Directory for Worship, a Book of Simple Forms and Services which shall be proper and helpful for voluntary use in Presbyterian churches in the celebration of the Sacraments, in marriages and funer-

ADJUSTMENT TO SOCIAL AND CULTURAL CHANGE

als, and in the conduct of public worship.

Resolved, 2. That in the preparation of these voluntary services the Committee be instructed to draw from the Holy Scriptures and the usage of the Reformed Churches; to avoid those forms which savor of ritualism; to embody sound doctrine in the language of orderly devotion, and to keep ever in mind the end of Presbyterian worship which is that all the people should join in the service of God as He is revealed in Jesus Christ. (*Minutes of the G. A.*, 1903, 113–114.)

The opinion is prevalent that there has been a movement among Presbyterians in the direction of a more thoughtful and beautiful worship; and that this movement, beginning in the Sabbath-schools with various "exercises," and proceeding among the churches with "orders of service" and more or less elaborate forms, has become so widespread as to need recognition, wise guidance, and perhaps some measure of prudent restraint. . . .

Therefore we sent out a letter of inquiry to the churches. . . .

From 26 Synods, 2001 ministers report for their church as follows:

		PER CENT. OVER
Sunday-schools:		
Using Responsive Service	1673	83
Using Lord's Prayer	1740	86
Using the Creed	746	37
Churches:		
Using Lord's Prayer	1432	71
Using Psalter responsively	1377	68
Using Creed regularly or occasionally	1017	51

Furthermore, of these 2001 ministers, 1774 or 88 *per cent.*, say that "there is room for improvement in the orderly and reverent conduct of worship generally." 1888, or 94 *per cent.*, say that "the people should participate." 1752, or over 87 *per cent.*, say that "a more general, voluntary agreement in regard to the parts of public worship and their order would be a help in this direction." A book of forms is used as follows: marriages 1627, funerals 1619, baptisms 1503, Lord's Supper 1457; and 1634, or over 81 *per cent.*, say that they "feel the need of such a book."

These figures show beyond question: first, that the movement toward an order of service with responsive features is already going on in three-fourths of our churches; second, that nine-tenths of our ministers desire improvement and better order in the conduct of worship generally in our Church; third, that almost all of our ministers wish the people to take part in the service; fourth, that more than four-fifths of our ministers wish for more unity in Presbyterian worship, if it can be voluntarily brought about; and finally, that all but about fifteen *per cent.* feel the need of a book of forms. (*Minutes of the G. A.,* 1904, 66–67.)

We have searched the Holy Scriptures, the usage of the Reformed Churches, and the devotional treasures of early Christianity, for the most noble, clear, and moving expressions of the Spirit of Praise and Prayer; and we have added to these ancient and venerable forms and models, such others as might serve, under the guidance of the same Spirit, to give a voice to the present needs, the urgent desires, and the vital hopes of the Church living in these latter days and in the freedom of this Republic. (*The Book of Common Worship,* Philadelphia, 1906, Preface, iv–v.)

5. Woodrow Wilson on Individual Responsibility

Industrialization with its interdependence led some to the so-called "social gospel" (see Ch. 10, art. 8). But Woodrow Wilson (1856–1924), son of a Southern Presbyterian minister and himself a ruling elder in the Presbyterian Church, U.S.A., during his earlier years was representative of the many clergymen and laymen who sought to meet the new social forces with a re-emphasized individualism. Wilson's ethical emphasis always remained strong and religiously motivated, but a little later, when as Governor of New Jersey (1911–1913) and President of the United States (1913–1921) he came face to face with powerful social forces, he drastically modified the individualism seen in the quotation below.

No doubt Christianity came into the world to save the world. We are privileged to live in the midst of many manifestations of the great service that Christianity does to society, to the world that now is. All of the finest things that have made history illustrious seem to have proceeded from the spirit of Christ. . . .

But Christianity did not come into the world merely to save the world, merely to set crooked things straight, merely to purify social motives, merely to elevate the program according to which we live, merely to put new illuminations into the plans we form for the regeneration of the life we are living now. The end and object of Christianity is the individual, and the individual is the vehicle of Christianity. There can be no other vehicle; no organization is in any proper sense Christian;

no organization can be said itself to love the person and example of Christ. No organization can hold itself in that personal relationship to the Saviour in which the individual must hold himself if he would be indeed one who lives according to the Christian precepts.

You know what the distinguishing characteristic of modern society is, that it has submerged the individual as much as that is possible. In economic society particularly we see men organized in great societies and corporations and organic groups, in which each individual member feels that his own conscience is pooled and subordinated, and in cooperating with which men, as you know, constantly excuse themselves from the exercise of their own independent judgment in matters of conscience. . . .

The minister has the very difficult and responsible task of enabling the individual to find himself amidst modern thought. This evening I must call your attention to the fact that it is also his business to enable the individual to find himself amid modern action. There are daily choices to be made, and the individual must make them at the risk of the integrity of his own soul. He must understand that he cannot shift the responsibility upon the organization. The minister must address himself to him as his counselor and friend and spiritual companion; they must take counsel together how a man is to live with uplifted head and pure conscience in our own complicated age, not allowing the crowd to run away with or over him.

You know that the law has shirked this duty. Sooner or later the duty must be faced. The law tries nowadays to deal with men in groups and companies, to punish them as corporate wholes. It is an idle undertaking. It never will be successfully accomplished. The only responsibility to which human society has ever responded or ever will respond, is the responsibility of the individual. The law must find the individual in the modern corporation and apply its demands and its punishments to him if we are to check any of the vital abuses which now trouble the world of business. . . .

As I see the opportunity of the church, it is to assist in bringing in another great age. Ministers are not going to assist very much in solving the social problems of the time, as such. Their attitude toward the social problems of the time is always supposed to be a professional attitude, and they are not of as much assistance in that matter as the average serious-minded layman is. But the opportunity of the church is to call in tones that cannot be mistaken to every individual to think of his own place in the world and his own responsibility, and to resist the temptations of his particular life in such ways that if he be central to anything the whole world will feel the thrill of the fact that there is one immovable thing in it, a moral principle embodied in a particular man. . . .

The minister ought to see to it that with infinite gentleness, but with absolute fearlessness, every man is made to conform to the standards which are set up in the gospel, even though it cost him his reputation, even though it cost him his friends, even though it cost him his life. Then will come that moral awakening which we have been so long predicting, and for which we have so long waited; that rejuvenation of morals which comes when morals are a fresh and personal and individual thing for every man and woman in every community; when the church will seem, not like an organization for the propagation of doctrine, but like an organization made up of individuals every one of whom is vital in the processes of life. . . .

You will see, therefore, that there is a sense in which the minister is set against modern society. Modern society is collectivist. It says "Unite." The minister must say: "Not so. You can unite for certain temporal purposes, but you cannot merge your souls; and Christianity, come what may, must be fundamentally and forever individualistic." For my part, I do not see any promise of vitality either in the church or in society except upon the true basis of individualism. A nation is strong in proportion to the variety of its originative strength, and that is in proportion to the vitality of its individuals. It is rich in direct proportion to the independence of the souls of which it is made up. And so every promising scheme that unites us must still be illuminated and checked and offset by those eternal principles of individual responsibility which are repeated not only in the gospel but in human nature, in physical nature. . . .

He ["the minister of the gospel"] must preach Christianity to men, not to society. He must preach salvation to the individual, for it is only one by one that we can love, and love is the law of life. And the only person living through whom we shall love is our Lord and Saviour, Jesus Christ. (Woodrow Wilson, "The Ministry and the Individual," in *McCormick Theological Seminary Historical Celebration . . . November . . . Nineteen Hundred and Nine*, Chicago, 1910, 163 ff.)

6. A Social Milestone

In dealing with social problems caused by industrialization, the Presbyterian Church was near the forefront of the American denominations. Examples of the Church's interest in industrial relations are Labor

ADJUSTMENT TO SOCIAL AND CULTURAL CHANGE 279

Temple (see Ch. 11, art. 3) and the Church's social pronouncements of 1910, reproduced below, which came two years after the "Social Creed of the Churches" of the Federal Council of the Churches of Christ in America. Paradoxically, this same Assembly of 1910, which in these social pronouncements implied that society is fluid, set forth five "essential and necessary" doctrines which implied that theology is rigid and fixed (see Ch. 11, art. 7).

We hold that our Church ought to declare:
 1. For the acknowledgment of the obligations of wealth.
 The Church declares that the getting of wealth must be in obedience to Christian ideals, and that all wealth, from whatever source acquired, must be held or administered as a trust from God for the good of fellowman. The Church emphasizes the danger, ever imminent to the individual and to society as well, of setting material welfare above righteous life. The Church protests against undue desire for wealth, untempered pursuit of gain, and the immoderate exaltation of riches.
 2. For the application of Christian principles to the conduct of industrial organizations, whether of capital or labor.
 3. For a more equitable distribution of wealth.
 We hold that the distribution of the products of industry ought to be made such that it can be approved by the Christian conscience.
 4. For the abatement of poverty.
 We realize that much poverty is due to vice, idleness or imprudence; but, on the other hand, we hold that much is due to preventable disease, uncompensated accidents, lack of proper education, and other conditions for which society is responsible, and which society ought to seek to remove. We believe that Christianity requires that adequate provision be made to relieve from want those, who through no fault of their own, but by reason of old age or incapacity, now suffer the brunt of losses incurred in the service of society as a whole.
 5. For the abolition of child-labor—that is, the protection of children from exploitation in industry and trade, and from work that is dwarfing, degrading, or morally unwholesome.
 6. For such regulation of the conditions of the industrial occupation of women as shall safeguard the physical and moral health of themselves, the community, and future generations.
 7. For adequate protection of working people from dangerous machinery and objectionable conditions of labor, and from occupational disease.
 8. For some provision by which the burden imposed by injuries and

deaths from industrial accidents shall not be permitted to rest upon the injured person or his family.

9. For the release of every worker from work one day in seven.

The Church holds that in a Christian society these things should prevail: (a) One day of rest for every six days of work secured to every worker; (b) this one day of rest made to be, wherever possible, the Lord's Day; (c) the pay of every worker for six days' work made sufficient for the needs of seven days of living.

10. For such ordering of the hours and requirements of labor as to make them compatible with healthy physical, mental and moral life.

11. For the employment of the methods of conciliation and arbitration in industrial disputes.

12. For the removal of unsanitary dwellings and the relief or prevention of congestion of population, so that there may be the proper physical basis for Christian family life.

13. For the application of Christian methods in the care of dependent and incapable persons, by the adequate equipment and humane and scientific administration of public institutions concerned therewith.

14. For the development of a Christian spirit in the attitude of society toward offenders against the law.

The Church holds that a Christian society must seek the reformation of offenders, and that it must endeavor to prevent the commission of crimes by furnishing a wholesome environment, and by such education as will develop moral sense and industrial efficiency in the young. (*Minutes of the G. A.*, 1910, 230–232.)

7. "Essential and Necessary" Doctrines

Cultural and theological change in the Presbyterian Church has inevitably related itself to the "subscription" formula. Candidates for the Presbyterian ministry adopt the Westminster Confession of Faith "as containing the system of doctrine taught in the Holy Scriptures." What does this formula require them to believe? The old Adopting Act of 1729 (see Ch. 1, art. 11) allowed a candidate who could not affirm a particular article of the Confession to state his "scruple" concerning it, and the ordaining body would then decide whether or not this scruple involved an "essential and necessary" article. In 1910, the General Assembly, after debate as to whether certain candidates for the ministry were sufficiently orthodox, set forth the five "essential and necessary" doctrines reproduced below, and declared that all candidates for the ministry must affirm them. But later the Assembly of 1927 in effect said that the Assembly may not thus categorically designate certain doctrines as essential and necessary.

1. It is an essential doctrine of the Word of God and our Standards, that the Holy Spirit did so inspire, guide and move the writers of the Holy Scriptures as to keep them from error. Our Confession says (see Chapter i, Section 10): "The Supreme Judge, by whom all controversies of religion are to be determined, and all decrees of councils, opinions of ancient writers, doctrines of men, and private spirits, are to be examined, and in whose sentence we are to rest, can be no other but the Holy Spirit speaking in the Scriptures."

2. It is an essential doctrine of the Word of God and our Standards, that our Lord Jesus Christ was born of the Virgin Mary. The Shorter Catechism states, Question 22: "Christ, the Son of God, became man, by taking to Himself a true body and a reasonable soul, being conceived by the power of the Holy Ghost, in the womb of the Virgin Mary, and born of her, yet without sin."

3. It is an essential doctrine of the Word of God and our Standards, that Christ offered up "himself a sacrifice to satisfy divine justice, and to reconcile us to God." The Scripture saith Christ "once suffered for sins, the just for the unjust, that he might bring us to God, being put to death in the flesh, but quickened in the Spirit." (See also Shorter Catechism, Question 25.)

4. It is an essential doctrine of the Word of God and our Standards, concerning our Lord Jesus, that "on the third day he arose from the dead, with the same body in which he suffered; with which also he ascended into heaven, and there sitteth at the right hand of his Father, making intercession." (See Confession, Chapter VIII. Section 4.)

5. It is an essential doctrine of the Word of God as the supreme Standard of our faith, that the Lord Jesus showed his power and love by working mighty miracles. This working was not contrary to nature, but superior to it. "Jesus went about all the cities and villages, teaching in their synagogues, and preaching the gospel of the kingdom, and healing every sickness and every disease among the people" (Matthew ix. 35). These great wonders were signs of the divine power of our Lord, making changes in the order of nature. They were equally examples, to his Church, of charity and good-will toward all mankind.

These five articles of faith are essential and necessary. Others are equally so. . . .

Resolved, That, reaffirming the advice of the Adopting Act of 1729, all the Presbyteries within our bounds shall always take care not to admit any candidate for the ministry into the exercise of the sacred function, unless he declares his agreement in opinion with all the essential and necessary articles of the Confession. (*Minutes of the G. A.,* 1910, 272–273.)

8. The Church and World War I

Fluctuations of public opinion, including Church opinion, between America's neutrality and her entrance into World War I were extreme. A revealing study of Church opinion is found in Ray Abrams, Preachers Present Arms, *New York, 1933. Dr. Robert E. Speer, Secretary of the Presbyterian Board of Foreign Missions (1891–1937) and chairman of the General Wartime Commission of the Churches, was more moderate than most in his effort, quoted in part below, to set forth the proper attitude of an American Christian toward the war.*

The fundamental question which was alive before the war and which is alive to-day again and which will be alive when the war is over is: Can war ever be right, or is war in moral principle always wrong? . . .

The past is a record of how God actually has shaped human history. Can any one deny that there have been wars which on one side at least were right? If there is any truth at all in the Old Testament records it is clear from them that again and again men were convinced that they were fighting with the very help and warrant of God. In our own national history, who is prepared to say that both the Revolutionary and the Civil Wars represented no right principle for which the nation was justified in contending even to the death? The New Testament itself recognized the legitimacy of military service for Christian men as it certainly could not have done without sacrifice of its moral authority if it be true that war cannot be morally allowed in human life. And in all later days many of the noblest and purest Christian spirits have been soldiers.

This fact that God has allowed wars in human history and that Christian men have been soldiers does not prove that war is a good thing and that it is to be accepted as a lasting human institution, a part of the divine order of the world, any more than the existence of polygamy in the Old Testament times and of slavery in New Testament times and for centuries afterwards proves that polygamy and slavery are good things and divinely ordered permanent institutions. There is such a thing as world progress. What was allowable and even necessary in one day becomes wrong and intolerable in another. . . .

Not only does the past refuse to justify the view that Christianity and war are irreconcilable as yet, although God intends and we intend, by His help, that they shall be, but the fundamental Christian principles of trusteeship and unselfishness require resistance to wrong directed against the weak and the innocent. . . .

He clearly bade us to yield our own rights, but he did not bid us to yield our duties. If one smites us on our own cheek we are to turn to him the other, but if he smites a little child on one cheek he will not smite it on the other if we have the strength and love of Christ in us. . . .

Another New Testament conception which makes it impossible for us as yet to set up the thesis of the absolute indefensibility of war is the conception of the state as an ordinance of God. Paul held this conception firmly (Romans xiii, 3–7) and he did not hesitate to appeal to the state for military protection against violence and crime (Acts xxiii, 17–23). The Christian Church in the first century was not called, and never as a Church has been called, to go to war; but nations and ordered governments, whether then or now, are to do justice and to prevent wrong. Paul said this was the divine purpose of government in the case of Rome (Romans xiii, 4). It is not possible that God should intend a heathen government to prevent evil, but Christian governments to permit it.

And we cannot absolutely rule out war from the universe on the ground that it employs force and costs human life if at the same time we believe in God. If the universe is not moral, then, of course, no ethical question will trouble us. But if it is moral, if a personal God is back of it, must not the use of force and of human life in the progress of the world be warrantable if He uses them so? Can He not allow and authorize this war? When he has educated us a little more we may be sure He will rule war out. The God in Whom we believe would have destroyed it long ago if He could have done so without destroying man too. But until mankind comes to the stage where war can be abandoned without abandoning the world to the armed wrong-doer, we cannot say that the use of war for righteous defense is wrong. . . .

If this view now allows and warrants war, it also warns and cautions and sobers us. It bids us be rid of our prejudice and passion, to chant no hymns of hate, to keep our aims and our principles free from selfishness and from any national interest which is not also the interest of all nations, to refrain from doing in retaliation and in war the very things we condemn in others, to avoid Prussianism in our national life in the effort to crush Prussianism. (R. E. Speer, *The Christian Man, the Church and the War*, 11, 25 ff. The Macmillan Company, 1918. Used by permission.)

9. Auburn Affirmation

*During the widely publicized "fundamentalist-modernist" controversy in the American Churches in the 1920's and 1930's, the chief issue among Presbyterians was how much divergence from **traditional theological views the Church should tolerate**. The strict constructionist party insisted that candidates for the ministry must **be able to affirm the five** "essential and necessary" doctrines of 1910 (see art. 7, above). A broader view was championed by "An Affirmation" (popularly called the "Auburn Affirmation"). On its governmental side, the Affirmation said that for the General Assembly to declare certain doctrines of the Confession "essential and necessary" is virtually to amend the Confession, which cannot be done without the concurring action of two thirds of the presbyteries. On its theological side, the Affirmation, very much after the manner of "A Plea for Peace and Work" of 1892 (see Ch. 10, art. 5), said that the Assembly's five doctrines were theories about certain Christian facts. The subscribers affirmed adherence to the facts, but claimed the right, contrary to the Assembly's pronouncement, to hold differing theories about those facts. The Affirmation was first published in January, 1924, and republished in May, 1924, with the signatures of 1,274 Presbyterian ministers. The General Assembly of 1927 said in effect that the Assembly may not categorically declare certain doctrines to be "essential and necessary" (see G. A. Minutes, 1927, 70, 77–78).*

An Affirmation
designed to safeguard the unity and liberty of the Presbyterian
Church in the United States of America

Submitted for the consideration of its ministers and people

We, the undersigned, ministers of the Presbyterian Church in the United States of America, feel bound, in view of certain actions of the General Assembly of 1923 and of persistent attempts to divide the church and abridge its freedom, to express our convictions in matters pertaining thereto. At the outset we affirm and declare our acceptance of the Westminster Confession of Faith, as we did at our ordinations, "as containing the system of doctrine taught in the Holy Scriptures." We sincerely hold and earnestly preach the doctrines of evangelical

ADJUSTMENT TO SOCIAL AND CULTURAL CHANGE 285

Christianity, in agreement with the historic testimony of the Presbyterian Church in the United States of America, of which we are loyal ministers. For the maintenance of the faith of our church, the preservation of its unity, and the protection of the liberties of its ministers and people, we offer this Affirmation.

I. By its law and its history, the Presbyterian Church in the United States of America safeguards the liberty of thought and teaching of its ministers. At their ordinations they "receive and adopt the Confession of Faith of this Church, as containing the system of doctrine taught in the Holy Scriptures." This the church has always esteemed a sufficient doctrinal subscription for its ministers. Manifestly it does not require their assent to the very words of the Confession, or to all of its teachings, or to interpretations of the Confession by individuals or church courts. The Confession of Faith itself disclaims infallibility. Its authors would not allow this to church councils, their own included: "All synods or councils since the apostles' times, whether general or particular, may err, and many have erred; therefore they are not to be made the rule of faith or practice, but to be used as a help in both." (Conf. XXXI, iii). The Confession also expressly asserts the liberty of Christian believers, and condemns the submission of the mind or conscience to any human authority: "God alone is lord of the conscience, and hath left it free from the doctrines and commandments of men which are in anything contrary to his Word, or beside it, in matters of faith or worship. So that to believe such doctrines, or to obey such commandments out of conscience, is to betray true liberty of conscience; and the requiring of an implicit faith, and an absolute and blind obedience, is to destroy liberty of conscience, and reason also." (Conf. XX, ii).

The formal relation of American Presbyterianism to the Westminster Confession of Faith begins in the Adopting Act of 1729. This anticipated and provided for dissent by individuals from portions of the Confession. At the formation of the Presbyterian Church in the United States of America, in 1788, the Westminster Confession was adopted as the creed of the church; and at the same time the church publicly declared the significance of its organization in a document which contains these words: "There are truths and forms, with respect to which men of good characters and principles may differ. And in all these they think it the duty, both of private Christians and Societies, to exercise mutual forbearance towards each other". (Declaration of Principles, v).

Of the two parts into which our church was separated from 1837 to 1870, one held that only one interpretation of certain parts of the Confession of Faith was legitimate, while the other maintained its right to dissent from this interpretation. In the Reunion of 1870 they came together on equal terms, "each recognizing the other as a sound and orthodox body." The meaning of this, as understood then and ever since, is that officer-bearers in the church who maintain their liberty in the interpretation of the Confession are exercising their rights guaranteed by the terms of the Reunion.

A more recent reunion also is significant, that of the Cumberland Presbyterian Church and the Presbyterian Church in the United States of America, in 1906. This reunion was opposed by certain members of the Presbyterian Church in the United States of America, on the ground that the two churches were not at one in doctrine; yet it was consummated. Thus did our church once more exemplify its historic policy of accepting theological differences within its bounds and subordinating them to recognized loyalty to Jesus Christ and united work for the kingdom of God.

With respect to the interpretation of the Scriptures the position of our church has been that common to Protestants. "The Supreme Judge," says the Confession of Faith, "by whom all controversies of religion are to be determined, and all decrees of councils, opinions and ancient writers, doctrines of men, and private spirits, are to be examined, and in whose sentence we are to rest, can be no other but the Holy Spirit speaking in the Scripture". (Conf. I, x). Accordingly our church has held that the supreme guide in the interpretation of the Scriptures is not, as it is with Roman Catholics, ecclesiastical authority, but the Spirit of God, speaking to the Christian believer. Thus our church lays it upon its ministers and others to read and teach the Scriptures as the Spirit of God through His manifold ministries instructs them, and to receive all truth which from time to time He causes to break forth from the Scriptures.

There is no assertion in the Scriptures that their writers were kept "from error." The Confession of Faith does not make this assertion; and it is significant that this assertion is not to be found in the Apostles' Creed or the Nicene Creed or in any of the great Reformation confessions. The doctrine of inerrancy, intended to enhance the authority of the Scriptures, in fact impairs their supreme authority for faith and life, and weakens the testimony of the church to the power of God unto salvation through Jesus Christ. We hold that the General Assembly of 1923, in asserting that "the Holy Spirit did so inspire, guide and move the writers of Holy Scripture as to keep them from error," spoke without warrant of the Scriptures or of the Confession of Faith. We hold rather to the words of the Confession of Faith, that the Scriptures "are given by inspiration of God, to be the rule of faith and life." (Conf. I, ii).

II. While it is constitutional for any General Assembly "to bear testimony against error in doctrine," (Form of Govt. XII, v), yet such testimony is without binding authority, since the constitution of our church provides that its doctrine shall be declared only by concurrent action of the General Assembly and the presbyteries. Thus the church guards the statement of its doctrine against hasty or ill-considered action by either General Assemblies or presbyteries. From this provision of our constitution, it is evident that neither in one General Assembly nor in many, without concurrent action of the presbyteries, is there authority to declare what the Presbyterian Church in the United States of America believes and teaches; and that the assumption that any General Assembly has authoritatively declared what the church believes and teaches is groundless. A declaration by a General Assembly that any doctrine is "an essential doctrine" attempts to amend the constitution of the church in an unconstitutional manner.

III. The General Assembly of 1923, in asserting that "doctrines contrary to the standards of the Presbyterian Church" have been preached in the pulpit of the First Presbyterian Church of New York City, virtually pronounced a judgment against this church. The General Assembly did this with knowledge that the matter on which it so expressed itself was already under formal consideration in the Presbytery of New York, as is shown by the language of its action. The General Assembly acted in the case without giving hearing to the parties concerned. Thus the General Assembly did not conform to the procedure in such cases contemplated by our Book of Discipline, and, what is more serious, it in effect condemned a Christian minister without using the method of conference, patience and love enjoined on us by Jesus Christ. We object to the action of the General Assembly in this case, as being out of keeping with the law and the spirit of our church.

IV. The General Assembly of 1923 expressed the opinion concerning five doctrinal statements that each one "is an essential doctrine of the Word of God and our standards." On the constitutional grounds which we have before described, we are opposed to any attempt to elevate these five doctrinal statements, or any of them, to the position of tests for ordination or for good standing in our church.

Furthermore, this opinion of the General Assembly attempts to commit our church to certain theories concerning the inspiration of the Bible, and the Incarnation, the Atonement, the Resurrection, and the Continuing Life and Supernatural Power of our Lord Jesus Christ. We all hold most earnestly to these great facts and doctrines; we all believe from our hearts that the writers of the Bible were inspired of God; that Jesus Christ was God manifest in the flesh; that God was in Christ, reconciling the world unto Himself, and through Him we have our redemption; that having died for our sins He rose from the dead and is our ever-living Saviour; that in His earthly ministry He wrought many mighty works, and by His vicarious death and unfailing presence He is able to save to the uttermost. Some of us regard the particular theories contained in the deliverance of the General Assembly of 1923 as satisfactory explanations of these facts and doctrines. But we are united in believing that these are not the only theories allowed by the Scriptures and our standards as explanations of these facts and doctrines of our religion, and that all who hold to these facts and doctrines, whatever theories they may employ to explain them, are worthy of all confidence and fellowship.

V. We do not desire liberty to go beyond the teachings of evangelical Christianity. But we maintain that it is our constitutional right and our Christian duty within these limits to exercise liberty of thought and teaching, that we may more effectively preach the gospel of Jesus Christ, the Saviour of the World.

VI. Finally, we deplore the evidences of division in our beloved church, in the face of a world so desperately in need of a united testimony to the gospel of Christ. We earnestly desire fellowship with all who like us are disciples of Jesus Christ. We hope that those to whom this Affirmation comes will believe that it is not the declaration of a theological party, but rather a sincere appeal, based on the Scriptures and our standards, for the preservation of the unity and freedom of our church, for which most earnestly we plead and pray. (*An Affirmation*, Auburn, N. Y., May 5, 1924, 3–6. The text of the Affirmation is here given in full. The Foreword, names of signers, and Supplementary Note are omitted.)

10. United Presbyterian Church's Preamble to the Confessional Statement

This Preamble and the Confessional Statement which follows it are notable in securing greater freedom for officers of the United Presbyterian Church, particularly with reference to the relation of God's sovereignty to his love and to man's freedom (compare arts. 1 and 11).

The United Presbyterian Church of North America declares afresh its adherence to the Westminster Confession of Faith and Catechisms,

ADJUSTMENT TO SOCIAL AND CULTURAL CHANGE 289

Larger and Shorter, as setting forth the system of doctrine taught in the Scriptures, which are the only infallible and final rule of faith and practice. Along with this it affirms the right and duty of a living Church to restate its faith from time to time so as to display any additional attainments in truth it may have made under the guidance of the Holy Spirit. Accordingly, by constitutional action consummated June 2, 1925, it adopted the following Confessional Statement. This Statement contains the substance of the Westminster symbols, together with certain present-day convictions of the United Presbyterian Church. It takes the place of the Testimony of 1858, and wherever it deviates from the Westminster Standards its declarations are to prevail.

Subscription to the foregoing Subordinate Standards is subject to the principle maintained by our fathers, that the forbearance in love which is required by the law of God is to be exercised toward any brethren who may not be able fully to subscribe to the Standards of the Church, while they do not determinedly oppose them, but follow the things which make for peace and things wherewith one may edify another.

In keeping with its creedal declaration of truth, the United Presbyterian Church believes that among the evangelical communions of the world there is "one Lord, one faith, one baptism," and therefore, shunning sectarian temper, it cherishes brotherly love toward all branches of the Church Universal and seeks to keep the unity of the Spirit in the bond of peace. (*The Confessional Statement of the United Presbyterian Church of North America*, Pittsburgh, 1926, 7–8. By permission.)

11. The Southern Presbyterian Church's Amendment to the Confession of Faith

The Presbyterian Church in the U.S. (Southern), in 1942, amended the Westminster Confession of Faith by the adoption of Chapter IX, "Of the Holy Spirit," and Chapter X, "Of the Gospel," the latter reproduced in full below. These creedal changes are very similar in import to creedal changes adopted by the Presbyterian Church in the U.S.A. (see Ch. 11, art. 1) and by the United Presbyterian Church (see Ch. 11, art. 10).

I. God in infinite and perfect love, having provided in the covenant of grace, through the mediation and sacrifice of the Lord Jesus Christ, a way of life and salvation, sufficient for and adapted to the whole lost race of man, doth freely offer this salvation to all men in the Gospel.

II. In the Gospel God declares His love for the world and His desire that all men should be saved, reveals fully and clearly the only way of salvation; promises eternal life to all who truly repent and believe in Christ; invites and commands all to embrace the offered mercy; and by His Spirit accompanying the Word pleads with men to accept His gracious invitation.

III. It is the duty and privilege of every one who hears the Gospel immediately to accept its merciful provisions; and they who continue in impenitence and unbelief incur aggravated guilt and perish by their own fault.

IV. Since there is no other way of salvation than that revealed in the Gospel, and since in the divinely established and ordinary method of grace faith cometh by hearing the Word of God, Christ hath commissioned His Church to go into all the world and to make disciples of all nations. All believers are, therefore, under obligation to sustain the ordinances of the Christian religion where they are already established, and to contribute by their prayers, gifts and personal efforts to the extension of the Kingdom of Christ throughout the whole earth. (*Minutes of the . . . G. A. of the Presbyterian Church in the United States, 1942, 68–69.*)

12. The Great Depression

The depression of the 1930's deeply affected the American Churches. Some congregations still in debt from ambitious building programs in the 1920's became bankrupt. Missionary, educational, and promotional programs of the denominations were cut to the bone. The failing of traditional American optimism stimulated some to shift from the optimistic "liberal" theology toward the more realistic "neo-orthodox" theology coming from the European Continent under the leadership of Karl Barth and Emil Brunner. Contributions to economic relief were more often on an individualistic basis through community chests and welfare agencies than on an ecclesiastical basis. Some, like Rev. Dr. Edmund B. Chaffee, director of Labor Temple in New York, quoted below, were led to challenge, in the name of the Christian gospel, shortcomings which the depression was revealing in the existing social order.

As I write this the Welfare Council reports that there are 633,000, most of them children, in need of clothing in New York City. Millions in our great cities are without food except as it is given them by private or public charity. From 12,000,000 to 15,000,000 men and women able to work and willing to work cannot find employment. In the face of such an appalling situation there is one obvious duty which rests upon every Christian man and woman in the land. That is the duty of giving to the limit of his ability. It is easy in these days to sneer at charity and it has too often been made a cloak to cover injustice but it is terrible to contemplate the depths of human suffering without it. While the giving of the American people has not been adequate to meet the needs yet the fact is clear that the hungry have been fed and the needy have been clothed and shelter has been provided because men were unwilling to see their fellows in want. Ever since the beginnings of the Christian faith and down through the ages Christians have been taught to give for the relief of human suffering. It is probably due to this fact more than any other that a complete collapse of our civilization has not occurred. . . .

Next to the duty of love there is no more important task laid upon the individual Christian today than that of understanding this era, of grasping the significance of this moment in human history. We are literally at the end of an epoch. For the last few decades one of the greatest changes in all human history has been taking place. . . .

In the last few decades and particularly in this very century men have learned how to harness the energy resources of nature. . . .

We have come into a new epoch in human history. It is now possible as it has never been possible in the past to give every man, woman and child in this land, the material basis for the good and satisfactory life. It is the manifest duty of the Christian to understand this fact, to realize this stupendous change and to help others to realize it. And yet there is more in the present problem than the rôle of high power machinery. That is but one of the two chief elements with which we must deal. As Christians we must also understand that we have not yet shaken loose from the chains put upon us by chattel slavery. It was slavery that cut society in twain. It was slavery that divided mankind into classes. . . . It is this old, old evil of slavery that still prevents us from thinking in terms of the essential oneness of mankind. It is this old, old evil that makes it tolerable to us that the few should have much and the many little. It is this evil which has made us so complacent of the inequitable division of the profits of our high-power machinery. . . .

It is the duty of the follower of Jesus to give sacrificially to feed the hungry and clothe the naked in this hour of black distress and it is his duty also to understand the nature of the crisis now upon us. It is also his duty to do his share of the world's work. No one can consume unless some one first produces. The hours of human labor can be much shortened and they will be but still we can never have the material basis for the good life unless each one will pull his share of the load. . . .

It cannot be too often pointed out that all socially necessary work is holy work, work done unto the Lord. The old division of work into secular and religious is an intolerable division. . . .

It is not enough that we do our share of the work both in quantity and quality. We must not overdo our consuming. There is an obligation upon the Christian to live simply. Particularly do we in America need this reminder. Jesus taught men to value the things of the spirit. He taught simplicity of life. When other people have not the necessaries of life our right to luxuries may well be questioned. In the face of the present world tragedy there surely is an obligation laid upon us as disciples of Jesus to spend upon ourselves only that which will keep us at the highest efficiency. . . .

We face a vast reorganization of human society. It must and will come. It is perfectly possible to let matters so drift that the changes will come with the violent overthrow of existing governments and institutions. It may be better to get to the new day that way than not to get there at all, but the costs of that way will make the Great War seem child's play. That way will wreck the delicate industrial mechanism we have built up. . . . Because of all these dangers the Christian must fight valiantly for the new order, but he must fight with the weapons that are consistent with the ethic of love. This is going to lose him friends. It cannot be otherwise. He will put the whole strength of his life and purpose against the injustices and stupidities of the present and those who believe in that present will consider him subversive. He will not engage in violent revolution and many a sincere fighter for social justice will call him yellow and traitorous. . . .

What then can the individual Christian do in this fearful time of economic catastrophe? He can give; he can understand; he can do his share of the work and he can do it well; he can live with becoming simplicity; he can fight for the new order with weapons consistent with the world of love he seeks to build. He can and must do these things as an individual, but most of us will need to go still further and unite with our fellows politically and industrially, that we may have the power which comes from such united action. And yet all of these things are meaningless to the Christian unless they are inspired by something far deeper, which lies at the heart of the gospel. That something is the spirit of love with which all our mighty economic and industrial problems can be solved, but without which our efforts are foredoomed to disappointment and failure. . . . It is this which must guide our consciences today and every day as we face a world which the spirit of God is destroying that He may make it new. (E. B. Chaffee, *The Protestant Churches and the Industrial Crisis*, 207 ff. The Macmillan Company, 1933. Used by permission.)

CHAPTER

12

INTIMATIONS OF FRESH CREATIVITY
1937–1956

1. The Church and Industrial Relations

In its attitude toward industrial relations the Church no longer implies that social righteousness is synonymous with the economic status quo of which the Church is the divinely commissioned spokesman. The Church's most recent pronouncements do not find the social norm in any static pattern, but in values—in particular in those values which foster free, Christian, ethical personality. The Church's own social shortcomings are freely acknowledged. Thus, the ideal is an "open" and unpredictable future, limited only by God's Word and Spirit. The Department of Social Education and Action, set up by the General Assembly in 1936, has supplied vigorous leadership in industrial and other social problems.

The Church must confess that too often in its prevailing social attitude, as in so much of its membership, it is middle and upper class. Often it has failed to make real for those in the ranks of labor the spirit of Christian fellowship. . . .

Surely, it is incumbent upon members of our Churches to acknowledge that in matters pertaining to industrial relationships and economic practices, the Church has signally failed to speak and to act, without fear and favor, out of its own genius as a fellowship committed to loyalty to God as revealed in Christ Jesus. . . .

The economic order is not an autonomous system, outside of and apart from the moral order as conceived in the Christian faith. It is one aspect, and a neglected aspect, of the moral order. The essential dignity of human personality, recognized in family and other personal relations, demands the same respect in economic and industrial relations. . . .

The divine purpose in human history, in part, is executed by great social groups, the members of which are often unaware that they are fulfilling a divine mission. . . .

The individual and society are together a living unity. Personality is socially conditioned, socially nurtured, and socially expressed. The economic and industrial order tend to make us what we are in character. . . .

Every increase in power must be matched by a corresponding sense of social responsibility. The winning of gains for one's own group must be viewed as only a partial victory until similar gains have been won for those still in depressed circumstances. . . .

Democracy in industry is something other than benevolent paternalism. It concerns the independent status of the individual worker in relation to his employer. . . .

The labor movement has helped many an individual to find himself in meaningful cooperation with his fellows. In the opportunity to participate in the life of the labor union, the worker has the chance to develop capacities for leadership, and, thereby, he feels he has more to give as neighbor and as citizen. . . .

Broadly speaking, social experience, insight into human nature, and the character of our industrialized society point to the social desirability of labor unions. . . .

We believe that there is nothing in Christian faith and principle that either supports or denies the closed shop, as such, on ethical grounds. . . .

One of the dangers of our present social order is found in the development of blocs or pressure groups, each intent on its own advancement. The Church must demand that all economic groups—industry, labor, agriculture, consumers—shall voluntarily join in seeking the welfare of all. . . .

Either we shall show initiative in this direction or the Government will be compelled to extend its social controls, and this we should regret. . . .

The need is . . . for the reinforcement of the spiritual and moral basis for constructive and cooperative group relationships. . . .

The Church cannot accept existing injustice as inevitable, but, rather, must proclaim God's will for justice in the economic dealings of men. . . .

The payment of a socially adequate wage should be the first charge against the earnings of any business enterprise. . . .

The mandate upon the Church to extend its ministry into the industrial and economic order is to be found in the sovereignty of God over the whole of life. . . .

Now and in the immediate future the Church must act vigorously upon its divine mandate. . . . It must discern and support those who would deal more justly in the economic order. It must stand with the humble and with all those who would lift up the humble. (*Minutes of the G. A.,* 1944, 197 ff.)

2. Service in World War II

In World War II the Presbyterian Church provided numerous special ministries. "Hospitality houses" were opened for service personnel; many pastors, temporarily released by their congregations, labored as service pastors at the great training camps; missionaries sometimes ministered to servicemen overseas. Most important of these special ministries was the Army and Navy chaplaincy, in which a total of 802 Presbyterian ministers served.

Chaplain Eben Cobb Brink, after serving in Presbyterian pastorates in the United States, entered the Army chaplaincy. The opening part of the quotation below describes an attack in North Africa by the American troops with whom he was serving.

Covered by the thick darkness that hangs heavy just before the dawn breaks, vehicles and men respond. Thank God for the protection of the blackout! No! rather let the light come—O God, where art thou? What's going to happen?

Out over the plain they spread, crawling slowly forward, now around a wadi, now cautiously approaching a barren hill. Slowly the advance vehicles inch their way to the crest of the hill, delaying as long as possible the inevitable silhouette that may first draw enemy fire.

Suddenly out of the sun they come—roaring down in their hellish dive. Guns blaze, bullets stream from planes as they mercilessly strafe vehicles and men who have flattened themselves on the ground. Who will ever know the thoughts or the prayers of a man when first he is the target of a strafing attack? Can those marks there on the ground just an arm's length away really be the pattern of the bullets sprayed by the fast-passing plane? What about the other men? Mustn't stay here! Must get going!

Down! Here they come again—zooming back for another attack. O God! How many times are they going to try for us? That truck there! It's hit! It's burning! Get the gunner off—he's shot! . . .

The chaplain too kneels beside the stretcher. He speaks into the ear of the wounded man the words of faith—words which he had always known would be the words to speak at such a time. A jeep drives up, bringing two more wounded men. Stretchers are placed for them on the ground. The doctor looks hurriedly at their injuries and turns back to the first, more serious case. The chaplain speaks to each of them—carefully chosen words—just the right words at such a time! Finally the wounds are dressed—the ambulance has moved off to the field hospital. Medical men and chaplain move forward to rejoin the others. . . .

The battlefield offers, to those who are able to listen amidst the turmoil of conflict, a stirring study of men's souls. During engagements the opportunities of holding worship services are of course rare, if such opportunities present themselves at all. But it is during such days that the chaplain comes nearest to the hearts of men. Kneeling beside the wounded as the doctors care for them, speaking words of assurance, sharing the privilege of prayer, taking down some message for the loved ones at home—a thousand and one little intimacies reveal so often the true soul of a man.

The chaplain bent over one, lifting his head that he might quench the burning thirst from the canteen held to his lips. Others lay beside him on the ground while doctors and aid men gave them emergency treatment. "Tell the doctor to take care of the others first; I'll be all right. But I am not so sure of the others." His voice was weak, breath came in short gasps. . . .

That night the corporal who took his place came to the chaplain's pup tent. "He used to talk to us about God, Chaplain, and we never paid much attention to what he said. But somehow tonight I feel he was right. I've got to take his place, but I want to know what he knew about God." Men need sleep, but the stars that looked down that night had circled far in the heavens when finally chaplain and corporal knelt together in prayer: "Lord, I believe; help thou mine unbelief." . . .

Frequently the men would come to the chaplain before going into an engagement, bringing an envelope, a package, a trinket, or some other possession: "Chaplain, please hold this for me until it's over. If I don't come back, please send it home for me." And when, sometimes, the lad did not come back, the chaplain opened the envelope, as censorship required, before it could be sent home. The tender confidences contained therein cannot be betrayed. But one had a message that ought to be known. The mother to whom it was sent has told the chaplain he might share it, for this is what the lad wrote:

"I have tried in my letters not to worry you, for I have known how you must fear daily for my safety. But I want to leave one final message for you if anything should happen to me. Somehow I feel I will not come home again. It is a strange feeling, with no fear in it. It is a quiet feeling, that I want you to understand, as I think you can. Every day since you taught me to pray as a little child at your knee, I have always prayed to God. My happiest thoughts are of you and father praying at home for me as I over here am praying for you. And lately, as I have said my daily prayers, I have felt that God was nearer to me than ever before. We've had some pretty dirty jobs to do, but still God has been very close to me. In spite of what goes on around me, I still feel he is nearer every day. And tonight I feel that he is so near I can almost see him. If anything does happen, and I don't come home to you, I want you to know that I am not afraid, for I will be safe with him."

A few hours after he had written that letter, and deposited it with the chaplain for safekeeping, the lad had gone out on another reconnaissance mission. Later as we turned away from the rough cross marking another hallowed spot, one of his comrades who had come back from the mission, laid some desert flowers on the new-turned soil, and stood for a moment in final salute before the grave. Everyone there understood: those who had come back owed their safety to the comrade who had volunteered to stay that they might return. "If anything does happen, and I don't come home to you, I want you to know that I am not afraid, for I will be safe with Him." (E. C. Brink, *And God Was There*, 41 ff. Copyright by The Westminster Press, 1944. Used by permission.)

3. Restoration Fund

As World War II came to a close, the Presbyterian Church set up what was later called a Restoration Fund for reconstruction work in war-devastated Europe and Asia, as well as for educational, pension, and mission needs in the United States, most of which were related to wartime dislocations. By the time of the final report in 1952, $23,680,-931.75 had been raised.

Dr. Hugh T. Kerr, whose letter in behalf of the Fund is quoted below, was a former pastor of the Shadyside Church, Pittsburgh, and Moderator of the General Assembly in 1930.

HUGH THOMSON KERR · European Letter VI

En Route,
American Transport Co.,
Azores, October 30, 1945

Dear Friends:

I am on my way home after three months in Europe, and my mind is full of tragic and unforgettable pictures. The quiet flight over the fleecy mountains of clouds contrasts vividly with the desolations of war swept Europe. My last journey took me into Germany. The cities of Frankfort, Mannheim, Stuttgart, Ludwigshaven, Saarbruchen are a haunting memory. From the hills around the once fascinating city of Stuttgart one looks over a city of destruction, and the American officer with me said, "Did you ever see a finer piece of precision bombing?" My answer was "No". It was such devastation that brought the World War in Europe to an end. Death came not only to Germans but to Americans, British, French, Canadians, Russians. The sacred dust of the dead sleeps in the vast cemeteries marked with thousands of white crosses.

The retreating Germans as they passed through to their homeland left a trail of destruction behind them. Bridges were blown up. Churches were wrecked. Even the cemeteries of World War I were desecrated. Bullets and shrapnel were trained against the lovely monument of the Aisne-Meuse American Cemetery near Chateau Thierry, and the white marble stars marking the graves of the Jewish dead were broken down. In speaking with Col. Stubblebein, who has charge of American Cemeteries, and whose honored father was a member of our Pittsburgh Presbytery, he said that only eternal vigilance could ensure peace.

Since concluding my itinerary, I have been turning over in my mind day and night the question, "And what now must the American churches do?" It is, of course, not merely a question for the American churches, but for all the Christian churches of all lands. It is significant that the British churches, out of their own great need, have pledged and are paying one million pounds sterling into the Reconstruction program of the World Council of Churches. The churches of Denmark and Sweden and Switzerland are making sacrificial contributions, as are also the churches of Australia, New Zealand, Canada and South Africa. We are not alone, but we carry the heaviest load. Our Lutheran Churches have already at hand a sum of five million dollars. They have a peculiar stake in Lutheranism in Germany and Norway. Our American churches must, however, carry the heaviest responsibility. The Anglican Church in England is particularly interested in the Eastern Orthodox Church, and is undergirding reconstruction in Greece, and the Balkans. Never before in history has the Christian Church been so united in a single task. We pray and work for Church Union, but in a practical sense, unity is already here. Let us acknowledge this fact and thank God and take courage.

I have been asked repeatedly if there are signs of a religious revival in Europe. While it is true that suffering does throw men back upon God, it is still true that war instead of awakening new interest in religion has always produced a decline. If a graph is made of the history of Evangelism in America it will soon become evident that the curve goes steadily and often sharply down after every war. It is true of the Civil War and the First World War, and it is apt to be true of this war. How can people be deeply interested in spiritual things when material subsistence—food, clothing, comfort,—haunts their daily life. They are hungry, cold, dismayed. Up until now thousands upon thousands of German prisoners have had no word from their homes, and their families guess and wonder and pray about them. This situation is being remedied, but the German prisoners with whom I spoke knew nothing of their home folks. These pressing anxieties do not make for trust and faith. Nevertheless suffering, if it does not lead to despair, does lead men to God, and everywhere in France, Holland, Czechoslovakia, Germany there is a stirring of spiritual interest in the churches, and the clergy and church leaders, dissatisfied with the past are eagerly feeling after recreation and spiritual revival. By the way, it is 10% not 2% as stated in one of my letters that are related to the Churches of England. In this situation, what can the churches do?

The Church can initiate and supplement efforts so that hunger and disease and cold may be overcome among all the people of Europe. This is a big task and involves the work of UNRRA and the Red Cross. But the churches can lead in awakening the conscience of America. It cannot be that Christians can live in an American economic heaven and be satisfied for others to endure in an European economic hell. I do not think, much as the German people deserve punishment and should endure justice, that we can administer justice by means of starvation. The principle of the Army, following the instructions of our Government, is that Germans must not receive food, etc., above the level of the occupied countries. That is a just principle, but the answer to it is that the standard of all countries should be brought up to a comfortable subsistence level.

There is work to be done in the area of reconstruction. It is, of course, impossible to subsidize the rebuilding of the $1,500,000,000 property destroyed, but we can help. I have been often struck by the fact that the first building to receive restoration in a destroyed area is the church. We can supply wooden chapels, obtainable in Switzerland for devastated areas. We can create a revolving loan fund to help churches to help themselves. Above all we can inspire and encourage. I was frequently overwhelmed by the expressions of gratitude because Christians from afar were vitally concerned in the present and future of the churches, ruined by the war, and stood ready to help.

The first request made by the churches of Holland, Belgium, Czechoslovakia, France, was for Bibles and Christian literature. The Christian churches and colleges have been isolated for six to ten years. Pastors and people are both physically and mentally hungry. They long to know what is being thought and said by the Christian people of other lands, especially America. It is a hopeful and a distressing sign when people demand Bibles in their own tongue and Christian books, prayer books, hymn books, missionary books, and must await the response of the World Council of Churches acting on behalf of the Christians of all lands. The problem is not only money, but transportation, but that situation will quickly change.

Everywhere there is evidence that a new day is dawning for theological education. There is a deep conviction that the ministry and the church has been out of touch with the life and needs of the people. Evangelism has been neglected. Theological faculties appointed by the State have been satisfied with academic and professional interests. Dr. Kraemer of Leyden University is so concerned over the situation that he is sponsoring a Christian daily paper called "The New Dutchman" and also a Christian Institute for the training of laymen and theological students in evangelism, so as to win the contemporaneous pagan world. This problem, in my judgment, lies at the root of all reconstruction programs.

Europe needs our money. It needs big money. It has become our primary missionary concern, and it is heartening that through our Board of Foreign Missions it is alert to the pressing necessity of getting European churches back into the stream of Christian and missionary activity; and that stream, there as here, must be fed at the fountain of evangelism. At the same time, much can be done and is being done through the fellowship of the churches. Europe is especially sensitive right now to sympathy. This opportunity must not pass without action on our part. Everywhere the interest and practical value of the church is recognized. The officers of the Army understand and are cooperative. The representatives of the American Government in the Embassies and Consulates are most sympathetic. Certainly the Church has come to the Kingdom for such a time as this.

The Presbyterian Church faces its greatest opportunity and its greatest challenge in its long and splendid history. It was the great French preacher, Bossuel, who presided over the diocese of Rheims, whose cathedral stands largely unharmed by this war, who said, "When God wipes out he is getting ready to write." We are confident that the story about to be written will be one of triumphant faith.

Very sincerely yours,
HUGH THOMSON KERR
(Letter VI of Dr. Hugh T. Kerr, in P.H.S.)

4. A Dynamic View of the Church's Message

Closely paralleling a social, cultural, and theological change in the United States as a whole, a marked change of atmosphere in the Presbyterian Church can be dated from about the middle 1930's. A new dynamism, strongly colored by Christian existentialism, came to the American Churches somewhat belatedly from disillusioned, postwar Europe. Keenly aware that everything human is in continuous process of change, and skeptical about the powers of human reason, this dynamism denied that authoritative theological systems or social programs can be elaborated by rational processes. But, by a salutary paradox, this Christian existentialism insisted that the Christian can have personal knowledge of the unchanging God who encounters man in revelation. This new view gave wide scope to social and cultural change while at the same time retaining essential Christian truth which is God himself as revealed in Christ.

The document presented here, which admirably illustrates the influence of this dynamism on theology, was part of a discussion of the Presbyterian new curriculum of church school materials which went into operation on October 1, 1948. A number of the other documents of the present chapter also reflect the influence of the new dynamism.

The content of the Church's teaching is determined always in the light of two considerations. On the one hand, the essential content has been given once and for all in God's revelation of himself in the Scriptures. The word which the prophets and the apostles heard and spoke and which for them had in it the decisive truth concerning the whole of life is the word which the Christian teacher must hear and speak today. The Church has no choice in the matter; its commission is not to teach anything and everything that it may find interesting or valuable in human life, but specifically to teach the Gospel. All Christian teaching must be measured by the standard: Is there to be heard in it the same message of God which is the center and heart of the Scriptures? On the other hand, everything that is said and done by the Church in teaching must proceed from a sympathetic understanding of the particular situation and needs of those who are to be taught. It must be characterized, not by abstraction and generalities, but by pertinence to the actual problems and issues of life. It is not enough for the pupil to hear that God once spoke and once redeemed his people and once pardoned sinners and transformed their lives. He must hear God speaking to him today through the teaching of the Church, and it must be for him immediately true that God redeems his people, that God pardons sinners, that life can be transformed by God's grace.

Two major errors have been made in recent years concerning the content of the Church's teaching, each seizing upon half of the truth and treating it as though it were the whole truth. One viewpoint is based soundly upon the importance of the Bible and Christian doctrine in all teaching, but it proceeds as though all that is necessary is to communicate a body of information concerning the Bible and doctrine. The assumption is that there is a body of objective Christian knowledge which needs only to be conveyed to another person in order to make him more Christian. Learning is thus conceived as a mere storing in the mind of information. There is indeed a very real place in the curriculum for the learning of facts—about the Bible, about Jesus Christ, about the history of the Church, about the world in which the Christian has to live—for right thinking is impossible if a person is without the facts or has a distorted or inaccurate knowledge of them. But it must be recognized that even where there is the completest knowledge of the facts there may at the same time be the completest ignorance of God or denial of God. The content of the curriculum is not information but a Person, Jesus Christ, and the information is valid only in so far as through it he becomes known to man in his need today.

The second error arises by way of reaction from the first. Too often the pupil has been placed at the center as though the content of the teaching can be determined by examining the needs and problems of the pupil. He is to be taught whatever will promote his healthy growth as a person toward mastery of his life situation. The self-development of the pupil thus becomes the organizing principle and the goal of the process. But as Christians we know that the true needs and problems of life can be seen only in the light of the Gospel. We have no right understanding of our human situation until in Christ there is unveiled to us both the extremity of our need and the adequacy of the remedy which God has supplied. Also, the overconcentration upon the pupil to the neglect of the Gospel and the Church results in a development that moves ever farther away from the Christian faith in the direction of a general cultural ideal. We do not find the answer to the need of man or child by even the most carefully scientific examination and analysis of the need. The answer is always found elsewhere, and unless it has its source in the Gospel it is likely to be something other than the Christian answer.

What the Church teaches abides always the same, and yet it is no contradiction to say that it changes with every shifting situation of life. What God claims from man, what he proposes for him, what he expects of him, what he offers to him, is always the same, but man is never twice at the same point in his understanding and response in relation to God. Therefore there is bound to be an infinite variety of approach in a teaching which takes the human situation in earnest, and a constant freshness and newness, while at the same time it will have a consistency which is a reflection of the consistency of God's truth and justice and love.

There can be no right understanding of Christian teaching, however, without the recognition that it is God who teaches, guides, enlightens and redeems, and that all our human endeavors are secondary and conditional upon his activity. To put it most strongly, that which we are commanded as Christians to teach we are unable of ourselves to teach successfully to anyone, regardless of how correct our understanding may be or how wise our methods. All right teaching begins, continues, and ends with an acknowledgment that no person is rightly taught in the things of faith until in a real and personal sense he is taught of God. The knowledge of God is not a subject matter that is at our disposal, to be controlled and communicated by us as we see fit. That God is known is ever afresh an act of his grace and love whereby he himself comes today to be the God of those who are willing to receive him in repentance and faith. Therefore we must teach always with a consciousness of the limitation that is upon all that we do. We cannot of ourselves and out of our own resources communicate to others a truly Christian faith and life; we can at most be instruments through which persons are led to the place where God meets with men, takes away their blindness, and redeems them into fellowship with himself.

What shall we teach? We receive the answer only as we stand with heart and mind open on the one side to the revelation of God in the Scriptures and on the other to the fullest possible understanding of those to whom we minister. (*Annual Report of the Board of Christian Education*, 1947, 83–84.)

5. New Life Movement

Following World War II, there was concern not only for physical rehabilitation (see art. 2, above), but also for the strengthening of spiritual emphasis in the Church. With this in view, a "New Life Move-

ment" followed close on the heels of the Restoration Fund, extending from January 1, 1947, through January 1, 1950. Twenty-four four-day training schools were held for pastors, more than four million pieces of literature were distributed in a single year, and 648,583 new members were won to the Church in the three-year period (annual average 219,194) compared to an average annual accession for the preceding five years of 154,930. The impulse continued to be felt after the formal ending of the effort. A typical pamphlet of the movement is reproduced below.

1. WHY A NEW LIFE MOVEMENT
    a. *The Need:* Failure to know Christ is life's most tragic loss.
       A secular society is doomed.
       The present moral crisis is a crisis in faith.
       Christian principles cannot be put into human affairs until Christian convictions are put into human hearts.
       A Christian's first duty is to help others have the blessings God has given him.
    b. *Facts:* One-half the adult Americans profess no interest in Jesus Christ nor in His Church.
       15,000,000 children in this country receive no religious training.
       Every church is a mission station surrounded by the unbelieving masses.
    c. *Our Church:* From 1926 to 1944 our country grew 17.9%, our Church grew 7.7%.
       We do not share our faith because we do not know how.
       In former times our Church has had a tremendous evangelistic power.
       New Life means regaining this power.
2. WHAT THE NEW LIFE MOVEMENT IS
    a. *Purpose:* The concentration of the whole Presbyterian Church, U.S.A., on every possible way of bringing people to faith in Jesus Christ and to membership in His Church.
    b. *Dates:* January 1, 1947–January 1, 1950
    c. *Goals:* 1,000,000 persons won. 100,000 lay workers trained. 300 new churches or church schools.
       The complete goal is *to gain during three years of specializing the ability to win other millions still unreached.*
    d. *Requirements:* Mobilizing our total manpower. We have only 4200 pastors but there are 2,200,000 members. It requires every one to make a significant impact on the world.
       A rediscovery of evangelism in terms of our own time and situa-

tion. The methods and vocabulary must be for today, not for the past.

A knowledge of the practical, normal, immediate things each one can do to help spread the Christian faith.

Preparation through a sense of urgency, increased power of prayer, clarified faith, a revitalized Church.

3. NEW LIFE TASKS FOR MEN

Here are some of the New Life Movement tasks which depend on men:

   a. *Sharing the Christian faith by conversation.* Men must be enlisted and trained both for assigned calls and for winning men through daily contacts.
   b. *Bringing hearers for the pulpit presentation of the claims of Christ.*
   c. *Reaching out through church organizations.* This is a work for men in the Sunday School, the Scout troop, the Men's Club or as youth advisers.
   d. *Establishing new churches, church schools or neighborhood centers.* Ministers are kept in their churches at the hours when much of this work is done.
   e. *Conservation of new members.* This needs men for house calls, sponsoring, supplying literature and watchful care.
   f. *The care of pastorless churches.* Laymen volunteers can take the New Life Movement to them.
   g. *Office work.* Building a prospect list, making assignments, keeping records, districting the parish make many jobs for men.
   h. *Block by block or rural area surveys.*
   i. *Advertising.* The use of newspapers, leaflets, posters and letters is especially understood by business men.
   j. *Parole, delinquency and youth club work.* This is a large evangelistic opportunity for men.
   k. *The church welcome.* Men greet visitors and make them feel at home.
   l. *Every member calling.* Men take the New Life Movement to church homes. They may become responsible for a definite section of the membership.
   m. *Public speaking.* The Movement greatly needs this.

The New Life Movement has limitless new jobs for men. It gives old jobs a new importance.

4. TRAINING

Each minister goes to a school to learn to be the teacher of his men. Conferences will gather men for training.

Leaders of men will go into churches to instruct and inspire.
Literature will be provided.
Learning comes with doing. The heart beat does not pick up until after exercise has started. Skill and enthusiasm come from the work.

5. RECRUITING

At the start keen interest in the Movement is built by sermons, men's club meetings, adult Bible classes, conferences, letters, literature.
The New Life Committee of the church lists all the needs there are for men.
The Men's Work Committee may share in that listing.
With every job the men it needs are named.
These men are then asked to serve.

6. RESULTS

Lives brought to Jesus Christ.
The Church revived.
Church members with a new vision of complete Christian living.
Recruits for the ministry and for other church vocations.
Dedication to Christian living in every area of life.
A new power for social righteousness in the Church.
FIND YOUR PLACE IN THE NEW LIFE MOVEMENT—IT NEEDS YOU NOW!
(Pamphlet entitled *New Life and Church Men*, n. p., n. d.)

6. Westminster Foundations

The Presbyterian Church is endeavoring to reach college and university students not only through its 41 Church-related colleges, but also through the work of its student centers, or Westminster Foundations, in 130 secular colleges and universities. (The figures are for 1955.)

A. Perspective on Student Work

Presbyterian-preference students constitute 20 per cent of all Protestant-preference students and approximately 12 per cent of the total student population at the universities where student work is sponsored by Westminster Foundations. This represents a constituency far in excess of the ratio of Presbyterians in total population, which is 1.6 per cent. Here is a concentration of intellectual ability, talent, and future leadership in national and world affairs. These students are the custodians and transmitters of the best that our culture contains. In this segment of our population is an evangelistic and educational potential unequaled among the multiplying opportunities of the Church. . . .

At those institutions where our work is established the attitudes of administrators are generally favorable to religion as manifested by the granting of use of facilities and in other ways giving encouragement to the local program. Testimony from university pastors at eighty-five centers refers to both administration and faculty as being more "favorable" and "co-operative" than "neutral" and "negative."

Nearby churches, with few exceptions, are friendly and co-operative. Forty student centers are in or attached to local church buildings. There are four other types of centers. . . . Co-operation between synod Westminster Foundation boards and local Student Work committees calls forth assistance in matters of policy, program and financial support on the part of an influential body of local ministers and laymen.

With the advantages of favorable "climate," co-operative administrators, friendly faculty, and some measure of adequacy in facilities, the student program attempts to focus upon the needs and interests of young men and women who are endeavoring to find a sustaining basis of faith and life within an atmosphere surcharged with feverish action and confused aims. The variety of claims upon the time and energy of students makes highly necessary this special ministry of the Church through which growth in the understanding of life's meaning and development of a heightened sense of the Christian vocation bring into focus new directions for living, increase in the store of knowledge, and improvement of practical skills. (*Perspective on Student Work; A Report on Westminster Foundation Work on University Campuses,* Philadelphia, 1952, 2–3.)

B. A Letter to Freshmen
[Philadelphia, Pa., October 1, 1954]
HI SLUG!

Now that you have completed all the necessary things—your roommate lined up to do as you tell him, your name signed one thousand times in triplicate, your dad's money handed over to the treasurer, a complete list of dating possibilities, your texts studied for four weeks in advance. . . . ! Who are we kidding? Well, it was a nice dream!!

All this is by way of saying "Welcome", a sorely tried word but nevertheless very genuine as it comes to you from us. We are awfully glad you decided to come here for your "higher" learning and "higher" other things. Next week your Presbyterian church on Campus will send you a fancy gadget telling all about what the "Presbys" are doing that you can get in on. In the meantime we want to *ask you one question* and *give you a thumbnail sketch* for the next few days.

The question is this, "*Are you going to mature in your faith as much as you will mature in your fields of study and your fields of conquest (socially)?*" Your whole future depends upon this. What we see so often is people in college or nursing school—of necessity!—[coming] to a mature understanding of sociology, engineering, biology, etc., but whose faith stays in the same old immature stage it was in when they arrived at school. What happens? Well gradually the faith doesn't stand up to the tests of maturity in other areas of life so many decide it doesn't have anything significant to say, or is not very important. See what happened? They never really tested the Christian faith because all they had to measure was a childish conception.

It is up to you. Actually the gospel of Jesus Christ can stand up to the stiffest test of any part of life and can answer your deepest questions on the most mature level. You will never find that out unless you take *and make the time* to avail yourself of the help the church is here and ready to give you. The struggle for Christian maturity is our business and we have a whale of a good time in it! Come on in!

Here's the hot dope for the week-end:

> TABERNACLE PRESBYTERIAN CHURCH Chestnut and 37th St. Sunday Morning Worship—11:00 a.m. Here you will find the largest student congregation in Philly.
>
> STUDENT SUPPER—At Tabernacle at 6:00 p.m. Sunday Evening, Supper, fun, worship, and programs that make you think.
>
> TUESDAY LUNCHEON—1:00 p.m. Tuesday at the C.A. Here you meet the commuter Presbyterian in one big Presbyterian Fellowship for discussions that are pertinent to student Christian life.

Hope to see you soon,
Ed Brubaker—Pastor—Director
Fran Weakley—Program Assistant
and Music Director

(Mimeographed Westminster Foundation letter.)

7. Alcohol Re-examined

After the ending of slavery, "temperance" was the chief social concern of the American evangelical Churches. Since the repeal of prohibition in 1933, the Presbyterian Church has shown open-mindedness and a desire to go beyond the slogans and strategy of the temperance move-

ment of a century ago and to utilize the best knowledge of the contemporary physical and social sciences on the alcohol problem, such as the material being produced by the important Yale Center of Alcohol Studies. Social Progress, *in which the material quoted below appeared, is a monthly publication of the Presbyterian Department of Social Education and Action.*

Q. Why did national prohibition fail?

A. National prohibition became a reality in 1920 with the adoption of the Eighteenth Amendment to the Constitution. It began as a popular cause among the people who were genuinely aroused by the irresponsible behavior and the unholy alliances of the saloons in many communities.

Prohibition's decline in popularity was influenced by two factors. First, American drinking constituted a multitude of different customs, each of which was interwoven with many practices, ideas, and organizations; the attempt to cut out and erase these many and varied customs proved to be far from a simple maneuver. Secondly, the problems, which so many people associated with drinking and which to some were held identical with drinking, were in fact not only difficult of solution but were also of great variety and complexity; the proposed solution, however, was single, simple, and inflexibly uniform.

Other factors often held to be of importance in the increasing ineffectiveness of this law were these. (1) A large segment of the public previously disinterested or "benevolently neutral" became hostile to the operation (or nonoperation) of the law; to label them wets is probably a mistake, but they might properly be called antiprohibitionists. (2) The enforcement of the law was rarely handled well and was often openly sabotaged by the very persons responsible for such action. (3) Temperance and other educational activity, essential for the success of any legislation so markedly affecting a widespread custom, not only was not increased but actually was greatly relaxed. (4) A well-organized and broadly based campaign for the repeal of the amendment was persistently and skillfully conducted.

Q. Can we use the same approach to the problems of alcohol that was used by the early temperance workers one hundred years [a]go in America?

A. . . . There has been a considerable change in the pattern of drinking in America over the last ten or twelve decades. Many of the approaches advocated by some present-day temperance workers seem to be related more to what was happening in 1850 than to the present situation. They are not very useful in providing realistic solutions to the problems of alcohol as we know them today.

The problem here is well stated by Dr. Robert Straus and Dr. Selden D. Bacon in the recent Yale publication, *Drinking in College:* "When it is recalled that between 1800 and 1850 the per capita consumption of absolute alcohol was slightly higher than today, but a much smaller proportion of the population drank—meaning that those who drank did so heavily and frequently—that drinking was almost entirely in the form of distilled spirits, and that the frontier type of drinking was at its peak, it is not difficult to understand why the Temperance Movement came to consider alcohol, drinking, drunkenness, and alcoholism as one concept, and all productive only of evil. The proportion of instances of drinking accompanied by socially unacceptable behavior was far, far greater then than it is today, or has been for generations. But the conception of drinking based on the unfortunate manifestations of 1800 to 1850 remained frozen, so to speak, in the Temperance Movement—and the Temperance Movement was the only movement. No other conceptions based on objective study of custom and behavior and other types of facts have been available for those who have had to deal with the problems of drinking. The power of the movement has been so great that many who are not sympathetic with it, including numbers even in the alcohol beverage industry, unconsciously accept its definitions of problems."

Q. Well, what should be our approach today?

A. Is it not time for us in the churches to recognize that there is not a single solution for all the problems of alcohol?

We need to know much more than we do now about the drinking customs in various segments of the American population, and about the problems related to drinking. We need to be objective in getting and interpreting the facts, and realistic in finding solutions.

We believe that some of the churches have made a step in the right direction in their promotion of a threefold program: (1) concern for alcoholics and their families and other victims of alcohol; (2) scientifically oriented and ethically sensitive alcohol education, upholding the standard of voluntary abstinence; (3) appropriate public action, realistically conceived, to restrict and control the distribution and use of alcoholic beverages.

Q. To what extent should the churches co-operate with temperance organizations?

A. It is important for churches to take initiative in developing their own programs of education and action relating to the problems of alcohol. The task cannot be assigned to agencies over which the churches have little or no control. The responsibility of the churches in this matter is a fact which must be recognized and accepted by the temperance groups and their leaders.

In doing their own thinking and planning, the churches are able to deal with problems that lie outside the direct concern of most of the temperance groups. In the field of pastoral help for the victims of alcohol, for example, the churches have a unique contribution to make.

The General Assembly of the Presbyterian Church in the U.S.A., in 1954, encouraged the churches "to participate in the work of state and national temperance organizations whose purposes and programs are in harmony with the goals of our Church." The General Assembly went on to ask the churches "to withhold endorsement of such temperance groups as do not support our concern for alcoholics, or which in other ways exhibit an unrealistic or partial view" of the problem of alcohol.

Q. Why do the churches uphold a standard of voluntary abstinence?

A. Let it be said first of all that not all the churches uphold this standard. Many churches in the Lutheran and Anglican traditions advocate the "moderate" use of alcoholic beverages. Jewish and Roman Catholic groups likewise advocate moderation, although there are notable exceptions on the part of some members of the Catholic clergy who encourage total abstinence. Most churches in the evangelical tradition, however, uphold abstinence as a Christian ideal for their members. (*Social Progress*, Mar. 1955, 29–31. Pres. Bd. Chr. Ed. By permission.)

8. Needed: Peace That Provides for Change

John Foster Dulles is the son of a Presbyterian minister and himself an active Christian layman. Before becoming Secretary of State he had, among many other activities, served as chairman of the Commission on a Just and Durable Peace of the Federal Council of the Churches of Christ in America. In the address quoted in part here, he seeks foundations of a dynamic peace in two concepts to which Christianity has contributed, namely, moral law and the value of man.

This is a time for the churches to expose the evil of war and its futility. Many are talking about war as though it were an unpleasant, but necessary, remedy for existing ills. The fact is that another world war would engulf all humanity in utter misery and make almost impossible the achievement of the good ends for which, no doubt, the combatants would profess to be fighting. At times, war may have to be risked as the lesser of two evils. But there is no holy war.

War is evil. Over the ages violence has repeatedly been invoked for noble ends. That method is dramatic and exciting. It seems to promise quick and decisive results and, at times, it inspires fine and sacrificial qualities. But violent methods breed hatred, vengefulness, hypocrisy, cruelty and disregard of truth. Because of such evils, wars have seldom accomplished lasting good and there is no reason to think that new war now would accomplish any good.

The Organization of Change Through Law

The churches can and should say these things and develop a stronger public opinion against war. But that part of the churches' task is the easier part. War has been recurrent throughout the ages, despite its generally acknowledged evilness and most men's preference for peace. For that there must be some basic cause. The churches' further and harder task is to discern that cause and show how it can be overcome.

The Oxford Conference of 1937 pointed out the most basic cause of war. That is the fact that, in a living world, change is inevitable and unless there are political institutions that make provision for peaceful change, there is bound to be violent change.

It is possible to have a peace of exhaustion or a peace of tyranny. But such peace is not true peace and it seldom lasts long. If peace is to be durable it must be organized on the basis of laws that are made peacefully and that can be changed peacefully.

That is a basic conclusion; but nothing practical can be done about it unless certain other matters can be settled. If the organization of peace is dependent on law, it is necessary to have some understanding as to the nature of law. Are laws merely what the most powerful want, or are they an effort to carry into effect moral principles of right and wrong? And if law-making is relied upon to effect change, who are to control that process and how are non-assenters to be treated? Without agreement on these matters there can be no adequate organization of international peace.

Moral Law and Individual Dignity

At this point the churches can make a decisive contribution. Two great principles are here involved. One is recognition that there is a moral law and that it provides the only proper sanction for man-made laws. The other principle is that every human individual, as such, has dignity and worth that no man-made law, no human power, can rightly desecrate.

Both of these concepts rest on fundamental religious assumptions. Belief in a moral law flows from the assumption that there is a divinely ordained purpose in history, that moral considerations are ultimate and that man, through his laws, cannot disregard the moral law with impunity, just as he cannot disregard the physical laws of the universe without wrecking himself.

Belief in the dignity and worth of the individual flows from the assumption that the individual is created by God in His image, is the object of God's redemptive love and is directly accountable to God. He therefore has a dignity and worth different than if he were only a part of the natural order. Men, born to be children of God, have rights and responsibilities that other men cannot take from them.

Experience shows that when men organize a society in accordance with these two basic beliefs, they can, within such society, have peace with each other.

Christian Influence on Political Organization

The Western democracies have never created, internationally, adequate institutions for peaceful change. But domestically they do have institutions that, to a large extent, reflect the two principles to which we refer. . . .

Social and economic changes have been immense and they have, in the main, been peacefully effected. . . .

The world situation is serious because of a sharp division. On the one hand are those who claim to be seeking the welfare of the masses but who reject the moral premises necessary to make their efforts peaceful and fruitful. On the other hand are those who accept the moral premises necessary for the organization of peace but who have allowed their practices to seem routine, materialistic and spiritually unfertile. That division will gradually become less sharp if those who believe in moral law and human dignity will make it apparent by their works that their political practices are in fact being made to serve their faith. (J. F. Dulles, *Address . . . on August 24, 1948, at the Assembly of the World Council of Churches at Amsterdam, Holland,* pamphlet, n.p., n.d., 2 ff.)

9. "Ecumenical Presbyterianism"

Many forces, both physical and cultural, were bringing men into closer relationship in the nineteenth century. Similarly, factors both economic and mystical were bringing the Churches closer together (cf. Ch. 10, art. 1). The twentieth century, which saw the new interrelatedness produce the League of Nations and the United Nations in the international sphere, witnessed also the rise of the modern ecumenical movement among the Eastern, Protestant, and Anglican Churches of the world. The ecumenical movement aspires after a Christian unity based on the best of the total Christian heritage, rather than a unity of mere expediency which would be without principles or roots. The task is both facilitated and complicated by the fact that the great denominational types or "families" have their own world federations. Thus the Presbyterian and Reformed group of Churches in 1875 formed what is now known as the World Presbyterian Alliance, discussed in the article below.

Dr. John A. Mackay, president of Princeton Theological Seminary and president of the World Presbyterian Alliance, and a leading exponent of the ecumenical movement, here discusses the relationship between Presbyterianism and the ecumenical movement as a whole.

The title of these reflections is obviously ambiguous. I have made it ambiguous intentionally, because Presbyterianism today is ecumenical in a double sense.

I

Presbyterianism, we might say, is *naturally and natively ecumenical*. It is so when it is true to its own spiritual genius and to the thinking and spirit of John Calvin. Just as it is the true nature of the Christian Church to be an instrument of God's glory and not to be an end in itself, it is the true nature of Presbyterianism never to be merely an end in itself, but to serve the Church Universal of Jesus Christ, the Church which is His Body.

This was the spirit and viewpoint of the Executive Committee of the Alliance of Reformed Churches Holding the Presbyterian System, when it met at Cambridge last July. This meeting, which it was my privilege to attend, went on record as maintaining that the supreme purpose of the Alliance is not to promote Presbyterianism as an end in itself, but to make our great tradition serve the redemptive purposes of God in and through the Church Universal. Many of us in these days can say, with pride and gratitude, that we are both more Presbyterian and less Presbyterian than ever before. We are *more* Presbyterian because we thank God increasingly for our heritage, and for what He has done and has still to do through the Presbyterian churches. We are *less* Presbyterian because we believe that the highest glory of Presbyterianism consists in having a vision of the Church Universal, and in contributing our part to its visible unity upon earth, in accordance with the mind of the Head of the Church and through the power of the Holy Spirit who indwells the Church.

II

It is equally true that Presbyterianism is *ecumenical in its world outreach and dimensions*. Presbyterian missions have encompassed the globe and new sister churches, members of the great Reformed family, are found today in all the representative regions of the world. It is about this that I want to write chiefly in this brief article. I do so because it was my privilege during the past year to attend ecumenical gatherings in South America and in Asia where the representatives of Presbyterian churches played a prominent part.

The first of these gatherings took place in Buenos Aires, the great metropolis of the Southern Hemisphere, and the leading contemporary center of Spanish culture. In Argentina one of the most cynical dictatorships in Latin American political history has its seat. In Buenos Aires a phrase is current which sheds a lurid light, and makes a devastating comment, upon the religious history, past and present, of the Spanish-speaking world. When an ordinary citizen of Buenos Aires wants to say about somebody that he represents a type of sub-humanity, a poor beggar or a poor devil, he says, "He is a poor Christ," (un pobre Cristo). Whence this terrible phrase? The type of Roman Catholicism which has prevailed in the Iberian Peninsula and in the lands of America which have been influenced by Iberia, has committed a great religious betrayal. It has represented the death of Christ, unlit by the Resurrection, as the culminating episode in the life story of the Redeemer. In Latin America, so far as the problems of the present life are concerned, the Virgin Mother is much more important than Jesus Christ. In Argentina the Virgin has actually been elevated to the rank of General in the Argentine Army. The new official Patroness of the Americas is the Mexican Virgin of Guadalupe, a childless Madonna who is thereby divine in her own right. It was in the chief center of this vast area that there took place last July the first ecumenical gathering ever to be sponsored by Latin American evangelicals themselves. It was a revealing side-light on the political situation in Argentina that the condition upon which authority was given for the meeting to be held, was that a secret service man sent by the Government should watch the proceedings and overhear what was said.

In this gathering the representatives of the national Presbyterian churches in Chile, Brazil, Colombia and Venezuela and Spain played a prominent part. A Presbyterian gave the opening address of the Conference upon the subject, "Our Evangelical Heritage". Two things moved me. I was thrilled to see how loyal those Presbyterians are to the great essentials of our Protestant faith and how real a contribution Presbyterian churches are making to the evangelization of the Latin world. Yet how un-sectarian and cooperative they are in their ecclesiastical spirit! I was equally thrilled to discover that Latin American Presbyterians want to become more closely bound together in a federation of Presbyterian churches. They want Presbyterians to come to know one another better; they want to rediscover what it means to be Presbyterian in the most vital sense. They want this, in order that, under the guidance of the Holy Spirit and in loyalty to the Head of the Church, they may be able to make a Presbyterian contribution to Protestant Christianity in Latin American lands. The circulation of *The Presbyterian World* throughout the Presbyterian churches of Latin America can do a very great deal to promote this new vision, and to strengthen the spirit of consecration to a great task which awaits to be accomplished within the unity of the common faith.

III

Bangkok, the capital of Thailand, is one of the great centers of the Buddhist faith in Asia. Here the visitor may see the famous Recumbent Buddha, the symbol of perfect detachment from the realities of life. In Bangkok last December there took place the first gathering ever held by East Asian Christians under their own leadership. Evangelical Christians were present from Japan, Korea, China (evan [sic] though the official Chinese delegation was unable to come), the Philippine Islands, Indo-China, Malaya, Indonesia, New Zealand, Australia, Thailand, Burma, India, Pakistan and Ceylon. The meeting was held under the joint auspices of the World Council of Churches and the International Missionary Council. It was sobering to realize that the General Secretary of the World Council and the Chairman of the International Missionary Council, both of whom were present, belonged to the Presbyterian family. A Presbyterian gave the closing address. Today in Korea, Siam and Indonesia Protestant Christianity is chiefly represented by branches of the great Reformed family. A Presbyterian minister was also the first Moderator of the United Church of Japan. Presbyterians occupy leading positions in the cooperative enterprises of Protestantism in the Philippine Islands. A Presbyterian minister is the Secretary of the National Christian Council of Korea. The largest Protestant congregation in East Asia, consisting of 5,000 members, is in Indonesia where Dutch Presbyterians gave birth to a church of marvelous vitality. In Seoul, the Korean capital, there is a vigorous Presbyterian congregation of 4,500 members.

I found among Presbyterians in East Asia the same spirit that I found in Latin America. They are all desirous to be related more closely and organically to fellow Presbyterians in East Asia and the world. At the same time, they are all committed to Christian unity and to the promotion of Christ's Church Universal. It is their aspiration, and this is especially true among youth, to be ecumenical Presbyterians. They want to be Presbyterian, but they do not want to be sectarian Presbyterians. They want to bring into the common heritage of the Christian Church what God has said to, and done through, Presbyterianism in all ages. They want to bring, as their contribution to the ecumenical movement, to the upbuilding of the Church of Jesus Christ throughout the world, and to the coming of God's everlasting Kingdom, a Presbyterianism which has been scrutinized by the eyes of Christ and purified by the Holy Spirit.

IV

As I see the situation, we Presbyterians in the world of today have a very special task. We are charged by God to see to it that the resurgence of denominationalism, which is manifest around the globe, shall not become sectarian, but shall become and remain ecumenical in character. The new ecumenical denominations, of which there are now six in the Protestant world, can make or wreck the ecumenical movement. If they pursue denominational preeminence and make their great world bodies ends in themselves, they will betray Jesus Christ. But, if they desire, and succeed in their desire, to make denominational emphasis an enrichment of, while remaining subservient to, our common evangelical heritage, they will, by so doing, fulfill the designs of the one Head of the Church and be true organs of His Holy Spirit. As for us Presbyterians, let us be ecumenical Presbyterians. Grasped afresh by Jesus Christ Himself, let us dedicate ourselves to propagate the one holy Faith throughout the world and to seek the unity of the one Church of Christ. Let us do what John Calvin wanted to do. Let us cross "seven seas", and the great terrestrial spaces as well, to make Jesus Christ known as the World Saviour, as the sovereign Lord of life and death, in whom all His true followers are one. (J. A. Mackay, "Ecumenical Presbyterianism," in *The Presbyterian World*, XX, 1950, 52–56.)

10. "A Letter to Presbyterians"

During the "cold war" between the West and lands dominated by Russian Communism which followed World War II, an almost hysterical alarm over Communism for a time sanctioned practices contrary to

American democratic principles. The General Council of the Presbyterian Church, feeling that Christian ideals were involved, circulated the letter quoted in part below. The letter attracted wide attention in the press, appearing shortly before opinion among the American Churches and among the general public began to turn sharply against the spirit and methods protested against.

Serious thought needs to be given to the menace of Communism in the world of today and to the undoubted aim on the part of its leaders to subvert the thought and life of the United States. Everlasting vigilance is also needed, and appropriate precautions should be constantly taken, to forestall the insidious intervention of a foreign power in the internal affairs of our country. In this connection Congressional committees, which are an important expression of democracy in action, have rendered some valuable services to the nation.

At the same time the citizens of this country, and those in particular who are Protestant Christians, have reason to take a grave view of the situation which is being created by the almost exclusive concentration of the American mind upon the problem of the threat of Communism.

Under the plea that the structure of American society is in imminent peril of being shattered by a satanic conspiracy, dangerous developments are taking place in our national life. Favored by an atmosphere of intense disquiet and suspicion, a subtle but potent assault upon basic human rights is now in progress. Some Congressional inquiries have revealed a distinct tendency to become inquisitions. These inquisitions, which find their historic pattern in medieval Spain and in the tribunals of modern totalitarian states, begin to constitute a threat to freedom of thought in this country. Treason and dissent are being confused. The shrine of conscience and private judgment, which God alone has a right to enter, is being invaded. Un-American attitudes toward ideas and books are becoming current. Attacks are being made upon citizens of integrity and social passion which are utterly alien to our democratic tradition. They are particularly alien to the Protestant religious tradition which has been a main source of the freedoms which the people of the United States enjoy. . . .

1. The Christian Church Has a Prophetic Function to Fulfill in Every Society and in Every Age

. . . While it is not the role of the Christian church to present blueprints for the organization of society and the conduct of government, the Church owes it to its own members and to men in general, to draw attention to violations of those spiritual bases of human relationship which have been established by God. It has the obligation also to proclaim those principles, and to instill that spirit, which are essential for social health, and which form the indispensable foundation of sound and stable policies in the affairs of state.

2. The Majesty of Truth Must Be Preserved at All Times and at All Costs

Loyalty to truth is the common basis of true religion and true culture.... The state of strife known as "cold war," in which our own and other nations, as well as groups within nations, are now engaged, is producing startling phenomena and sinister personalities. In this form of warfare, falsehood is frequently preferred to fact if it can be shown to have greater propaganda value.... According to the new philosophy, if what is true "gives aid and comfort" to our enemies, it must be suppressed. Truth is thus a captive in the land of the free....

It is being assumed, in effect, that, in view of the magnitude of the issues at stake, the end justifies the means. Whatever the outcome of such a war, the moral consequences will be terrifying. People will become accustomed to going through life with no regard for rules or sanctities.

A painful illustration of this development is that men and women should be publicly condemned upon the uncorroborated word of former Communists. Many of these witnesses have done no more, as we know, than transfer their allegiance from one authoritarian system to another....

3. God's Sovereign Rule Is the Controlling Factor in History

... Social disorder and false political philosophies cannot be adequately met by police measures, but only by a sincere attempt to organize society in accordance with the everlasting principles of God's moral government of the world....

That we have the obligation to make our nation as secure as possible, no one can dispute. But there is no absolute security in human affairs, nor is security the ultimate human obligation.... In the world of today all forms of feudalism, for example, are foredoomed. So too are all types of imperialism....

Let us frankly recognize that many of the revolutionary forces of our time are in great part the judgment of God upon human selfishness and complacency, and upon man's forgetfulness of man. That does not make these forces right; it does, however, compel us to consider how their driving power can be channeled into forms of creative thought and work. . . .

On the other hand, just because God rules in the affairs of men, Communism as a solution of the human problem is foredoomed to failure. No political order can prevail which deliberately leaves God out of account. Despite it[s] pretention to be striving after "liberation," Communism enslaves in the name of freedom. . . .

Let us always be ready to meet around a conference table with the rulers of Communist countries. . . .

In this connection such an organization as the United Nations is in harmony with the principles of God's moral government. . . .

While we take all wise precautions for defense, both within and outside our borders, the present situation demands spiritual calm, historical perspective, religious faith, and an adventurous spirit. Loyalty to great principles of truth and justice has made our nation great; such loyalty alone can keep it great and ensure its destiny. (Issued through the Office of the General Assembly, October 21, 1953.)

APPENDIX

APPENDIX
List of Documents Quoted

The Address of the Board of Education . . . to the Presbyteries, Ministers, Churches, People, Under the Care of the Assembly, Philadelphia, 1819, 125–127.

An Affirmation, Auburn, N.Y., May 5, 1924, 284–288. The text of the Affirmation is here given in full. The Foreword, names of signers, and Supplementary Note are omitted.

"Alcohol Re-examined," *Social Progress,* March, 1955, 308–311.

The American Biblical Repository, 1839, 2d series, 158–162.

Annual Report of the Board of Christian Education, 1947, 301–303.

S. J. Baird, *Assembly's Digest,* rev. ed., 1855, 151–152, 153–156.

A. Barnes, *The Way of Salvation, A Sermon, Delivered at Morris-town, New-Jersey, February 8, 1829,* 7th ed., New York, 1836, 146–149.

C. Beatty, *The Journal of a Two Months Tour,* ms. in P.H.S., 74–75.

Lyman Beecher, *A Plea for the West,* 2d ed., Cincinnati, 1835, 140–143.

The Biblical Repertory and Princeton Review, 1837, 162–166.

The Biblical Repertory and Theological Review, 1834, 114.

S. Blair, *A Short and Faithful Narrative of a Remarkable Revival of Religion in the Congregation of New Londonderry and other Parts of Pennsylvania, etc.* Reprinted, Baltimore, 1836, 37–39.

The Book of Common Worship, Philadelphia, 1906, 275–276.

In C. A. Briggs, *American Presbyterianism,* New York, 1885, 19–20, 21–22.

C. A. Briggs, "The Barriers to Christian Union," in *Presbyterian Review,* VIII, 1887, 244–246.

C. A. Briggs, "The Inaugural Address," in *The Edward Robinson Chair of Biblical Theology in the Union Theological Seminary New York,* New York, 1891, 251–253.

C. A. Briggs, "Presbyterian Worship," in *New York Evangelist,* April 12, 1888, 2, 254–255.

C. A. Briggs, "Revision of the Westminster Confession," in *Andover Review,* XIII, January–June, 1890, 248–249.

APPENDIX

E. C. Brink, *And God Was There*, 295–297. The Westminster Press, 1944.

Joseph Brown, *Sabbath-School Missions in Wisconsin*, Philadelphia, 1904, 233–234.

J. Caldwell, *A Trial of the Present Spirit*, Boston, 1742, 44–47.

E. B. Chaffee, *The Protestant Churches and the Industrial Crisis*, New York, 1933, 290–292.

The Christian History, Containing Accounts of the Revival and Propagation of Religion in Great-Britain, America & for the Year 1744, Boston, 1744, 36–37.

A Circular Letter Addressed to the Societies and Brethren of the Presbyterian Church Recently Under the Care of the Council by the late Cumberland Presbytery . . . , Russellville, Ky. Printed by Matthew Duncan, at the office of the Farmer's Friend, 1810, 117–118.

Clipping from Board of Home Missions promotional literature, n.p., n.d., signed by H. Kendall and Cyrus Dickson, Secretaries, and O. D. Eaton, Treasurer, in Sheldon Jackson's Scrapbook, Vol. 55, 229–233, in P.H.S.

The Confessional Statement of the United Presbyterian Church of North America, Pittsburgh, 1926, 288–289.

The Constitution of the Presbyterian Church in the United States of America, 1950, 268–269.

"Narrative of James Hutchinson, Esq.," in F. R. Cossitt, *The Life and Times of Rev. Finis Ewing*, Louisville, Ky., 1833, 114–116.

S. Davies, *Sermons on Important Subjects*, A. Barnes, ed., New York, 1854, 62–65.

Diary of David Mc Clure, F. B. Dexter, ed., New York, 1899, 75–76.

J. Dickinson, *A Sermon Preached at the Opening of the Synod at Philadelphia: September 19, 1722, etc.*, Boston, 1723, 25–27.

J. F. Dulles, *Address . . . on August 24, 1948, at the Assembly of the World Council of Churches at Amsterdam, Holland*, pamphlet, n.p., n.d., 311–313.

J. Edwards, *Memoirs of the Rev. David Brainerd; Missionary to the Indians etc.*, S. E. Dwight, ed., New-Haven, 1822, 49–53.

Extracts from the Minutes of the General Assembly, 1811, 118–120.

Familiar Letters of John Adams to his Wife etc., ed. by C. F. Adams, New York, 1876, Letter, June 11, 1775, 85.

Fifteenth Annual Report of the Board of Publication of the Presbyterian Church in the United States of America, 1853, 186–187.

In W. H. Foote, *Sketches of Virginia*, Philadelphia, 1850, 89–92.

Glad Tidings, 1804, 108–109.

APPENDIX 325

Diary of Timothy Hill, ed. by J. B. Hill, *Journal P.H.S.*, XXV, 181–182.

A. A. Hodge and B. B. Warfield, "Inspiration," in *Presbyterian Review*, II, 1881, 239–240.

In C. Hodge, *The Constitutional History of the Presbyterian Church in U.S.A.*, Philadelphia, 1851, Part I, 27–30.

C. Hodge, *What Is Darwinism?* New York, 1874, 234–236.

The Home and Foreign Record, Vol. III, 1852, 195–197.

Sheldon Jackson to Henry Kendall, 1877 (no month given) in Sheldon Jackson, "Correspondence—1856–1908," Vol. 7, in P.H.S., Philadelphia, 225–229.

Fellenberg or An Appeal to the Friends of Education on Behalf of Lafayette College, 1835, probably by George Junkin, 139–140.

S. H. Kellogg, in *Charges and Addresses at the Inauguration of Rev. W. H. Jeffers, D.D., and Rev. S. H. Kellogg, D.D. . . 1877*, Pittsburgh, 1878, 241–242.

"A Letter to Presbyterians." Issued through the Office of the General Assembly, October 21, 1953, 317–320.

Letter VI of Dr. Hugh T. Kerr, in P.H.S., 297–301.

H. Kollock, *Christ Must Increase*, Philadelphia, 1903, 105–106.

Letter Book of Presbytery, 1714, 19.

Letters of William Montague and Amanda White Ferry, ed. by C. A. Anderson, *Journal P.H.S.*, XXV, 130–134.

John Lyle, "Narrative of a Mission," *The General Assembly's Missionary Magazine*, 1807, 112–113.

In M. W. Mc Alarney, *History of the Sesqui-Centennial of Paxtang Church*, Harrisburg, 1890, 60–61.

J. McCosh, *Development: What It Can Do and What It Cannot Do*, New York, 1883, 236–239.

J. A. Mackay, "Ecumenical Presbtyerianism," in *The Presbyterian World*, XX, 1950, 313–317.

Manuscript letter in P.H.S., 152–153.

S. J. Mills and Daniel Smith, *Report of a Missionary Journey Through that Part of the United States which Lies West of the Allegany Mountains*, Andover, 1815, 121–123.

"The Ministry and the Individual," in *McCormick Theological Seminary Historical Celebration . . . November . . . Nineteen Hundred and Nine*, Chicago, 1910, 276–278.

Minutes of the Auburn Convention, Held August 17, 1837, to Deliberate Upon the Doings of the Last General Assembly etc., Auburn, 1837, 166–171.

APPENDIX

Minutes of the Corporation for Relief of Poor and Distressed Presbyterian Ministers etc., mss. in P.H.S., 68–73, 74.

Minutes of the . . . G. A. of the Presbyterian Church in the United States, 1942, 289–290.

Minutes of the General Assembly, Presbyterian Church in the U.S.A., 1801, 102–104; 1802, 104–105; 1803, 109–110; 1816, 123–125, 136–137; 1818, 134–136; 1819, 136; 1837, 156–158; 1861, 211–212; 1883, 242–243, 256; 1886, 256–257; 1889, 257; 1893, 249–251, 253; 1898, 265–266; 1903, 274–275; 1910, 278–282; 1927, 284; 1944, 293–295.

Minutes of the General Assembly, N.S., 1857, 202–204.

Minutes of the General Assembly, O.S. 1849, 187–188; 1845, 200–202; 1865, 218–220.

Minutes of Texas Presbytery, Journal P.H.S., 173–176.

A Narrative of a New and Unusual American Imprisonment Of Two Presbyterian Ministers . . . One of Them for Preaching One Sermon at the City of New-York, By a Learner of Law and a Lover of Liberty, 1707, 13–18.

Pamphlet entitled *New Life and Church Men*, n.p., n.d., 303–306.

New Themes for the Protestant Clergy, Philadelphia, 1852, 193–195.

New York Evangelist, November 21, 1835, 199–200.

B. M. Palmer, *Thanksgiving Sermon Delivered at the First Presbyterian Church, New Orleans, On Thursday, December 29, 1860*, New York, 1861, 204–209.

C. H. Parkhurst, sermon preached in Madison Square Presbyterian Church, February 14, 1892, in Parkhurst, *Our Fight with Tammany*, 1895, 260–263.

F. L. Patton, *The Revision of the Confession of Faith*, read before Presbyterian Social Union, New York, December 2, 1889, 248.

Perspective on Student Work; A Report on Westminster Foundation Work on University Campuses, Philadelphia, 1952, 306–307.

Absalom Peters, in *Report of the Society for the Promotion of Collegiate and Theological Education at the West*, 1847, 172–173.

A. T. Pierson, in *Presbyterian Review*, I, 1880, 240–241.

Plan for Circulating the Books of the Presbyterian Board of Publication, n.d., 184–186.

A Plea for Peace and Work, n.p., February 17, 1893. A copy is in Box No. 174, Henry van Dyke Papers, Princeton University Library. Signed by 235, 253–254.

Presbyterian, March 4, 1896, 263–264; April 27, 1898, 264; May 4, 1898, 264; May 18, 1898, 264–265; July 13, 1898, 265.

Presbyterian Reunion: A Memorial Volume, 1837–1871, New York, 1870, 220–221.

Records of Old Londonderry Congregation, manuscript in P.H.S., 22–25.

Records of the Presbyterian Church of Booth Bay, Maine, 1767, printed in *Journal of the Presbyterian Historical Society*, XVI, 77–78.

Records of the Presbyterian Church, U.S.A., W. H. Roberts, ed., Philadelphia, 1904; [1706], 11–13; 1710, 19; 1716, 20–21; 1738, 34–36, 39–40; 1741, 47–49; 1743, 54; 1753, 54–57; 1758, 65–68; 1766, 78–80; 1775, 80–85; 1786, 95; 1787, 95–96; 1787, 96–97; 1788, 96.

Records of the Presbytery of New Castle Upon Delaware, mss. in P.H.S., I, 25.

Records of the Presbytery of Redstone, 1784, in Smith, *Old Redstone*, 100–101; 1789, 101.

Records of the Synod of Pittsburgh, Oct. 24, 1831, 149–151.

Renewal of the Covenants, National and Solemn League; A Confession of Sins; An Engagement to Duties; and a Testimony; as they were carried on at Middle Octorara in Pennsylvania, November 11, 1743, n.p., 57–60.

Report of the Board of Education on Parochial Schools, Philadelphia, 1847, 188–190.

Report of Board of Education, 1856, 190–191.

Report on an Inquiry in *Church Service Society Papers, No. 1, The Report of an Inquiry into the Present Conduct of Public Worship*, n.p., *1899*. A copy is in the Presbyterian Historical Society, Philadelphia, 255–256.

Second Annual Report of the United Domestic Missionary Society, New York, 1824, 128–129.

J. R. W. Sloane, *Review of Rev. Henry J. Van Dyke's Discourse on "The Character and Influence of Abolitionism,"* N.Y., 1861, 209–211.

In J. Smith, *Old Redstone*, Philadelphia, 1854, 76–77, 97–100.

R. E. Speer, *The Christian Man, the Church and the War*, New York, 1918, 282–284.

Robert E. Speer, *Presbyterian Foreign Missions*, Philadelphia, 1901, 269–270.

Letter of J. G. M. Ramsey, M.D., 1849, in W. B. Sprague, *Annals of the American Pulpit*, New York, 1868, III, 101–102.

Personal Reminiscences of the Life and Times of Gardiner Spring, 1866, II, 137–139.

"Statement of Principles" of the Church Service Society, in *The Church*

Service Society of the Presbyterian Church in the U.S.A., n.p., n.d. [1897]. A copy is in the Henry van Dyke Papers, Presbyterian Historical Society, Philadelphia, 255–256.

A Statement of the Reasons which Induced the Students of Lane Seminary to Dissolve their Connection with that Institution, Cincinnati, 1834, 143–145.

Charles Stelzle, *A Son of the Bowery; The Life Story of an East Side American*, New York, 1926, 270–274.

R. Stuart, "Reminiscences," 1837, reprinted in *Journal P.H.S.*, XXIII, 111–112.

Gilbert Tennent, *The Danger of an Unconverted Ministry*, Philadelphia: Printed by Benjamin Franklin, in Market-street, 1740, 40–44.

Third Annual Report of the United Domestic Missionary Society, 1825, 129–130.

Thirty-third Annual Report of the Board of Education, 1852, 191–193.

R. E. Thompson, *De Civitate Dei. The Divine Order of Human Society*, Philadelphia, 1891, 257–260.

R. E. Thompson, *A History of the Presbyterian Churches in the United States*, 1895, 197–198; Appendix, 212–218.

Transactions of the Twenty-First Annual Reunion of the Oregon Pioneer Association for 1893, 176–181.

H. van Dyke, *The American Birthright and the Philippine Pottage; A Sermon Preached on Thanksgiving Day, 1898*, New York, n.d., 263–267.

H. J. Van Dyke, "God's Infinite Love to Men," in *Presbyterian*, October 5, 1889, 247–248.

H. J. Van Dyke, "Revision of the Confession of Faith," in *Presbyterian*, August 17, 1889, 246–247.

The Watchman, San Francisco, April 1, 1850, reprinted in *Journal P.H.S.*, XXIII, 182–184.

The Weekly Recorder, Chillicothe, Ohio, April 17, 1816, reprinted in *Journal P.H.S.*, XXX, 127–128.

The Western Missionary Magazine, Washington, Pa., 1803, I, 110–111.

Mimeographed Westminster Foundation Letter, 307–308.

Whitefield's Fifth Journal, Nov. 22, 1739, 33–34.

W. Williamson, "Journal," in *Journal P.H.S.*, XXVII, 106–108.

J. Witherspoon, *The Dominion of Providence Over the Passions of Men*, reprinted, London, 1778, 85–89.

INDEX

INDEX

Abbott, Lyman, 235
Abrams, Ray, 282
Academies. *See* Schools
"Act and Testimony," 151–152
Adams, John, 85
Adopting Act, 28, 30–32, 65, 280, 282, 285
Alaska, 231
Alcohol, 23, 134–135, 144, 182, 308-311
Alison, Francis, 78
American Home Missionary Society, 128
Anderson, Charles A., 8, 134
Anderson, James, 19–20, 21, 32
Andrews, Jedediah, 11, 12, 13, 19, 21, 32
Apostles' Creed, 248
Arminianism, 29, 113, 167, 245
Atheism, 208
Auburn Affirmation, 284–288
Auburn Declaration, 166–171
Auburn Theological Seminary, 128

Bacon, Sumner, 173–174
Baird, Charles W., 255
Baptism, 99
Barnes, Albert, 146–149
Beatty, Charles, 71, 74–75
Beecher, Lyman, 140–143
Benevolent Empire. *See* Voluntary Societies
Bible, 26; and Holy Spirit, 286; inerrancy of autographs of, 239–240, 249–251, 253–254, 281, 286; study of, by laity, 136–137, 181, 300; supply of, 123, 124; taught to children, 190

Blackburn, Gideon, 108–109
Blair, Samuel, 36–39
Boudinot, Elias, 104
Boyd, John, 11, 12
Brainerd, David, 49–53
Briggs, Charles A., 20, 22, 239, 244–246, 248–249, 255; "heresy" case, 251–253
Brink, Eben C., 295–297
Brown, Joseph, 233–234
Brubaker, Edward, 307–308

Caldwell, John, 44–47
Call. *See* Ministers
Calvinism, 29, 146, 245, 246, 247, 259. *See also* Westminster Confession of Faith: revision of
Camp meetings, 111–112. *See also* Revivalism
Card playing, 101, 186
Catechism, 187; catechetical instruction, 99, 137, 191
Censoriousness, 40–48, 66–67
Centralization, 244
Chaffee, Edmund B., 290–292
Chaplaincy, 295–297
Chinese, 266
Christian education. *See* Education
Church, conception of, 254, 258. *See also* Organization, Church
Church Erection Board, 231
Circuit rider, 106–108, 128, 233
Civil liberties, 317–320
Civil War, 209, 211–218, 242, 282. *See also* Reconstruction
Coldin, Alexander, 12
College of New Jersey, 54–57, 62, 85, 235

331

INDEX

Colleges, 54–57, 101–102, 242–243; need of, 141–142; religion in, 191–193. *See also* College of New Jersey; Log College; Manual Labor in Education; Westminster Foundations
Colporteur, 186–187
Colwell, Stephen, 193–195
Communion. *See* Lord's Supper
Communism, 317–320
Confession of Faith. *See* Westminster Confession of Faith
Congregationalists, 162–164. *See also* New England; Plan of Union; Puritans; Voluntary Societies
Cornbury, Lord, 14–18
Covenants, renewal of the, 57–60
Craighead, Alexander, 57
Creeds for congregations, 153–154
Cross, Robert, 47
Cumberland Presbyterian Church, 113, 114, 117, 173–176, 286

Dancing, 100–101, 135–136
"Danger of an Unconverted Ministry," 40–44
Darwin, Charles, 235–236. *See also* Evolution
Davies, Samuel, 55, 62–65
Davis, Samuel, 11, 12, 21
Deism and "Infidelity," 29, 118, 186, 187
Depression, economic, 290–292
Dickinson, Jonathan, 26–27, 32, 55
Dickson, Cyrus, 229–233
Discipline, 22–25, 100–101, 155–156
Doak, Samuel, 101–102
Drury, Clifford M., 123, 176, 225
Duffield, George, 74, 85
Dulles, John Foster, 311–313
Dwight, Timothy, 171

Ecumenical movement, 246; "Ecumenical Presbyterianism," 313–317. *See also* International Missionary Council; Unity, Christian; World Council of Churches
Education, Board of, 125–127, 152–153; religious, 123. *See also* Catechism; Colleges; Ministers: education of; Publications, Religious; Schools; Sunday Schools
Edwards, Jonathan, 53, 171
Elder, John, 60
Elder, ruling, 154, 159, 160, 163
"Essential and Necessary" doctrines, 248–249, 253–254, 280–282, 284, 287–288. *See also* Adopting Act
Ethics. *See* Alcohol; Card Playing; Censoriousness; Dancing; Gambling; Morality; Sabbath Observance; Social Problems; Theater
Evangelical Alliance, 246
Evangelism, 303–306. *See also* Revivalism
Evans, David, 18–19, 21, 25
Evolution, 234–239
Ewing, Finis, 114–117
"Exercises" in revivals, 112–114. *See also* Revivalism
Existentialism, 301
Exscinding Acts, the, 156–158. *See also* Old School Presbyterianism

Faust, Harold S., 130
Female Cent Society, 127–128
Ferry, Amanda, 130–134
Foreign Missions, 121, 149–151, 160, 266, 268, 269–270, 282, 300, 315–317. *See also* Indians; International Missionary Council; Western Foreign Missionary Society; Women's Work
Freedmen. *See* Negroes
Freedom of religion. *See* Liberty, Religious
Freethinking, 29
French and Indian War, 62–65, 70–72, 78–79
Frontier, 60–61, 64, 69–71, 74–77, 90, 101–102, 105, 126, 254, 257; sod house, 181–182. *See also* Circuit Rider; Home Missions; Indians; Revivalism; Voluntary Societies; West, the American
Fundamentalism, 239, 280–282, 284. *See also* Bible: inerrancy of autographs of

INDEX

Gambling, 135
General Assembly organized, 95–96, 285
Gillespie, George, 32
Glasgow University, 19–20
Great Awakening. See Revivalism
Great Britain, 68–69, 79. See also Revolutionary War; Scotch-Irish; Scotland

Hampton, John, 11, 14, 21
Hanover, Presbytery of, 89–92
"Haystack" prayer meeting, 121
Hazard, Ebenezer, 104
Henry, Patrick, 62
Hill, Timothy, 181–182
Hodge, A. A., 239–240, 249
Hodge, Charles, 30, 211, 235–236
Home Missions, 13, 19–20, 102–108, 109–110, 174, 225–234, 271; Board of Missions, 123–125, 172; Standing Committee of Missions, 104–105; United Domestic Missionary Society, 128–130. See also Colporteur; Frontier; Indians; Sunday Schools; Women's Work
Hopkins, Charles H., 258
Hunt, T. B., 182–184
Hymns, 187. See also Psalmody

Immigration, 172–173, 195–197, 240, 256–257
Imperialism, 265–267, 319
Indians: missions to, 49–53, 106, 108–109, 130–134, 176, 180, 231; trade with, 179; "vices" of, 69, 72, 78, 106; war with, 62–65, 70–74, 227–228
Individualism, 257–260, 276–278. Cf. Social Problems
Industry, industrialization, 240, 258; industrial relations, 293–295. See also Labor
Infidelity. See Deism
International Missionary Council, 316
Ireland. See Scotch-Irish
Itinerant preacher, 39–40, 46, 47, 65, 67. See also Circuit Rider; Revivalism

Jackson, Sheldon, 225–229
"Jerks," the, 112–113. See also Revivalism
Jews, 256, 311

Kellogg, Samuel H., 241–242
Kendall, Henry, 225, 229–233
Kennedy, John L., 271
Kerr, Hugh T., 297–301
Kingdom of God, 258
Klett, Guy S., 23
Kollock, Henry, 105–106

Labor, 241, 279–280; Labor Temple, 270–274, 290. See also Industry
Laggan, Irish Presbytery of, 13
Laissez-faire, 257. See also Individualism
Lane Theological Seminary, 140, 143–145
"Letter to Presbyterians, A," 317–320
Liberty of conscience, 25–27
Liberty, religious, 13–18, 69, 89–92. Cf. Theocracy
Loetscher, Lefferts A., 225, 239
Log College, 33–34, 36, 47
Lord's Supper, 77–78, 98–99
Lyceums, 144
Lyle, John, 112–113

Mackay, John A., 313–317
Makemie, Francis, 11, 12, 13, 14–18
"Manifest Destiny," 172–173. See also Nationalism; West, the American
Manual labor in education, 139–140, 176
Marx, Karl, 258
Mather, Cotton, 13
Maxwell, William D., 255
Mc Clure, David, 75–76
McCormick Theological Seminary, 278
McCosh, James, 235–239
McKemie. See Makemie

McMillan, John, 76–77
McNish, George, 11, 12, 21
Mexicans, 231
Mills, Samuel J., 121–123
Ministers: call of, to a pastorate, 12–13; education of, 18–19, 29, 33–36, 56–57, 118–120, 125–127, 152, 175–176; need for, 141, 188, 243; ordination of, 11–12, 19, 25, 65, 67, 118–120, 153–154; support of, 20, 68–73. See also Education, Board of
Minority, rights of, 66
Missions. See Foreign Missions; Home Missions
Morality, 21–25, 37, 45, 79. See also Ethics
Mormons, 231
Murray, John, 77–78

National Missions. See Home Missions
Nationalism, 95, 140, 257, 263, 265. See also "Manifest Destiny"; Wars
Nativism, 140
Negroes, 105, 144, 266; freedmen, work for, 231. See also Slavery
Neo-orthodoxy, 290, 301–303
New England, 35, 49, 57. See also Plan of Union; Puritans
New Life Movement, 303–306. See also Evangelism
New London Synodical Academy, 54
New School Presbyterianism, 146–149, 152–153, 158–162, 164–171, 202–204, 285; reunited, 220–221
New Side Presbyterianism, 33–34, 36–39, 44–47, 49–57, 65–68; reunited, 65–68
Newman, John Henry, 258

Oberlin College, 143, 163
Old School Presbyterianism, 149–152, 153–158, 162–164, 200–202; reunited, 220–221
Old Side Presbyterianism, 34–36, 39–44, 47–49, 65–68; reunited, 65–68

Ordination. See Ministers: ordination of
Organization, Church (polity), 153–156. See also Centralization; Church, Conception of; Discipline; Education; Elder, Ruling; Foreign Missions; General Assembly Organized; Home Missions; Itinerant Preacher; Ministers; Plan of Union; Presbytery, the First; Synod, the First; Unity, Christian; Voluntary Societies; Women's Work

Palmer, Benjamin M., 204–209
Parkhurst, Charles H., 260–263
Parochial schools. See Schools: parochial
Patton, Francis L., 248
Peace, 311–313. Cf. Wars
Peters, Absalom, 172–173
Pierson, Arthur T., 240–241
Piety, 119–120, 137–139. See also Ethics; Revivalism
Plan of Union (of 1801), 102–104, 152, 153, 156–162, 164, 166
"Plea for Peace and Work," 253–254
Polity. See Organization, Church
Poor, concern for the, 128, 193–195, 240–241, 279, 290–292
Pragmatism, 253–254
Prayer, day of, 211
Preaching, 188
Premillennialism, 241
Presbyterian Church in the United States, 212–218, 289–290
Presbyterian Ministers' Fund, 69
Presbytery, the first, 11–13, 18–20
Princeton Theological Seminary, 118–120, 128, 235, 239, 314
Princeton University. See College of New Jersey
Protest, right of, 66
Protestation of 1741, 47–49, 65, 66
Psalmody, 75, 96–97, 99–100, 198. See also Hymns
Publications, religious, 183, 184–186
Puritans, 26, 254, 258, 263. See also New England

Railroad, transcontinental, 225
Reconstruction after Civil War, 218–220
Redstone Presbytery, 76–77, 97–101
Reform, municipal, 260–262
Reformed Presbyterian Church in America, 58
Religious education. *See* Education
Restoration Fund, 297–301
Reunion, Presbyterian, in 1758, 65–68; in 1869, 220–221, 286
Revision. *See* Westminster Confession of Faith: revision of
Revivalism: at college, 191–193; Great Awakening, 33–53, 62, 65, 67–68, 167, 254, 258; Kentucky revival, 111–118. *See also* Circuit Rider; Ethics; Evangelism; Piety
Revolutionary War, 78–92, 282
Roman Catholics, 121, 140, 181, 186, 189, 193, 245, 256, 286, 311
Rush, Benjamin, 109

Sabbath observance, 22, 136, 174–175, 183, 208, 280
"Salvation, the Way of," 146–149
Sanctification after death, progressive, 252
Schools, 54, 101, 108–109, 122, 144, 180; parochial, 188–190, 243
Scotch-Irish, 13, 21–22, 26, 27–28, 69, 75
Scotland, 12, 18, 19–20, 22, 25, 45, 55, 57, 70, 72, 75, 197, 255
Seminaries, theological. *See* Ministers: education of
Sherrill, Lewis J., 188
Slavery, 143–145, 164–166, 181–182, 198, 199–211, 213–217, 219–220. *See also* Negroes
Sloane, J. R. W., 209–211
Slosser, Gaius J., 225
Smith, Adam, 258
Smith, Daniel, 121–123
Smith, Joseph, 97–100
Social Education and Action, Department of, 293, 309
Social problems, social change, 241–242; social gospel, 193–195, 257–260, 278–280. *See also* Civil Liberties; Communism; Depression, Economic; Education; Ethics; Immigration; Imperialism; Indians; Individualism; Industry; Labor; Laissez-faire; Liberty of Conscience; Liberty, Religious; Lyceums; Nationalism; Nativism; Negroes; Poor, Concern for the; Reform, Municipal; Slavery; Social Education and Action; Sociology, Christian; Theocracy; Vaccination; Wars
Socinianism, 29
Sociology, Christian, 257–260
Spanish-American War, 263–267
Speer, Robert E., 269–270, 282–284
Spring, Gardiner, 137–139, 211–212
Stamp Act, repeal of, 78–80
"Star of Texas," 175
Stelzle, Charles, 270–274
Stuart, R., 111–112
Subscription. *See* Westminster Confession of Faith
Sunday schools, 128, 136, 144, 183, 275; new curriculum, 301–303; Sunday school missions, 233–234. *See also* Bible; Catechism; Home Missions; Publications, Religious
Sweet, W. W., 164
Synod, the first, 20–21

Taylor, Nathaniel W., 11, 12, 13
Temperance. *See* Alcohol
Tennent, Gilbert, 32, 33, 40–44, 47, 55; John, 36; William, 32, 33, 34; William, Jr., 36–37
"Testimony and Memorial," 153–156
Tewksbury, Donald D., 242
Texas, Republic of, 173–176
Theater, 135
Theocracy, 259, 263. *Cf.* Liberty, Religious
Theological education. *See* Ministers: education of
Theology. *See* Adopting Act; Arminianism; Bible; Calvinism; Church,

Conception of; Deism; "Essential and Necessary" Doctrines; Evolution; Existentialism; Freethinking; Fundamentalism; Neo-orthodoxy; New School Presbyterianism; New Side Presbyterianism; Old School Presbyterianism; Old Side Presbyterianism; Premillennialism; Sanctification After Death, Progressive; Social Problems; Socinianism; Universalism; Westminster Confession of Faith

Thompson, Robert E., 197–198, 258–260

Thomson, John, 28, 32

Thornwell, James, 212–218

Token, Communion, 77–78, 99

Toleration. See Liberty, Religious

Trinterud, L. J., 36

Union Theological Seminary, 244, 251

United Domestic Missionary Society, 128–130

United Presbyterian Church, 197–198, 288–289

Unity, Christian, 129, 244–246, 248, 252, 313–317. See also Ecumenical Movement; Evangelical Alliance; International Missionary Council; Voluntary Societies; World Council of Churches

Universalism, 187

Vaccination, 109–110

van Dyke, Henry, 255, 266–267

Van Dyke, Henry J., 209–211, 246–248

Van Rensselaer, Cortland, 172, 188

Voluntary Societies, 121–123, 128–130, 151, 158, 160–161, 175, 176

Warfield, Benjamin B., 239–240, 249

Wars. See Civil War; French and Indian War; Indians; Revolutionary War; Spanish-American War; World War I; World War II. Cf. Peace

Weld, Theodore D., 143

Wesley, John, 258

West, the American, 140–143, 172–184, 225–234, 256. See also Frontier; Redstone Presbytery

Western Foreign Missionary Society, 149–151

Western Missionary Society, 110–111

Western Theological Seminary, 239, 241

Westminster Confession of Faith, 187; as basis of reunion in 1869, 220–221; revision of, 246–249, 268–269, 288–290; subscription to, 25–32, 66, 67, 75, 95–96, 118, 163, 167, 247, 248, 268, 280, 284, 289. See also Adopting Act

Westminster Foundations, 306–308. See also Colleges

Whitefield, George, 33–34

Whitman, Dr. and Mrs. Marcus, 176–181

Williamson, William, 106–108

Wilson, John, 11, 12, 13, 19, 32

Wilson, Woodrow, 276–278

Witherspoon, John, 85–89, 171

Women's work: leading public worship, 155; women's boards, 229–233. See also Female Cent Society

World Council of Churches, 298, 300, 313, 316. See also Ecumenical Movement

World Presbyterian Alliance, 314

World War I, 282–284

World War II, 295–301. See also Restoration Fund

Worship, 19–20, 187–188, 245, 254–256; Book of Common Worship, 274–276. See also Baptism; Hymns; Lord's Supper; Prayer, Day of; Preaching; Psalmody; Revivalism